W9-BZE-733

STRONG PRESIDENTS

S·T·R·O·N·G

PRESIDENTS

A Theory of Leadership

PHILIP ABBOTT

EMERSON COLLEGE LIBRARY

The University of Tennessee Press / Knoxville

E
176.1
.A29
1996

Copyright © 1996 by The University of Tennessee Press / Knoxville.
All Rights Reserved. Manufactured in the United States of America.
First Edition.

"At Sagamore Hill" from *Starved Rock* by Edgar Lee Masters,
originally published by the Macmillan Co. Permission by Ellen C. Masters.

The paper in this book meets the minimum requirements of the
American National Standard for Permanence of Paper for Printed Library Materials.
∞ The binding materials have been chosen for strength and durability.

Library of Congress Cataloging-in-Publication Data

Abbott, Philip.
    Strong presidents : a theory of leadership / Philip Abbott.—1st ed.
    p.   cm.
    Includes bibliographical references and index.
    ISBN 0-87049-931-9 (cloth: alk. paper).
    ISBN 0-87049-932-7 (pbk.: alk. paper)
    1. Presidents—United States—History. 2. Political leadership—United States—
    History. 3. United States—Politics and government.
    I. Title.
E176.1.A29 1996
973'.099—dc20   95-41758
                                                                      CIP

To Josh and Julie

◆　◆　◆　◆　◆　◆　◆　◆　◆　◆　◆　◆　◆　◆　◆　◆　◆　◆　◆

"... most of us need the eggs."
—Woody Allen, *Annie Hall*

CONTENTS

•   •

PREFACE

✦ ✦

I n *Richard III*, one of Shakespeare's finest examinations of leadership, ghosts
come to visit both the king and his challenger the night before the great
battle of Bosworth. Each reminds the sleeping Richard III of his crimes. The
ghosts, after all, are those whom Richard has killed or has had killed. To the
Earl of Richmond, soon to be Henry VII, these apparitions urge revenge and
the restoration of a peaceful kingdom. The two young boys murdered by Richard assure the Earl that "God and good angels fight on Richmond's side." Both
are strong leaders, but one is good and the other bad. In fact, it is hard to find
a more villainous king in Shakespeare's plays. Richard's withered arm, blood-
stained cloak, and gnawed lip are only outward signs of his inner moral deprav-
ity, and interestingly, Richard frankly tells us as much. He admits to his evil
intent in his very first speech and in his very last. Richmond, on the other hand,
wishes only to avenge those treated so unjustly and to restore a divided kingdom to its proper "smoothed face peace." On the night before the great battle
the ghosts haunt Richard and comfort Richmond.

No one knew better than Shakespeare the moral ambiguity of strong kings,
but in Richard III the moral symmetry is perfectly drawn: a bad man with bad
intent commits bad acts and a good one with good intent does good deeds.
Many writers have told us that this narrative is not always the case or not frequently or not even ever so. Yet there is a powerful attraction to this kind of
account, and it is one, I contend, that forms the poetry of the strong president
in America. Americans have historically been distrustful of authority and even
cynical about those who claim goodness in their exercise of power. Yet they
do acknowledge, and even revere, strong presidents who defeat evil men in
pursuit of good causes, and they are often willing to grant them purity of thought
as well. Washington, who defeated a venal imperial power in an anticolonial
war and designing politicians after the Revolution; Lincoln, who led an army

against the slavocracy; FDR, who defeated predatory capitalists at home and Hitler and the Axis powers abroad are the most monumental examples, but there are others as well. While I do not wish to dismiss this poetic narrative, I hope to show that good strong presidents are haunted by ghosts and that, at least in their imagination, they have slain as many as did Richard III. Of course, American presidents do not exhibit the same forthrightness about themselves as Richard III showed, and thus it is, I argue, the task of the student of the presidency to move aside the moral veils that cloak their personas, not to ridicule the great poetic narratives of their feats, but to show that their achievements are of necessity based upon less than benevolent intent. In the theoretical account I offer, strong presidents have always been aware of this conjunction of good and evil, though they have not dared to tell us so. In fact, I argue that they speak frequently and obsessively to one another on the nature and costs of greatness. Of course, even this knowledge will not make us secure in our liberties from the actions of strong presidents. Strong presidents will always be dangerous, but we may be in a better position to see why this is so and to judge them on these terms.

I have incurred a great many debts in this project. This book has been read in whole or part by Erwin Hargrove, Richard Pious, Mark Rogell, Arthur Schlesinger Jr., George Graham, and Chris Duncan. I am very grateful for their suggestions. Special mention is owed to Richard Waterman and Marilyn Kallet, who read the manuscript for the University of Tennessee Press with great care and sympathy as well as with invaluable advice. Meredith Morris-Babb has been an especially supportive editor. Finally, I thank my wife, Patricia, and children, Josh and Meg, who followed my interactions with the imaginary president who stalks the pages of this book with amusement and interest.

Philip Abbott
Detroit, Michigan

INTRODUCTION

I n the days before William Clinton was inaugurated forty-second president
of the United States, he visited Monticello, retraced Jefferson's route to
the capital as president-elect, and held a ceremony before the Lincoln Memorial. *New York Times* editorialists surveyed these movements and concluded
that while the new president might not be able to match the achievements of
Jefferson and Lincoln, they were "surely worth emulating."[1] The notion that
later presidents draw strength and support from their predecessors is at the core
of a major ritual of American political culture, which Clinton ostentatiously
performed. It is prudent for a new president, as the *New York Times* reiterated,
to systematically emulate other presidents.

In a much more intense performance, Richard Nixon, in his last moments
as president, reviewed the tragedies that had befallen him in his life before a
stunned staff. He concluded by saying that he had been reading a letter by
Theodore Roosevelt the night before. He read of Roosevelt's inconsolable grief
at the death of his young wife: "As a flower she grew and as a fair young flower
she died. . . . And when my heart's dearest died, the light went from my life
forever." Drawing strength from Roosevelt, the president claimed the former
president's grief subsided and that his own dark moment would too pass.[2]

THEORIES OF BELATEDNESS

Clinton had acted prudently in suggesting that he would follow Jefferson, and
Nixon had revealed the sources of his resolve in reading Roosevelt. What if,
however, a president regards his predecessors not as exemplars to be imitated
but as models to be surpassed? What if a new president stands before his predecessors as Harold Bloom argues poets confront their forebears? Bloom contends
that the creative process of poets since Milton can be understood in terms of
experiencing a sense of "belatedness." Having arrived "late in poetic history,"

they fear that their "poetic father" has exhausted creative opportunities. Only the most "strong" poets can overcome this dread of belatedness. Weaker poets avert their attention from the task required and continue to suffer from the "anxiety of influence." Only the strong poet overcomes the "poetic influence" of the master and joins them in influencing others even from the grave.[3]

Bloom is not the only literary critic to examine belatedness. Robert Weisbuch has argued that entire generations of American literati suffered from belatedness in their effort to find their own culturally autonomous poetic voice. Faced with the achievements of a "mature" culture whose projects were complete and whose achievements were monumental, Americans struggled, often with a sense of hopelessness, to find independent poetic forms and to voice their desire for originality.[4] Another student of poetic belatedness has identified a broad cultural challenge in the confrontation of the English neoclassical poets with their predecessors. W. Jackson Bate contends that the entire struggle of a generation of English poets with belatedness is emblematic of a larger cultural dilemma in the arts. The task of the artist is to confront two processes "crazily split down the middle by two opposing demands." On the one hand, he is required to learn from the "great examples that, from childhood up, are viewed as prototypes." Having engaged in this exercise until it is "gradually absorbed into the conscience and the blood stream," he is confronted with a "second injunction": "You are forbidden to be very closely like these examples." The poet is thus enjoined to "admire and at the same time to try, at all costs, not to follow closely what you admire." To Bates, the agony of the poet mirrors the problem of culture itself: "How to use a heritage . . . and how to acquire our own identities."[5]

Presidents are not generally regarded as poets, although the greatest efforts of some of them are accorded this description. Yet even if we grant that what presidents speak is not poetry (at least most of the time), they do seem to be confronted with the same challenge: how to cope with what Bloom calls "poetic influence," how to find their own voice (Weisbuch), "how to use a heritage" (Bate). In fact, it is the argument of this essay that since presidents face precisely the same crises as aspiring poets, they act like the poets illuminated by these critics and by their acts of imitation and exceptionalism some learn to speak and write poetically.

Certainly the contradictory demands for both imitation and exceptionalism are recognized as characteristics of leadership in general. Machiavelli suggested that would-be leaders "follow in the path trodden by great men and imitate those who are most excellent" as a solution.[6] Alexander Hamilton's famous defense of a "vigorous executive" reflects both aspects of leadership. He defined the presidency as a limited institution with less authority than many governorships as well as an outlet for those whose "love of fame" would prompt "extensive and arduous enterprises for the public benefit."[7]

To the extent that the American presidency is conceived as a clerkship, presidents can escape a sense of belatedness. But even before the emergence of the modern presidency, central features of the American political system have often limited this option. As revisionist as the founding fathers might have been in regard to republican theory, their creation of the presidency rested upon republican understandings of the "patriot-hero" as a figure whose leadership epitomized virtue.[8] The very mechanisms created in the Constitution to restrain the exercise of political power produce crises of governance which generate demands for presidential leadership. The electoral process itself focuses attention on the capabilities and agendas of the presidential office seeker.

When crises become imminent, however, the American president is confronted with a series of obstacles that make the sense of belatedness acute. The president who finds himself in the midst of crisis is confronted with the cultural ambivalence to the office itself, which opponents to the Constitution called the "fetus of monarchy." He is challenged by the fragmentation of political authority and the limited resources of the presidency. Not least, a president is faced with extremely strong cultural dispositions against giving legitimacy to granting any new exercise of political power. Thus, as Bert Rockman has recently observed, presidents are required to govern "without a government" and exercise statecraft "without a state."[9]

This systemic and cultural tendency to both demand and restrict the exercise of presidential leadership leads both presidents and citizens to turn both conceptually and psychologically to "strong" presidents in the past who have been able to overcome these obstacles. Innumerable problems confront a president who turns to successful predecessors to resolve a crisis. He not only must adapt his predecessor's policies to his own situation. He must often convince others that the problems at hand constitute a crisis requiring imitation of exemplary presidents. Even the most exemplary presidents were contested figures (every "strong" president has been accused of tyrannical ambition) since they pushed at the margins of American political culture. Clinton Rossiter captures this poetic enterprise and attempts to resolve its moral ambiguity in his classic *The American Presidency*, when he observes that "a strong President is a bad President, a curse upon the land, unless his means are constitutional and his ends democratic, unless he acts in ways that are fair, dignified and familiar, and pursues policies to which a 'persistent and undoubted' majority of the American people has given support. We honor the great presidents of the past, not for their strength, but for the fact that they used it wisely to build a better America. And in honoring them we recognize that their kind of Presidency is one of our chief bulwarks against decline and chaos."[10] Once a president initiates a process of imitation he opens up the application of the same negative narratives to himself. Thus to be "like" a Washington or a Jackson or a Lincoln or an FDR, a president is driven to create an arena of independence from the very exemplars he is implementing much as the poet, who in setting out to write poetry "like Milton," finds he must create a zone of autonomy from figures such as Milton in order to be a poet. The crisis at hand becomes at once a personal crisis. A president seeks to give rebirth to himself as new political persona and to add his name to the list of strong presidents. This dramatic process of imitation with the goal of exceptionalism is an extremely high risk venture not only because exceptional presidencies are rare but also because a president is actually engaging in a public process of psychological transformation. The language of presidential studies, both academic and journalistic, which describes the "burdens" of leadership and the "testing" of a president, form part of a public "watch" of an agonic process that, like Bloom's poet, involves "not so much a man speaking to men as a man rebelling against being spoken to by a dead man (the precursor) outrageously more alive than himself."[11]

THE IMAGINARY BELATED PRESIDENT

Suppose, then, we test the proposition of the presidency as a poetic institution by constructing an imaginary "belated president" who performs the ritual task of emulation while at the same time secretly hoping to surpass his predecessors. The belated president does not employ past presidents as exemplars in any casually opportunistic way as filler for addresses or even as simple policy legitimization. Nor does he cite past strong presidents out of piety. Rather, he studies and speaks of other strong presidents out of a desire to overcome their influence. He, in fact, is deeply resentful of their influence, although he cannot express this *resentment* lest he be exposed as a "bad president." Thus publicly he draws "strength" from the fact that "he holds Lincoln's office, lives in Lincoln's house, and walks in Lincoln's way."[12] Privately, his envy of Lincoln's mythic status is aggravated by the demand that he imitate the man whose presence is felt in what is rightfully "his" office, his house, his way.

The imaginary president is, of course, the suffering president of presidential scholarship, but his agon is one driven by a sense of belatedness. He suffers greatly from the fact that despite achieving the truly exceptional status itself of holding the presidency, his fame is eons away from the limited pantheon of great presidents and he shudders at the prospect that he will be forever unable to join them. This poetic distance infuriates him; it saddens him; it challenges him.

Suppose, then, we imagine an imaginary poetic president who is suffering so at some time in the near future, perhaps as president-elect. We need not assume that he is a scholarly person, although we can assume that he is familiar with poets proper. We need not place some veil of ignorance before him. He is familiar with literary criticism as well as with the great theorists of resentment, Nietzche and Freud. We need not give him a party identification since, although his own public ideological predispositions might create some obstacles, imitation of strong presidents generally transcends partisanship. We give him no "presidential character" on the assumption that his sense of belatedness overwhelms any particular aversion to risk taking and that his confidence is already shredded by his affliction and the task required to alleviate it. We give him a range of political experience and political adeptness as well as training in lawyerly and/or capitalist pursuits. He may have the most astute counselors at his disposal, for while they are largely irrelevant to his secret desire to excel monumentally, why not give him every opportunity to implement his strate-gies in overcoming belatedness?

Some questions we leave to fate. We assume that he is in reasonably good health, although he may be stricken with illness at any moment. We are pre-pared to give him a background of great wealth, great economic mobility, or simply material comfort. We grant him any number of ethnic heritages. We care not whether he had a strong or weak father, whether he was a first or only child, nor do we make an assumption about his gender, although we generally write of him as a man in deference to historical precedent. Thus while we try to keep the insights of both Freud and feminism as a point of reference, we aim to carry these theories to both higher abstraction and narrower focus by framing belat-edness only, on the assumption that the encounter with poetic influence con-fronts both men and women and that psychoanalytic constraints inform rather than determine the challenge. Similarly, we assume the belated president is white while granting that an African American president would face a special confrontation with belatedness but a confrontation nevertheless. In fact, were the imaginary president a woman and/or an African American, certainly any belated analysis of strong presidents would be filtered through this monumen-tal, unknown journey. New opportunities for "firstness" might well be tossed before her only to be matched by monumental constraints. Would this "new" president still find common cause with the *resentment* of predecessors, especially one like Washington, who so magnificently constructed a special kind of firstness? Or would this new president confront past ones with a kind of double resentment, one derived from their greatness and another from their maleness or whiteness? Or would this new president be freed from at least some of these belated fantasies, since this new one would have the opportunity to explore sources of strength in race and gender unavailable to *all* the others? Belated-ness experienced in terms of selected, duplicated, conflated, or distanced resent-ment would be only one puzzle of this unknown journey, which, when it be-gins, will add significantly to the poetry of presidents.

READING BELATEDLY

We thus send this imaginary belated president upon a quest to alleviate his belatedness through a analysis of the strong presidents he is determined to imitate and excel. The belated president's analysis is a thorough one, at least in terms of examining those aspects of each president's confrontation with belatedness. His study, however, is driven by one central tenet. He assumes that each strong president, like him, has battled belatedness. Thus when he reads the material presidents have uttered—addresses, speeches, conversations, let-ters—he searches for evidence of hidden belated motives. He knows that the great bulk of presidential speech is what might be called genre.[13] Presidential genre, of course, has its own subdivisions: inaugurals and farewell addresses (in which poetry is acknowledged and even expected), the State of the Union as constitutionally generated speech, the crisis address, the campaign stump speech, speeches set in the Rose Garden, press conferences, "minor" speeches to the innumerable groups that compose a pluralist society, ritual proclamations of fasting and thanksgiving. The presidential genre seems capable of being divided endlessly and curiously, almost like Borges's fantastic encyclopedia.

The belated president also learns that the occupants of the office are required to speak more often than they once were and presidents' speech now is often institutionally managed by speech-writing teams. He knows that presidential speech has grown to such remarkable proportions that one commentator has contended that it is the grounding principle of a "second constitution" in which rhetoric, supported by mass media, is a central means of governance.[14] Hence, presidential discourse has been of necessity institutionalized and subjected to the restrictions of communications technology. As, so this argument might proceed, individual craftsmanship was all but obliterated with the advent of factory production, so too any claim of the president as poet has been replaced by the communications staffs and sound-bite restrictions. Yet there is a sense in which even the sternest critics nevertheless acknowledge "all [modern presidents] labor under the expectation of great oratory,"[15] and thus the belated president regards the norm of increased volume as another obstacle in overcoming belatedness and in uncovering poetic intent.

He understands, for example, that presidential speech has always assumed collective proportions. Washington's famous Farewell Address underwent various drafts by Madison, Hamilton, and others, as did Jackson's bank veto. Lincoln's famous phrase, "the mystic chords of memory," was added by Seward, and while FDR worked assiduously to frame his first inaugural as a lonely individual act, the speech was the product of several revisions by aides. The question about authorship, then, surmises the belated president, turns upon the subgenre of presidential speech itself in which some are virtually decentered in terms of authorship to others in which the presidential hand is in evidence as copy editor, originator, instigator, assembler, or employer of talent and still others in which the president assumes responsibility as composer.[16] President Reagan, for example, had his old speeches delivered to his speechwriting office with instructions to imitate style and substance.[17] The belated president will also be delighted to discover that the analysis of the relationship between a president and his "ghosts" can actually reveal, not erase, poetic intent as well as poetic cunning. The ghosts Washington sought in creating his Farewell Address, and his own subsequent revisions, permitted him to gauge the range of alternatives available to him in his pursuit of firstness, as did FDR's implicit "contracts" (and his complex reneging of them) with his own speechwriters, such as Moley and Berle.

In truth, concludes the belateded president, the de-authorship of presidential discourse may be too heavily emphasized as the primary model and is a reaction, in part, to the strong president's very creation of the myth of the poet who composes in stark isolation (and, in part, to the ghosts' attempts to figure too prominently in any awarded poetic achievement). In fact, one sign of a strong president is the ability to capture and defend his authorship of selected texts against the efforts of ghosts, critics, and historians. It is part of the task of relieving belatedness that the strong president aspires to be his own court historian, often in the persona of the exited politician now statesman in the farewell address and the memoir. Thus there is often a looped character to the authorship question with the president as creator, as filter, and as author in some Homeric sense. The task then of the belated student of the presidency is to locate those sources most likely to bear personal composition and to identify, if sometimes only through patterns of repetition, the mark of presidential authorship conceived in terms of assemblage, editorship, and contract while recognizing that one can peer at the loop from various vantage points depending upon the purpose at hand.

However, for all the variations in presidential discourse which require a president to speak now majestically, now with resolve, now with humor, now with reassurance, and now with greater quantity, the genre itself generates its own requirements. Presidents speak with authority, not only in the constitutionally created sense of *in authority* which the president shares with several other offices, national and local, but in the more inclusive sense of *an authority*. Indeed, strong presidents are not even content to argue that they hold particular expertise in addition to their legal authority; they argue that they are *the authority*. The contested nature of the assertion that the president knows more than other officials or has knowledge others do not have is revealed by the fact every strong president must make this claim anew. Woodrow Wilson's statement that "there is but one national voice in the country and that it is the voice of the President" is often given precedential privilege (perhaps because of his early "modern" status and also perhaps because he singularly failed to convince the Senate and the American people of this truth in the treaty ratification struggle), but, as we shall see, Washington's warning against the "spirit of party" and his review of the agon he undertook in behalf of the country was certainly an eighteenth-century assertion of the unique authority of the president.

This combination of in authority and the authority, contested though it is, gives presidential discourse its configuration as genre. Perhaps the closest type of discourse which forms a parallel genre is that of the Supreme Court. The judge is in authority and his expertise places him as an authority. Like the strong president, the strong justice makes the assertion that he is actually *the* authority in matters of the Constitution. It is no accident, then, that strong presidents have regarded the institution as mortal enemy. But every strong president knows intuitively that in addition to his elected status in a democracy, executive power always has the potential of trumping the judicial, for as in Jackson's challenge to Marshall, executive power can be exercised without juridical authorization and not vice versa.[18] Despite this ultimate advantage, presidents are engaged in a continual process of constitutional interpretation, claiming themselves as the authority both when the Constitution speaks and when it is silent.[19]

When Lyndon Johnson (again a notable failure in mastering the genre) asked, "How does a public leader find just the right words or the right way to say no more and no less than he means to say—bearing in mind that anything he says may topple governments and may involve the lives of innocent men?" he expresses in poetic fantasy the central core of presidential discourse as genre.[20] For he asserts as fact the potential that in authority/an authority/the authority will coalesce at any historical moment so that the word becomes the deed or, more properly, word and deed become synonymous. Of course, very rarely does this essence of presidential genre appear. How many times does a president assert that the nation must "go forward" or "move" or give "rebirth" to "renew" itself or start "anew" and nothing happens? No governments are toppled and no innocents suffer. These poetic invocations, actually institutionalized and centered in some portions of the genre, thus give rise to the claim that presidential speech is a conceit harbored by both the president and the American people. Yet a belated president knows full well that there are occasions in which the genre shakes off its Borgian picaresque and word and deed converge. In these moments the president speaks as the genre demands. He says move and the nation moves; he says fight and the nation fights; he says pray and the nation prays.

From the perspective of the imaginary belated president, the genre in these moments speaks truth and he is prepared to assign these rare moments the status of poetic achievement. He marvels at these achievements much as an aspiring poet marvels at the accomplishments of Shakespeare or Milton. But when his poetic intent emerges to a conscious level, he is struck with a sense of catastrophe. How can he possibly capture the essence of the genre the way that Washington, Lincoln, or FDR did? He can, of course, imitate these men much as a poet might imitate Milton. This, after all, is Machiavelli's advice. But, however clever a Milton sound-alike might be, he would never be a poet. A president who imitates a strong president without transcending him, that is, without exhibiting *his* strength, mimics the strength of his predecessor and, like the poet manqué, fails to master the genre.

If we continue to pursue the thoughts of an imaginary belated president, we would conclude that this sense of catastrophe would be so extreme that he would be driven to learn to read past strong presidents belatedly. The belated president may have begun his study of his predecessors like any diligent student. His own belatedness is not yet a centered one and he marvels over the *poetic achievements* of monumentally strong presidents. He is awed by their assertion and capture of authority, their mastery of the presidential genre, their forging of word and deed. He reads the great speech-acts that form the essence of the genre and represent the poetic achievement of strong presidents: Washington's Farewell Address, Jackson's bank veto, Lincoln's inaugurals and his Gettysburg Address, FDR's 1933 and 1937 inaugurals. He studies the *poetic narrative* that informs each achievement: Washington's construction of the first presidency, Jackson's creation of himself as tribune, Lincoln's insistence that the Republic remain intact, Roosevelt's fearlessness when a nation was enveloped by fear. He extends the narrative to include each president's years of preparation for these moments, the origins and development of their extraordinary poetic vision, and above all, the agon that characterizes their monumental achievements.

Having studied poetic achievement and its narrative, the belated president is prepared, eminently prepared, to engage in his own monumental acts, thus contributing to the presidential genre in some monumental way. He approaches his own presidency much the same way that the young John Kennedy envisioned his: The president "must above all be the Chief Executive is every sense of the word . . . a Chief Executive who is the vital center of action in our whole scheme of government." He now confronts his own sense of catastrophe directly, for he realizes that however much he might imitate his poetic predecessors, their achievements remain remote and inaccessible to him. He can never be the first president, the first tribune, the first Civil War president, the first president to face global depression and provide security through the first creation of the welfare state. Heretofore the belated president's actions have been no different than those of any admiring American. Now he feels like the English poet after Shakespeare empathetically described by Goethe: "Had I been born an Englishman, and had those manifold masterworks pressed upon me with all their power from my first youthful awakening, it would have overwhelmed me, and I would not have known what I wanted to do! I would never have been able to advance with so light and cheerful a spirit, but would certainly have been obliged to consider for a long time and look about me in order to find some new expedient."[21]

This disjunction between two intense cravings, the desire to imitate and the desire to excel, represents a traumatic moment for the belated president. The strong presidents he so fervently admires now become obstacles to the assertion of his own strength. These poetic achievements and their narratives now become barriers to his own monumental aspirations. The strong presidents become, in short, his enemies. There are, of course, several general strategies in the face of belatedness other than confrontation. The belated president can end his study of these great poet-presidents and accept an inferior status. He might hope for lesser achievements well done. The memorable comment by President Ford that he was not a Lincoln constituted just such a plea. Ford abdicated poetic status and claimed reliability and serviceability. Most presidents, however, do not so directly accept poetic defeat. Instead, they avert their glance from strong presidents, preferring to ignore their dominance. The belated president who cannot or will not divert his attention accepts his "mediocrity" less gracefully. He might resent strong presidents deeply but may not be able to focus his anger. He stands in the shadow of strong presidents striking out sporadically like a vanquished slave.

Recognizing that some some presidents are never struck with belatedness and that others in varying degrees learn to live with or are unable to overcome the affliction, the imaginary president concludes that he must confront his condition. He surveys his dilemma. Strong presidents are recognized for their monumental accomplishments in the mastery of the presidential genre which are reflected in poetic achievements recorded as narratives of greatness. While he has studied these achievements closely, he has experienced an excruciating remoteness between himself and strong presidents. He can quote strong presidents extensively, he knows their agonic narratives by rote but he still does not know how he can become like Washington or Lincoln or FDR, for he realizes to be "like" Washington/Lincoln/FDR he must somehow become different from them. He wants to show strength and become a strong president like them, but he knows that in order to do so he must produce some poetic achievement the strong presidents have not yet created.

It is at this point that the imaginary belated president makes what he regards as a major discovery and what the student of a theory of belatedness would call a grand assumption. Perhaps he concludes that the key to closing the distance between himself and the strong ones rests not in imitating their poetic achievements, which he decides, in his moment of supreme resentment, is an act of deception on their part, but in imitating their *poetic intent*. If I suffer from belatedness, he asks, why not the strong presidents? Why should not Washington/Lincoln/FDR and others have suffered the same catastrophe as me? If this is the case and men like Lincoln once concluded that poetic opportunities were closed to them, then I am in part already like strong presidents. The belated president knows that such an assumption (which he is convinced is a major truth) is diametrically opposed to the poetic narratives which surround strong presidents. How could one assume that the great George Washington, the "father" of our country who sacrificed his own fortune and fame, was driven by such feelings of resentment? How could one conclude that the long-suffering Abraham Lincoln sought fame at the price of thousands of war dead? How could one conclude that the confident FDR cared more about his own belatedness than the plight of a terror-stricken population? He defends himself against the charge that his resentment is a destructive one that damages the reputations of great men in order to salve his own malady by noting that these same charges were raised against Washington/Lincoln and FDR in their own lifetimes. The strong presidents produce poetic achievement so monumental that these critiques are crowded out by poetic narratives and what the belated president sees as glimpses of insight into poetic intent come to be regarded as the ravings of cranks and ideological malcontents. Besides, rationalizes the imaginary belated president, belatedness produces good deeds which he too hopes to do.

The belated president does not dwell upon these matters (which we will take up ourselves at the conclusion of this essay) since his drive to become a poet-president is his exclusive focus. He concludes, rather, that behind the poetic achievement of every strong president lies a poetic intent which is hidden. Instead, he constructs an alternative narrative of poetic achievement based upon the poetic intent to alleviate belatedness. For example, as we will outline in the next chapter, he reviews the poetic narrative of George Washington: the revolutionary general resigns his commission at the height of his military and political power and returns to private life; the private citizen agrees to come out of retirement to preside over an attempt to save a troubled nation from a defective Constitution; the presiding officer of the successful convention is forced to become its first executive officer; the first president reluctantly undertakes a second term but refuses a third bequeathing to a thankful nation his advice in a farewell address. The belated president then constructs his own narrative based upon poetic intent: an ambitious colonel establishes his reputation for military skill and obeisance to civilian authority with the new revolutionary Congress, which bestows upon him the authority of commander-in-chief; faced with a polity paranoid about standing armies and Cromwellianism, he refuses to encourage mutiny on the part of the professional army he himself has built, but he publicly and repeatedly criticizes the government; when the time is right, he presides over a bloodless coup d'état which creates an office which he fills; as president, he initiates the policies which could not be implemented under the old Constitution and leaves office with a stern farewell to hold fast to his personal vision.

The construction of alternate poetic narratives such as these are more or less difficult exercises depending upon the character of the poetic achievements of each strong president. But in each case, from the standpoint of the belated president, they provide a link between achievement and intent that permits him to examine how he might overcome his own belatedness. He has, however, only begun to learn to read belatedly. Since the achievements of strong presidents are read by others on the basis of standard narratives and only the assumption of poetic intent reveals the existence of other narratives, he concludes that the poetic achievements themselves contain one or more *poetic veils*, structures which serve to hide the intent of the strong president. Naturally, an aspiring strong president cannot say, "Follow me so that I might be a monumental poet-president." His great addresses veil his intent.

As the belated president considers the notion of poetic veil he realizes that reading belatedly directs him to the difficult and arcane world of "secret" texts. Despite the predominance of treating texts esoterically in the history of Western thought by religious, Freudian, and deconstructionist scholars, the practice is a controversial one. How does a reader know when a text must be read esoterically? In this case, however, the belated president's task is a more limited one than some other esoteric reading strategies. He does not assume that the author is ignorant of the relationship between the esoteric and the exoteric, nor does he assume that the text itself produces the unanticipated relationships. He assumes only that the intent is disguised on the part of the poet-president and that the esoteric element is readable to a persistent and knowledgeable student.

Reading belatedly is somewhat like the model advanced by Leo Strauss in his famous essay "Persecution and the Art of Writing."[22] Strauss contends that in many periods, presenting arguments exoterically is not possible due to persecution or social ostracism. His imaginary example is one in which a historian living in a totalitarian country, a member of the ruling elite, has come to doubt the government-sponsored interpretation of religion. Permitted to attack the liberal view of religion, he would make a "quiet, unspectacular and somewhat boring case." He would use "many technical terms, give many quotations and attach undue importance to insignificant details." Buried in this verbiage, however, would be a statement of his putative adversaries of "three or four sentences in that terse and lively style which is apt to arrest the attention of young men who love to think." Once the attentive young reader caught a glimpse of the "forbidden fruit," he would reread the text many times and "detect in the very arrangement of the quotations from the authoritative books significant additions to these few terse statements which occur in the center of the rather short first part."[23] He would learn then to read esoterically. Strauss contends that a large number of writers wrote esoterically, including Plato, Aristotle, Averoes, Maimonides, Hobbes, Locke, Rousseau. He extends his analysis, however, to offer the claim that the ancient writers were more likely to write esoterically not simply from fear of persecution but from the belief that "public communication of the philosophic or scientific truth was impossible or undesirable, not only for the time being but for all times." Such works then had two teachings: "A popular teaching of an edifying character, which is in the foreground and a philosophic teaching concerning the most important subject, which is indicated only between the lines."[24]

Does a strong president believe that certain truths must be disguised? We leave the implications of this question to our conclusion. For now, we need only grant that the belated president, who has extended his reading apparatuses from poetic achievement and narrative to alternative narratives based upon poetic intent, believes that the discourse of strong presidents necessarily contains poetic veils which must be read esoterically to be truly understood. His own belatedness is the praxis for his study, and he does not consider consequences beyond it. But even this more limited vision permits him to draw up for himself a way to read presidential texts belatedly. He begins with the exoteric aspects of presidential texts. Strong presidents cite past strong presidents frequently and with emphatic commendation. They seek exoterically to imitate their strong predecessors. From the standpoint of belatedness, however, this persistent honoring of past presidents contains an esoteric element of hostility. Let us give one example here which we will discuss in detail in chapter 3. In 1859, Lincoln praised Jefferson effusively: "All honor to Jefferson—to the man who, in the concrete pressure of a struggle for national independence by a single people, had the coolness, forecast, and capacity to introduce into a merely revolutionary document, an abstract truth, and so embalm it there, that today and in all coming days, it shall be a rebuke and a stumbling block to the very harbingers of reappearing tyranny."[25] In an exoteric reading of this portion of a letter to a party leader (which many commentators offer), Lincoln acknowledges his debt to Jefferson. But the belated reader would note that Lincoln describes the Declaration of Independence, the greatest of American texts, as a "merely revolutionary document" written under pressure in which its poetic achievement lay "embalmed."

Among strong presidents these parallel offerings, one exoteric and commendatory and the other esoteric and hostile, constitute a standard structure. In addition to these combative remarks which are hidden behind poetic veils, if one reads belatedly, as does our imaginary president, strong presidents offer readings of other strong presidents that entail systematic (mis)readings of their achievements. Again, these "teachings" are not public ones; strong presidents do not announce that they (mis)read and hence revise the texts of other strong presidents. Indeed, as did Lincoln, they assert quite the opposite. Take, for example, FDR's honoring of Jefferson as a nationalist-democrat. Jefferson was "no local American! He was no little American!" exclaimed Roosevelt, and he restricted his reading to two of Jefferson's accomplishments, his building of a national party system and his purchase of the Louisiana Territory, in order to make his case.[26]

Why did Lincoln and FDR (mis)read Jefferson? An exoteric reading, a reading in which both Lincoln's and FDR's remarks were taken as homages to Jefferson, would answer that both presidents hoped to draw sustenance from Jefferson's achievements. Jefferson's Declaration was *the* document in which the revolutionary crisis was framed, and each man attempted to apply Jefferson's poetic achievement to the crisis he faced. Thus Harry Jaffa, who engages in some important esoteric examinations of some of Lincoln's works, nevertheless insists that Lincoln had changed not a jot in the Declaration. An exoteric reading, then, quietly makes the connection between the strong president and the good president. Yet there is the incontrovertible fact that Lincoln wrote that he was retrieving only a portion of the Declaration (the remainder was a "merely revolutionary document") and that the timeless or "poetic" portion was dead ("embalmed"). As we shall see, Lincoln not only ignored the assertion of the right to rebel in the Declaration (a right claimed by secessionists partly on Jefferson's authority) but (mis)read the Declaration as a work whose poetry lay embalmed and could only be brought to life by a providential test of which he was the agent. Roosevelt too (mis)reads Jefferson by way of silence. He fails to cite the Declaration at all as one of Jefferson's monumental achievements and instead frames Jefferson's project in terms of a historical battle between elitists and democrats in which Jefferson is honored as founding but not realizing. A permanent "shared public life" was Jefferson's poetic goal in this (mis)reading, which "great leaders of every generation" sought to achieve but failed. Then comes FDR.

These (mis)readings of strong presidents in which the poetic achievements of strong predecessors are reinterpreted by way of silences and selected emphases are, from a belated perspective, attempts to create a poetic space which has been denied to the later poet-presidents. The poetic achievements of strong presidents are monumentally successful because they bar those who come later from any future achievements. A (mis)reading opens up an arena for poetic achievement which the aspiring strong president hopes to capture as he too closes off poetic opportunities for others. Perhaps the classic case of poetic resentment against closed texts, one which has received much attention because it is so thinly veiled and because it is offered by what many regard as America's most monumental strong president, is Lincoln's Lyceum address. Here the young

Lincoln spoke eloquently of the the belated poet's dilemma. By the third generation of the Republic the monumental achievements had been completed and the task of the present generation was to tend to institutions bequeathed to them. Scholars have argued violently about whether Lincoln's observation that the "field of glory is harvested and the crop is already appropriated" requires an esoteric reading. The case, however, for reading the young Lincoln in terms of belatedness is strengthened not only by imagining how a belated president might approach the address but also by considering how common statements of poetic resentment appear among strong presidents.

ELEVEN POET-PRESIDENTS

Theorists of belatedness have offered us maps of strategies by which strong poets overcome their predecessors. Harold Bloom outlines a general process of "limitation" (taking a new look), "substitution" (replacing one form by another), and "representation" ("restoring a meaning") by which "sons" attempt to gain an imaginative distance from their "fathers." Bloom identifies six strategies, which he calls "revisionary ratios," by which later poets attempt to achieve independence.[27] In the clinamen an aspiring poet (mis)reads a poem in such a way that the precursor poem was accurate up to a point "but then should have swerved precisely in the direction that the new poem moves." In the tessera the challenged poem is treated as a fragment which the new poet pieces into a new work. In kenosis the belated poet empties himself of his poetic aspiration in such a way that the precursor poet is so emptied also but the later poem ends with much less deflation than was apparent. In daemonization the belated poet focuses not on the poem itself but stations himself on some meaning just beyond his precursor "as to generalize away the uniqueness of the earlier work." In askesis the later poet gives himself over to uniqueness and secretly too gives the precursor poem the same (mis)reading and thus curtails its effects. Finally, in apophrades the belated poet holds his own poem so openly before the precursor that the latter when measured against the revisions of the former makes it seem as if the precursor were writing it.

Bloom's revisionary ratios emphasize the enormous creative weight of poetic fathers and the enormous determination of the poetic sons to free themselves from this burden. Dead poets not only speak to young ones but actually are part of the late-comers' voice, a "voice which cannot die because it has already survived death." Young poets are engaged in a monumental battle in "wrestling with the greatest of the dead," and their poems are "refusals of mortality."[28] In each of his ratios the young poet risks envelopment by the fathers, for "to live, the poet must misinterpret" and rewrite the fathers. If he forgets them, he writes "very forgettable poems"; as he remembers, he risks reading "too deeply" and thus silencing his own struggling voice.[29]

Robert Weisbuch too categorizes the heroic struggle of the belated poet in nineteenth-century America. Open poetic resentment of the domination of

British literary achievement is rare, but when it is expressed, its hostility is virulent. America's great, still-unacknowledged revolutionary poet, Philip Freneau, seethes: "Can we never be thought to have learning or grace / Unless it be brought from that damnable place / Where tyranny reigns with her impudent face." Emerson complained in his journals that none of his British precursors—Landor, Coleridge, Carlyle, Wordworth—has "a mind of the very first class" once one ceases to view them from an "idealized" perspective. Mark Twain insisted that he was ultimately disappointed by the British storyteller Dickens (not just a "good deal" disappointed as he corrected himself but a "great deal" disappointed).[30] Yet these resentful assertions that British precursors are falsely revered and claim their authority by aristocratic insouciance did not in itself empower the angry Americans to become poets in their own right. They must somehow find their own poetic voice and turn away the critique that their inspiration originating from British poets amounted to colonial authorization. Weisbuch discovers the ingenious strategies of the American belated poets: "correcting," parodying, and revising their precursors until their influence is diminished. Melville rewrites Othello in *Benito Cereno*; Whitman replaces Arnold in *Democratic Vistas*; Emerson reorders Coleridge in *English Traits*. Each struggle he recounts is refreshingly individual, but Weisbuch finds a common constellation of images: "British writer-Britain-outmoded past-deadening present-unfounded repute-conventional living-blinkered literature."[31] The great absence, then, that so infuriated the belated American poet when he confronted British culture was made into a presence, indeed, a monumental presence, as Americans, especially in the great works of emancipation—*Walden, Moby Dick, Leaves of Grass, The Scarlet Letter*—were able to overcome belatedness by asserting that American newness was an independent source of creativity and a morally superior authorial stance.

Bate's mapping of the eighteenth-century belated poets (ironically some of the very same men that Americans regarded as so outrageously self-confident in their firstness) reveals a more problematic resolution to late-coming. According to Bate, a generation of English poets, faced with the enormity of the achievements of the Elizabethans, collectively committed themselves to the project of "neoclassicism." They attempted to achieve a perfection of style and form based upon their immediate poetic heritage and the accomplishments of classical culture. But, although Bates praises the eighteenth-century poet for his commitment to decorum as a monument to Greek arrete and contends that neoclassicism permitted the rise of the romantic and modern poet, he notes that the poets themselves began to feel the anxiety of influence with agonizing acuteness, epitomized by Dryden's poem of self-criticism: "Our Age was cultivated thus at length / But what we gain'd in skill we lost in strength, / Our builders were, with want of Genius curst; / The Second Temple was not like the first."[32] For the most part, the eighteenth-century poet accepted his belatedness with resignation and even with grace. But he wondered why work in whole genres seemed now impossible to undertake, whether his project of perfection was not just imitation, whether he had over idealized the past, and whether he was not in some historical sense part of a generational social contract which had traded away monumental poetic achievement for social stability.

There is, then, in these maps of overcoming belatedness a combination of shrewdness and audacity that marks the strong poet as well as a forever nagging lack of confidence that particularly afflicted Bate's poet. We have not attempted to replicate these poetic strategies as the belated president surveys strong presidents, but several of them do appear with striking similarity. Many others are original ones, not mapped by Bloom, Weisbuch, or Bate.

Presidential hagiography historically shifts in its designation of "great" presidents. But its central purpose, the identification of great presidents = strong presidents = good presidents, is the structure of this theory as well. We send out an imaginary belated president to identify and examine strong presidents with the assumption that strength is defined in terms of those presidents who speak to their precursors poetically by reading belatedly and writing esoterically. The model for our search, the imaginary belated president, distinguishes eleven poet-presidents and groups them roughly into three categories. first are the truly most monumental strong presidents, strong presidents who gave definition to the greatest challenges a nation can confront: founding, civil war, and economic collapse. It may seem untoward to treat George Washington, the monumentally "first" of the presidents, in terms of belatedness. But Washington's great poetic achievement was his poetic construction of "firstness." Eighteenth-century presidential portraiture invariably placed Washington at the center or top of the growing collection of presidents (certainly much to the private agony of early belated occupants of the office).[33] This initial hagiography could not have been offered had not Washington not just poetically succeeded in preventing the collapse of the second founding but also successfully created himself as a poet-president that leaned upon his "first" roles as revolutionary commander-in-chief and presiding officer of the Constitution, achievements which he reiterated in his Farewell Address. Belatedness as president, Washington, of course, never confronted, but his poetic firstness had to be constructed, and the young Washington, who could not yet even see the outlines of the opportunities that opened before him, experienced belatedness acutely as he faced his status as colonial on the fringes of a great imperial empire.

No president was more successful in overcoming belatedness than Abraham Lincoln, for he, in fact, eclipsed even the epitome of firstness, Washington. But, not surprisingly, no president seemed to suffer more from the affliction than Lincoln and no president exposed his poetic intent, at least to some, more than our great Civil War president. Lincoln's mastery of the presidential genre is so complete that his exoteric and esoteric readings are examples of perfect symmetry. In fact, the map of belatedness that the imaginary president discovers in the esoteric aspect of his texts, which we call "double-crossing," covers every major figure of the Republic.[34] Lincoln spoke esoterically, (mis)reading and (re)writing, not only Washington but also Jefferson and as well as Douglas, Clay, and Calhoun.

Perhaps the most difficult task of the belated president involves reading FDR esoterically. Every president develops his own persona, his own person-in-the-poet so to speak, and Roosevelt's image of geniality appears to have formed an almost perfect poetic veil. FDR happily appropriated the voices of Jefferson, Jackson, and even Lincoln. Indeed, his monumental achievement rested upon his multiple employment of presidential exemplars. FDR imitated but he imitated so profusely that he excelled.

All presidents are ephebes as they stand belatedly before their poetic fathers. But with some presidents this youthful status is so centered that it forms a belated stance of spiritedness. Spirited presidents can barely contain their eagerness to excel and thus barely contain their frustration toward their poetic fathers. For spirited presidents poetic intent is thus barely containable and they are only able to disguise it by idealizing their ephebian status. Spiritedness, perhaps the most dangerous of presidential virtues, is nevertheless highly prized in presidents. Every president enjoys and commends to the public his spirited moments of anger and impetuosity (Truman's firing of MacArthur, Reagan's dismissal of the air controllers, even Carter's reaction to the Soviet invasion of Afghanistan), but only a few presidents have been able to carry their spiritedness to levels which overcome belatedness. The archetype of the spirited president is, of course, Andrew Jackson, the man of "iron will" whose poetic strategy actually involved a (mis)reading of Jefferson into a spirited figure and who engaged in mortal combat with America's central economic institution, the "monster" Bank of the United States. Theodore Roosevelt, immensely frustrated as only a spirited president can be, set his poetic ambition upon foreign affairs as an outlet, successfully (mis)reading Washington and longing for an opportunity to excel Lincoln. Fate is largely responsible for the poetic success of our third spirited president, John F. Kennedy, whose youthful energy is forever captured in the poetic trope of "The Promise."

Perhaps the most difficult designation of literary achievement is the one of minor poet, and we thus employ this category as something of a test case in the theory of belated leadership. Are there presidents who struggle with the poetic eminence of their precursors and succeed partially though not monumentally? Jefferson's greatness is attested to by the extent to which he has been (mis)read by his fellow presidents. But as president, Jefferson could never quite overcome the influence of his poetic father, although he showed brilliant flashes of poetic accomplishment while never quite mastering the genre. Ronald Reagan too struggled with the poetic memory of his own poetic father, FDR, and partially broke through from his status as late-comer through an ingenious (mis)reading of Roosevelt's poetic accomplishments.

A minor poet is a failure, at least from the standpoint of belatedness, but what of the failed poet? Along with our category of minor poets we have the belated president consider monumental failures, presidents whose failure is so great that they stand as negative exemplars among presidential poets. Yet like Milton's Satan, the failed poet has his own consolation, and we examine an esoteric puzzle in the presidencies of Woodrow Wilson, Herbert Hoover, and Richard

Nixon. What attracted these men to one another, and are there linkages dis-
coverable esoterically among them?

We present, then, three categories of strong poet-presidents: monumental
ones (Washington, Lincoln, and FDR), spirited ones (Jackson, TR, and JFK)
and minor ones (Jefferson and Reagan), and failed ones (Wilson, Hoover,
Nixon). Of course, other categories and identifications are possible, but revisions would still permit us to gauge the character of presidential leadership from
a belated standpoint. We now report in detail analyses of strong presidents as
poets who read belatedly and write esoterically as they might be surveyed and
judged by an imaginary belated president, one whom presidents themselves write
for (or, more properly, against). For the most part we let the belated president
speak exclusively, much as game theoretic participants or actors perform their
parts, and return only in the last chapter to evaluate his insights and hence the
theory of belated leadership.

Part I

MONUMENTAL PRESIDENTS

· ·

The fewer the men, the greater share of honour.

—*Henry V*

◆ ◆

As the belated president begins the daunting task of examining strong presidents, he is immediately drawn to what can be called the monumental ones: George Washington, Abraham Lincoln, and Franklin Roosevelt. Although the American Republic is only little more than two hundred years old, it is these men whose achievements are so monumental that their poetic personas exude a heroic quality of such great proportions that they appear impossibly remote as objects of successful imitation. The belated president learns almost immediately that their distance from him—which he angrily admits appears as moral as well as political—results from the poetic focus on their monumental achievement. Washington's firsts—his role as revolutionary general, founder, and president—highlight his monumental contribution to the birth of a great nation. Lincoln "saved" the nation from dismemberment from civil war and FDR from collapse from economic disintegration. The achievements rest not upon the speculation that without Washington, Lincoln, and Roosevelt there would be no America or America no more (who knows if some other monumental figures might not have arose) but that it is impossible to imagine America without their achievements.

The belated president reaches for Machiavelli's *The Prince* as consolation, since it is this work which forthrightly acknowledges poetic intent as the basis for great achievements. But then he realizes that however helpful Machiavelli will be to his project, he must confront narratives of poetic achievement, in which intent is neglected or hidden, in order to fully appreciate the task before him. He has available to him Plutarch's *Lives* and Homer and Virgil as accounts of heroic figures, but he selects an epic of more recent history, Shakespeare's *Henry V*, a play which some commentators regard as a British *Aeneid*, as the initial basis for his study of monumental achievement. Shakespeare examines poetic intent in his portraits of King Richard II and the villain-king Richard III, and Henry V can fairly be called the dialectical opposite of both Richards. Henry's motives are pure, his actions are resolute; he is indeed the "mirror of all Christian kings." There is certainly an inescapable attraction in Prince Hal, but he fits the role of one kind of the spirited leader, too young, too inexperienced, to be the mirror. Henry V is Hal grown up, "reclaimed and sobered."[1]

Henry V is very much a narrative of kingly literature, but the belated president knows that the connection between the two offices is complex especially in regard to strong presidents. Besides, there is a strong democratic element in Henry V's character, particularly in terms of battlefield comradeship. He knows, too, about Shakespeare's own aristocratic predispositions, his fear of disorder and respect for authority. What impresses him—and infuriates him—however, is his poetic portrait of Henry V's achievement. For Henry V not only won the Battle of Agincourt against enormous odds. He gave it poetic meaning by so naming the event in honor of the Feast of St. Crispian. The holiday would "ne'ver go by / From this day to the ending of the world / But we in it shall be remembered."[2] He did so also in the spirit of piety and self-control. He listens patiently to his scheming advisors and responds with threats only after receiving the taunts of the Dauphin. Even Henry V's agon is other-regarding as he prays before the great battle, beseeching pardon for his father's "crimes." Not until he learns of French atrocities does he show anger. But Henry's moderation is one of self-restraint rather than compromise. Once he decides, he is fiercely resolute. Once assured by the Archbishop that the claims against France are just, Henry resolves to "bend it to our awe, Or break it all to pieces."[3] At Harfleur he utters terrible threats to the town's inhabitants when they try to negotiate a peace. He approves of the execution of a looter, even though he learns he was a member of Falstaff's party-goers of which he was a participant, without hesitating. And then, of course, there is that reprisal order ("we'll cut the throats of those we have, And not a man of them that we shall take / Shall taste our mercy"[4]). The order at Agincourt, remarkable for its furiousity and scope, forms the core exemplar of Henry's decisiveness, moving Shakespeare's Fluellen to compare him to Alexander the Great.[5]

King Henry is not philosophically inclined, although he is so informed. When the troubled Williams asks him about the sin of killing in an unjust cause, Henry acknowledges the moral imperfections of leaders but announces that "every subject's duty is the King's, but every subjects' soul is his own."[6] He is unconcerned with the legal intricacies of England's title to France, demanding only the bottom line from his advisors: "May I with right and conscience make this claim?"[7]

Everyone loves King Harry. Even the traitors exposed before the battle acknowledge his greatness, and, of course, the "angel" Catherine proclaims her love in the final act. This monumental achievement at Agincourt seems to expand to suffuse first his army ("we few, we happy few, we band of brothers"), then his country ("Harry England"), and finally, as Shakespeare announces in the epilogue, an entire epoch of British history. Herein, concludes the belated president, is the real achievement of monumental leaders: the ability to convince others to participate and share in their achievements. Henry's prediction before the battle that "this story shall the good man teach his son" shows the monumental president as the monumental storyteller who constructs a narrative in which everyone has a part "as household words" but the greatest is reserved for him.

Not every reader of Henry V has accepted Shakespeare's centering of achievement and neglect of poetic intent. Yeats concluded that Henry's goodness slightly bored Shakespeare and that in his heart he preferred Richard II. Others regret that more of Prince Hal did not survive and find Henry's piety wearing, and still others claim that poetic intent can still be discerned as far back as Hal's rejection of Falstaff.[8] Moreover, it is abundantly clear to the modern reader that England's claims in France were specious ones in which the recondite recitation of Salic law covers not only the Church's interests (which Shakespeare permits us to view) but Henry's interests as well. In fact, Shakespeare acknowledges the objective, the nonpoetic character of the achievement at the close of the play as the Chorus tells us that Henry VI "lost France and made his England bleed" and prepares the audience for another chapter of British kingship.

These objections aside, Henry V is a monumental leader. He is fair and pious, practical, resolute, and loved. He is indispensable to British history. His achievement illuminates this poetic persona. The belated president knows that the monumental figures he is about to study are not, except for Washington, soldier-kings, and that the personas they develop are not precisely the same as King Henry's. But he thinks that Henry's qualities of piety, resoluteness, and practicality, qualities that inform and magnify great achievements, will emerge in his studies of Washington, Lincoln, and Roosevelt. He is determined, however, to connect in some systematic fashion their versions of Agincourt/Feast of St. Crispian to poetic intent.

Chapter 1

GEORGE WASHINGTON: THE FIRST

＊　＊　＊　＊　＊　＊　＊　＊　＊　＊　＊　＊　＊　＊　＊　＊　＊　＊

When presidents who are afflicted with belatedness confront George Washington, they face not a single obstacle to greatness but a pantheon of men remembered for monumental achievements. Look at the leaders to which Washington has been compared: Moses, Joshua, David, Elijah, Noah, Josiah, Ezekiel, Hezekiah, Samuel, Solon, Cato, Cincinnatus, Fabius, Cicero, Cyrus, Darius, Mohamet, Alexander, Charlemagne, Henry IV.[1] The list is so long and so imposing, containing narratives of the colossal achievements of men across civilizations, that the belated president seems to confront not a single monumental figure to which he can aspire to overcome but the monumental leader himself magnified and abstracted into a figure of universal achievement.

Central to Washington's monumental status is his "firstness." The comparisons to Moses, Cyrus, Charlemagne capture this unique position. Even if the belated president can resist confrontation with Washington as the epitome of the universal leader, he is still faced with the multiplication of firsts with which Washington is credited. He was the revolutionary commander-in-chief; he was the chair of the constitutional convention; he was the first president of the Republic. He was, in the words of Henry Lee's eulogy, "first in war, first in peace, and first in the hearts of his countrymen." These multiple roles of revolutionary military hero, law giver, and founding leader, encapsulating feats that even Plato, Machiavelli, and Rousseau did not theorize in terms of a single person, permitted Washington's idolizers to fold in monumental figures like Joshua and Cincinnatus, who had accomplished only one of Washington's achievements.

The belated president who examines Washington's firstness in terms of monumental achievements also cannot avoid examining the context in which these feats were performed. For Washington's feats reveal to the belated president the historical opportunities available to the general and denied to them. Each of his achievements were undertaken under conditions of severe political extremity which permitted the seizure of power and its concentration in his own hands. The very monumental status accorded Washington has decentered the multiple opportunities available to him, but they were vividly perceived by Washington himself, his contemporaries and the first generations after the founding. Upon his death one eulogist remarked upon both Caesar and Washington. The former's "great talents would have made him the first citizen of Rome; but he disdained the condition of subject."[2]

The afflicted president faces even more obstacles to the alleviation of belatedness when he studies Washington's approach to these opportunities for firstness. For Washington became thrice first not by seeking power but by refusing it. He was, in the words of Gary Wills, "a virtuoso of resignations. He perfected the art of getting power by giving it away."[3] Washington elaborately resigned his commission as revolutionary general, declined several times the offer to preside at the constitutional convention, undertook the first presidency reluctantly. He consciously and painstakingly reversed Machiavellian advice that the caprice of fortune required the aggressive seizure of opportunity. In fact, his monumental achievements always focus on the caution and deliberation that attended new initiatives and on those occasions in which he left office.

Then, of course, the belated president must confront Washington as the first occupant of his House. The president suffering from belatedness, who feels like an intruder or guest in the office, views the presidency as one constructed by another. Even here, the way this monumental project was achieved appears doubly difficult to overcome. For Washington, confronted with few models on which to build, created an institution that epitomized his own unique pattern of leadership. Washington's presidency did not seem to be *his* presidency but rather an efflorescence of factional struggles in the new Republic. Hamilton once said that Washington was the "aegis" for his policies. The classical reference to wisdom and shield is intriguingly ambiguous. If Washington is Athena, then who is Zeus? Certainly, the ambitious Hamilton does not object to the implication. But given Washington's artful exercise of power in other circumstances, is the presidency by aegis a Washingtonian invention? Was Hamilton Washington's shield? There are then two presidencies which challenge the belated occupant of the office: the "personal" presidency of Washington himself, who is disdainfully tolerant of the belated contestants who would fill it, and the institutional legacy of the "Federalist" presidency. One contemporary student of the presidency captures Washington's poetic achievement (though not his poetic intent) in regard to the former when he observes: "Washington's determination to be the patriot leader was frustrated in practice, however, by unyielding partisanship around him . . . He had no choice, he thought, but to support the advisors who best coped with the problems facing the nation. Nothing more troubled and upset him, though, than the barrage of charges in the last two years of his presidency that he had himself become the creature of a party and thus no longer the patriot leader of the whole nation."[4] But is it possible that the personal presidency, the presidency of the patriot leader, was a shield for the creation of Federalist dreams, dreams to which Washington himself aspired? Through his actions against Indians and rebellious farmers and his reactions to a factious Congress at home and his policies toward intrigue and conflict abroad, Washington developed the concept of executive privilege, personal diplomacy and executive action independent of the will of Congress.

THE BELATED PRESIDENT'S NARRATIVE

Let us consider for a moment, the imaginary president severely stricken with belatedness. Standing before a bust of Washington he is overcome with terror and dread at the prospect of overcoming his monumental achievements. He surveys Washington's achievements, his many firsts, the opportunities apparently forever unavailable, the creation of the office he now occupies. Another wave of terror strikes him when he examines how Washington succeeded not by seeking and seizing power but by rejecting it. It is at this point, after imbibing Washington's poetic achievement, that the belated president finds no relief from his affliction. Indeed, the stricken president is even more discomfited. With a great act of will, he confronts his affliction at still another level. What, he asks himself, was the intent of this great poet whose achievements I cannot even conceive of matching?

The imaginary president might be able to construct two entangled narratives of the source of his affliction. He reviews the poetic achievement in narrative form: the revolutionary general resigns his commission at the height of his military and political power and returns to private life; the private citizen agrees to come out of retirement to preside over an attempt to save a troubled nation from a defective constitution; the presiding officer of the successful convention is forced to become its first executive officer. Driven by the terror of belatedness, the president then constructs a narrative which might reveal the poet-president's intent: an ambitious colonel establishes his reputation for military skill and obeisance to civilian authority with the new revolutionary Congress, which bestows upon him the authority of commander-in-chief; faced with a polity paranoid about standing armies and Cromwellianism, he refuses to encourage mutiny on the part of the professional army he himself has built but he publicly and repeatedly criticizes the government; when the time is right, he presides over a bloodless coup d'état which creates an office which he fills; as president, he initiates the policies which could not be implemented under the old constitution and leaves office with a stern farewell to hold fast to his personal vision.

That the narrative of poetic intent may not be the "real" Washington, cannot be denied. There are certainly other narratives which explain poetic achievement. But the point in this imaginary reconstruction is how the belated president would be forced to read the monumental achievements of Washington, for it is on the basis of these readings that the suffering occupant of the office attempts to become a poet in his own right. His narrative of poetic intent is his secret knowledge. Indeed, it is his secret medicine, since any public revelation of his discovery pushes the belated president's terror to catastrophic proportions. He who would be able to read the monumental poet Washington thusly would violate the standards set for the aspiring poet. If Washington's achievements were pronounced the manifestations of poetic ambition, then what are the desires of the belated poet but envy? Who else could read the monumental poet's intent but the aspirant consumed by monumental resentment? Armed then with knowledge of poetic intent which must remain covert, the belated president might examine Washington's achievements in light of the second narrative he has constructed. He might divide his career into four chapters, much as did the early eulogists: the actions of the colonel Washington, the revolutionary commander-in-chief, the founder, and the president.

COLONEL WASHINGTON

There is a small sense of relief as the belated president reviews the life of the colonel. Here too is the same aspiring poet as the present occupant in the office. Colonel Washington faces the same indignities, frustrations, and blocked opportunities that men of his rank have always historically endured and struggled to overcome. The young Washington is a man born on the periphery of a great empire who finds himself the inheritor of an estate divided seven ways among his brothers. His early models are not Cicero or Cato but "Rules of Civility and Behavior" and "The Young Man's Companion," eighteenth-century survival manuals for aspiring gentlemen. Whatever forms of conduct he might acquire, however, young Washington was acutely aware that he lacked the "interest," the feudal euphemism for economic mobility through sponsorship. Indeed, if one were to add an additional "first" to Washington's vitae, it could be constructed from the fact that he rose the farthest from an aristocratic world, refracted through colonial structure, that would be shattered within a generation.

In the 1750s, however, the young Washington's aspirations were firmly encased in a peculiar politico-economic complex of aristocratic sponsorship, nascent bourgeois opportunity, and imperial condescension. Washington's early sponsors exemplify his predicament. His elder brother, Lawrence, a colonel in the colonial army, was Washington's first sponsor. Lawrence held the status of first as the commander of Virginia's "American regiment." One of his biographer's surmises that it was Lawrence's image of a "cosmopolitan adventurer" that so attracted George to him rather than John Augustine, the sibling with whom he had more contact.[5] Lawrence married well and was elected to the House of Burgess, and "to the young George, it must have seemed that there were no worlds left for Lawrence to conquer."[6] Lawrence died of tuberculosis in 1752, but his brother's father-in-law, Colonel William Fairfax, assumed the role of his benefactor. Fairfax told the young George that a military career was his only route away from Ferry Farm, and Washington himself was undoubtedly aware that surveying, which provided him with the capital for land speculation but forced him to live "like a Negro," held limited possibilities.

Imperial rivalry provided him with his first opportunity and Washington set out "to push his Fortune in a Military Way." Furnished with Fairfax's "interest," the young Washington traveled to Williamsburg in order to convince the colonial governor, Robert Dinwiddie, to give him a part in the British assertion of sovereignty in the Ohio Valley. Dinwiddie was old enough to be George's grandfather, completing the young Washington's trinity of sponsorship that began with an elder brother and a father surrogate. The Washington-Dinwiddie relationship lasted five years and ended acrimoniously with his benefactor making the sponsor's ultimate accusation—"ingratitude."

Washington was given the assignment of delivering a message to the French that the Ohio Valley was British territory. The French were cordial but patronizing to "the buckskin general" and stated their intention to remain in the territory. When the young Washington returned east he stopped by the Fairfax estate to inform his benefactor of his mission and then went to Williamsburg, where he wrote a report which emphasized the danger of French designs which Dinwiddie used as a basis for calling a special session of the House of Burgess. The report was subsequently printed in colonial newspapers and distributed in London.

The whole adventure seemed to work to perfection for the twenty-one-year-old officer. His name was now known in the other colonies and even in London. He had successfully placed himself at the center of the political/military conflict between two great empires. His subsequent mission, however, resulted in a disaster that the elder Washington could never quite erase from his record. Based in part on Washington's own report on French intentions, the governor ordered the young officer to raise troops to build a fort in the Ohio Valley. Much to his disappointment, Washington soon found that his own "interest" was not strong enough to prevent Joshua Fry, an aging teacher, from actually receiving the command. But after learning that the French had the same goals, Dinwiddie ordered Washington to race to the Ohio River forks. Subsequent events are still contested, but if one were to construct the secret narrative as the belated president might do, Washington acted so rashly and unwisely that he launched the Seven Years' War, whatever were French or British intentions, and raised questions about his character and military ability. In a skirmish with the French the elated Washington reported that he "heard the bullets whistle" and found "something charming in the sound."[7] But the French commander had been killed on what the French regarded as a diplomatic mission. Certain of a counterattack, Washington asked for reinforcements and began building a stockade which he poetically called Fort Necessity. When help arrived, the ambitious colonel wrote Dinwiddie that he would not accept the command of the officer in charge even though his royal captaincy outranked his colonial military status. Soon the French arrived in force, and the battle lasted only an hour. One-third of Washington's troops fell and he accepted the terms of surrender offered by the French commander on July 4. The terms seemed generous enough, an escort of his troops back to Williamsburg in return for repatriation of French prisoners, but the agreement, signed by Washington, included acknowledgment of the Virginian's "assassination" of the French officer in the earlier skirmish.

Washington never accepted, nor did he receive, direct blame for the surrender. His second in command was criticized for retreating into the stockade, and Washington blamed his translator for leading him to accept the assassination charge. Still, the belated president who is constructing this narrative might emphasize Washington's inexperience in fort building (the Indian sachem at the site called it "that little thing in the meadow") and his indecision in the days after the skirmish as to where the colonials would make a stand. And if the young Washington suffered at the hand of an incompetent translator, why had he taken three hours to accept the surrender? One biographer offers comfort for the belated president: "No one could suggest that Washington had not acted bravely. On the other hand, he also had behaved like the ambitious young man that he was, so anxious and impatient for recognition that he sometimes acted injudiciously and recklessly."[8] Whatever assessment might be made, the young Washington paid a price. His sponsor, the governor, broke up the Virginia regiment into companies with none led by an officer higher than the rank of captain. Colonel Washington entered the first of what became one of many retirements rather than accept demotion.

The young Washington's civilian status was quite short, however. He felt, despite the calamity at Fort Necessity, that he had "opened the way" for settlements in the Ohio Valley and he yearned for the "laurels" an officer could receive. When he learned that General James Braddock had arrived in America with orders to secure fortifications in the valley, Washington saw his opportunity to "merit . . . royal favor, and a better establishment as a reward."[9] Braddock took on Washington as a volunteer with duties in camp that seem to have consisted largely of errand work and a listener to his stories in the evenings. The general was soon to be defeated and killed in the Battle of Monongahela. Washington survived unscathed, although two horses were shot from under him.

Braddock's defeat represented a turning point in colonial psychology. The colonial mind, as a mixture of inferiority and resentment toward the imperial power, frequently discovers victory in defeat and thus Braddock's expedition represented a turning point in American opinion. Although now exposed to French forces, the Virginians regaled in the bravery of their recruits. The young Washington himself spoke of the Virginians who "behav'd like Men, and died like Soldier's" in contrast to the Crown regulars who "eposd" provincial troops as "they broke and run as Sheep pursued by dogs." Washington, who helped organize the retreat, concluded that "it was impossible to rally them."[10]

The "defeat" at Monongahela forced the governor to reconstitute the Virginia regiment, and the young Washington as the provincial hero of the battle was the logical choice as commander. But Washington soon found that heroism was still no firm substitute for interest. His demands for control of officer selection, aides, and a war chest were resisted by Dinwiddie. The young man and his grandfather surrogate eventually came to terms, but their relationship was irrevocably altered. The Virginia colonel's command was characterized by irresolvable frustrations. Settlers on the frontier were driven to panic by marauding Indians, but they refused to join the militia in sufficient numbers or to relocate in more defensible locations. Washington was driven to apoplexy by unruly recruits and instituted a brutal system of five hundred lashes for infractions of rules. His complaints to the governor became peevish and resentful as he ignored Dinwiddie's advise for patience and calm. Washington's anger was out of control when he learned that a Maryland captain with a royal commission was given command of Fort Cumberland. He refused to enter the area rather than be subject to his command since a royal captaincy outranked his provincial status of colonel. Dinwiddie even gave the inconsolable Washington permission to take his grievance to British headquarters in New York, where he used the occasion to attack the governor as incompetent and to request a commission for himself and his officers.

When the Crown sent Brigadier General John Forbes to capture Fort Duquesne, Washington insisted upon a longer route south from Philadelphia. The colonel knew that the road cut through the forest would be followed by more settlements and complained that Forbes had become the "dupe" of Pennsylvanian "Artifice." He was clearly embarrassed when the expedition succeeded. When the Virginia regiment was disbanded, Washington again resigned his commission and again returned to Mount Vernon.

Washington's biographers, at least those who have (like our belated president) been able to examine his poetic intent, have long puzzled over the transformation of the colonel whose frustration and ambition overflowed from the sponsorship system that demanded deference to the ever patient revolutionary commander-in-chief. For example: "How do we explain his transformation?" asks Don Higginbotham, who regards Washington's legacy of "respect and understanding of superior authority" as "his most admirable soldierly quality in the War of Independence and his foremost contribution to the American military system." "How did the twenty-six-year-old colonel of the Virginia Regiment, so hotheaded and critical of his superiors, obtain the breadth for which he is properly remembered today?"[11] Even Marcus Cunliffe, whose study of Washington would provide the most solace to the belated president and who concludes that "there is something unlikable" about the George Washington of 1753–58, since he is "raw and strident, too much on his dignity, too ready to complain, too nakedly concerned with promotion," finds in the 1772 Peale portrait a man grown in "moral statue," a man "poised, almost benign—the master of himself and his surroundings." If an artist had painted him fifteen years earlier we would probably "almost imagine him scowling a little and adopting a belligerent stance, like those anonymous, pathetic young heroes, a century later, in daguerreotypes of the Civil War."[12]

But while both these examinations open up biographically Washington's poetic intent, they also quickly close off the view. Higginbotham erases poetic intent by focusing upon Washington's maturity: "Thank goodness Washington in 1775 was forty-three rather than twenty-six. Everything we know about him indicates that during those intervening seventeen years he became a more sober and judicious person."[13] Cunliffe admits that the "mature" Washington did not undergo any dramatic conversion—"the road back to Mount Vernon was not for him the road to Damascus"—and he also rejects the notion that Washington underwent the kind of transformation precipitated by war weariness that explained the new life of Ignatius Loyola and Francis of Assisi. But still, despite the absence of evidence, Cunliffe returns to the conversion narrative in order to explain the erasure of poetic intent: "The most we can say (and it is a good deal) is that, like Loyola or Saint Francis, he showed a capacity for growth; his character improved, if not to the point of sanctity."[14]

Yet these assessments would not satisfy the belated president. He would not want to know how the young Washington defeated ambition but how he disguised it. Just when these students of Washington reveal poetic intent they seal it under the cloak of youthful indiscretion, so the belated leader might complain. What the belated president wants to know biographically is why the young Washington ordered six busts for Mount Vernon (Alexander the Great, Julius Caesar, Charles XII of Sweden, Frederick II of Prussia, Prince Eugene, and the Duke of Marlborough) and rejected the supplier's substitute offer of poets and philosophers when they were not available. These men were hardly republican heroes, and they were precisely the men the Washington eulogists of 1800 distinguished from their departed leader.

Can we provide any comfort for the president stricken with belatedness? The seventeen years that elapsed between Washington's resignation of his commission and his assumption of commander-in-chief of the American revolutionary forces provide a key. There was indeed a change in Washington's personality, but can we describe the transformation in a language that does not hide poetic intent? The retired colonel spent a great deal of his energies in remunerative pursuits. He first attempted to produce premium tobacco at Mount Vernon. When the soil proved recalcitrant, Washington began experimenting with other cash crops and managed to make arrangements for wheat contracts with a Virginia firm. Careful attention to overseers and slaves also permitted Washington to reduce his London debt. But Washington knew that the solution to economic independence and wealth lay less in sound management and more in land speculation. The Proclamation of 1763 forbade settlement beyond the Allegheny watershed. Ambitious planters like Washington were suspicious that London was adopting a French model of colonization, preserving the colonial periphery for fur traders and limiting immigration to the coast. He quietly began surveying western land through a process of "Silent management" lest word of his activity "give alarm to others" and "set the different Interests aclashing, and probably in the end overturn the whole." He claimed his own colonel's bounty of five thousand acres offered by Dinwiddie in 1754 and secretly bought shares from enlisted men and Indian traders. In all, Washington managed to procure about thirty-three thousand acres in a process that one biographer described as one which "verged on, if it did not move into, the unethical."[15] In 1758 Washington was elected to the House of Burgess, where he served diligently throughout the prerevolutionary crisis with Britain. He never positioned himself in the forefront of colonial protest but moved in almost perfect lockstep with his Virginia counterparts.

In 1775, when he was selected by the House of Burgess to represent Virginia in the second Continental Congress, Washington epitomized the traits of many Virginia planters. He was acquisitive and daring in his pursuit of economic advantage and deliberative and paternal in politics. This combination of bourgeois and aristocratic values converged in the prerevolutionary period toward an assault on British policy. The Washington of the 1770s was both a self-made man and man who governed by virtue of his standing in the community. In short, Washington no longer needed sponsors in an aristocratic sense; he himself was now part of the interest that others sought. He now derisively referred to "our lordly masters" and asserted in 1774 that "the crisis is arrived when we must assert our rights, or submit to every imposition that can be heaped upon us, till custom and use shall make us as tame and abject slaves, as the blacks we rule over with such arbitrary way."[16]

"As the blacks we rule over" is a phrase that our belated president might stop to ponder. Certainly Washington did not really believe that his status would be reduced to one of chattel slavery. Yet every Virginia planter vividly and personally understood from their daily experience the Hegelian dynamic of master and bondsman. Washington himself constantly complained of the "idleness and mischief" of slaves as well as their "cunning and roguish" behavior. His solution was extensive supervision. "I expect my people will work from daybreak until it is dusk," he told an overseer and once complained that even his managers had a tendency to fall to the "level with Negroes."[17] Thus while the equation of British "enslavement" and black slavery might have required an empirical leap even given the most negative interpretation of the designs of the empire, its connection in psychic terms was real and intimate. Washington could not bear to imagine the loss of his newly created economic independence (and thus actively supported the nonimportation movement as a response to the Townshend Acts) nor could he bear to imagine the loss of the arena of political autonomy that the Virginia planters had so carefully constructed at Williamsburg. "Custom and use" could "tame" him once again in his imagination and he would have no more Dinwiddies whom he must supplicate.

WASHINGTON: COMMANDER-IN-CHIEF

Up to this point the belated president might come to understand Washington's revolutionary commitment, but the colonel is, after all, not yet a poet. Washington's maturity, if that is the word that is to be used, is in a general sense an aspect of America's maturity. If Washington, as had many other Americans, been able to cast off large chunks of colonial frustration and dependency through revolutionary self assertion, his ambition still existed though in another guise. The self assurance that shown through in Peale's portrait still required the creation of routes of access in the emerging new society for his ambitions to flourish. Washington's approach to the position of commander-in-chief is instructive on this point because it is his first discernable step in the formation of monumental achievement and the first instance of his capacities as poet.

The poetic rendering of Washington's acceptance of the command of the Continental army emphasizes the enormity of the challenge that was thrust upon this indispensable man who reluctantly accepted the burden of the defense of his country. The belated president, however, who searches valiantly for poetic intent could reconstruct another narrative. In the portrait that Washington chose to sit for in 1772 he selected the garb of a soldier even though he had not commanded a military force for fifteen years. Washington alone attended meetings of the Continental Congresses in uniform (one which he designed) and impressed a delegate with his "easy, soldier like air and gesture." At the first Congress, Washington is reported to have offered to raise and financially support a regiment from Virginia. The gesture overwhelmed the delegate, who noted breathlessly that "his fortune is said to be equal to his undertaking."[18] At the second Congress, Washington made no such offer (although he spent his time when the Congress was in adjournment training a militia with own funds) but chaired two committees dealing with military questions in 1775. Washington thus had advertised his availability and suitability in a variety of ways: he visibly promoted his persona as soldier in both appearance and behavior; he illustrated grandly his economic status by lending his fortune to the cause; he demonstrated his competence in military issues in congressional committee. The appointment still required more than a little bit of luck. Fate required a commander from the South to solidify national resistance.

The statement accepting the command is not poetry but it does reveal all the elements that were to make Washington a great poet. The brevity of his acceptance is at least indirect reference to his poetic intent. Poets compress utterance and Washington magnified the "monumentous duty" imposed upon him by offering just three short paragraphs. Washington had already understood that on certain occasions the act and speech coincide and he attempted to pack into this performative all the symbolism the circumstance permitted. This "extensive and important Trust" was evidence of congressional recognition of his talents for which he gave "cordial thanks." Washington, however, reminded his audience that he "may not be equal" to the task, and the belated president could not fail to note the repetition of this disclaimer: "But lest some unlucky event should happen unfavourable to my reputation, I beg it may be remembered by every Gentn. in the room, that I this day declare with utmost sincerity, I do not think my self equal to the Command I am honored with."[19] The address concludes with a gesture. Washington refuses to accept any pay for the command.

The belated president who is confronted with this pre-poetic, though majestic, statement might do well to review Washington's reaction to his commission as commander-in-chief of Virginia forces in 1755. Here, the belated president would find a Washington who with partial success negotiated with his civilian superior. Amidst salary matters and the demand that he be given the authority to select his own officers is Washington's statement about the public blame in case of military defeat: "How little does the World consider the circumstances, and how apt are mankind to level their vindictive Censures against the unfortunate Chief, who perhaps merited least of the blame." Washington pleaded with Dinwiddie to give authority to the "Man whose powers and what is still dearer, whose honor depends upon their good Examples." The request was all the more urgent because the present situation constituted an "unhappy Dilemma" in which "no Man can gain any Honour by conduct'g our Forces at this time, but rather lose his reputation."[20]

The belated president could not fail to see the same concerns on Washington's part in 1775 as those he had twenty years earlier: the offer of a military command without appropriate authority with a charge that was nearly impossible to successfully complete. The "mature" Washington, however, no longer complains, no longer negotiates, or, more properly, elevates these resentments to the level of poetic discourse. He acknowledges the honor, warns his sponsors that the assignment is an impossible one (twice), and then offers an honorific gesture validating his own disinterestedness in any "pecuniary consideration" as a motive for his acceptance. In short, Washington accedes to the superior position of his sponsors by asserting his own superior position to them.

Although Washington, Commander-in-Chief, was constantly confronted with prideful generals, jealous provincials, and a recalcitrant and even critical Congress, he no longer treated these as sponsors who presented obstacles that thwarted his ambition. Against his old sponsors, of course, Washington was waging war. But in a central way, Washington recognized that his new sponsor was American political culture. The mature Washington learned to epitomize that culture in the same way he had attempted to epitomize aristocratic sensibility. Expressed as maxim, Washington's strategy was a response as old as the structures of domination themselves: copy your oppressors.

The key, however, to Washington's monumental achievement as General did not rest simply with his identification with the emerging republican consensus that formed America's early national identity. If it had, Washington would have pursued the policies that the Congress and the new states wanted, which he did not. No, so learns the belated president, the mature Washington rejected central portions of American culture and systematically fought to alter them while at the same time offering himself as its exemplar.

Since the belated president is most interested in poetic intent and its relationship to poetic achievement, he might find some comfort in the criticisms, both contemporary and current, of Washington as a General. General Washington won few battles and made many mistakes. An unkind British observer noted that "any other General in the world other than General Howe would have beaten General Washington; and any other General in the world other than General Washington would have beaten General Howe."[21] Washington's tactics were later compared to Fabius's. The analogy fit the General nicely into republican iconography, but seen from the angle of belated frustration, the comparison is clearly post hoc. If there was criticism of Washington in Congress it was based upon his caution and the unfavorable comparisons between the successes of his generals and their absence with troops under his command. Only after Trenton could Washington claim a personal victory, and even here the rout of the Hessians covered what was essentially a botched military operation. Moreover, Washington himself, although he came to see the unique advantages of a citizen army late in the war, was not by personal inclination a Fabian warrior. Like the decisions that were the result of his frame of mind at Fort Necessity, the General always preferred the coup de main, although he was restrained by his own council of war or his low regard for the fighting capacity of his recruits. Robert T. Jones's conclusion in this regard is an apt one: "Fabian by necessity, he was a gambler by instinct."[22] Near the end of the war, Washington himself seemed puzzled by the reasons for victory. Later historians, he told Nathaniel Greene, would be forced to "bestow on our labors . . . marks of fiction . . . for it will not be believed that such a force as Great Britain has employed for eight years in this Country could be baffled in their plan of Subjugating it by numbers infinitely less, composed of Men oftentimes half starved; always in Rags, without pay, and experiencing at times, every species of distress which human nature is capable of undergoing."[23]

So our afflicted president learns that while Washington was the first general, he was not a great general nor perhaps even our greatest general. But this moment of relief soon fades when he jealously examines not simply battles won and lost and military opportunities not seized, but also surveys the institution Washington almost singlehandedly created, the Continental army. When the General assumed command in 1775, there was no army to command. Washington was generously provided by Congress with four major generals and eight brigadiers and instructed to rely on local militia. After Yorktown, the Continental army was a formidable force, well trained and reasonably well equipped, commanded by a highly professional officer corps. The French officers who came to the aid of the Americans were happily surprised to find a *European* army in the field in 1782.[24] In fact, it would not be a serious overstatement to suggest that the Continental army was the first and only American national institution before the second founding and it was created by Washington.

What is so amazing about Washington's achievement in this regard is that it was undertaken in the context of a culture which was both obsessively preoccupied with the danger of a standing army and committed to the militias as the primary means for its defense. Republican theory was confirmed by recent American experience with British troops. A standing army was an "armed monster," an "infernal engine" from the "powers of hell" that stripped a free people of their freedom and bent government to its own will.[25] Its replacement was the militia, which also had American precedent. The American pride in its militias had almost no bounds. The militia epitomized both ancient and current republican virtue. "Native courage" substituted for money and career advancement. Americans even rejected standard training techniques as smacking of unrepublican professionalism. "Away then," said John Pickering, "with the trappings (as well as the tricks) of parade; *Americans* need them not: *their* eyes are not to be dazzled, nor their hearts awed into servility, by the splendour of equippage and dress; *their* minds are much too enlightened to be duped by a glittering outside." General Charles Lee accepted this notion of the militia as an anti-army army when he claimed that without drilling in "the tinsel and show of war" he could train a fighting force in three months.[26]

The long war forced many patriots to modify their fears of a standing army and support for a militia but Washington never accepted these tenets from the inception of his command. He insisted that congressional fears of the "Evils" resulting from a standing army were "remote" and in the present case "not at all to be dreaded."[27] Washington, in fact, came to see the concern about creating a national army as so unfounded that he attributed the fear to "narrow politics" and warned that an overzealous effort to subordinate military to civilian authority could produce "a contrary effect."[28] For militias, he had almost complete disdain. "To place any dependence upon militia, is, assuredly, resting upon a broken staff," he told Congress. Near the end of the war, he insisted that the militia had not been helpful in a single battle. They were useful only as "light parties to skirmish the Woods, but incapable of making or sustaining a serious attack."[29]

Washington's support of a professional, national army and his denigration of militias entailed a serious revision of the concept of virtue so central to republicanism. Six months after accepting the command, he complained that enlistments were sluggish because potential volunteers were "playing off to see what advantages are to be made, and whether a bounty cannot be extorted either from the public at large, or individuals, in the case of a draft."[30] Washington's pessimistic predictions were based upon a decidedly Hobbesian conception of human motivation. He told Congress in 1776 with "sincerity" and "candor" that "it is vain to expect, that any (or more than a trifling) part of this Army will again engage in the Service on the encouragement offered by Congress."[31] As the war dragged on, his critique of republicanism grew more generalized. "Men may speculate as they will; they may talk of patriotism; they may draw a few examples from ancient story of great achievements performed by its influence; but whoever builds upon it, as a sufficient Basis for conducting a long and [bloody] War, will find themselves deceived in the end." Washington insisted that "we must take the passions of Men as Nature has given them."[32]

There were three reasons which motivated men to fight: "natural bravery, hope of reward, and fear of punishment." Washington believed he could not rely on bravery for soldiers to "discharge their Duty in time of Action" any more than he could rely on patriotism as a reason for enlistment. As he had done as a colonel of the Virginia regiment, he recommended more severe punishments for enlistees. A man receives no more than thirty-nine lashes for "the most atrocious offences," he told Congress, and soldiers regard the whipping as "rather a matter of sport than punishment."[33] He favored financial inducement but complained bitterly about the short terms of commitment favored by Congress and the states. Six months was not enough time to discipline men "accustomed to unbounded freedom, and no control."[34] "Subordination and Discipline" were "the Life and Soul of an Army," and short term enlistments made officers too much under the control of their troops: "A kind of familiarity takes place which brings on a relaxation of discipline" as officers attempted to induce second enlistments.[35]

Washington's assessment of the revolutionary soldier was quite clear: he must be induced to enlist with promises of bounty or cash ("for notwithstanding all the publick virtue which is ascrib'd to these people, there is no nation under the sun [that] pay greater adoration of money than they do"), he must be forced into as long a tour of duty as possible to ensure discipline, and he must be confronted with severe punishments in order to fight ("a coward, when taught to believe, that if he breaks his Ranks, and abandons his Colours, will be punished with Death by his own party, will take his chance against the Enemy").[36]

If these were the conclusions Washington reached by taking the passions of men as nature has given them, he drew a different assessment concerning officers. "Good officers" were essential to any army. "An Army formed of good Officers moves like Clock-work," Washington informed Congress, and good officers were "Gentlemen" and "Men of Character" who were "actuated by Principles of honour, and a spirit of enterprize."[37] The model that Washington had in mind, of course, was a European officer corps. French and Prussian officers were members of the nobility; the British extended admission to the ranks of gentility. But Washington was directly confronted with a brute fact of American exceptionalism when he sought to build his national army. Where were the gentleman in America to be recruited? Washington himself had mirrored the aristocratic model when he refused to accept any pay as commander-in-chief, but how many young men could afford to buy commissions (even if the republican Congress permitted the practice)? Washington's solution was to demand significant financial inducements. "They ought to have such allowances as will enable them to live like, and support the Characters of Gentleman; and not be driven by a scanty pittance to the low, and dirty arts which many of them practice, to filch the Public of more than the difference of pay would amount to upon an ample allow," he told congress in 1776. Why should a Continental captain, "performing the same duties of an officer of the same Rank in the British Service," receive lower pay?[38] But the belated president can not fail to see that Washington had put the cart before the horse. The gentleman officer was to be a man of independent means for whom pay was an incidental feature of his service. As one military historian notes, Washington and his young officer corps "kept turning the theory around. While they were eager to serve their country as gentlemen officers, they worked harder to make their military rank prove they were gentleman than to use their social status as an instrument of command."[39]

It is easy to see why Washington created the Continental army the way that he did. The young Washington had had his fill with the Virginia militia, including the frustrations in "managing a number of self-willed, ungovernable people."[40] His young officers were in many ways images of himself as a young man. Washington would be their sponsor before an indifferent Congress. In fact, the complaints of his officer corps which Washington continually placed before civilian authority became his aegis. The "patience" of the officers was "exhausted," Washington repeatedly warned as the war neared its end. He outlined to his most ambitious young officer, Alexander Hamilton, his "critical and delicate" position as standing as "Citizen and Soldier" between "the sufferings of a Complaining Army" and the "inability of Congress" to redress their grievances.[41]

How might our belated president view Washington's "critical and delicate" position in the spring of 1783? Washington, whose poetry had not yet been exhibited, had indeed succeeded in a monumental task. He created an army which defeated the army of an empire under the most disadvantageous of circumstances. He overcame the obstacles before him by sucking all the principles of republican political culture into his own person. Washington was an ever-patient citizen-soldier reluctant to assume and exercise power and motivated solely by consideration of patriotism. These qualities, enormously magnified as they were in the character of a single person, were, however, lacking in the American people at large. The enlisted man was a tangle of Hobbesian interest and the "good officer" must be monetarily assisted to be "Actuated by Principles of honor." Between the consequences of "the extinction of public spirit, the increasing rapacity of our times, the want of harmony in our councils, the declining zeal of our people, the discontents and distresses of the officers of our army" stood only General Washington, the patriot commander.[42] How could these historians fail to see that Washington had not abandoned ambition but sharpened it to the point where Americans could not even feel its rapier, wonders the belated president?

Oh! how far ambition can take a man! exclaims the belated president. But as he reads on, the belated president sees a crisis looming before the Commander. British forces had surrendered at Yorktown, but no treaty had been signed and His Majesty's troops were still on American soil. For two years Washington was faced with a situation that terrified republicans had predicted: managing a standing army in repose. To disband the Continental forces risked a resurgence of British military action. To keep the army in place made republicans more skittish. Most importantly, as republicans had warned, an army in repose has time to think. The young officer corps that Washington created began to doubt congressional commitments to compensation. Washington, in a brief moment of self-doubt, wondered if the Commander-in-Chief should not have been "let more into the political and pecuniary state of affairs than he is." He continued, however, to press for the "just claims of the Army" before Congress.[43]

The crisis (and the poetic opportunity) came in March. Two young officers circulated letters which urged an end to "the meek language of entreating memorials," demanded postwar compensation from Congress, and warned that the army might withdraw to the interior and "mock when their [Congress's] fears cometh forth."[44] An officer's meeting was scheduled to discuss the proposal. Historians have experienced great difficulty assessing the significance of the Newburgh conspiracy. If it was an attempted coup d'état, why then the Lockean-style warning of withdrawal rather than a threat against the Congress sitting in Philadelphia? Who were the conspirators? Were they from General Gates's command? Was the army a pawn of nationalists in Congress? What was Hamilton's role and why did he warn Washington of the meeting? Unable to sort these questions, analysts have relegated the Newburgh conspiracy to a relatively minor, late-war dispute.[45] But the belated president would not view the event from this angle. What he would see is the possibility of a complete collapse of Washington's political agenda. Either his officers had turned on him, preferring a more popular general, or figures in Congress had judged him as an obstacle to the nationalist cause. In either case, the patriot soldier was being discarded by either the military or Congress. The irony of a political strategy which was premised upon soothing republican fears of a Cromwell and then facing replacement by a Cromwell is certainly appreciated by the belated president, as it was also appreciated by Washington himself. Or perhaps, so might the frustrated belated president wonder, Washington himself was a co-conspirator, if not in an actual at least in a moral sense. He, after all, had repeatedly criticized current constitutional arrangements and forcefully conveyed the justness of the army's cause. If the army's case was just, as Washington had shown, and if Congress was politically or constitutionally unable to finance its commitments, as Washington had also intimated, then were not the events at Newburgh those partially of his own making?

Whatever Washington's responsibility, the belated president will find that his response was one of monumental achievement. When Washington called a meeting on March 15, spoke before his assembled officers and so disarmed the coup, he spoke for the first time as a great poet. The Commander employed a variety of arguments to convince his officers to ignore the exhortation to rebel. Washington was an adept scold and he began his address by berating the author of the circular: "How inconsistent with the rules of propriety! how unmilitary!" He even pointed out the practical problems with the plan. Would the officers leave their families unprotected? Would they be willing to "perish in a Wilderness, with hunger, cold and nakedness?" But what cut most sharply for Washington was the officer's warning to avoid men who would counsel moderation. This, of course, was meant for Washington. His whole persona was built on moderation. What else would he be expected to do but plead patience? And patience indeed did the Commander plead, but Washington encased his argument for moderation in the world of the passions. It was Congress that moved slowly since "there is a variety of interests to reconcile." The army, however, was animated by other concerns. Its moral credit rested with a sense of honor which the author of the circular was certain to dissipate. Washington spoke of Congress as an honorable body which moved on a different moral plane than the military. Why then "distrust" civilian authority when it acted differently than the military, especially when the consequence of such distrust would be to "cast a shade over the glory which, has been so justly acquired?" No soldier who had a regard for the "Military and national character of America" would wish to "open the flood Gates of Civil discord, and deluge our rising Empire in Blood."[46]

The poetic conclusion of Washington's address came when he began to read a letter as proof of Congress's good intentions. Reaching for his glasses, the General said: "Gentlemen, you must pardon me. I have grown grey in your service and now I find myself going blind."[47] Many officers wept.

Twentieth-century commentators may not weep, but even a historian who has raised suspicions about the conspiracy has succumbed to Washington's poetry. "The tension, the imposing physical presence of the Commander-in-Chief, the speech, and finally the act that emotionally embodied the whole army's experience, combined all at once," writes Richard H. Kohn.[48] The belated president, however, looks harder past the tears. What he sees is an argument against coup d'état that is actually based upon military values. The object (the belated president is not so sure about the intent) may have been to assert civilian supremacy, but the actual argument asserts the opposite. The military is the guardian of the Republic. Look! murmurs the afflicted president, he even designates the army as the interpreter of the American national character as he announces the military as the protector of the Revolution! And look! who best exemplifies the patriotism of the army than Washington himself! To the Continental army, Washington stood between them and a slow moving Congress apt to be forgetful of soldierly glory. To Congress, Washington stood before an army ready to mutiny.

The events after Newburgh constitute one poetic narrative that Washington set in motion by his address. His officers received a commutation of five years at regular pay. A treaty was signed in September followed by the complete withdrawal of British troops. Washington announced his resignation in December. In June, however, two months after the aborted conspiracy, the General presented his "Circular to the States." The circular immediately became known as "Washington's legacy." The belated president confronts once again Washington's peculiar exercise of power. The General stated his intention to resign and "return to that domestic retirement, which is well known, I left with the greatest reluctance, a Retirement, for which I have never ceased to sigh through a long and painful absence."[49] Cincinnatus is Washington's model, and if there were the slightest doubt that a Cromwellian alternative would be fashioned, Washington closed off the fear. In 1779 William Tudor, in a speech delivered in commemoration of the Boston Massacre, warned of republics in the past in which "a despot, who from private station, rose to uncontrolled dominion, at a time when [the people] were sternly virtuous." Tudor stated that the likely moment of crisis would emerge "at the close of a successful struggle for liberty, when a triumphant army, elated with victories, and headed by a popular General may become more formidable than the tyrant that has been expelled." "Witness the aspiring Cromwell!," exclaimed Tudor, who offered this advice: "resist beginnings."[50]

The belated president sees how Washington anticipated such fears and dispelled them by his announcement of resignation. But he will also note that Washington in this "last official communication" spoke very much in Cromwellian terms. He asserted a right to step "out of the proper line of my duty" even though "those who differ from me" might "possibly ascribe" his remarks to "arrogance or ostentation." Washington declared that an independent America was under "political probation." He described America as in a state of crisis, a state in which "a spirit of disunion or a temper of obstinacy and perverseness" could emerge in the states. To meet this crisis he recommended additional powers for Congress and a uniform militia as the "Palladium of our security."[51] Had Washington made these remarks with an intact army under his command and without his intention to resign, he would have fulfilled the fears outlined by Tudor. That he did not is, of course, the Washington legacy. But to the belated president it is the message that fascinates.

CHAIRMAN WASHINGTON

The message itself, the "crisis" of present constitutional arrangements and the need for a strengthened national government, has now been attached to the next portion of the Washington narrative. From the standpoint of a successful second founding, Washington's "legacy" is the "centerpiece of his statesmanship" and a "coherent vision of the unfinished work" of the revolution.[52] The belated president, however, does not accept the relationship between the circular and the convention as an allusion. He sees the exercise of power. He sees Washington seizing a political opportunity by apparently rejecting one.

This resignation, the third in Washington's career, was undertaken with much bravado. Washington did not stand for election in the Virginia legislature and he even resigned his seat from the vestry of his parish. But the pastoral image of his retirement that he conveyed as one of resting "under the shadow of my own Vine and my own Fig tree, free from the bustle of a Camp and the busy scenes of public life" did not quite correspond to his activities.[53] Washington threw himself into that same bourgeois "symbiosis between private gain and public weal" that characterized his last "retirement."[54] He worked assiduously on improving the productivity of both his crops and slaves at Mount Vernon and avidly pursued his activities as a land speculator including assuming a leading role in the formation of the Potomac Company, which took as its project the building of a canal which would eventually provide a trade route to Ohio. To Washington, while he was not economically "disinterested" in the venture, the company would provide an essential component in the prosperity of the new nation.

The narrative of Washington's desire for freedom from the "busy scenes of public life" is so strong that only a belated president is able to discover some evidence of restlessness. He told Lafayette in 1784 that he was "solacing himself with those tranquil enjoyments" which a "soldier who is ever in pursuit of fame" can have "very little conception." Two years later, Washington wrote Jay that though "it is not my business to embark again on the sea of troubles," he could not "feel myself an unconcerned spectator" to the affairs of the Republic.[55]

The retired Washington retained extensive contacts with those nationalists who either doubted the viability of or had abandoned any hope in the confederation. Washington seemed to fall into the former camp. He, in fact, seemed to have worried most that political instability and even a counterrevolution might come from the "better kind of people." Shays's Rebellion dramatically altered Washington's weak support for the confederation. When he received reports of the resistance, Washington concluded that this was "a formidable rebellion against reason [and] the principles of all government." He looked upon the protests with all the horror that a bourgeois experiences when economic structure is challenged. "Good God!" exclaimed Washington when he was told that the farmers seemed to think that America was "the common property of all." "If there exists not a power to check" these "desperate characters," what "security has a man for life, liberty or property"?[56]

But when Washington was invited to attend the convention in Philadelphia, he hesitated. The hesitation is so extended, so painfully expressed, so fully examined that the belated president cannot fail to be visibly excited. Washington expressed many reservations about participating. He had already told the Society of Cincinnatus that he would not be able to address their meeting in Philadelphia. He complained of rheumatism in his shoulder. Perhaps not enough delegates would attend or perhaps those who did would not be distinguished enough or perhaps they would be too "fettered" with instructions from their states to act independently. Attendance would be "considered inconsistent" with his pledge "never more to intermeddle in public affairs." He told John Jay, almost in a whisper: "In strict propriety a Convention so holden may not be legal."[57]

The belated president might compare Washington's hesitation with his earlier instances of reluctance to assume power. Clearly in this instance Washington did not feign hesitation while actually seeking a prize. Washington *was* hesitant and his poetic ambition emerged in his hesitation. Douglas Southall Freeman notes that Washington reveals "an amazingly egocentric strain" and displays a "patent regard for himself, as distinguished from his country."[58] "He could never have won the war," he concludes, "in the spirit he displayed in this effort to secure the peace." Not since the days of the young colonel Washington is poetic intent so fully revealed in the letters of the retired General in the spring of 1787, for the belated president has already concluded that Washington had acted in an "egocentric strain" during the Revolution, indeed, throughout his whole career.

In fact, the belated president is somewhat surprised that contemporaries and even later commentators could not see the extent to which poetic intent so clearly exposed. For example, the regret that the General must leave his precious private station beneath his fig tree is barely noted. Washington is plainly more concerned with the impact of his attendance upon his pledge to retire from private life than the loss of private life itself. As to the argument that he could not attend because he had already declined an invitation from the Society of Cincinnatus to address their meeting on the grounds that personal business required his presence at Mount Vernon, Washington was confronted with a minor dilemma. Washington had indeed "fibbed himself into an embarrassing corner,"[59] but dates could be altered, as in fact they were. His refusal to attend due to his rheumatism is an old student trick that no one took seriously.

What was Washington so worried about that he so exposed his poetic intent? The belated president discovers that both contemporaries and later commentators were able to discover two of Washington's concerns, although only through affliction with belatedness can their extent be appreciated. The legality of a convention was very much on the minds of each of its proposers. Madison was to directly confront the convention's authority in Federalist #40, and even today the ingenuity of his arguments cannot itself fully cover the nature of the convention as the "dark conclave" of which the anti-Federalists spoke. A sanguine view developed from historical patina notes the deep theoretical inconsistency in any founding, but for Washington and the conventioneers the meeting in Philadelphia constituted a real risk. The best they could manage in regard to this problem was actually stated by Washington himself. If the Congress should call for a convention, it could provide a "coloring" of legality.[60] The secrecy of the convention proceedings, the extent of changes and the mode of ratification certainly did little to erase the concern that the resort to legal coloring was in fact a veneer for conspiracy.

What the belated president finds so intriguing is not the problem per se. He, after all, yearns to have opportunities such as Washington had. What he finds so interesting is the nature of the General's hesitation. As Freeman notes, Washington hesitates primarily out of concern for his reputation. He seems more worried about the damage to his reputation that a failed convention would bring than the consequences of a failed convention in itself. Harsh though the belated president's assessment might be, he is confident about his conclusion on this matter. Washington finally agreed to go to Philadelphia because he had concluded that a *refusal* to attend might actually damage his reputation. Many commentators have concluded that his decision to attend rested upon congressional authorization of the convention. Legal the meeting might not be, but it did have legal coloring, and thus the scales of calculation inclined toward his attendance. But the belated president has noted that even this development did not remove a dilemma that Washington also faced. He had so carefully constructed the role of Cincinnatus, the reluctant participant who undertakes public duties when circumstances indicate his indispensability, that Washington had difficulty finding a way to justify his return to politics. In fact, Washington never did meet this dilemma. While it is true that "no one, it turned out, invoked against Washington his earlier renunciation of public office,"[61] why, wonders the belated president, was Washington's attendance so indispensable? Clearly the proposers were anxious that Washington attend. They had already had Franklin's assent, and with Washington's they would have America's great philosopher and warrior as symbols of the convention's moral, if not legal, legitimacy. Would the proposers, however, have been willing to receive the General's blessing in the absence of his presence? Would it have been possible for the General to write comments to be read at the first session?

To the belated president, Washington's real reasons for attendance can be plucked from the ritual repetition of the Cincinnatus role. A refusal to attend, said Washington, might be considered a "dereliction to republicanism, nay more, whether other motives may not . . . be ascribed to me for not exerting myself on this occasion."[62] Aha! says the belated president. Washington attended the convention, became its presiding officer and thus "first in peace" after being first in war because he was worried that if he did not attend—and the convention succeeded—he would have lost his firstness to the younger men who were writing the constitution.

PRESIDENT WASHINGTON

The belated president enviously reviews Washington's role at the convention and the events which led to his election as the first president of the United States. Even though the proceedings were secret, Washington as presiding officer was able to avoid participation in the debates.[63] To the belated president, Washington's elevated position is yet another instance of his hidden-handedness. How especially resentful must the belated president be when he reviews the point when the convention approaches the question of a single executive and reads that there was a "considerable pause" before the debate ensued since delegates were so conscious of the embarrassment to the presiding officer who was almost certain to be its first occupant. And how the belated president's anger must rise when he learns that a delegate later concluded that the powers of the presidency would not have "been so great had not many of the members cast their eyes toward General Washington as President; and shaped their Ideas of the Powers to be given to a President, by their opinions of his Virtue."[64]

The belated president, of course, knows that Washington will express his desire to be bypassed for the position only to be forced to accept. Jefferson, in fact, politely remarked that despite Washington's "vast reluctance," he "will undertake the presidency if called to it." There is hesitation then on Washington's part, but it shows none of the genuine apprehension that he showed about participating at the convention. Most of all (from the belated president's vantage), Washington worried about the outside chance that he might indeed be overlooked: "If the friends of the Constitution conceive that my administering the government will be a means of its acceleration and strength, is it not probable that the adversaries of it may entertain the same idea? and of course make it an object of opposition? That many of this description will become Electors, I can have no doubt of. . . . It might be impolite in them to make this declaration previous to the Election, but I shall be out in my conjectures if they do not act comfortably thereto—and from that seeming moderation by which they appear to be actuated at present . . . a finesse to lull and deceive."[65] Despite these "conjectures," Washington held firm in his refusal to state whether he would serve if elected. Anti-Federalists were only able to create a semblance of opposition and that in regard to the vice-presidency. When informed of the Electoral College's choice, Washington replied: "I am so much affected by this fresh proof of my country's esteem and confidence, that silence can best explain my gratitude."

When the belated president attempts to assess the first president, his initial reaction is one of limited relief. He might read, for example, Forrest MacDonald's assessment that "the harsh reality of Washington's presidency is that the Father of his Country was not, except in a symbolic sense, particularly efficacious in establishing the permanence of his country, or even of the executive branch." For MacDonald, many of Washington's practices were quickly revised or abandoned by his immediate successors. Under Adams, cabinet members assumed independent executive responsibility; under Jefferson, the presidential practice of refusing to interfere in legislative proceedings was abandoned; under Jackson, the notion of reserving the presidential veto for constitutional questions was broadened; "and so on," concludes MacDonald. Each of Washington's successors "talked about the infallible example that Washington had set, then departed from it."[66] Even the achievements of the Washington administration were largely fortuitous. Washington's banking policies were framed independently by Hamilton. "President Washington's role in creating it, apart from giving his implied blessing, was nothing at all." Washington signed Jay's Treaty in a "fit of rage against Randolph." "No American could take credit" for Pinckney's Treaty, which opened the Mississippi to settlement. The successful removal of Indians from the Northwest Territory was the result of a military campaign waged by Wayne contrary to Washington's instructions. How delighted the belated president must be to learn the "secret" that MacDonald tells: "No one who followed Washington in the presidency could escape the legends that surrounded his tenure in the office, but the more perceptive among them shared a secret: Washington had done little in his own right, had often opposed the best measures of his subordinates, and had taken credit for achievements that he had no share in bringing about."[67]

To the belated president the dread which overcomes him when he confronts Washington as president now seems to dissolve. Washington was first, but only first. His firstness is only that; it is a firstness which is not monumental. Armed with this "secret" he can offer symbolic obeisance to a symbolic presidency and go about creating his own firstness on his own terms. But perhaps it is at this moment that the worst kind of fear, the kind of fear that emerges after a moment of relief, settles upon the belated president. Our belated president has by now reviewed Washington's career quite thoroughly. He knows how limited was Washington's role in Braddock's defeat, how mediocre were his talents as military strategist during the revolution, how small were his actual contributions to the convention. He also knows the enormous credit Washington received as colonial military hero, as revolutionary commander, as father of the Constitution. Is the Washington presidency too in some way a monumental one, independent of any particular achievement on Washington's part, or worse, engineered by Washington himself? Is there a secret behind the secret that MacDonald has told?

First, the belated president reviews Washington's role in Hamilton's financial policies and wonders if Hamilton is not the shield for the president. Then he reviews the neutrality proclamation. Washington had indeed followed Jefferson's advice to water down its language and he had indeed signed the treaty with great reluctance. On the other hand, he had also dismissed Genet only when he openly challenged his presidency and humiliated one of his cabinet members most opposed to the treaty. His decades-old interest in westward expansion was realized in the Pinckney Treaty, however fortuitous were its circumstances. The actual victories of General Wayne were achieved without Washington's direct supervision, but for four years Washington engaged in day-to-day management of Indian relations, exercising a constant policy of personal diplomacy.

Next, the belated president finds other evidence of Washington's hidden "personal" presidency. He discovers Washington's systematic appointment of Federalist bureaucrats and he is forced to pause when he reviews Washington's policies toward protesting farmers in western Pennsylvania. The president insisted that the Whiskey Rebellion was the work of dangerous "self created societies" which required forcible repression. Despite Madison's charge that the action was an excuse to create a standing army and assurances from the governor that a militia call-up was unnecessary, Washington personally led troops as far as Carlyle to confront the "rebels." Jefferson had argued that "an insurrection was announced and proclaimed and armed against, but could never be found." Indeed, the army (which approached the size of the revolutionary Continental forces) found no resistance. One contemporary observer concludes that "perhaps it is just coincidence that Washington, after having ridden into western Pennsylvania, decided to return before that army went into the areas in question. Or it may have be that the genuine hero of such battles as Princeton, Trenton, and Yorktown knew the difference between a real victory and a counterfeit one."[68] Washington, however, later told Congress that the farmers threatened to "shake government to its foundation." On January 1, 1775, he declared a day of national thanksgiving.[69]

At least, notes the belated president, there is no poetry in Washington's personal presidency. But, of course, he knows about the famous Farewell Address. When he finally gathers the courage to carefully read the text, he is directly challenged by Washington's masterful closure of his firstness as president. The many subsequent readings of the Farewell Address focus upon its monumental influence as a statement of American foreign policy, as a statement of Federalist ideology, as a statement of American exceptionalism. The belated president, however, treats the document as a statement, or rather as a monumental poem, of ambition. He notes, of course, Washington's enunciation of the "great rule" of American foreign policy, his defense of the Jay and Pinckney Treaties, his rendering of Federalist prejudices, his remarks on the uniqueness of the American experiment. What impresses and terrifies him so, however, is Washington's success in collecting all these concerns around his own persona.

He notes first the voice through which Washington speaks. Washington begins by informing his audience that he intends to retire and acknowledges a "debt of gratitude . . . for the many honors" his countrymen have bestowed upon him. "Here, perhaps I ought to stop," says the President as he switches to another voice. "A solicitude for your welfare," however, requires that he continue, and the President offers his advice in terms of the "disinterested warnings of a parting friend who can possibly have no personal motive to bias his counsel." Washington's form of address as a "parting friend" is repeated when he closes with a second self-description as an "old and affectionate friend."[70] The Farewell Address thus has two parts: a short and very Washingtonian preamble from which he speaks as a Cincinnatus who announces his decision to return to private life and the longer analysis from which he speaks as a departed figure, indeed, as the lawgiver of antiquity.

Washington lays the foundation for his second voice just before this second section: "If benefits have resulted to our country from these services, let it always be remembered to your praise and as an instructive example in our annals that under circumstances in which the passions, agitated in every direction, were liable to mislead; amidst appearances sometimes dubious; vicissitudes of fortune often discouraging; in situations in which not infrequently want of success has countenanced the spirit of criticism, the constancy of your support was the essential prop of the efforts and a guarantee of the plans by which they were effected."[71] The belated president, whose own ambition has driven him to understand Washington's in all its complex forms, knows quickly how to translate this passage. He sees first that Washington does not review the great events of a young nation, its suffering under colonial dependency and its sacrifices in the revolutionary struggle and its efforts to found a workable Constitution. Instead, he reviews in only slightly disguised form, his own *personal* sufferings: a people whose resolve to support him is challenged by agitators who have awakened passions, questioned appearances, criticized his failures. Now the belated president is ready to translate in order to expose poetic intent. He reviews his effort which now reads something like this: "Remember that the support and honor you have given me has benefited this country in the past and it will do so in the future."

When Washington offers specific counsel in the second section about rejecting the spirit of party, supporting the Constitution, and avoiding European conflict, he is, so concludes the belated president, demanding that Americans follow him departed though he now is. The belated president, of course, does not accept the fiction that Washington speaks in a "disinterested" voice any more than he accepts the fiction that Washington has departed. In fact, he knows for certain in his ever-envious heart that Washington is very interested and never intends to depart from the thought of his countrymen.

What so impresses the belated president, however, is how Washington speaks in the second section. By departing six paragraphs into the address, Washington not only speaks in the voice of "an old and affectionate friend" but now further separates himself from the "sweet enjoyment" of public life. For now his fellow citizens are often referred to in the second person. Washington speaks of the unity of government which constitutes "*you* one people," "*your* union" and how "*you* have improved" upon the first Constitution. In fact, thinks the belated president, the further Washington departs, the more that he demands that he and his policies be followed. Americans are his other, and Washington grasps the central persona of his career, his patriotism, his "disinterestedness," his position "above" the political controversies of the Republic and contrasts it against all others who would manage the Republic after him. The "truly enlightened and independent patriot," the "real patriots," are imitations of his persona. All others, all who might dare to pursue policies different from the President's, are "ambitious, corrupted and deluded citizens" for the "love of power and proneness to abuse it . . . predominates in the human heart."[72]

Finally the belated president considers the counsel that Washington offers. He reviews the President's warning to avoid sectional rivalry and stops for a moment when he sees that Washington announces that it is the Constitution that is the basis for continued union that "presupposes the duty of every individual to obey." He notes how certainly Washington speaks of the Constitution as the "offspring of our own choice" considering his earlier hesitation regarding its legality. But what he finds most interesting is that the Declaration of Independence is unmentioned in the Farewell as a basis for political unity. The address is replete with reference to the Constitution as a "pillar," "prop," and "foundation" of America as a nation. It is the Constitution which demands "respect for its authority, compliance with its laws, acquiesce in its measures." Why, wonders the belated president, does Washington insist upon the Constitution as the sole text for the nation? Certainly Washington had no fears that Jefferson might overcome belatedness. The belated president concludes that Washington has perceived that the Declaration as a revolutionary text was ambiguous as a foundation for order. Writing as a founder, indeed as *the* founder, he is not anxious to recommend a document that focuses upon the right of people to change governments. From the perspective of the belated president, although Washington was first in war, another revolution or radical change in government would result in a diminution of his status as first revolutionary leader and, of course, erase his status as the first president under the present Constitution. Thus the President closes up the revolutionary alternative in his idea of a nation: "The very idea of the power and the right of the people to establish government presupposes the duty of every individual to obey the established government."[73]

The belated president has little difficulty translating Washington's criticism of factions. In fact, he sees the warning as an extension of the President's strategy of Constitution worship. According to the belated president, Washington knows very well the motives of "cunning, unprincipled and impatient" men. Here were men who would challenge Washington's own firstness by dismembering his experiment or initiating another. As Lenin insisted that unions were unnecessary institutions for protection in a workers' state, Washington argues that parties are unnecessary in a Republic.

Washington's final counsel has certainly received more subsequent discussion than the others he offered. Certainly Washington's "great rule of conduct" in avoiding political connections with other nations can be traced to his own defense of his foreign policy and his partisan goals. But Washington's admonitions are also a reflection of his own sense of firstness. One of the most common avenues for the advancement of "cunning, unprincipled and impatient" men involves the effort to seduce a citizenry to oppose or support foreign governments. Driven by "sinister and pernicious motives," these politicians would lead citizens to adopt policies which "reason would reject." By following "the great rule of conduct" laid down by Washington, others would be unable to advance themselves in ways that might overcome the President's firstness.

WASHINGTON I

As we have watched the belated president study George Washington, we have discovered some preliminary answers to two important related questions: What does the belated president learn and what do we learn about the belated president? First, by imagining the struggles of the belated president and viewing how Washington appears to him, we have learned how he might conclude how Washington came to possess his multiple firstness and thus became, if we were to employ kingly description, Washington I. To the belated president, Washington's firstness is achieved through two sets of actions. To be a great poet-president, the belated president has learned from Washington that a monumental ability to hide monumental ambition is as essential as ambition itself. Washington did not learn this truth until the 1770s, when he first exhibited these characteristics successfully in his campaign to be chosen as commanding general of the American revolutionary forces. That Washington came to this achievement through the very particular combined circumstances of confrontation with a declining aristocratic colonial order and an adaptation to an emerging republican and entrepreneurial one, is intriguing to the belated president but not in itself worrisome. Once he knows Washington's secret, he need not to follow this actual path, nor even one like it. His own method of analysis discovered what it took the young Washington decades to achieve. For he realizes he finally is in possession of *his* Washington. This thought by itself greatly pleases him and eases the pain of belatedness, for the narrative he constructed exposed Washington's poetic intent and thus the two presidents are now psychically paired in a very special way. Only a greatly afflicted president could have discovered this common bond. For other presidents, Washington's poetic intent remains a secret that they are unable to unearth.

The belated president learns other secrets from his analysis of Washington. He learns how the contours of American political culture are an enemy to his monumental ambition, but he now knows at least one way in which they were overcome by Washington. Washington's strategy of so exemplifying cultural constraints that the future of the Republic rested upon him he sees as one avenue. He notes by way of confirmation John Adams's complaint concerning Washington's status that "some of our members" are "disposed to idolize an image which their own hands have molten." He knows now how Washington's

firstness in this regard actually aids him, for he too is now in a position to engage a people suspicious of the exercise of political power but willing on occasions, and indeed anxious, to be convinced that those who have imbibed their
truths can exercise strong leadership.

The belated president has also learned from Washington that his firstness
was not simply the result of historical opportunity but also the result of
Washington's talent in closing up those opportunities to preserve his firstness.
For the moment the belated president, armed with *his* Washington, sees his
presidency so connected with Washington's in terms of their mutual ambition
that he is able to admire the first President's achievements in closing off future
pretenders to firstness. He marvels at Washington's rejection of the
Cromwellian alternative in his Newburgh address and circular letter and the
preservation of his firstness as a leader who rejects monumental opportunity.
One of his eulogists grasped Washington's uniqueness in this regard when he
asserted that Washington was "superior to ancient and modern examples" of
great leaders. Others may have rejected such opportunities, "but generally, the
vicissitudes of fortune, and the disappointment of their favorite schemes, urged
them to abdicate power, which they found inadequate to their ambition."[74] He
marvels at his actions under circumstances, such as in accepting the invitation
to attend the constitutional convention, when his firstness was in danger of
recession. He marvels, of course, most of all at Washington's monumental assertion of firstness at the moment of his final departure in his Farewell Address.

If these are some of the lessons the belated president has learned from his
analysis of Washington, what do we learn from the efforts of the belated president? We learn foremost that he who suffers from belatedness is so filled with
what Harold Bloom calls a sense of catastrophe that in his efforts to uncover
poetic intent he will attribute any action and any text in terms of monumental personal ambition. For the belated president, no aspect of Washington's
career, no aspect of his multiple firstness is accorded any other weight. The
belated president is a desperate man whose confrontation with the achievements of others is so monumental and so catastrophic that his study of his predecessors drives him to an interpretation of presidential texts that invariably
drips with resentment. This envy will be the central motivation of the belated
president when searches for esoteric elements in other president's speech.

We also learn that the relationship between the belated president and his
predecessors is a uniquely intimate one. We have not speculated upon the belated president's attitude toward Washington before his affliction. Perhaps he
too once venerated Washington and loved his poetry. Once stricken, the president, of course, is driven to reinterpret Washington on the basis of a narrative
of resentment, but when this project is completed the belated president returns
to the arms of his former love, since they are now reunited in a common bond
of poetic achievement.

In a sense, however, this embrace is a very momentary one, and in terms of
the belated president's enterprise, it is not very significant. For once the belated
president has satisfied himself that he has uncovered poetic intent, he very

shortly comes to understand that he must still achieve monumental poetry. Thus Washington returns to the status of an enemy of the belated president's own ambition. It is probably true that the relationship between Washington and the belated president has been substantially transformed. He now regards Washington and his firstness as a challenge that is at least theoretically or psychically capable of resolution, and thus Washington now stands before him as a very formidable adversary rather than as an evil god who blocks his ambition. But the belated president's prenarrative image will reemerge as he attempts to achieve monumental ambition.

We also learn from the belated president's analysis of Washington's firstness that the belated president is of necessity in open rebellion against his predecessor and his reputation and is a potential destroyer of his texts. We have not yet learned precisely how actual belated presidents challenge and sometimes overcome Washington's firstness, but we do know that this project will involve a reinterpretation and tearing apart of Washington's achievement so that the belated president can make room for his own firstness, and we do know that this monumental battle will be fought in secret. Yet as the imaginary belated president unearthed Washington's poetic ambition, we will strive to unearth the secrets of those who attempted to excel him.

Chapter 2

ABRAHAM LINCOLN: THE DOUBLE CROSS

◆ ◆

A braham Lincoln is not the first president to suffer from belatedness. He deserves, however, the designation of the textbook case. Moreover, Lincoln overcame belatedness more successfully and more completely than any other president. His personal rise to greatness mirrored but exceeded Washington's. Washington built his fortune and his reputation from modest beginnings, but Lincoln's rise was incomparably more steep. His mother may have been illegitimate and his father was an illiterate peripatetic frontier farmer-carpenter and sometime whiskey merchant. While recent scholarship has challenged Herndon's description of his frontier life as a "stagnant, stinking pool," Lincoln lived his youth under the most primitive of conditions. It is from contemplation of these origins that Lincoln came to be eulogized as the "first" great American president. Lincoln was no "gentleman" as Washington had been. He was a new American man, a "man of the people," the "new birth of our new soil."[1]

Of course, Lincoln's besting of Washington in terms of ascent represents only a portion of his status as a great poet-president. Previous presidents, including Andrew Jackson, employed the log cabin motif and democratic origin. What so distinguishes Lincoln and so erases even the trace of belatedness is his monumental feat and his poetic interpretation: He preserved the union under conditions of civil war. No worse calamity can befall a nation than civil war and dismemberment. Even military occupation and a revolution gone astray permit opportunities for retrieval through heroic effort. But civil war unleashes the Hobbesian terror of a human violence that is perpetual and fratricidal. Lincoln undertook the monumental task of providing poetic meaning to this violence and successfully closed this horrible wound in the body politic. Thus the status of equal to Washington, and even superior, was bestowed upon Lincoln. He became "Father Abraham." For which is greater, the founder or the savior?

In the context of this monumental achievement, it seems positively malodorous to interpret Lincoln in terms of any sort of quest to relieve belatedness. Yet despite the fact that Lincoln is granted the role of America's greatest poet-president, there have been persistent questions raised about Lincoln's poetic intent. Recall that the imaginary belated president (who certainly theoretically could have been Lincoln) learned from his analysis of Washington's narrative that he must hide his affliction and make, as did Washington, his poetic intent a secret shared only psychically with his predecessors. Yet Lincoln seems to have achieved greatness and at the same time made his intent at least partially visible to his contemporaries and succeeding generations. Does Lincoln's status as America's greatest poet rest ultimately upon his achievement and the visibility of his poetic intent?

The insistence that Lincoln's actions and words could be explained in terms of a poetic intent of the most destructive sort has been so historically persistent that it constitutes an alternate mythology to the Lincoln legend. Herndon, who himself seems to have suffered from resentment in regard to his former law partner, raised the issue of Lincoln's "restless ambition," and southern commentators, of course, consistently made claims about Lincoln's poetic intent. Albert Bledsoe, to cite a single example, concluded that while Lincoln's success "has been the wonder of all nations . . . perhaps the wonder of all ages," it was the outcome of a "ruling passion" for distinction, not a love of freedom or hatred of oppression. "The one thought . . . that haunted and tormented his soul, was the reflection that he had done nothing, and might die without doing anything, to link his name and memory forever with the events of his time."[2] In fact, during Lincoln's lifetime, it was southerners who systematically spoke of his poetic intent while northern critics doubted his resolve and tended to relegate him to the status of an ordinary politician.

While southern complaints might be explained in terms of natural animosity, there remain the repeated explorations of poetic intent from subsequent generations that seem to parallel each adoring tribute. There are dozens of them. And again while these critiques can be partially interpreted in terms of efforts to redraw history in terms of current controversy, there is an earnestness to the participants of the anti-Lincoln tradition that make their assertions jarring and unsettling. The imaginary president reviews them. In 1931 Edgar Lee Masters in his ferociously hostile biography, which stood beside Sandburg's recently published admiring portrait, compared Lincoln to Robespierre as a ruthless leader driven by ambition and cruelty. Edmund Wilson compared Lincoln to Lenin and Bismarck in 1961. In 1985 M. E. Bradford drew parallels between Lincoln and Roman emperors.[3]

If we framed each of these commentators' conclusions in terms of the theory of belatedness (which involves only the slightest effort at translation), their common assessment would centrally involve the claim that Lincoln was a man so obsessed with overcoming the affliction of belatedness that he was driven to slay his predecessors and managed to do so through the creation of a new American political language. To Masters, Lincoln "armed" himself with the "theology of a rural Methodist" and "crushed the principles of free government."

("He saw Jehovah ruling the insane scene because he rules it.") Wilson's Lincoln is one who attributes to himself a "heroic role" in providential history and in so doing provided the "stimulus for a fanaticism almost Mohammedan." Bradford's "bill of particulars contra the Lincoln myth" rests with the damage that he wrought to American political discourse. In his "universe of discourse, this closed linguistic system, all questions are questions of ends, and means are beside the point."[4]

The belated president discovers that two recent additions to the anti-Lincoln tradition provide an alarming specificity to these kinds of claims. According to George B. Forgie, Lincoln was overwhelmed with his resentment and envy of the founding fathers and the fate which relegated him to life in a "post-heroic age." Lincoln was only able to repress his anger through a complex psychological process which ultimately led to his designation of Stephen Douglas as the "bad son" who would destroy the project of the fathers. Thus Lincoln devised for himself a heroic project of his own: the stalking and "symbolic murder" of the evil son and the preservation of the union at the cost of civil war.[5] According to Dwight G. Anderson, Lincoln struggled to imitate Washington, but after his attempts at "filial piety" were unacknowledged by the American citizenry, his heart filled with "malignant passions" and he set out with a "revolutionary vengeance" to destroy and replace Washington through the destruction of civil war.[6]

Surveying these assessments, the belated president will conclude that both Forgie and Anderson are correct, that Lincoln attempted to slay both Douglas and Washington. But he will also conclude that Lincoln was so afflicted by belatedness that his poetic ambition led him to a project that involved not simply the poetic murder of his nation's father or one of its sons but that Lincoln was a slayer of many fathers and sons. In order, however, to appreciate the characterization of Lincoln as some kind of mass murderer, the belated president turns to a small piece of psychoanalytic theory upon which both Forgie and Anderson implicitly rely. In Freud's tale of the origins of culture, he spoke of a group of imaginary sons who were so resentful of the primal father's authority that they murdered him.[7] Freud's account includes two great acts after this revolutionary violence. Overcome by guilt, they recast the father in terms of totems to be revered and faced with sexual anarchy, they constructed the incest taboo which preserved in a small way the power of the primal father in themselves but permitted some measure of regulation among themselves. Both Forgie and Anderson capture Lincoln's destructiveness, but both fold in his poetic intent with his poetic achievement. For if Lincoln represents a son gone completely berserk from belatedness, he would have erased the achievements of the other sons and restarted the history of the primal father. This Lincoln did not do. He defeated Stephen Douglas the son and he overcame Washington the father as he did with other fathers and sons who crossed his path, including Jefferson, Jackson, Polk, Taylor, and Clay. But Lincoln accorded all these men a place in his poetry, albeit a place lesser than his own. Seen from the standpoint of belatedness, Lincoln's many speeches and addresses involve a complex strategy of reordering in which the achievements of each are (mis)read so as to give him an exceptional role. This strategy involves extremely close readings, expressed esoterically, of the texts and character of those who stand in the way of his poetic achievement. These intersections created by moving forward and backward from text to a consideration of his poetic intent and back again, the imaginary president calls "double crosses" to denote both the actual method Lincoln employed and the moral ambiguity of his enterprise. A recognition and exploration of this strategy can, the imaginary president feels, help solve the puzzle of Lincoln by offering a solution of how to combine both the Lincoln myth and the anti-Lincoln tradition, how, in other words, to acknowledge both poetic intent and poetic achievement.

DOUBLE-CROSSING THE FATHERS: WASHINGTON

Lincoln's career is studded with flashes of poetic intent which tantalize his critics. He often spoke of his lifelong fascination with Macbeth, the exemplary text of the tyranny of ambition. Days before his assassination, he ruminated on a dream which haunted him like "Banquo's ghost." Yet it is his Lyceum speech, delivered when he was a twenty-eight-year-old state representative, that stands as the monumental public expression of poetic intent. There is certainly a pattern of development in Lincoln's political thought, but his first major speech, the Lyceum address delivered in 1838, contains all the elements of his later theory. The speech had fascinated scholars for generations not only because of a belief that it represents a key to Lincoln's poetic achievement but because for some it offers tantalizing insights into his poetic intent, and thus it comes as no surprise that the belated president should latch onto the address with even more determination to discover its esoteric message than have the scholars of the two Lincoln traditions.

In 1838 Lincoln was a two-term representative of the Illinois legislature and a rising young politician in the Whig Party. The subject upon which he chose to speak was "the perpetuation of our political institutions." Lincoln reviewed a series of recent violent incidents that had occurred in the country. These included accounts of black lynching and the murder of Elijah Lovejoy, an abolitionist editor. But Lincoln also discussed the hanging of a group of gamblers in Vicksburg, thus treating both politically motivated and ordinary crimes as part of a general problem of law and order. A "mobocratic spirit" was "now abroad in the land." Some men had "no restraint but the dread of punishment"; some "having ever regarded government as their deadliest bane, make a jubilee of its suspension"; some "good men" who "love tranquility" and "who desire to abide by the laws and enjoy their benefits" see their property and families endangered, and "seeing nothing in prospect that forebodes a change for the better . . . imagine they have nothing to lose."[8]

Lincoln, at this point in his career, exclusively focused upon the effects of antislavery activity rather than upon its immediate causes. And what were the effects? For Lincoln, under such conditions "men of sufficient talent and ambition will not be wanting to seize the opportunity, strike the blow, and overturn that fair fabric which for the last half century has been the fondest hope of the lovers of freedom throughout the world."

According to Lincoln, the Republic was at a crucial juncture. His speech began with recitation of familiar July Fourth rhetoric. America was "in the peaceful possession of the fairest portion of the earth" and "under a government of a system of political institutions more essentially to liberty than any of which the history of former times tells us." But Lincoln reminds his audience that the present and future generation are not responsible for this fortune: "We toiled not in the acquirement or establishment of them; they are a legacy bequeathed to us by a once hardy, brave and patriotic, but now lamented and departed race of ancestors."[9]

Employing both republican symbols of virtue and corruption, Lincoln argued that the very success of the American experiment in free government was in danger in its third generation. In the first and second generations the success of the Republic was itself at stake. "Theirs was the task," said Lincoln, "to create a political edifice of liberty and equal rights." Ours is to "transmit these . . . undecayed by the lapse in time."

The problem of maintaining a republic across time had long been a preoccupation of republican political theory. Lincoln reiterates this republican theme and suggests that the threat to regime maintenance comes not only from the decline in virtue (the traditional republican argument) but the disjunction between the political ambition of leaders in the third generation and the requirements of the Republic. The republic requires a shoring of its foundations on the part of the leaders, a reminder to the people of their duties.

But what ambitious person would be satisfied with this chore of tending established institutions? In the first two generations, personal fame coincided with the needs of the Republic: "Their ambition aspired to display before an admiring world a practical demonstration of the truth of a proposition which had hitherto been considered at best no better than problematical—namely, the capability of a people to govern themselves. If they succeeded they were to be immortalized; their names were to be transferred to counties, and cities, and rivers, and mountains; and to be revered and sung and toasted through all time." But now the "field of glory is harvested, and the crop is already appropriated."[10] For Lincoln, however, human nature is unchanging. Each generation produces ambitious men, and leadership is now a threat to the Republic:

New reapers will arise, and they too will seek a field. It is to deny what the history of the world has told us is true, to suppose that men of ambition and talents will not continue to spring up amongst us. And when they do, they will as naturally seek the gratification of their ruling passion as others have done before them. The question is: Can that gratification be found in supporting and maintaining an edifice that has been erected by others? Most certainly it cannot. Many great and good men, sufficiently qualified for any task they should undertake, may ever be found to aspire to nothing beyond a gubernatorial or a presidential chair; but such belong not to the family of the

lion, or the tribe of the eagle. What! think you these places would satisfy an
Alexander, a Caesar, or a Napoleon? Never! Towering genius disdains a beaten path.
It seeks regions hitherto unexplored. It sees no distinction in adding story to story
upon monuments of fame erected to the memory of others. It denies that it is glory
enough to serve under any chief. It scorns to tread in the footsteps of any predecessor,
however illustrious. It thirsts for distinction; and if possible, it will have it, whether
at the expense of emancipating slaves or enslaving free men.[11]

How were the American people to "fortify" (to use Lincoln's expression)
against this danger? In the early days of the Republic, memories of the sacrifices in the Revolution acted as a barrier against usurpation by ambitious men.
"Nearly every adult male had been a participator in some of its scenes . . . in
the form of a husband, a father, a son, or a brother, a living history was to be
found in every family—a history bearing the indubitable testimonies of its own
authenticity, in the limbs mangled, in the scars of wounds received." Now "the
silent artillery of time" had accomplished what "invading foeman could never
do." These memories functioned as "pillars of the temple of liberty" but they
had crumbled. Unless this generation found "other pillars," the Republic was
imperilled.

The memory of revolution had functioned successfully for Lincoln as a natural support for republican institutions. Battlefield death and valor had made the
revolutionary experience an immediate and concrete symbol of American political culture. Lincoln admitted that those memories would never be "entirely
forgotten," but they would never again be "so universally known nor so vividly
felt as they were by the generation just gone to rest." To the extent to which
political culture could still function as an important foundation, it must now
emanate from a exercise of rational will. "Passion has helped us," said Lincoln,
but "in the future it will be our enemy." Only "reason—cold, calculating, un-
impassioned reason" can help us now.

Lincoln, in essence, calls for a reaffirmation of the American social contract
which emphasizes obedience to the law:

> Let every American, every lover of liberty, every well-wisher to his posterity swear
> by the blood of the Revolution never to violate in the least particular the laws of the
> country, and never to tolerate their violation by others. As the patriots of seventy-six
> did to the support of the Declaration of Independence, so to the support of the
> Constitution and laws let every man remember to violate the law is to trample on the
> blood of his father, and to tear the charter of his own and his children's liberty. So
> important is this pledge to the future of the republic that Lincoln insists that it must
> become the "political religion of the nation" taught by every family, every school and
> college, every clergyman and legislator.[12]

It is certainly possible to read the Lyceum address solely in terms of poetic
achievement. Harry Jaffa, who confronts and then rejects the position that
Lincoln suffered from a monumental case of belatedness, contends that the
description of the leader who disdains beaten paths is so strikingly vivid and

morally ambivalent because Lincoln "as every true strategist imagines himself in the position of his enemy."[13] Lincoln, according to Jaffa, prophetically determined that leadership of monumental magnitude was soon to be required and that "his warning against Caesar is sincere." Edmund Wilson, on the other hand, while he accepts the Lyceum speech as prophecy, cannot find any other explanation for the "fire that seemed to derive as much from admiration as from apprehension" which characterizes his account of the forthcoming Caesar. He concludes that "it is evident that Lincoln has projected himself into the role against which he is warning."[14] To the imaginary belated president, these commentaries raise this question: Had Lincoln undertaken an exercise in which he imagined the impulses of a belated presidential aspirant in order to warn and protect the Republic or had Lincoln esoterically confessed his poetic intent in his account of the problems faced by the postrevolutionary regime and the threat posed by Caesarism? There are several discernable rearrangements in the address that suggest that Lincoln was indeed suffering monumentally from belatedness. The opening of the address is as frank a confession of belatedness as one could write. Lincoln lists the achievements of the founders and flatly states that "we toiled not in the acquirement or establishment of them" and tells his audience that it is the task of his and succeeding generations to only "transmit these." Filial resentment, not filial piety can be the only accurate characterization of these remarks.

This resentment is relieved by a series of attacks on the motives and achievements of the founders so severe that one must wonder how much gratitude is owed. Look simply at what Lincoln said. The founders were motivated by "celebrity, fame, and distinction." They knew that were the experiment in creating a new government successful they would be "immortalized; their names transferred to counties and cities, and rivers and mountains; and to be revered and sung, and toasted through all time." Of course, such ambition is no longer beneficial to the Republic. "The field of glory is harvested, and the crop is already appropriated." When the "new reapers" rise they will seek to tear down the edifice of their predecessors. The eighteenth-century commentator gave due moral weight to the desire for fame which readers of his poetic achievement contend the young Lincoln was acknowledging, but Lincoln has in this instance equated the founders with Alexander, Caesar, and Napoleon. The Washington eulogists were fascinated with the difference between the first president's leadership, especially his exercise of restraint under conditions of monumental opportunity, and the great conquerors. Lincoln asserts that the difference between Washington and Caesar is simply one of political time. Is it possible that were Washington born in 1800 and not 1732 he would be a threat to the Republic?

The belated president reasons that if Lincoln were suffering from belatedness his psychic identification with Washington as first would be intense and intimate, since he would have discovered his antagonist's poetic intent as well as his achievement and regarded himself equal at least in regard to the former. In the Lyceum speech Lincoln announces to his audience his discovery without directly telling his own secret. By attributing moral weight to leadership solely in terms of political time and defining it in terms of the morally ambiguous motives of ambition and risk taking, he places himself on a par with Washington. Washington (unnamed until the penultimate paragraph of the essay) sought distinction through the demonstration of "the truth of a proposition" considered "at best no better than problematical." Had he failed he would have been called a knave and a fool and his name would "sink and be forgotten." The young Lincoln may be denied the harvest that Washington reaped, but so too would Washington had he lived in the next generations of the new regime. Then it would be Washington not Lincoln whom history would have cast in the role of destroyer. If, in the language of belatedness, Washington and Lincoln are equals at least in terms of poetic intent it matters little that Lincoln fantasized himself a Caesar as part of political exercise or psychic instability. From the perspective of belatedness, Lincoln tells his audience that Caesarism is poetic intent confronting historical contingency and that both he and Washington are equally both Caesars and not-Caesars.

If in his account of the monumental ambitions of great leaders the young Lincoln makes himself an equal to Washington, he undertakes an enormously bold maneuver in terms of Washington's poetic achievement. From Washington's perspective the goals of the Revolution were realized in the second founding, and he urged successive generations to offer filial obedience to the Constitution in his Farewell Address. Lincoln offers filial obedience alright, but he completely omits the object of Washington's urgings and focuses exclusively on the Revolution as the event to be revered. It is the "scenes" of the Revolution—"in limbs mangled, in the scars of wounds received"—that form the connection among generations, not the struggles of the men who met in the summer of 1787. Although Lincoln does not say so (he does not need to say so), it is the Revolution that constitutes the heroic event in American history that is the key to the nation's survival. "As the patriots of seventy-six did to support the Declaration of Independence, so to the support of the Constitution and the Laws, let every American pledge his life, his property, and his sacred honor; —let every man remember that to violate the law, is to trample on the blood of his father" was Lincoln's pledge. This "misreading" of Washington's instructions would form the central trope of Lincoln's political thought throughout the 1850s.

The young Lincoln had taken the "pillar" and the "foundation" of the pledge that Washington had urged generations to undertake, substituted the Revolution as the contractual object as one of the "pillars of the temple of liberty," and then argued that any violation of its terms would entail trampling on the blood of the fathers. Washington's firstness of course remains as the revolutionary general. Lincoln had peeled away only one of his adversary's inaugural acts. But the young Lincoln's last message attacks this aspect of Washington's firstness. In the first paragraph of the speech in which Lincoln announces his belatedness, the achievements of the founders provided only the transmissions of the edifice to new generations. By the end of the address, the young Lincoln has made clear his conclusion that the monumental project of Washington and the founders was not only incomplete but rapidly disintegrating. The edifice "must fade, is fading, has faded." The great pillars erected by the "departed race of ancestors" were a "Forest of giant oaks; but the all-resistless hurricane has swept over them, and left only, here and there, a lonely trunk, despoiled of its verdure, shorn of its foliage, unshading and unshading, to murmur in a few more gentle breezes, and to combat with its mutilated limbs, a few more ruder storms, then to sink, and be no more."[15] What greater announcement of his own independence could any young poet assert? From the perspective of belatedness, the young Lincoln sees his predecessors' influence as minimal and declining and his own opportunities for poetic achievement conversely growing.

Of course, the fadedness of Washington and the founders is achieved through the young Lincoln's own strategy of rearrangement. Washington knew quite well that revolutionary commitment was an inadequate basis for the founding. He questioned public regardedness as a basis for enlistments and support for the struggle and was terrified by his own knowledge of the directions in which revolutions could progress. The Constitution was recommended as the pillar for precisely these reasons. As a second effort in reflection upon the nature of human beings, Washington demanded "respect for its authority, compliance with its laws, acquiescence in its measures." The young Lincoln, however, asserts that the Revolution was the legacy of the founders and that its success rested with the "passions" it exerted upon the people to create circumstances in which "the basest principles of our nature" were made to "lie dormant." These passions, however, were already fading. "But those histories are gone," Lincoln tells his audience as he announces the focus of his own poetic achievement. We must "supply their places with other principles" since the passions provided by the founders can no longer help us. Political time, which Lincoln used to compare his own poetic intent to that of Washington (the "glory that Washington harvested" came from the same "ruling passion" as his), now is on his side since the project, as Lincoln had rearranged it, of the founders had eroded and needed new pillars. Thus from the perspective of poetic achievement, the vivid description of the "towering genius" and Caesarism is not the conflated Washington-Lincoln of poetic intent but now an avoidable figure. Remember the Caesarist threat to the Republic originated in circumstances in which poetic intent could find no outlet for poetic achievement. The one who belongs to "the family of the lion, or the tribe of the eagle" sees "no distinction in adding story to story, upon the monuments of fame, erected to the memory of others" and is impelled to destroy the Republic. But the young Lincoln of poetic intent has found a project worthy of his poetic intent in the creation of "new pillars." He is free of the historical guilt that a Caesar must assume as he strives to slake his thirst for distinction.

It is at this point that the imaginary belated president begins to appreciate the beauty of the young Lincoln's poetry. For if the young Lincoln in his struggle against belatedness has found an opening for poetic achievement that marks him off from the figure that he has constructed out of his fantasies of poetic intent, he has also found an adversary worthy of his poetic achievement. There will be men, he prophesied, who would seek to fulfil their poetic intent indifferently as to consequence. They will "have it," he tells his audience, "at the expense of emancipating slaves, or enslaving freemen" and the young Lincoln, with the monumental project of constructing new pillars before him, will be in a position to poetically confront them.

Evidence that the young Lincoln had not abandoned his strategy to alleviate belatedness can be seen in his Temperance address delivered three years later. Ostensibly the object of the speech is a commendation of a new approach to the treatment of alcoholism, but commentators who have searched for what we call evidence of poetic intent have had little difficulty decoding the esoteric messages in the speech. Harry Jaffa has argued that the young Lincoln's criticism of temperance reformers is a veiled critique of public opinion as the sole standard of moral evaluation and a general rebuke of the Enlightenment project. "When the people insist," Jaffa learns from Lincoln, "that the people become regenerate, when what is required is not good behavior but purity, then the requirement for participation in political life will be dramatically changed." The goals of the reformers, warned Lincoln, led to the "despotism of Cromwell or Massachusetts Bay. In the foreground we can discern Lenin or Stalin."[16]

Anderson's reading comes a bit closer to an appreciation of Lincoln's poetic intent, for he focuses upon the trope of intemperance as a veil for ambition. The alcoholic suffered from the same disease as the Caesarist leader of the Lyceum address. Indeed, in support of Anderson's interpretation on this point, the belated president can point to the common "thirst" of the men of the family of the lion and the alcoholic, their common pursuit of an object at any cost, their common inability to contain their extraordinary appetites. For Anderson, however, Lincoln's pairing of the Washingtonian Society of reformed drunks with his concluding comments on Washington himself at the close of the address (Washington is the "mightiest name on earth . . . still mightiest in moral reformation") is evidence for him that Lincoln had not yet abandoned Washington as a model for imitation. "Despite Lincoln's ironic detachment and tone," concludes Anderson, "he ended this speech, as he had the Lyceum Address, still formally committed to Washington as the moral exemplar and ultimate authority. There is nothing in the content of the speech inconsistent with this conclusion either, suggesting that his demonic impulse, though not suppressed, was firmly under the control of his reason."[17]

But is there nothing in the content of the speech, wonders the belated president, that suggests that the young Lincoln had not already arrived at an accommodation with his own poetic intent that involved a reordering of Washington's poetic achievement? Both Jaffa and Anderson agree that temperance and intemperance in the narrow sense is only the formal subject of the address, the exoteric aspect of the speech. But what is the young Lincoln telling himself, if not his audience, about "burning appetites" and the "citadels of the great adversary"?

Let us suppose, says the belated president, that the alcoholic is a veil for one who suffers from belatedness. Let us assume, in other words, that the alcoholic is the young Lincoln himself. The conclusion that Lincoln was fascinated with the Caesarist leader in the Lyceum address is largely based upon the vividness of his description and his veiled conflation of his motives with "good" leaders such as Washington and the founders. In the Temperance speech the alcoholic actually receives a warm depiction. The "demon of Intemperance" attacks those who are "brilliant and warm-blooded," men of "genius and generosity." It is the temperance reformers who are the object of the young Lincoln's scorn and ridicule. The "preachers, Lawyers and hired agents" who compose the movement have no real interest in those who suffer. The preacher advocates temperance because he is "a fanatic and desires a union of Church and State; the lawyer, from his pride and vanity of hearing himself speak; and the hired agent, for his salary." There was in the reformers "something so repugnant to humanity, so uncharitable, so cold-blooded and feelingless, that they never did, nor ever can enlist the enthusiasm of a popular cause."[18] The Washingtonians, on the other hand, as a society of reformed alcoholics, "desire to convince and persuade" as "their old friends and comrades." "They know that generally they [the alcoholics] are not demons, nor even the worst of men. They know that generally, they are kind, generous and charitable, even beyond their more staid and sober neighbors. They are practical philanthropists; and they glow with a generous and brotherly zeal, that mere theorizers are incapable of feeling."[19]

The young Lincoln thus speaks of three classes of men: the old reformers, the drunks, and the reformed drunks. If the address is at least partly poetically autobiographical, to which class does he belong, wonders the belated president? There is certainly a Nietzschean strand to Lincoln's classification if one interprets the address from the perspective of belatedness. His expressions of positive revulsion toward the men who govern society, the ministers, lawyers, and the hired agents, is based upon their incapacity to judge those whose "genius" and "generosity" make them vulnerable to drink. In Nietschean terms, these reformers have interpreted what is "bad" as an "evil." Excessive drink (the frustration derived from belatedness) arises "from the abuse of a very good thing." But while Lincoln announces considerable sympathy for the drunkard, he reserves his highest accolades for the alcoholic who has overcome his affliction.

It is true, as Anderson notes, that the young Lincoln, ends his address with a paean to Washington, but what, asks the belated president, does this reveal about Lincoln's poetic intent? He had already concluded that the temperance pledge was an ineffective device of the old reformers. When an alcoholic "bursts the fetters that have bound him," he does so not because he is a member of a church, or because he is "vain of hearing himself speak," or because he has been compensated monetarily. He does so from the example and persuasion set by men of humanity. In the language of belatedness, Lincoln has said that his frustration could only be alleviated by the example of men like him, hence the pairing of the project of the Washingtonians and of Washington himself. But it must be noted, however, that the Washington who saves Lincoln is the Washington whose poetic intent as well as poetic achievement has been revealed. In other words, Lincoln has been saved from a "desolating career" by Washington, the reformed drunkard. Both Washington and Lincoln are equals in the sense that both possess unquenchable thirsts and as only a Washingtonian can understand an alcoholic and place himself in a position to aid him, only a Washington can understand a Lincoln and too provide him guidance. Lincoln and Washington now proceed hand in hand. Lincoln's own "tyranny [is] deposed" and his slavery (before belatedness) "manumitted." Is it not more plausible to suggest that the puzzling conclusion to the address ("Happy Day, when, all appetites controlled, all passions subdued, all matters subjected, mind, all conquering mind, shall live and move, the monarch of the world")[20] is less a satiric comment on the excess of reformers than an autobiographical celebration of Lincoln's poetic independence?

The belated president concludes that the young Lincoln's Lyceum and Temperance addresses constitute a complete statement of his pain of belatedness as well as his general strategy for overcoming it. He had experienced in a monumental way the frustrations of participating in a political arena in a "post-heroic" era, and by uncovering the poetic intent of the greatest father of the founders, George Washington, he opened for himself means for overcoming belatedness.

This is not to say that Lincoln never again was forced to confront the agonies of belatedness. He struggled with the enormous obstacle of historical contingency and at several points in his career was despondent when he thought that he had been defeated by chance. When Lincoln returned from Washington to Springfield in 1849, he thought his political career was finished. According to Herndon, his depression "dripped from him as he walked." Six years later the repeal of the Missouri Compromise "aroused him as never before" and he reconfronted his belatedness by attacking the Kansas-Nebraska Act. His general strategy for overcoming belatedness through a "rededication" of the American experiment was complex and delicate, involving as it did reinterpretations of the two great texts of the Republic. Moreover, Lincoln was never quite able to find the Caesarist leader that he prophesied to confront and slay. This did not, however, prevent Lincoln from battling a whole range of antagonists whom he was willing to accept as substitutes.

DOUBLE-CROSSING THE FATHERS: JEFFERSON

What is important in understanding Lincoln's battle with belatedness is that never again does the anger with the fathers that so animated the Lyceum address surface, nor does he continue to explore his affinity toward the fathers in terms of common poetic intent. His later speeches reveal a continuation of his struggle to find the appropriate discourse to express his strategy, but they are firmly directed toward implementing a presidential version of poetic achievement.

The belated president now focuses upon what all students of Lincoln acknowledge as his poetic achievement: his reading of the Declaration of Independence. But to him the Declaration of Independence became the central metonymy with which Lincoln moved from a (hostile) imitation of Washington as well as his "sons" to an act of exceptionalism. Lincoln's assertion that the Declaration was the "immortal emblem of Humanity" and the "central idea" of nationhood involved more than simply moving back America's origins by eleven years. This trope involved a serious misreading of Washington's Farewell Address, which was designed to promote the second constitution as the founding moment to be preserved. Washington had urged citizens to "properly estimate the immense value of your national union to your collective and individual happiness." Lincoln's own conception of national union grew progressively more majestic until he reached his poetic apogee in the Gettysburg Address. His July 4 speech before Congress after the attack at Fort Sumter in which he claimed that the war was a "People's Contest" contained his determination to prevent the destruction of a union that was "made by Washington." But what in Lincoln's reordering of Washington's poetic achievement was the exceptional act of the first president? The union came into existence ("conceived" in the poetry of the Gettysburg Address) "even before [the states] cast off their British colonial independence." The July 4 speech also reiterated the history of the nation first narrated in terms of belatedness in the Lyceum address. The Republic was an "experiment" in which two points—"the successful establishing, and the successful administering"—had "already been settled."[21] It was certainly no hyperbole in 1861, however, for Lincoln to argue that its "successful maintenance" involved much more than routine transmission across future generations. From the perspective of poetic achievement, Lincoln had erased (or at least reordered) the Constitution as the basic text of the Republic, replacing it with the Declaration, and at the same time made its maintenance a heroic act. By placing the Declaration as the idea to be preserved, Lincoln created his own monumental project, a project as monumental as that undertaken by Washington.

As Lincoln pursued the implications of his act in terms of slavery he was always careful to remind his audience that this in fact was the same project as that of the founders. "I fully endorse" Douglas's statement that "our fathers, when they framed the government under which we now live, understood this question just as well, and even better, than we do now" was the beginning of the Cooper Institute address, and he proposed to "adopt it as a text for this discourse."[22] But to the belated president, Lincoln knew full well that the manner in which he had defined filial piety required monumental acts, acts in the famous chilling words of the speech that involved a conviction that "might makes right."

Lincoln, however, was also intent on avoiding replacing the shadow of one dead poet with another. He also set out to complete this project by (mis)reading the Declaration itself. In 1859 he praised Jefferson thusly: "All honor to Jefferson—to the man who, in the concrete pressure of a struggle for national independence by a single people, had the coolness, forecast, and capacity to introduce into a merely revolutionary document, an abstract truth, and so embalm it there, that today and in all coming days, it shall be a rebuke and a stumbling block to the very harbingers of reappearing tyranny and oppression."[23]

Encased in this allocation are the aims of the strong poet. The Declaration could have been "merely a revolutionary document" had not Jefferson had the foresight to introduce the idea of an "abstract truth." Taken out of the evasive strategy, Lincoln says that the work is simply a revolutionary pamphlet written under "concrete pressure" except for a singular abstract idea. But the idea is "embalm(ed)." Lincoln frequently referred to the document as "old." The striving monumental poet-president, must bring a dead thing to life.

When Lincoln as president-elect said that he never had "a feeling politically that did not spring from the sentiments in the Declaration of Independence," he reflects the evasive aspect of his poetic strategy. In the Gettysburg Address, which all Americans recognize as a literal poetic form, we see, however, the monumental achievement of Lincoln's project. The Declaration constituted a providential test for Americans. The founding fathers gave birth to an idea of nationhood; the war was now a trial to determine if that idea would endure; victory would assure a rebirth. Lincoln had not only given meaning to a war with half a million casualties, he had transfigured an eighteenth-century Enlightenment project into a miraculous event of biblical proportion. For while the founders had conceived the idea that all mean all created equal, it was Lincoln, through the apocalyptic struggle of civil war, who had given the idea a new life.

If Lincoln's strategy involved a reordering of America's great poet-presidents from the conventional Washington-Jefferson to Lincoln-Jefferson-Washington, the theory of belatedness that the imaginary belated president represents needs to account for the particular nature of his (mis)reading of the document. Such an account need not demean Lincoln's poetic achievement in successfully asserting that the Declaration contained a broader meaning than the one Douglas had assigned to it in his response to Lincoln's poetic act of reordering. That the Declaration was in danger of completely losing its moral force if it were read as a text which guaranteed the rights of white males of European descent was a reading which would have satisfied his desire to overcome Washington. Moreover, although Lincoln scrupulously defended the founders, including Jefferson, of complicity in protecting the institution of slavery, their historical role in this regard was ambivalent enough to give Lincoln enormous room for his own exercise of poetic achievement. The mere act of retrieving the embalmed document from both the caution of the founders and its neglect by Douglas and the southern radicals was a heroic task in itself.

The question, then, which faces the theorist of belatedness is why Lincoln gave the document such a monumental reading. If one were to focus only on the Gettysburg Address in this regard, an argument could be made that the horror of civil war demanded religious poetry. But while Gettysburg represents the height of Lincoln's achievement as poet, he offered a reading of the Declaration as colossal as the one after the great Civil War battle in his debate with Douglas in 1858. This (mis)reading of the Declaration is particularly informative in terms of those commentators who do not accept the argument of his poetic intent by asserting that Lincoln had no other motive in the election other than the senate seat. But it also requires an explanation from the theorist of belatedness.

The belated president thus quotes from Lincoln's account of the meaning of the commemoration of the signing of the Declaration:

> We hold this annual celebration to remind ourselves of all the good done in the process of time of how it was done and who did it, and how we are historically connected with it; and we go from these meetings in better humor with ourselves—we feel more attached the one to the other, and more firmly bound to the country we inhabit. In every way we are better men in the age, and race, and country in which we live for these celebrations. But after we have done all this we have not yet reached the whole. There is something else connected with it. We have besides these men—descended by blood from our ancestors—among us perhaps half our people who are not descendants at all of these men, they are men who have come from Europe—German, Irish, French and Scandinavian men that have come from Europe themselves, or whose ancestors have come hither and settled here, finding themselves our equals in all things. If we look back through this history to trace their connection with those days by blood, they find they have none, they cannot carry themselves back to that glorious epoch and make themselves feel part of us, but when they look through that old Declaration of Independence they find that those old men say that "We hold these truths to be self-evident, that all men are created equal," and then they feel that that moral sentiment taught in that day evidences their relation to those men, that it is the father of all moral principle in them, and that they have a right to claim it as though they were blood of the blood, and flesh of the flesh of the men who wrote that Declaration and so they are. That is the electric cord in that Declaration that links the hearts of patriotic and liberty-loving men together, that will link those patriotic hearts as long as the love of freedom exists in the minds of men throughout the world.[24]

Certainly one can read this statement in nonpoetic terms. Lincoln is appealing to immigrant sentiments and he could always deftly mix self-interest into even his most majestic arguments as he did when he claimed that slave states are places whites move from and free states places whites move to. But one cannot fail to be struck by the religious metaphor that pervades this selection. The July Fourth commemoration is an act of communion in which each participant partakes of "the blood of the blood and flesh of the flesh" of the signers and also becomes "whole" and "connected" with one another. Three paragraphs later Lincoln quotes Scripture, "As your Father in Heaven is perfect, be ye also perfect," and claims that the Declaration asserts a common standard which Douglas's reading denies and he is determined to "resist."

It is Lincoln's (mis)reading of the Declaration as a mystical text, far removed from its Jeffersonian Enlightenment origins, that drives those who write from the anti-Lincoln tradition into a fury. Thus Bradford writes that Lincoln's "calculated posturing" about the Declaration and its pledge "hidden in that document" had consequences far beyond civil war: "Even after the passage of over a century, with each new day they unfold with additional and ever-deepening iteration and threaten to produce divisions that make those explored on the battlefields of Virginia, Maryland, and Tennessee seem mild indeed."[25] At this point the belated president wonders if Lincoln's monumental ambitions led him into a strategy of overkill. Indeed, Bradford himself seems to accept the thesis that Lincoln encouraged secession as part of his strategy to rationally transform the Republic as he laid out originally in the Lyceum speech but expected only a short-lived insurrection. However, the answer to the monumental escalation in the stature of the Declaration can be traced to the tenacity of the meaning of the document itself. For the Declaration of Independence was foremost a revolutionary document which justified rebellion. Thus when Lincoln described the text as a "merely revolutionary" one, he not only unveiled his poetic intent in regard to his reordering of Jefferson but also expressed the fundamental obstacle to his reading. However much he might insist that the key to the text was its message of equality, he could not avoid the counterreading that the Declaration asserted an inalienable right to rebel. Lincoln's repeated utterance of the phrase "all men are created equal" involved a Pauline expansion of the document, but he never accepted the assertion that "it is the right of the People to alter or abolish" a government that came only two sentences later. That the southern reading of the text was dramatically inconsistent did not alter Lincoln's own dilemma. How could he place a text at the center of political discourse and deny its own raison d'être as an assertion of the right to rebellion? He spent many pages of lawyerly text attempting to show that the Declaration conferred no such right. His most successful reading of this question, however, is the poetic one. For what Lincoln asserted was that the Declaration represented such a foundation of national identity that it permitted no such act. Its meaning involved no "mere matter of separation."[26] His poetic feat seen on these terms was incredible; Lincoln literally erased the right to rebellion from the meaning of the text. To validate this interpretation, however, required him to offer a conception of American identity more collectivist and more intense than any other American had ever conceived. Thus Lincoln denied the revolutionary import of the Declaration and substituted for it another revolutionary doctrine. The South had not engaged in rebellion but "simply the wicked exercise of physical power." The North was not suppressing rebellion but engaging in a revolutionary "struggle for maintaining in the world that form and substance of government whose leading object is to elevate the condition of men."[27] It was as if Lincoln had taken Washington's 1774 observation that the British would "make us as tame and abject slaves" and replaced it with the South as the source of tyrannic ambition. In his House Divided speech Lincoln raised the specter that a citizen could "lie down pleasantly dreaming" that Missouri was free and awake to find Illinois a slave state and spoke in the same conspiratorial terms that the revolutionaries did.

As the war lengthened, Lincoln's interpretation of the Declaration expanded to include many of the elements of the Jacobin project that Tocqueville had contended Americans had avoided. In 1861 Lincoln warned against a war that would "degenerate into a violent and remorseless revolutionary struggle." But if one views the Civil War as delayed Jacobinism which Lincoln's battle against belatedness had unleashed through his extraction of the truth embalmed in a revolutionary pamphlet, he found himself challenged by a "Left" which urged the President to "free every slave—slay every traitor—burn every rebel mansion."[28] Certainly to many abolitionists, Lincoln was a Danton, and the belated president needs to ask if Lincoln ever wondered if he himself would be superseded by a leader with greater revolutionary resolve.

Indeed, there were moments in which Lincoln seemed to actually undertake the transformation to another level of revolutionary leadership himself. He declared his impatience with those who would engage in "temporizing and forebearing" in regard to the South. A war could not be fought "with elder-stalk squirts, charged with rose water." He also employed what later became the classic metaphor of revolutionary morality. "Broken eggs cannot be mended," he told August Belmont when he complained that his critics "will not read and understand what I have said."[29] The assassination sealed Lincoln's victory against belatedness in part because it left the question of his revolutionary resolve against the South a matter of historical speculation. But it should be noted that even the assassination did not immediately guarantee Lincoln's status as the monumental savior. The New England ministry gave its imprint to the myth of the "Black Easter" Lincoln when it was asserted that "it was no blasphemy against the Son of God that we declare the fitness of the slaying of the second Father of our Republic on the anniversary of the day on which he was slain." Others, however, saw Lincoln's murder as a sign that "God . . . has withdrawn [him] at the moment when . . . the nation needed a sterner hand for the work God has given to do."[30]

The focus of those who later commemorated Lincoln's poetic achievement has rested with his Christian foundational plea to "bind up the nation's wounds" in a spirit of "charity for all." Yet standing immediately before this statement is a poetic utterance of the revolutionary: "Yet, if God wills that it continue until all the wealth piled by the bondsman's two hundred years of unrequited toil shall be sunk, and until every drop of blood drawn from the last shall be paid by another drawn from the sword, as was said three thousand years ago, so it must be said, 'The judgments of the Lord are true and righteous altogether.'"[31]

DOUBLE-CROSSING THE SONS: POLK, TAYLOR, CLAY, DOUGLAS

To the belated president, Lincoln's (mis)reading of the Declaration and the Constitution constituted a monumental reordering of the fathers of the Republic. Lincoln's analysis of these texts, his double-crossing of their meanings, opened up a place for himself connected with but superior to the greatest of men. Yet this battle constitutes only one narrative of Lincoln's multiple poetic achievement. For if as a belated man he yearned to be unfettered from his frustrated ambitions, he was guarded not only by Washington and Jefferson, the fathers, but by those jailers who called themselves their sons. Thus Lincoln's struggle with his contemporaries was concurrent with his battle against the monumental figures of the Republic. In a sense, Lincoln as a belated general was thus forced, as are all aspiring poets, to fight on two fronts. The military metaphor fits, however, only if one keeps an eye on the fact that these two lines of battle represented regiments of a single army. For from the standpoint of belatedness, the sons carry (or claim to carry) the banners of the fathers. The belated poet must therefore both challenge the fathers and at the same time seize the banner from competing sons in the name of the fathers. Yet on this very confusing battlefield, one which brings all but the strongest of belated figures to the point of defeat and despair, the belated general must adopt a different set of tactics against his opposition. The demands of poetic achievement prevent the destruction of the fathers in anything like an open sense. In Lincoln's strategy their status is shifted and reordered, demoted to be sure, but never directly slain however much poetic intent so wishes. The sons, on the other hand, are not afforded this protection. The belated poet can simply reorder the line of preference in terms of filial affection but he can also drive his competing brother from the public arena in symbolic annihilation. Lincoln, as one of the greatest American poet-presidents, engaged in both tactics. He pushed aside aspiring sons like Polk, Taylor, and Clay and set out to "murder" his rival, Stephen Douglas.

The most universally recommended military strategy must acknowledge historical context and Lincoln's own circumstances are worth noting. From historical hindsight the second party system of the Republic was in the process of disintegration and transformation in the 1840s and 1850s, but from the vantage point of a participant afflicted with belatedness, it offered institutionalized opportunities to strike out at those who stood in the way of his aspirations. Lincoln pursued this acceptable convention of attacking party opponents with great skill. Party rivalry was an ideal structure to hide poetic intent, but as Lincoln noted in his Lyceum speech, there were two kinds of men, those content to hold a congressional seat or a governor's chair and those for whom such rewards were trivial, and he himself seemed to feel constrained by the role of "hack politician" and "above average" legislator.[32] Lincoln always searched for monumental rivals to battle in apocalyptic struggles. In a campaign speech against Van Buren in 1839, Lincoln attacked a Democratic opponent who offered the moderate claim that his party might err in practice but was sound in principle. Lincoln responded violently by asserting a Van Buren victory would represent the end of the Republic. "Free countries have lost their liberty; and ours may lose hers," said Lincoln, "but if she shall, be it my proudest plume, not that I was the last to desert, but I never deserted her."[33]

He appeared to have overreached himself in what Democrats derisively called his "Spot Resolutions." Even Whig politicians winced when he charged that unless President Polk could show the actual spot where Mexico invaded the United States, "the blood of this war, like the blood of Abel, is crying to Heaven against him."[34] Lincoln hoped that the speech would provide the occasion to "distinguish" himself and vehemently defended himself against Herndon's reservations. Both Herndon and "other good friends" misunderstood him. Lincoln was especially anxious to argue that any other position placed him in the ranks of the ordinary politician: "Would you have gone out of the House-skulked the vote? . . . If you had skulked one vote, you would have had to skulk many more, before the end of the session."[35]

Lincoln's defensiveness in regard to his attacks on Polk represented the delicate nature of the Whig party in general in regard to the Mexican-American War. Anxious not to be considered unpatriotic, most elected officials were forced to vote for appropriations but were driven to rage when Polk and the Democrats interpreted their votes as evidence of support. Lincoln, for example, sharply accused one friendly critic who questioned the political prudence of Whig opposition to the war for falling into "one of the artfully set traps of Locofocoism."[36]

The war itself both sharpened and began the unraveling of the second party system. Polk's war aims, in which the demand for indemnities on the part of the Mexicans were thinly disguised attempts to expand American territory, brought into focus the Democrat-Whig controversy over the pace of expansion. The threat of a war debt was regarded by some as an indirect maneuver to close down the Whig agenda of internal improvements (much in the manner that later liberals contended that Reagan's defense buildup and subsequent deficits would prevent the expansion of the welfare state if only through lack of revenue). And then, of course, there was the question of the impact of expansion on the slavery issue. Radical northern Whigs had come to the conclusion that the war was another part of the conspiracy of the Slave Power.[37]

The belated president is, of course, intensely interested in all facets of this complex political struggle, but he cannot help but be especially intrigued by Lincoln's assessment of Polk. Polk had won his party's nomination in 1844 as a dark house largely because of Van Buren's strategic error in indicating opposition over the annexation of Texas. The outraged Jackson gave his support to the young governor of Tennessee. Partly in response to his relative national obscurity, the Democrats began a concerted and successful campaign to tie Polk ideologically and mythically to Jackson. The response to the question "Who is James K. Polk?" was "Young Hickory." As one campaign speaker intoned: "We have had one old hickory tree . . . sixteen millions of Americans have reposed under its shade in peace and happiness. It is yet vigorous—but it cannot live forever. And now to take its place, is springing up at its side a tall and noble sapling. . . . Its growth cannot be checked. It is destined to reach a correspondent elevation with the parent stem. We and our children will yet live in prosperity under the broad branches of this new young hickory tree. On the 4th day of March next, that young hickory tree will be transplanted by the people to the people's house at Washington; and you and I, and all of us, will assist in that transplanting."[38] Upon election, the Young Hickory seemed to act as if the clock had been turned back a generation. He referred to Whigs as "Federalists," pledged a return to hard money, debt and tariff reduction, cheap land, and the annexation of Texas as an extension of Jeffersonian policy in regard to Louisiana and Jackson's Indian removal.[39]

What other conclusion, thinks the belated president, could Lincoln, the young Whig congressman and aspiring poet-president, have reached other than one which saw Polk as Jackson Recidivus? If Polk could revive the Democracy as a transplant from Old Hickory, would this "son" block the political landscape for the indefinite future? Lincoln insisted upon referring to Polk in the diminutive as "Little Hickory," but in his "spot resolutions," Lincoln attacked Polk along the very same lines that he would attempt to destroy the filial pretender that emerged in Polk's place, Stephen Douglas. In his Springfield address, Lincoln portrayed Douglas as either a conspirator for the Slave Power or a "toothless lion." In his February 1848 address before Congress, he contended that Polk's war was being carried on by the "sheerest deception," a deception "by design." Alternately, Lincoln layed out the image of Polk the incompetent, a man "bewildered, confounded, and miserably perplexed."[40] To Lincoln, the opening, which might seem small—even comically so to the Democrats and even some Whigs—but which would expose either Polk's poetic intent or his ineptness, centered on the question of where precisely hostilities began. If "the first blood of the war was shed" on Texan soil, Lincoln would be "with him." If not, the president was a bumbler or a usurper of the honor of the fathers. In either case, he was no exemplar of filial piety. The belated president notes how Lincoln insists that Polk respond to his queries "fully, fairly, and candidly" and that he do so in open awareness of his filial responsibilities: "Let him remember he sits where Washington sat, and so remembering, let him answer, as Washington would answer."[41] Should Polk be unconvincing (or even confess, since Lincoln believed Polk was "deeply conscious of his transgressions"), poetic intent would emerge in full view. The image Lincoln selected to convey what he thought were Polk's aims is as vivid a description of poetic intent exposed as any the belated president has ever seen. Polk's addresses justifying the war will be seen as an attempt on his part to seize glory for himself by "fixing the public gaze upon the exceeding brightness of military glory—that attractive rainbow, that rises in showers of blood—that serpent's eye, that charms to destroy."[42]

Polk never did respond to Lincoln's demands nor his charge of poetic intent, never even bothering to note the young congressmen's speech in his voluminous diary. But then neither did Polk initiate a reign of Jackson II. The war only exasperated the slave question and its impact on the party system. Polk represented the last of the Jacksonians and Jacksonian Democracy and not the first of a new generation. Caught by is own pledge to serve only one term, Polk left the presidential political scene as quickly as he rose to it. Though he was "the father of the states of Oregon, Washington, Idaho, California, New Mexico, Arizona, Nevada, Utah, and parts of Colorado, Montana, and Wyoming," Polk ceased to be a competing son with Lincoln.[43] Not until his challenge to Douglas in 1858 could it be said that Lincoln found an opponent worthy of relieving his belatedness. To the belated president, Lincoln in fact said as much in his famous debates when he claimed in a language barely concealing his poetic intent that he thought he possessed no "insensibility to political honors," and that he had "prayed from the first that this field of ambition might not be opened."[44]

If the intensity of party competition provided Lincoln with both opportunities and frustrations in terms of campaigns against his rivals for distinction, his own political party presented him with complicated terrain. The Lincoln of the 1830s and 1840s may have suffered from belatedness, but he had no difficulties supporting the core of the Whig economic platform in regard to internal improvements. The Whig position in regard to the presidency and to political leadership in general, although more of a sensibility than a set of policy recommendations, demanded a more intricate strategy. The Whigs as a party originated in large part from their critique of the personal, democratic leadership of Jackson. Whigs resented the expansion of the electorate under Jackson's leadership, criticized his policies as reckless and his partisanship as divisive, and regarded his cult of personality as a danger to the Republic. Jackson's conception of the president as tribune who would defend the people against the "rich and the powerful" was evidence to the Whigs of a degeneration to "elective despotism" with whom they tended to conflate Polk in a negative reading of the Young Hickory trope. When the Whigs finally broke through to the presidency in 1840, their candidate William Henry Harrison promised a restrained presidency and warned Americans of "designing men" who would appeal to the "passions" for their own purposes. The Harrison victory was won in large part through Whig concessions to democratic sentiments not the least of which involved what became the party's addiction to nominating military heroes for the presidency. Thus Whigs, who were scolds on the question of the dangers of executive power, also placed professional soldiers at the helm of the Republic.

Lincoln seemed to have no objection to this strategy. He supported Zachary Taylor in 1848 over his professed idol Clay, and supported Winfield Scott in 1852, although he had placed himself in a conventional political dilemma as his party began to seek generals who had distinguished themselves in a war he had opposed. When a Georgia Democrat contended that the Whigs had deserted their principles by "taking shelter under Gen. Taylor's military coat-tail," Lincoln angrily retorted that the Democrats were in no position to make these sorts of allegations: "Like a horde of hungry ticks you have stuck to the tail of the Hermitage lion to the end of his life; and you are still sticking to it, and drawing a loathsome sustenance from it, after he is dead."[45]

Though Lincoln found some room to maneuver on this question, the issue did raise problems in his quest to alleviate belatedness. For if his party found electoral success in gathering generals to their cause, a practice which Lincoln was politically unable to resist, what were the implications for his personal efforts at distinction? The occasion of Taylor's death, however, permits the belated president a glimpse at Lincoln's sibling tactics in regard to the generals as the favored sons of the fathers. The Taylor eulogy begins with a long and

rousing narrative of the general's military experiences. He told of Taylor's gar-
risoning of Fort Brown against Arista's forces and captured the suspense of the
battle. Forces inside the fort could not tell if all those without had perished and
those outside did not know if their comrades inside had been "massacred to the
last man." Lincoln concludes his story thusly: "And now the din of battle nears
the fort and sweeps obliquely by; a gleam of hope flies through the half impris-
oned few; they fly at the wall; every eye is strained—it is—it is—the stars and
stripes are still aloft! Anon the anxious brethren meet; and while hand strikes
hands, the heavens are rent in a loud, long, glorious, gushing cry of victory!"[46]

Lincoln's assessment of Taylor as a military leader, however, is much more
restrained. The battles he fought would never "have been selected by an ambitious captain upon which to gather laurels." Taylor was not "distinguished for
brilliant military manoeuvres"; he had a "blunt business-like view of things";
his rarest military trait, was a combination of negatives—"absence of excitement and absence of fear." In short, Lincoln's Taylor was a plodder and Lincoln offers only a paragraph on his presidency, which he concludes was "no bed
of roses." This assessment provided a neat conjunction with his immediate
political objective and his larger battle against belatedness. Taylor was not a
general to be feared; he was a Whig soldier who "was always at his post." Thus
Lincoln tells the men of his party that they had not abandoned its principles
in selecting such a safe general of "unobtrusive qualities" as president. From the
standpoint of belatedness, Lincoln happily concludes that Taylor was not a rival.
Alive he was a dutiful son of the Republic; dead he would not collect "hungry
ticks" to his tail as Jackson had done. There was, of course, the possibility that
a belated Lincoln could be hemmed in by a succession of small men, Lilliputian
style, but he also had a resolution to this possibility. He paused to reflect what
would be the "effect, politically, upon the country" of the death of the general.
Taylor, even as Lincoln had defined him diminutively, was the last of a line.
The dead general's patriotism and wisdom could certainly be replaced, but Lincoln wondered whether his "confidence and devotion" would be imitated by
his successors. Lincoln has concluded that men like Taylor, honest but mediocre men, men unafflicted by belatedness, are unlikely to succeed in the future.
In the Lyceum address, he had praised the projects of great men (again as he
defined their achievements) but argued they had been so eroded by time as to
be relatively useless without monumental rededication. He closes his eulogy
with the very same assessment. The American people had been wise to elect
Taylor president. Youth should know that "unobtrusive qualities" like steady
devotion to duty "will be noticed and will lead to high places." But Taylor is
dead: "He is gone. The conqueror at last is conquered."[47]

The generals were not the only class of men who were in a position to claim
special status as favored sons. The third generation of the Republic had produced a set of extremely gifted politicians whose fame rested not on battlefield
exploits but upon their own talents in argument and persuasion. They too were
favorites of the Whigs, and the greatest of them all was Henry Clay.

In his debates with Douglas, Lincoln systematically employed Clay in defense of his positions regarding the evil of slavery, the moral significance of the Declaration, and his opposition to its extension in the new territories. In truth, the authority of Clay on these questions was ambiguous, as Douglas's rejoinders illustrated. For example, Lincoln argued that Clay's support for the Declaration's moral import in regard to slavery could be derived from his assertion that "as an abstract principle" there was "truth" to the Declaration's statement that all men are created equal and that his opposition to its extension could be supported by Clay's comment that equality was "desirable in the original construction of society, and in organized societies, to keep it in view as a great fundamental principle." But Lincoln was forced in the debates to quote the remainder of Clay's comments, which were written in response to a demand that he free his own slaves. Clay had continued by stating that "in no society that ever did exist, or shall ever be formed, was or can the equality asserted among members of the human race be practically enforced and carried out." He contended that "large portions" of any population would always remain "subject to the government of another portion of the community" and concluded that the claim that the Declaration had a "secret and unavowed purpose" which entailed the emancipation of slaves was a "fraud" upon "the noblest band of patriots that ever assembled in council" and a "fraud upon the confederacy of the Revolution."[48] In short, Clay (much like Jefferson) had often expressed anguish over the existence of slavery but could never bring himself to undertake any but the most cautious measures to eradicate the institution in practice. His support, therefore, for the Declaration on the question of equality was a formal one. If a "state of nature" existed, "no man would be more opposed" to the incorporation of slavery.

Despite these contortions, it is easy to see Lincoln's motives in attempting to appropriate Clay in terms of gathering electoral support within the disintegrating party system of the 1850s. He accused Douglas of the selfsame strategy at Springfield when he contended that the Judge's story of his deathbed encounter with Clay was designed to produce tears "drawn down the cheeks of all Old Whigs, as large as half grown apples."[49]

If one, however, studies Lincoln's use of Clay in terms of his poetic intent, his attitudes reveal a larger project. Lincoln always insisted that he loved Clay and "revered him as a teacher and leader." But as Douglas reminded Lincoln at Alton and Freeport, he had cut Clay's throat in 1848 and brought the Compromise of 1850 into disrepute "although the sod was not yet green on his grave." Three years earlier in his defense of Clay to an abolitionist, Lincoln argued that while Clay was a slaveholder a refusal to support him did not constitute a vindication of the rule that "an evil tree can not bring forth good fruit." For "if the fruit of electing Mr. Clay would have been to prevent the extension of slavery, could the act of electing have been evil?"[50] Lincoln clearly knew that Clay was a tainted politician on the slave question. He had fashioned a monumental compromise in 1820 and would be called again to repeat the feat in 1850. He was not a evil tree in the sense that he would characterize the Douglas-Pierce-Taney-Buchanan conspiracy. But in 1845 Lincoln was willing to examine the moral rule for his argument that Clay was not an evil tree focusing upon his assessment of the consequences of a Whig victory and not on Clay's personal taintedness. In 1852 he underlined Clay's career in terms of his actions on the slavery question (completely ignoring his economic policies) and noted the incongruity between his love of liberty and his complicity in the institution of slavery. "And yet Mr. Clay was the owner of slaves," Lincoln told his audience.

The belated president thus sees how Clay's taintedness made him an ally in Lincoln's quest to defeat belatedness. For here was a man whose eloquence, judgment, and will were unsurpassed, a man who had cast a "spell . . . with which the souls of men were bound to him" for a generation.[51] Yet here also was a loser, not just in the sense that the presidency had eluded him, but in the sense that all of his genius at compromise had failed to resolve the slave question. What better way to alleviate belatedness than to tether the great Mr. Clay, an acknowledged great failure, to his own project against belatedness? Lincoln closed his eulogy with the question, could the country "have been quite all it has been, and is and is to be, without Henry Clay?" Stripped of poetic evasion, Lincoln can be understood as saying, without Clay as a kind of John the Baptist how could Lincoln's poetic achievement be acknowledged?

As the belated president stops for a moment to briefly review the men whom Lincoln "honored," Lincoln's strategy in regard to Clay becomes even more clear. He "honored" Washington by acknowledging his poetic intent and then focused upon the poetic achievement of Jefferson. He "honored" Jefferson by acknowledging him as a minor poet whose achievement required his extraction and transformation. He "honored" Taylor for his "combination of negatives" since he was a man with neither poetic intent nor achievement. And now he "honored" Clay as a man who on four occasions (1812, 1820, 1832, 1850) came to the aid of his country to avert disaster. Four times he had saved the union. He was in Lincoln's words, "the man for a crisis."

Lincoln began his eulogy with the observation that Clay was born in the first year of the Revolution, the growth of the nation paralleled his own: "The infant nation, and the infant child began the race of life together. For three quarters of a century they have travelled hand in hand. They have been companions ever. The nation has passed its perils, and is free, prosperous, and powerful. The child has reached his manhood, his middle age, his old age, and is dead." Clay was dead and Lincoln carefully avoided carrying the parallel of Clay-America and birth-manhood-death to its conclusion. Clay was dead but America was "prosperous and powerful." Yet Lincoln so constructed his narrative of Clay's life (and the nation's) as to raise the question of who would save the country when the next crisis emerged. He quoted extensively from a Democratic eulogy that expressed the hope that "in the whole circle of the great and gifted of our land, there remains but one on whose shoulders the mighty mantle of the departed statesman may fall—one, while we now write, is doubtless pouring his tears over the bier of his brother and his friend."[52]

Lincoln had first produced a crisis narrative of the history of republics in the

Lyceum address. In his analysis of Clay's career he gave the narrative more historical specificity and "honored" his teacher as "the man for a crisis." But who could fail to reach the conclusion that Clay had averted multiple disasters rather than resolving them? Each time the American people were confronted with the "re-appearance of the slavery question" they turned to Clay to effect the "the task of devising a mode of adjustment." The unstated but clear conclusion is that Clay had failed each time to end the problem. Why else, despite the last task of adjustment completed, did another crisis then appear? Six years later Lincoln still spoke of a crisis politics but redefined the kind of resolution required. The Great Compromise (of which Clay was a major participant) had as its "avowed object, and confident promise, of putting an end to slavery agitation." But the conflict had "not ceased" and had actually been "constantly augmented." It would not cease "until a crisis shall have been reached, and passed." Thus Lincoln "honored" Clay by placing him as a central character in his crisis narrative. Clay's poetic achievement rested with the multiple moments to which the American people by "common consent" had "cast" him in the role of crisis manager. But Clay's real achievement, the "glorious consummation" of his efforts, would come when, as Clay himself had predicted, a captive people were freed. That task required a different approach to crisis from one who would come after him. Thus Lincoln could accept Clay's taintedness, his failure to achieve the presidency, his failure to resolve the source of the crises that repeatedly confronted the Republic, and his personal complicity in the institution of slavery as features of his leadership from which he was free.

One way to appreciate the brilliance of Lincoln's strategy in avoiding belatedness in regard to Clay, which the belated president finds helpful, is to consider Daniel Walker Howe's assessment of the relationship between Lincoln and his teacher. "Despite all the Clay influences on Lincoln," writes Howe, "when the chips were down in the 'great secession winter' he pursued no comprehensive compromise like one of Clay's close associate, John J. Crittenden, was proposing (and which Clay himself would no doubt have supported had he been alive)."[53] Translated into the language of belatedness, had Lincoln pursued the Crittenden plan, he could have been caught in Clay's web. He might have been known as Lincoln, the son of Clay. The American people still value men of Clay's type, men who are called upon to devise modes of adjustments to the great questions facing the Republic. But Lincoln had so supremely overcome any claim to poetic achievement on the part of Clay that the "test" which subsequent presidents are required to undertake are those which demand a Lincolnian definition of crisis.

Washington, Jefferson, Polk, Taylor, Clay—each had their fates reorganized and replaced neatly within Lincoln's own narrative. No figure in Lincoln's career, however, is more noticeably displaced than Stephen Douglas. If Lincoln's actions can be explained in terms of his struggle with belatedness, his double crosses are largely hidden. It is true that those who focus exclusively on Lincoln's poetic achievement acknowledge the momentousness of his defeat of Douglas and his philosophy. Thus Don. E. Fehrenbacher captures perfectly Lincoln's achievement: "In retrospect, the tall form of Lincoln dominates the scene; Douglas, originally the star of the show, is relegated to second billing; and the hard-fought battle for a Senate seat shrinks in proportions of a dress rehearsal." But Fehrenbacher continues his analysis with a denial of any poetic intent on Lincoln's part: "There is not the slightest evidence that any objective beyond the senatorship was in his [Lincoln's] mind." Any ambitions Lincoln might have had were "leavened by moral conviction and a deep faith in the principles upon which the republic had been built."[54] Jaffa too admits that Lincoln set out to "destroy" Douglas but contends that the objective was necessary in order to avoid what the prescient Lincoln saw as the logical conclusion of his policies, an American future that would resemble French Algeria.[55] Was Lincoln a man of moderate ambition who courageously and astutely saw in Douglas's doctrine of popular sovereignty a threat to the principles upon which the Republic rested and thus carefully devised in the debates a set of arguments derived from the Declaration to arrest the advance of slavery? Was the reordering of Douglas then simply a necessary consequence of Lincoln's project? Or, as Forgie argues, was Lincoln convinced that Douglas was the "evil son" whom he had predicted nearly twenty years earlier? Did he set out to destroy Douglas out of a psychically tortured errand of filial piety? "The bad son of the Lyceum address prophecy had at last appeared to make his assault upon the father's institutions" and Lincoln rose to kill Douglas "in order to save the father's work."[56] Or is it possible that Lincoln's debate with Douglas was only part of a larger psychological contest, as Anderson argues, in which Lincoln carried out his "personal vengefulness against constitutional fathers with the cause of equality."[57] The belated president considers each of these assessments as he reviews the Great Debates.

Like most of the readings of Lincoln, there emerges a great divide between those who will focus only on his poetic achievement in the debates and those who have riveted their analysis upon poetic intent. Those commentators who insist upon assessing the former emphasize the rationality of Lincoln's assessment of the growth of slavery and the forcefulness of his reading of the Declaration (as opposed to Douglas's). Those who have read the debates in terms of poetic intent insist that Lincoln's actions can only be understood in terms of Lincoln's monumental ambition. The problem with both readings, which the belated president is forced to confront, is that they are unable to account for significant questions about both intent and achievement. The achievement theorists are puzzled by what they admit are demagogic aspects of Lincoln's arguments. Did Lincoln really believe that there was a conscious conspiracy, of which Douglas was a member, to make slavery a national institution? And what does one make of Lincoln's repeated and overt racist statements throughout the debates? The intent theorists have failed to produce a consensus about Lincoln's motives. Was he attempting to protect the founders or was he engaged in a ritual act of patricide?

We have noted that those who strive to overcome belatedness become involved in a complex exercise in which the sufferer attributes belated motives on the part of those who block his relief. We have contended that Lincoln engaged in just this exercise in the Lyceum and Temperance speeches in terms of Washington. Did Lincoln undertake the same course in regard to Douglas? In 1852 Lincoln remarked that he "was reminded of old times"—of the times when Judge Douglas was not much "so much a greater man than the rest of us."[58] Thus Lincoln certainly acknowledged Douglas's ascent in national politics with not a little bit of resentment but did he perceive him to be the kind of person he described in the Lyceum speech? A positive answer is crucial to the theorists of poetic intent, for it would suggest that Lincoln was forcibly enacting his own prophecy offered in the Lyceum speech, however implausible events showed it to be. From the standpoint of belatedness, however, the question of Lincoln's perception of Douglas's Caesarism becomes a question of Lincoln's assessment of poetic intent. Actually Lincoln was thus faced with three possible conclusions in regard to Douglas. He could conclude that Douglas was a man without poetic intent, a man like Taylor who was marked by his "unobtrusive qualities." He could conclude that he was man like Clay, "the man for crisis." And, of course, he could conclude that Douglas was indeed a man much like Lincoln whose "field of ambition" had been "opened" for monumental tasks by the Kansas-Nebraska Act.

Let us think like a belated president for a moment. It is safe to say that Lincoln estimated Douglas more highly than he did Taylor. If Lincoln had any lingering doubts that he was dealing with a lightweight, they were erased in 1854 when the repeal of the Missouri Compromise "arose him as never before." But what if Douglas was a leader in the mode of Clay? Douglas was responsible for bringing the Great Compromise to fruition after Clay's failure to obtain passage of its provisions as a package. And it was Douglas who attempted to play the role of Clay as the man for a crisis in 1854. Douglas's rejection of the Lecompton constitution in 1857 cost him support in the South but also gained him the support of anti-Buchanan Democrats and the interest of some leaders in the Republican Party. Douglas's repeated insistence that he was the inheritor of Clay's policies and that it was Lincoln who followed "the example and lead of all the little Abolition orators who go around and lecture in the basements of schools and churches" would have confirmed Lincoln's supposition.[59] As we discussed above, Lincoln not only set out a reading different from Douglas's on Clay and the Declaration but also suggested that he could overcome any threat of belatedness in regard to Clay by demanding an approach to conflict resolution other than adjustment. Thus the debates focus and refocus on Lincoln's attempt to establish that there are moral limits to compromise which he insists that Clay recognized but which in practice would require a different kind of leadership.

If, however, Lincoln, would have been forced to consider the possibility that Douglas had the same poetic intent as he, a maximin strategy would prevent him from rejecting such a conclusion even if he regarded it as relatively remote. Lincoln's close reading of republican history in his own battle against belatedness led him to understand that men of monumental poetic intent are able to hide their ambitions. Suppose Douglas was only appearing to operate under the model of Clay to cover monumental aspirations for achievement. From the standpoint of the belated theorist, Lincoln was aware that he was using the model of Washington and Jefferson for his own projects. Combine, if you will, Lincoln's belatedly informed calculations with the mind of a Whig. Douglas's reverence for Clay was recent, but he had been known as a lifelong disciple of Jackson who Whigs had historically insisted was a Caesarist threat to the Republic. Douglas's entry into politics (and allegedly the origin of his nickname, "Little Giant") was marked by his rousing 1834 speech against rechartering the Bank of the Unites States in which he supported Jackson. A year later Douglas narrowly won his first election, and he attributed it to "the Lord, and the Legislature and Gen. Jackson." He defended Jackson's declaration of martial law in New Orleans in his first major speech in Congress. Douglas contended that there are "exigencies in the history of nations . . . when necessity becomes paramount to law . . . Talk not to me about rules and forms in court, when the enemy's canon are pointed at the door." The speech concluded with a tribute to Jackson as Douglas's "guiding star": "His stern, inflexible adherence to Democratic principles, his unwavering devotion to his country, and his intrepid opposition to her enemies, have long thwarted their unhallowed schemes of ambition and power, that they fear the potency of his name on earth, even after his spirit shall have ascended to heaven." Douglas finally made a pilgrimage to the Hermitage in 1844. He was struck speechless in the old man's presence, shook his hand "convulsively," and left the room.[60] Was Douglas (mis)reading Jackson as a tactic to defeat belatedness? Lincoln would have had enough evidence to reach such a conclusion, especially after a Democratic paper concluded that the spirit of Jackson lived in Douglas after the Little Giant eulogized the dedication of the general's statue across the street from the White House.[61]

At Freeport, Lincoln joked with the audience about "an evil genius" that had attended Douglas throughout his life. If Lincoln had supposed that Douglas carried with him an "evil genius" (read as poetic intent) he would have had some confirmation of Douglas's ambitions in his reply to the fourth question posed by Lincoln. Here Douglas described in the most vivid terms his vision of an expansive America: "This is a young and growing nation. It swarms as often as a hive of bees, and . . . there must be hives in which they can gather and make their honey. In less than fifteen years, if the same progress that had distinguished this country continues, every foot of vacant land between us and the Pacific Ocean, owned by the United States, will be occupied. Will you not continue to increase at the end of fifteen years as well as now? I tell you, increase, and multiply, and expand, is the law of this nation's existence. Any one of you gentlemen might as well say to a son twelve years old that he is big enough, and must not grow any larger, and in order to prevent his growth, put a hoop around him to keep him his present size. What would be the result? Either the hoop must burst and be rent asunder, or the child must die."[62]

Douglas's vision of an American empire is often neglected because scholars have focused upon the trap he fell into in response to Lincoln's first question.

But the first question—can a territory exclude slavery?—was designed to entrap the Douglas who had the ambition of a Clay (which it did). What Lincoln heard at Freeport in response to the fourth question was a confirmation of his fears that Douglas harbored monumental poetic intent. Rather than seeking fame through adjusting conflicts over slavery, Douglas outlined his real strategy in which slavery be removed as a restriction to territorial expansion. From the view of a belated figure, Douglas had exposed his poetic intent and outlined what he hoped would be his poetic achievement, the creation of a vast American empire. The reply at Freeport even contained the symmetrical opposite of Lincoln's own project in which he opened the debates. If American could not survive half-slave and half-free in Lincoln's terms, it could not survive bottled up in its youthful figure in Douglas's terms. Regrettably from the standpoint of poetic achievement, Lincoln's reply relied upon the same kind of racist fears that Douglas had raised in his objections to Lincoln's project. Should the United States annex Mexico, would Douglas permit people he had identified as "mongrels" the exercise of the doctrine of popular sovereignty?

Lincoln, of course, could not exactly anticipate Douglas's reply at Freeport, but he was forced to devise a strategy that recognized the existence of poetic intent on the part of his opponent. The famous House Divided speech thus reveals the strategy that Lincoln would employ through the debates. It was a dual tactic designed to meet both the assessment that Douglas conceived of himself as a great compromiser and that he carried with him an "evil genius." It is odd that the renowned metaphor which Lincoln employed at Springfield should receive so little extended analysis. Fehrenbacher, for example, simply notes that the metaphor was designed to polarize public opinion on the issue of slavery and Wills states that the function of the biblical figure of speech is to "pre-empt criticism of its premise."[63] It is important to note, however, how long and hard Lincoln worked to express the institution of slavery in metaphorical terms. He had described slavery as a cancer, as a snake, as an ant denied the crumb he has dragged to his nest, as a fenced meadow. The house-divided metaphor itself was in wide general use at the time Lincoln decided to use the term. Webster had warned that "if a house be divided against itself, it will fall and crush everybody in it." Lincoln, however, gave the expression a new reading that can only be appreciated by examining both its full biblical context and the remainder of his speech.

The concept of a house divided is discussed by Jesus in three versions of the New Testament. Jesus had already engaged in several acts of miraculous healing when a man possessed by demons was brought to him. Jesus cured him to the astonishment of a crowd that had gathered. The Pharisees, however, who had been observing Jesus' actions with suspicion, announced that "it is only by Beelzebub prince of devils that this man drives the devils out." Jesus replies: "Every kingdom divided against itself goes to ruin; and no town, no household, that is divided against itself can stand. And if it is Satan who casts out Satan, Satan is divided against himself; how then can this kingdom stand? And if it is by Beelzebub that I cast out devils, by whom do your own people drive them out? If this is your argument, they themselves will refute you. But if it by the Spirit of God that I drive out the devils, then be sure the kingdom of God has already come to you."[64]

Lincoln's use of a single expression from the incident in Jesus' ministry, "A house divided against itself cannot stand," does convey the discord that slavery had wrought in the Republic but a biblically informed audience could not fail to appreciate the focus of the narrative. Jesus is the figure under challenge in the text, and he is under question by the Pharisees in terms of his status as a healer. What makes the narrative one of the most difficult texts in the New Testament is the fact that it explores the motivations of the healer and good works. In fact, the suspicions of the Pharisees emerge in part because Jesus had already broken several rules of the Sabbath. Jesus had plucked and ate corn in a field and cured a man with a withered arm who had asked, "Is it permitted to heal on the Sabbath?" It is thus Jesus' status of a rule breaker that provokes his controversy with the Pharisees. In the Matthew version, Jesus summarizes his views: "Either make the tree good and its fruit good, or make the tree bad and its fruit bad; you can tell a tree by its fruit. You vipers' brood! How can your words be good when you yourselves are evil? For the words that the mouth utters come from the overflowing of the heart. A good man produces good from the store of good within himself; and an evil man from evil within produces evil." [65]

As we noted, Lincoln had considered the tree-fruit doctrine in his reply to an abolitionist in defense of Clay. What does the house-divided metaphor inform us about Lincoln's assessment of Douglas? Throughout the debates themselves Lincoln examines the likely consequences of Douglas's doctrine of popular sovereignty. At Springfield he raised the question of Douglas's motivations as a healer, and fully 90 percent of the address is devoted to this question. The longest section of the speech asserts that Douglas is part of a conspiracy to nationalize slavery. Here Lincoln returns to the house metaphor to draw a picture of the largely hidden edifice. He admits that he does not know if the election of Buchanan, the Nebraska bill and the Dred Scott decision are "the result of preconcert." But Lincoln has seen "a lot of framed timbers" gathered together by the conspirators and "we see these timbers joined together, and see they exactly make the frame of a house or mill." Lincoln concludes that it would be "impossible not to believe" that "all worked upon a common plan or draft."[66]

The last section of the speech involves an abrupt alteration of Lincoln's assessment. Here he assumes the existence of a slave owners' conspiracy but places Douglas outside it and considers the argument that he is the man for crisis. It would have certainly been possible for Lincoln to assert that Douglas's opposition to the Lecompton constitution was part of a complex conspiracy to raise Douglas to the status of a great compromiser only to later hand over the Republic to slave interests. Such an assessment is quite consistent with conspiratorial reasoning in general and Lincoln's conception of the abilities and tactics of an evil genius. Instead, the "living dog" section of the address attacks Douglas as a hopelessly tainted compromiser. Greeley had stated some sympathy for Douglas in view of his stand on Lecompton. Lincoln turned the assessment of Douglas's utility to the antislavery cause ("a living dog is better than a dead lion") into the derisive revision that Douglas, "if not a dead lion . . . is at least a caged or toothless one." The hostile rejection of the notion that Douglas would be an effective agent for the antislavery cause because "he is a great man, and that the largest of us are very small ones" shows more than a flash of Lincoln's own poetic intent. His willingness to consider Douglas in terms of a healer in the spirit of Clay, if only to conclude that he is incapable of performing such a role because he has "regularly voted with us on a single point" or that he was a man of "superior talent" suggests that Lincoln also planned for such an eventual role on the part of Douglas.

In either case, if Douglas was a conspirator or a toothless lion, Lincoln had raised questions about the source of Douglas's motivations. If he had evil designs, the house-divided doctrine established that no good could come from the house he and his conspirators were building since Satan could not drive out Satan. An American republic with slavery as a national institution would never find true unity and peace. If he hoped simply to seek a peaceful adjustment to the slavery crisis, Douglas would fail too because, while he may be free of malevolent intent, he was not possessed of good will. He was not, in other words, the man for a crisis. Thus throughout the debates Lincoln would give away enormous ground to Douglas by backing off from his conspiracy thesis only to assert that he might have been "used by conspirators, and was not a leader of them."[67] Douglas's indignant denials of a conspiracy, which also included his own efforts to assert that Lincoln was part of another one led by abolitionists, played to Lincoln's strategy. For while Lincoln insisted upon the humanity of the slave and his inclusion in the Declaration, he would give not one inch more. Several times during the debates Lincoln referred to African Americans as "niggers," denied that any implications of social or political equality were entailed by his reading of the Declaration, and insinuated that Douglas's position might involve a disguised sexual interest in black women. The repeated profession of racist sentiment, along with a general lack of history on the slavery question (Lincoln had not centered the question in terms of his public career until his speech at Peoria in 1854) permitted Lincoln to distance himself from the conspiracy countercharge. Lincoln's evaluation of Douglas's poetic intent, from which he was able to posit two likely interpretations of his opponent's motives, positioned him for a win-win outcome not only on terms which involved accusing Douglas of toothlessness if the conspiracy charge did not stick, but perhaps, most important, by aligning the debates in general in terms of human motivation. Thus when Douglas contended that only one whose "heart" was "corrupt" could charge him with conspiracy he led the debate straight back to the kinds of questions Lincoln raised in his opening Springfield speech about the relationship between good intentions and good actions on the part of a healer.

At Ottawa, Lincoln barred his poetic intent, still disguised as it was by the setting of partisan combat, when he said, "I know the Judge is a great man, while

I am truly only a small man, but I feel that I have got him."[68] It was reported that at Lincoln's inauguration, Douglas held his hat while the new president spoke.[69] This story has been only weakly substantiated, but it expresses perfectly Lincoln's achievement in regard to Douglas. The achievement is all the more monumental when one notes that during the debates Lincoln not only monumentally reordered the relationship between himself and Douglas but also "double crossed" the great and departed leaders of the Republic as well. For it was in the debates that Lincoln detailed his reordering of Washington through his (mis)reading of Jefferson's own monumental achievement.

LINCOLN FREED

There were subsequent events in Lincoln's assent to power, including his nomination, his election, and the various turns that any war takes, that can only be explained in terms of historical contingency. From the standpoint of belatedness, however, the monumental texts of his presidency, the two inaugurals, the message to the special session of Congress in 1861, and the Gettysburg Address are acts undertaken by a man already freed from belatedness. During his long journey from Springfield to his inauguration, Lincoln frequently spoke cautiously about the crisis he faced, reminding his audiences that his election did not ordain any particular course. But the president-elect also just as frequently spoke of the crisis that was now his and the project that was also now his. He faced "a task more difficult than that which devolved upon General Washington" at his Springfield farewell address. At Columbus, he defined his role even more exceptionally: "There has fallen on me a task such as did not rest even upon the Father of this country."[70] In Philadelphia, Lincoln told his audience that he "never had a feeling politically that did not spring from the sentiments embodied in the Declaration of Independence." He had "often inquired of myself" what was the "great principle or idea" of the Document and concluded that "it was that which gave promise that in due time the weights should be lifted from the shoulders of all men, and that all should be given an equal chance."[71] The president-elect, of course, has discovered the secret of the Declaration years before, but now he was in a position to recover it. He would be "one of the happiest men in the world" if he could "help save it."

In each of his great texts, written and delivered by Lincoln between 1861 and his death, it is his trope of the Founder that governs his poetry. It is Lincoln who is responsible for heroically maintaining a "government, which was made by Washington." It is his oath to "preserve, protect and defend" the constitution that now assumes monumental proportions. It is Lincoln who has plucked a revolutionary pamphlet from the controversies of the day to give "a new birth of freedom." And, of course, it is the Gettysburg Address itself that constitutes Lincoln's irrefutable evidence of his status as monumental poet. Every aspect of the speech has fascinated subsequent generations, but it is the audacity of the address that is responsible for the awe that it still conveys.

Commentators are enthralled by its brevity, its simplicity, its abstraction. A theorist of belatedness or a belated president could, of course, find traces of poetic intent in these elements. By studying the address in terms of what it does not contain (there is mention of no soldier's name nor any general, no mention of the enemy, no mention of slavery) and the themes of death and remembrance, he could note how Lincoln has, through abstraction and brevity, crowded out every aspect of this event but his own commemoration. For whom do you remember when you hear the name Gettysburg but the qualities of valor and purpose and the name Lincoln? Yet it is precisely the hiddenness of poetic intent that forces the listener to focus upon its poetic achievement, for Lincoln also never mentions himself. The reader of the address is rather propelled in rising crescendos to comprehend its messages: the war has a profound meaning; there is a national identity that has monumental historical meaning; there is a profound connection among generations of Americans. Each of these messages peel away to release their own higher levels of abstraction: the dead can and must be honored; humans are capable of monumental projects; one generation can atone for the actions of another. What remains is a statement of the horror and hope of human existence itself in which the recognition of birth and death is consoled by the prospect of rebirth. That a testimony of such grandeur can arise from the frustrations and anger of belatedness, contrary to all contending interpreters of Lincoln, adds to rather than subtracts from the poetic achievement. For Lincoln's case illustrates that it is possible that the struggle against belatedness can produce great achievements, although the price can be extremely high.

This conclusion, that good deeds (in fact, monumentally good deeds) can arise from resentment, is of some solace to the belated president since he learns, as did Lincoln as he esoterically spoke of his relationship to Washington, that the belated can thus imitate the great without automatically falling hopelessly under their influence. But, of course, the belated president grasps the fact that this is only the smallest of consolations as he reviews Lincoln's double crosses. Faint at heart, he nevertheless attempts to come to terms with the consequences of Lincoln's poetry. As he does so, he feels his own resentment rising ever more bitterly and he asks in derisive form: "So Lincoln was a great poet, but what did he do?" Determined to focus upon deeds only, pushing Lincoln's poetry into the background (although he knows in his heart the two cannot be separated), he first concludes that Lincoln created what he calls the "epic" presidency and he forces himself to consider its implications for men and women like him.

The belated president knows that Lincoln could never erase Washington's claim to heroic deeds and accepted the Platonic maxim that "the beginning is like a god," but he compares the hero as founder and as savior and notes how Lincoln in his Washington double cross privileged the later. He comes upon a fantasy offered by a young man (undoubtedly himself afflicted with belatedness) written in 1854 which he thinks holds a key to Lincoln's achievement. After acknowledging a bit too excessively Washington's achievement

("Washington's war was the noblest basis of a commonwealth and since the beginning of the world no nation eve had so splendid an origin"), he embarks upon this daydream:

> Still, we confess, when we consider what is due to the important picturesque of these things—or rather, due from that to the future sentiment of a nation—we feel inclined to make some change in the course of the war. We would . . . have Washington defeated, decisively, by overwhelming odds, like Aristomenes, Bruce, Vasa and the rest, and driven into the fastnesses of the Alleghenies, where he should live for some time, in a prowling condition, on wild animals and Indian corn, with a price upon his head, and surrounded by a few ever-faithful adherents—his adventures being too much enveloped by secrecy for an exact historical account, and amply suiting all the requirements of tradition—till the rallying of the Eastern States and the crowding of backwoodsmen to his standard, should enable him to march out again, scatter a number of detachments, and fall upon General Howe with determination, defeating him with great slaughter, in the renowned and beautiful valley of the Mohawk. This, certainly, would be an improvement.[72]

Here, thinks the belated president, is a fantasy which even the young Lincoln in his Lyceum and Temperance addresses did not share, even esoterically, with his audiences. For this belated young man engaged in the most thinly veiled fantastical patricide by imagining the humiliating defeat of his first president and criticizing him for not suffering such a fate. But here also is contained an opening from which the belated could exit. For while Washington was monumentally the first, he was, in terms of contemporary exemplars, no Mao or Castro. It is true that in Washington hagiography the winter of 1777–78 at Valley Forge suffices to count as the guerrilla retreat like the Long March and the encampments in the mountains of Oriente, but to the belated president, the key is "suffice." As president, from a belated standpoint, Washington's encounter with rebels in western Pennsylvania could have also sufficed as a heroic putting down of a Jacobin turn in the Revolution as did Washington's decision to return to public life as a result of Shays's Rebellion. But as all these forced parallels pile up, they show the exceptionalist nature of Washington's firstness, which is in a fundamental way more cerebral and sophisticated in its claim for his uniqueness than the above fantasy and some modern actualities. There is no real image of Washington in a "prowling condition" in the wilderness feeding on wild animals and Indian corn with a price on his head, and, of course, the two "rebellions" which Washington did himself suppress, one through his part in creating the constitutional edifice and another through minimal military force, reveal his persona as the revolutionary moderate, if not the revolutionary White.

The Civil War, on the other hand, with its incredible carnage and the ever-present possibility that the nation was on the brink of oblivion which no retreat to partisan combat could remedy, was the more direct emotive political experience and one which it could be said constituted the true functional replacement for the Revolution Tocqueville said America never had. It is true, of course, that Lincoln was not literally on the field and was not a general, but in his constant search for one he became the agent of the coups de théâtre of the great campaigns and battles, and in his wartime persona he took on the war guilt which even the righteous side shares.

There were other presidents after Washington and before Lincoln, who had these opportunities, and sometimes and in some respects, seized them. Jefferson in his pursuit of his embargo policies would come tantalizingly close to heroic emergency dictatorship in order to "save" America from foreign war. Madison actually found his nation reinvaded and its capital burned by former colonial masters, but the War of 1812 just gave America the jitters. Jackson's war on the Bank of the United States comes closest to a pre-Lincolnian epic presidency. But, as the belated president will soon learn, while there are elements in this battle which might have had revolutionary implications, the "Bank War" was at its core the kind of crisis which a commercial society produces. In other words, there are aspects of honor and valor, but it is foremost a fight over cash. And, of course, there was the possible heroism of the figure that briefly came across Lincoln's path, James K. Polk. But again, "Polk's War" said much about the opportunities which a young nation might take in regard to vulnerable neighbors but little more than that. No, concludes the belated president, Lincoln's action during the Civil War uniquely defined the presidency as an epic institution that leaned upon and then surpassed Washington's administration. Lincoln defined what the commander-in-chief clause could mean and gave the presidency a status as the agency of national salvation that, if occasionally conceived, had never been so tested before.

But Lincoln was not only an American Agamemnon, questioning valor as he came to epitomize and speak for it. He was also the Homer of the war. The wartime presidency thus rested as a time bomb or agency of grace (depending upon one's perspective on strong presidents) which could be, at great risk, brought forth in moments of monumental crisis. The meaning that Lincoln gave to the war, extending from his first (mis)readings of the Declaration to its poetic transformation at Gettysburg, had even more long-term consequences. For here Lincoln had unleashed elements in American culture that still require Americans to accept burdens they sometimes attempt to undertake and sometimes attempt to shirk. The belated president reviews Lincoln's (mis)reading of the Declaration and his phenomenal feat of rescuing this "embalm(ed)" revolutionary document. He notes that Lincoln gave the Declaration a sacred reading which was validated not only by the war itself but by the Gettysburg Address. He also insisted that (1) the Declaration could not be permitted the shrinkage that was the major consequence of Douglas's reading without destroying its moral meaning and that (2) the Declaration was fundamentally a commitment of equality. The latter provided a standard which confounded many presidents, belated and otherwise, after him. For, he concludes, if there is any truth to American exceptionalism, it must include a recognition of its twin original sins, the plunder of native peoples and the enslavement of Africans. Americans had been so successful in regard to the former that it could be for the most part tucked away from national consciousness. The latter, however, was a much more difficult task. Writers like Bradford might complain about this legacy of the ultimate belated president or, like Wilmoore Kendall, they might insist that Americans ought not to let Lincoln "'steal' the game" in his reading of the Declaration, but (as Kendall himself admits) "those who seize upon and stress the 'all men are created equal' clause, quite in keeping with the Lincolnian view of the tradition, have slowly, and understandably enough, fixed upon the symbol of 'equality' as supreme."[73]

The line that connects Lincoln's readings of the Declaration and later struggles over racial equality is not always a clear one. The Lincoln of the late war was clearly restrained on this question despite his supersession of Jefferson and Douglas. As Stephen Skrowronek reminds us, "In speculating about how things have turned out had Lincoln lived out his second term, it is best to be cautious."[74] It is, of course, the indeterminacy on this point created by the assassination that helps preserves Lincoln's firstness, and the belated president receives momentary solace from imagining the epic presidency of the second-term Lincoln unraveling as he makes concessions and compromises to racism in the face of demands from some in his own party and wonders what effect on race relations a failure of Reconstruction would have had for Lincoln's claim to greatness when it could be traced directly to him. Still, despite the failure of the "experiment" of Reconstruction; the Civil War amendments, Fourteen and Fifteen; the "second" Reconstruction; and the still-bleeding wound of racial inequality—all sans Lincoln—each is, if not inconceivable without his (mis)readings, very much dependent upon them. For Lincoln placed the obligation of the "unfinished work" of the war upon later generations of (belated) presidents. Thus belated presidents who come after Lincoln can see themselves as blessed that this project which he initiated was incomplete and hence amenable to their own efforts at bringing life to Lincoln's own embalm(ed) document or they can curse him for centering this moral standard from which they see no way of atoning and every way of failing.

This belated president stands before Lincoln aware of the fact that his two great deeds, the creation of the epic presidency and the moral confrontation with racial inequality, are infuriating obstacles because they are theoretically capable of replication and transcendence and practically utopian. He notes that FDR, whom he is ready to examine next, had the confidence to undertake (mis)readings of many strong presidents but chose only to challenge one of Lincoln's legacies despite the anticipation and loyalty of a hopeful people. He thinks he now understands John F. Kennedy, who would deal with both these legacies with some, but limited, success. The young president responded to the question on the morning after his first night as president if he had slept in Lincoln's bed by saying that he had: "I jumped in and just hung on!"[75]

Chapter 3

FRANKLIN D. ROOSEVELT: GENIAL MASKS

* *

Certainly Franklin Roosevelt achieved monumental status as president. He extricated the nation from the most harrowing crisis (save the Civil War) in the nation's history. He was the architect of the American welfare state. He guided America to confrontation and victory against two brutal powers who were on the verge of bringing the world to its knees. Rexford Tugwell made the appropriate assessment in terms of poetic achievement when he said: "We are a lucky people. We have had leaders when the national life was at stake. If it had not been for Washington we might not have become a nation; if it had not been for Lincoln we might have been split in two; if it had not been for this later democrat we might have succumbed to dictatorship."[1]

Perhaps what is so awesome about the Roosevelt presidency are the number of ways in which he pushed against the iron contours of American political culture. In a Lockean society, FDR attacked the moral authority of capital. Indeed, in 1936 he asserted that corporations were "aliens to the spirit of democracy." In a nation of laws, he attacked the Supreme Court as usurpers. In a culture fearful of executive power, he celebrated executive authority and broke the Washingtonian moral rule against third terms. In a nation in which all are Jeffersonians, he created a federal apparat and asserted that "the spirit of the frontier husking bee is found in carefully drafted statutes."

Of course, these altered contours were to shrink back toward their natural boundaries. Sometimes, as was the case with the attack on the Supreme Court and the 1937 attempted "purge" of the Democratic Party, Americans would not follow their leader. The élan of a federal apparat has since ebbed and flowed. But at least to the end of the Cold War, the structural elements of the Roosevelt presidency have remained—the altered economy and the welfare state, the United States as world power, the "modern" presidency as the center of the American political system—creating their own problems of belatedness for subsequent occupants.[2]

THE MASK OF GENIALITY

Each poet-president is a puzzle, and each president hides his own secrets. Washington encased his monumental ambition by appearing to accede to demands that he exercise power rather than by seizing it. Lincoln sheltered his ambition through exaggerated obeisance to his predecessors. But where is FDR's poetic intent? Despite these multiple monumental achievements, FDR appears to be the casual president. The Washington persona is premised upon sternness, sternness in regard to "ambitious politicians" and all those who would stray from the demands of the path of obedience to the Constitution. Lincoln became the mournful leader who carried the moral weight of thousands of battlefield deaths and the evils of slavery for the nation at large. But FDR? With the nation at peril, first from within and then from without, there stands the jovial president with the infectious smile, the cigarette holder cocked in the air, head tilted back, and hat worn rakishly off center.

One incident illustrates the Roosevelt persona. Even in 1944, after twelve years of presidential leadership and in seriously declining health, Roosevelt managed to recreate the old magic in his "Fala speech." After reviewing past partisan charges against his presidency ranging from plans for an American dictatorship to war mongering, he noted the claim that he had sent transport to the Aleutian Islands to retrieve his dog. The accusation was in a sense not a trivial one, for its subtext involved the observation that the president had created the isolated and sycophantic world that dictators have inhabited for centuries. FDR waved off the narrative. "Well, of course, I don't resent attacks, and my family doesn't resent attacks, but Fala does resent them."[3] His mock seriousness evaporated after delivering the line and that big smile, that smile that suggested a persona that is both oblivious to the frustrations of life and basks in life's pleasures, flashed once again.

This happy casualness was not FDR's only persona. He could don numerous masks which, as we shall see, formed his own secret strategy against belatedness. But should any slip away, beneath lay the good-natured Roosevelt, not the frustrated and angry face of the belated president. Those who would attempt to unmask FDR by laying bare the poetic intent behind his monumental actions have never quite been able to lift this veil. Few have dared to speak of monumental ambition in regard to Washington and few have failed to apply it in regard to Lincoln. But when suspicious minds have studied Roosevelt, they discover only geniality. The very first critique, and one that attained the exemplary status, was offered by Walter Lippman in 1932 when he said that FDR was "a very pleasant man who, without any important qualifications for office, would very much like to be president."[4] Many other characterizations of this sort followed. To both Edmund Wilson and Bernard Baruch, FDR seemed like a Boy Scout. George Creel called him "a gay, volatile Prince Charming" unfit to solve the problem of the Depression.[5]

Throughout the Depression this critique persisted with a large number of variations. To the radical Left and Right, FDR was an American Kerensky.

Roosevelt responded by offering his own jokes about the comparison. As capital was driven to a furious hatred of the president, the geniality persona was given macabre interpretation. James Hamilton spread the story that the laughter which echoed down the halls of the White House when FDR received visitors continued to grow louder and louder until it reached a maniacal pitch.[6]

Together, these assessments formed what Elliot A. Rosen has called the "country squire" thesis. Roosevelt was "at times a captive of his academic advisors, at times capricious as he played them off against one another as opposed to serious inquiry into their viewpoints, always superficial in his utterances and perception of the basics."[7] Later revisionist scholarship repeated this kind of New Deal criticism. Howard Zinn, for example, granted that "Roosevelt's social concern was genuine, his political courage huge, his generous spirit unfailing." "Beyond them," however, "his driving force weakened" and the "boldest programs often came from intellectuals not closely associated with the White House."[8] Even contemporary sympathetic biographers offer modified versions of FDR as genial squire. Thus Arthur Schlesinger Jr. wrote that Roosevelt "was unconsciously seeing America in the Jeffersonian image of Dutchess County and Hyde Park."[9] James MacGregor Burns concluded that "impatient of theory, insatiably curious about people and their ideas, sensitively attuned to the play of forces around him, he lacked that burning and almost fanatic conviction that great leadership demands."[10] In short, FDR was not afflicted with belatedness.

These perorations upon FDR's geniality—geniality as incompetence, geniality as shortsightedness, geniality as intellectual shallowness, geniality as conservatism, even geniality as madness—certainly all explain portions of the Roosevelt presidency. But as a theorizing concept they have hidden an assessment of FDR. This has always been the case with Roosevelt's critics. FDR sustained ferocious attacks, especially in 1936 and 1940, but his opponents were always confronted with the problem of his geniality. No president with the exception of Lincoln was subjected to more serious and more frequent charges of dictatorship than FDR. But it was his happy casualness that confounded his ideological opponents. Could this genial man really be an agent of capital or an instigator of a Soviet America? Critics thus were often forced to make their claims by indirection. Not only were they never sure FDR was "like" Kerensky or Leon Blum or Hitler or Stalin, but they were never sure precisely how he was like them. Thus Wendell Willkie, who had the great opportunity to present the charge of dictator in 1940, compared FDR to both Blum *and* Hitler.[11] One critic of the court-packing plan expressed this dilemma: "If the court as guardian and umpire is to be destroyed, let us not pretend that we are doing anything else. Let us frankly abolish the Constitution and adopt a system of parliamentary absolutism or its alternative, a dictatorship. For one who knows the president it is impossible to believe that he is aiming at a future dictatorship; but it is also impossible not to reconcile the packing of the Supreme Court as exactly what a dictator would adopt as a first step. The President may not know where he is going, but he is on his way."[12]

Jerome D. Green's lament that it is impossible to belief that FDR had monumental ambition and impossible to believe that he did not has blocked sustained consideration of poetic intent. Schlesinger concluded that "no one could guess" what Roosevelt really thought in his "rare moments of solitude," when he could not evade the ultimates. Perhaps James MacGregor Burns came the closest to confronting the paradox when he organized his biography around the Machiavellian advice about lions and foxes. Yet Burns could find very little of the new prince in FDR's actions: "He was always a superb tactician, and sometimes a courageous leader, but he failed to achieve the combination of tactical skill and strategic planning that represents the acme of political leadership."[13]

But what of the belated president who can see past the most complex and ingenious of disguises? If it is geniality that represents the center of the puzzle, then the belated president would ask: Is it possible that there is a connection between FDR's monumental achievements and his geniality? Certainly FDR's happy casualness could disarm critics and give confidence to a population terrified by the Depression. But the belated president soon discovers that geniality by itself is not a veil against poetic intent and a bridge to poetic achievement. For the Roosevelt critic, though he cannot quite find the origins of his achievements, would have us see geniality as incompetence and opportunism. Thus, the geniality persona seems like an invitation to an open critique. But it is in this very fact that it does not that lies FDR's secret. From the standpoint of the president determined to avoid belatedness, there must then be some project that FDR undertook that somehow partakes of geniality but that also somehow encases his happy casualness thus making it impossible to believe that he had monumental ambitions and that he did not.

We have by now become used to the frenzied and urgent process by which a belated president seeks to discover poetic intent. Unlike the belated president who confronts Lincoln, the post-FDR afflicted aspirant has no coherent critical tradition from which to proceed. He is thus driven to examine how FDR treats his own predecessors on his own. Surely, if Roosevelt was afflicted by belatedness he too had to make room for his monumental achievements, so wonders the person stricken himself with belatedness. The belated president then would look first at those moments when the opportunity for monumental achievement was possible or at risk. He thus reviews the hagiography of FDR: his privileged origins, his early political career and a fight against Tammany, his vice-presidential candidacy. There is, of course, his functional equivalent to modest origin: FDR was stricken by polio and thus learned about powerlessness. Driven into medical exile, the young Roosevelt examines his own personal challenges and those facing the Democratic Party. He loyally supports Al Smith for president and successfully runs for governor. When the Depression hits, he fashions an imaginative and supportive administration, a "little New Deal." He runs for president pledging a "new social contract" and vigorous experimentation in order to meet the economic emergency. He fashions a legislative agenda in his first hundred days that creates a permanent feature of presidential time. Through a variety of emergency measures, FDR saves the banking system, saves homes and homesteads, provides jobs and relief for the unemployed. Capital attempts to strike back in 1936, but FDR takes his case to the people and is reelected by a landslide. His attempts to reform the courts and the Democratic Party are unsuccessful but the president had already put into effect a "second New Deal" in 1935 seeking to create provisions for economic security in addition to economic recovery not the least of which includes social security and the economic enfranchisement of unions through the Wagner Act. Having defeated economic elites at home, he alerts Americans to the danger of dictatorships abroad. Declaring that the world cannot remain half-slave and half-free, he patiently educates the American people about the dangers of fascism. Reluctant to leave his responsibilities in the midst of war, he agrees to seek a fourth term and dies in office. His funeral train arrived in Washington, D.C., eighty years to the day after Lincoln was shot.

The belated president thus acknowledges Roosevelt's monumental achievements in narrative form. He tries to collect an alternative, a narrative of poetic intent. But he can only assemble bits and pieces. There are some tantalizing stories told by advisors: FDR's desire to have Adolph Berle call him "Caesar" in private conversation; his assertion to Moley that the 1936 election was about himself and himself alone; his comment to Tugwell that when conservatives strike they do so with a "closed fist" and progressives must learn to do the same. He finds one sustained critique by John T. Flynn. But *The Roosevelt Myth*, while it contains numerous stories of petty political corruption in the New Deal and even the charge that FDR, avid stamp collector, ordered die proofs sent to him, cannot quite develop an anti-Roosevelt myth of any proportion. The most that Flynn can manage is that the many terms in office "literally rotted the nature of Franklin Roosevelt," transforming him into an "Egyptian Pharaoh" concerned more about federal funding of his Hyde Park estate as a national monument than postwar policy.[14] Still Flynn acknowledges a pre-presidential FDR as a shallow, pleasant man who was actually humanized by his illness and an early presidential Roosevelt overwhelmed by the Depression and forced to rely on advisors and speech writers. The belated president also consults other postwar critiques chronicling FDR's naïveté at Yalta, but, like Flynn's, each is drawn back to that wall of Roosevelt's happy casualness.

THE JEFFERSON MASK

The belated president panics. Was FDR simply lucky? Is it possible that a man can be great without poetic intent? Questions such as these are more disturbing than the resentment that emerges when the belated president cannot discover poetic intent but knows that it must be secreted away somewhere. For how can an aspirant hope to overcome his adversary if his greatness rests simply on fortune? Poetic intent is the common bond between the two presidents. When the belated president cannot find it, he is terrified that greatness will always remain beyond his grasp.

But the belated president really has no choice but to continue to search since his affliction demands relief. He comes to despise that upturned face with the big grin. FDR's geniality infuriates him; that smiling face seems to be mocking him. "You will never find my secret," that damned pseudo-aristocrat seems to say. He searches for any patterns of belatedness. Fury rises in him when he reads FDR's comment to a questioner about his political philosophy. The bemused Roosevelt replies simply that he is a "Christian and a Democrat." He concludes that similar responses must be either apocryphal or further instances of the most remarkable cunning. Did FDR really say to Keynes that he could not understand his "rigmarole of figures"? He is enraged when he hears the campaign tune "Happy Days are Here Again" and when he learns that FDR allegedly kept the quote "Let Unconquerable Gladness Dwell" on his desk.

The belated president says to himself that he will read everything the president wrote. He pages through speech after speech from the Happy Warrior speeches and good government addresses in 1928 to the carefully calibrated remarks about the "forgotten man" in 1932 and the famous fireside chats. He studies four inaugural addresses. Nothing. Nothing but slogans about faith in America, the need for economic security, the perils from dictatorships abroad.

Exhausted and despondent, the belated president comes across an old book review in the _New York Evening World_, the only book review written by FDR, from 1925. The belated president is puzzled by FDR's enthusiasm for Claude Bowers's _Jefferson and Hamilton_. Roosevelt said the book was "thrilling" and should be studied in "newspaper editorial rooms as well as in homes and schools of America."[15] Bowers was a talented popular biographer and this effort vividly described the Jefferson-Hamilton rivalry. According to Bowers, the capital was on the verge of a coup d'état in the 1790s. Everywhere there was emerging the assertion of aristocratic power, not only in terms of a culture of dress and manner and money making from access to the party of the court, but in open conversation about the inevitable return to monarchy. To Bowers, it rested upon Jefferson, whom he described as a quiet westerner with interests in the solitary pursuit of philosophy and domestic life, to singlehandedly save the Republic from a Hamiltonian led counterrevolution. Jefferson, nearly defeated at every step he took, organized a republican press and a mass party system to awaken a public to the danger.

Roosevelt was captivated by both figures in the contest narrated by Bowers. He admitted that Hamilton was a "romantic and fascinating figure, albeit in his true character of aristocrat." Jefferson was both the "calm philosopher" and "the consummate politician" who successfully undertook the "colossal task" of "savior of the deeper ideals of the revolution." Jefferson could "count only on the scattered raw material of the working classes, difficult to reach, more difficult to organize." FDR concluded that it was 1790–1800 that was the most crucial period in American history, important in "every way" as the Civil War. He experienced a "breathless feeling" as he read of the "escape after escape which this Nation passed through in those ten years; a picture of what might have been if the Republic had been finally organized as Alexander Hamilton had sought." Roosevelt wondered with "breathless feeling too" if 125 years later "the same contending forces are not again mobilizing." He closed with the question,

"Hamiltons we have today," but "is there a Jefferson on the horizon?"

The belated president savors his own feelings of exhilaration after he reads this review. I've finally found you, you clever bastard! he exclaims. FDR had proclaimed he "felt like saying 'At Last'" when he read Bowers's book and now the belated president feels the same way. Here I have been searching for the "great" presidents and all along it was Jefferson who excites your poetic ambition! Of course, it is Hamilton, the aristocrat, who represents the source of your belatedness. For now that the belated president thinks that he has the key to alleviating his own belatedness, his theorizing feels like an explosive force. It is this "romantic" figure that you resent and you say as much when you admit that you were "fed up with the romantic cult which . . . surrounded the name of Alexander Hamilton." The imaginary belated president wonders, Is it possible that as Hamilton was allegedly Washington's aegis, so is Jefferson yours in your battle against belatedness? In any case, he is satisfied that he has discovered FDR's poetic intent. Roosevelt identified a "colossal task" in history, assayed the protagonists, and announced that a similar opportunity for monumental achievement worthy of Jefferson's lay on the horizon.

The belated president is pleased almost beyond his own hopes when he learns that Roosevelt proposed in a letter to hundreds of Democratic leaders across the country that the party after its recent defeat ought to consider returning to Jeffersonian principles. Democrats should examine "the difference between the Jeffersonian and Hamiltonian ideals for a method of government." Their "fundamental differences could be applied to present day policies," suggested FDR. His initiative was not well received. In fact, Herbert Croly, the editor of the *New Republic*, ridiculed the former Democratic candidate for the vice-presidency. He called the circular the "Great Jeffersonian Joke" and concluded that "a political party which, when asked to deal with difficult and novel political and economic problems, always answers by shouting, 'Hurrah for Jefferson,' belongs to musical comedy rather than to the sinister and tragic drama of politics."[16] But the belated president now knows that FDR had indeed an intimate grasp of the "sinister and tragic." He looks on approvingly at FDR's expression of poetic resentment. Many editors, said FDR in his review, "launched sneers at the mere suggestion that Jeffersonianism could, in any remote manner, bear upon the America of 1925." He confessed to "still boil[ing] inwardly when I think of these smug writers."

Now armed with not only evidence of Roosevelt's poetic intent but even with the general outlines of a strategy, the belated president returns to FDR's speeches. What he finds is a systematic application of Jefferson to the colossal task of confronting the Depression.

As the Depression deepened, the political climate seemed most receptive to campaign symbolism that emphasized a crisis vocabulary which relied either upon the martial rhetoric of Lincoln or the wartime Wilson or even political theories outside American political culture.[17] During the 1932 campaign, FDR periodically evoked both Lincoln and Wilson in his speeches but more consistently pursued the exemplar of Jefferson. His "Concert of Interest" speech reinterpreted an old debate in American political culture: the policy dispute between Hamilton and Jefferson on the role of the government in the promotion of economic policy. But Roosevelt ignored the usual grounding of the understanding of that debate in the questions of industrialization versus agrarianism and states' rights versus nationalism. Both Jefferson and Hamilton are portrayed as nationalists, Hamilton as a nationalist-elitist and Jefferson as a nationalist-democrat. Both were planners with a national vision, although Hamilton, "the great financial genius," sought to limit participation to "certain individuals . . . more fitted than others to conduct government."

FDR's case for a new Jefferson is based on three aspects of the original Jefferson's career. Jefferson "devoted years to the building of a political party" as a "definite act aimed at the unification of the country in support of common principles." Jefferson's cosmopolitanism is also emphasized. He worked "laboriously" to attain "an understanding of the people in this country" and came to know "at first hand every cross-current of national and international life" and consequently appreciated the "yearnings and lack of opportunity, the hopes and fears of millions." "He was," insists FDR, "no local American! He was no little American!" Finally, Jefferson's boldness as president is also recounted. He had been willing to "stake his fortunes on the stroke of a pen" when he purchased "an imperial domain which trebled the size of the country overnight." By contrast Hamilton and the Federalists are described as able but "local" Americans isolated by their elite perspectives.[18]

The immediate campaign objective of the St. Paul–Minneapolis speech was unmistakable. Hoover was a Hamiltonian and FDR a (would-be) Jeffersonian. But Roosevelt described in general terms how this debate, which he outlined as a reoccurring one in American political history, could be transcended. He offered Chesterton's joke about the British Empire as a metaphor for the Jefferson-Hamilton dialectic in American history. Chesterton had remarked that like the passengers on a omnibus, British subjects only get to know one another in the case of an accident. In "normal times" too, noted FDR, America is "a loose association of communities, with little common thought and little realization of mutual interdependence." Only in crises do Americans search for wider concerns. Then presumably the Jefferson-Hamilton battles are refought only to lead to truces in which the nation reverts again to the "isolation of sectionalism." Through the creation of a national political party based upon common participation and led by men who, like Jefferson, understood the "hopes and fears of millions of their fellow human beings," a "concert of interests" could be formed which could create a permanent "shared public life."

In his 1925 book review, FDR was thrilled to discover a crisis, a crisis greater than the Civil War, which he thought had been largely ignored in American history. Now the Depression had replicated the same conditions for his own participation. As Lincoln espied that a (mis)reading of Jefferson could create an opportunity to overcome belatedness, so did FDR. Lincoln (mis)read an embalmed abstract truth in Jefferson's revolutionary pamphlet that through his own monument effort could be brought back to life. FDR focused on a later

Jefferson, the Jefferson who fought off an ideological coup d'état, but he too found Jefferson's project incomplete, although in a different way. While Jefferson had "won," the "revolution of 1800" had been seriously incomplete. Jefferson was a monumental figure in a reappearing struggle. In "normal times" Americans thought in terms of local communities and private initiatives. In moments of crisis the Jeffersonian-Hamiltonian struggle reemerged only to sink once again to the "isolation of sectionalism." FDR spoke eloquently, as only a man convinced that a poetic opportunity lay before him, of the "great leaders of every generation," Jackson, Theodore Roosevelt, and Wilson, who strove to transcend the Hamiltonian perspective that had always reasserted itself. But in the language of belatedness these great leaders were really only minor poets or, in terms of the standard of monumental achievement, failed poets. Their efforts were incomplete because Americans lacked a "shared public life." It was the task of monumental leadership to create a "concert of interests" that would make public space constant.

The Concert of Interest speech thus reveals all the features of poetic intent veiled. Moley, the draft writer, later praised the speech for its attention to the contours of the American polity which he felt the president abandoned in 1935.[19] Indeed, FDR's depiction of America as a collection of interests that awaited collection into a "concert" seemed to respect the pluralism of a liberal society. Roosevelt had, in fact, portrayed the Jefferson-Hamilton struggle and its recurrent forms in terms of an expansion of interests which the elitists had blocked and assured his audience that he spoke not of an "economic life completely planned and regimented." But Roosevelt also (mis)read Jefferson as a nationalist and a planner and emphasized the swiftness of his executive decisions, although it was precisely this reading of a "democratic" Jefferson that formed the center of the Federalist critique. To men like Fisher Ames, for example, Jefferson "fomented a licentious spirit" among the populace. Though he spoke "the maxims of Cato," he acted "steadily on a plan of usurpation like Caesar."[20]

The general theme of the Jefferson Day address was repeated throughout the campaign. Roosevelt spoke of the need for "bold experimentation" under "true leadership which unites us all" at Oglethorpe University but reiterated his commitment to the "sacredness of private property" in Columbus, promised a "new deal" in Chicago. Each of these addresses included his emendations on the Jefferson-Hamilton debate.[21]

Jefferson formed the center of his famous Commonwealth Club address in September, although the belated president discovers that there are several steps between FDR and this text. Tugwell contends that Roosevelt never saw the speech until he opened it on the lectern in San Francisco.[22] The content of the speech is usually credited to Adolf Berle, its main drafter, and is regarded as reflecting more his economic views than Roosevelt's.[23] Thus the address fits neatly with the country squire narrative. Under the pressure of the campaign, FDR reads a speech that reflects the views of one of his contending advisors.

The belated president, however, simply will not accept a judgment that concludes that a speech of such import was treated so casually by a figure of such monumental achievement, especially so in Roosevelt's case in which he believes that the geniality persona is a veil to cover poetic intent. It does not take him long to discover a pattern of interaction between FDR and Berle. Both Berle and Roosevelt knew three aspects of the immediate future by late summer. A Democratic victory was likely. FDR's party was divided between a right wing and a liberal one that again divided over the old question fought by progressives over whether corporate power should be rationalized or dispersed. The Depression represented a real crisis for the Republic. FDR too knew two facts about Berle. Berle had been a fervent supporter of Newton Baker whom he regarded as a man of "finer and more precise intelligence" than Roosevelt. FDR was also aware of Berle's own ambitions. "An elegant young man" considered by many to be "arrogant and self-centered," Berle once confided that "his real ambition in life is to be the American Karl Marx—a social prophet."[24] The Depression was thus for both men an opportunity of monumental proportions.

The belated president asks, "Did these men form their own social contract in a mutual struggle against belatedness in 1932?" The first move came from Berle. In August, he wrote to Roosevelt about the campaign. Berle noted that the "chances were better than even" that FDR would win. Yet the "possibility of defeat" has "to be reckoned with" and Roosevelt must then "still have your political career to think of." Berle continued: "Should the campaign go off merely on a series of scattering issues, defeat would probably end your career, as it did the careers of Cox, Davis, and even Al Smith. Should you, however, quite definitely become the protagonist of an outstanding policy, your significance in American public life would continue—as did that of Bryan and Roosevelt." His counselor added: "The illustrations of course do not suggest any agreement with the policies of these men."[25]

The belated president ponders what a message such as this must have meant for his fellow sufferer. He has before him only FDR's genial response, "You are a wonderful help. See you soon."[26] If Roosevelt was afflicted, so concludes the belated president, Berle's argument that he *might* share a position with Cox, Davis, and Smith would have been terrifying and Berle's assertion that he had the chance to claim the "significance in public life" of Bryan, Wilson, and TR would have been regarded as a poetic opportunity that he *must* grasp. Indeed, Roosevelt accepted the advice that a speech "analogous to Woodrow Wilson's 'New Freedom'" address would "probably make your place in history." He was, in fact, willing to confront the central symbol of the American polity, "individualism," as Berle too suggested.

Yet the speech went through several drafts before its delivery. Berle complained privately about the editing but was satisfied. FDR, of course, remained silent, but his own revisions were carefully added to the text. Berle, the ambitious young man who so directly appealed to FDR's poetic intent, left Washington in 1934 unable to secure a major position in the administration although he continued to address his letters to the president as "Dear Caesar" until 1937, when Roosevelt told an aide, "Get hold of Berle and tell him to be darn careful in what he writes to me because the Staff sees his letters and they are highly indiscrete."[27] Shortly later, Berle was offered an undersecretaryship at State with hints from FDR that he would be part of a reconstituted brains trust.

The speech has many of the features of Lincoln's Lyceum address. FDR traces the morally ambivalent role that leaders have performed throughout history. In Europe, people supported national leaders in order to "put the unruly noble-man in his place," but they realized that new "limiting" structures, constitutions and parliaments, were necessary to hem in these "ruthless" men. In America, industrial leaders, men of "tremendous will and tremendous ambition," were "cheerfully" given power in order to build an industrial America. But now the railroads were built, the "dream of an economic machine" was over, and the people were faced with "great uncontrolled and irresponsible units of power within the state."[28]

The two major tropes of the address, ruthlessness/ambition and dreams, form a historical dialectic that provides belated men poetic opportunity. The people at large have their dreams; they are engaged in a "never-ending seeking for better things" and FDR attempts to provide a map of the "many roads" they pursue in their effort to achieve them. Desirous of economic opportunity or simply relief from "exploitation and cruelty," they happily contract with am-bitious leaders who in turn have their dreams fulfilled in terms of "free play and economic reward."

One of reasons the Commonwealth Club address is regarded suspiciously as a guide to later New Deal policy is the repeated rejection of American exceptionalism. Roosevelt not only asserts that the relationship between dream/ambition in America is fundamentally the same as the roads already taken in Europe, he declares that the "last frontier" in America has been reached. The safety valve in the western prairie is exhausted; "our industrial plant is built." The dream has been shut down: "We are not able to invite the immigration from Europe to share our endless plenty. We are now providing a drab living for our own people."[29] But a close reading of the argument suggests that FDR has not really abandoned American exceptionalism as dream but only its last contractual formulation. He assures his audience that "we have no ac-tual famine or dearth; our industrial and agricultural mechanism can produce enough and to spare." You can keep the dream, says Roosevelt, but look at the fact that "the central and ambitious financial unit is no longer a servant of desire, but a danger."

From the standpoint of belatedness, the Commonwealth Club speech thus announces the terms of a new contract offered by FDR and his counselor. Berle had warned Roosevelt that a certain kind of defeat might permanently frustrate FDR's ambitions and place him in the category of politician manqué along with Cox, Davis, and Smith. And Berle too, already suffering from his selection of a loser for the nomination, attempts to cast off the role of failed counselor by attempting to convince FDR that he must become the "protagonist of an out-standing policy." Thus, the dialectic of ambition and dream concluded by con-tract and outlined as the moving force of history is twice layered, consisting of the peoples' dreams and leaders' ambitions and, in this case, the dreams and ambitions of the aspiring president and his aspiring counselor.

The Depression, which had destroyed the dream of the economic machine, opened up an opportunity unparalleled in American history. For if the indus-trialist could no longer function as an agent of desire, who would take his place? Roosevelt could not be clearer on this point. The day of the "prince of prop-erty" was past and "the day of enlightened administration has come." The new leader's task would be one of "modifying and controlling our economic units." Whenever "the lone wolf, the unethical speculator, the reckless promoter, the Ishmael or Insull . . . threatens to drag industry back to a stage of anarchy . . . the Government must be swift to enter and protect the public interest."[30]

There was a tension in FDR's narration of this fall of one elite and rise of another that bedeviled both the New Deal and Roosevelt's own battle against belatedness. On the one hand, the failure of the economic machine seemed to suggest a permanent reorientation of the center of power and authority in America in which an apparat would govern the economy under a contract of "enlightened administration." Many of the New Dealers saw their historical roles in this light. Berle saw the New Deal in these terms. The Depression had "educated" the American people to seek economic safety as their prime value. Even "if . . . we were to adopt the Russian Soviet system entire, it would look a good deal more like the Rotary Club or the four railway brotherhoods than like the Moscow Soviet."[31] One the other hand, if history is a series of selections of leaders on the part of the people to save their dreams, then this subjection of the business class would be more charismatically based, one remarkably simi-lar to Locke's account of the people's turn to leaders in times of crisis in the Book of Judges.

FDR's account contained both these interpretations because each repre-sented a strategy against belatedness. The fact that he could never quite choose irrevocably between the two lies in the nature of the alternatives themselves. If the Depression represented a historical turn consisting of "the soberer, less dramatic business of administering resources and plants already built," FDR would be the founder of benevolent administration. If, however, his task was to keep a watchful eye on new Ishmaels, he assumed the role of a heroic figure. But as Locke noted, when the people chose judges they had no intention of anointing kings.[32] All they were concerned with was who could save them. Thus FDR was called upon as a belated figure to choose between permanence in the role of the sober administrator and the volatility of the charismatic leader.

Berle, as counselor, was quite prepared to accept the poetic opportunity opened by the Depression in terms of enlightened administration. His poetic intent, after all, was of necessity framed in terms of his role as a founding member of a new federal apparat. Since FDR's aims were more ambivalent, he would find himself in a nearly constant state of poetic competition between the bu-reaucracy he heroicly created and his continuing need to assert predominance over a new partially rationalized system. Thus when Walter Lippman com-plained in 1934 that the competitive proliferation of New Deal agencies proved that FDR had many plans but no Plan,[33] he was only partially correct, for it was from the context of bureaucratic incoherence that FDR was able to act heroically. To FDR's critics like Lippman, this constant experimentation with bureaucratic structures was illustration of drift, but to a president intent upon monumental achievement, it could have been conceived in precisely the opposite terms.

Even the belated president, however, might not grant that FDR fully realized the necessity of this strategy in 1932. But he could detect its elements in FDR's choice of Jefferson as a guide. In his 1925 book review, he discovered the heroic task that Jefferson had undertaken in the 1790s. To progressives like Herbert Croly, the symbol of Jefferson represented anachronistic tendencies in American culture. Convinced that it was Hamilton who conceived of a national purpose beyond "the parade of individualism," Croly concluded that the application of Jefferson, whose idea of democracy was "meager, narrow and self contradictory," to current problems was a great "joke." FDR, however, saw Jefferson in a different light. He was unconcerned about his individualism and localism. What so excited FDR about Jefferson was the "colossal task" he undertook as mobilizer of a sleeping people. That Jefferson "could rely only on the scattered raw material of the working classes, difficult to reach, more difficult to organize" animated Roosevelt because it provided a model of radical change in which the leader occupied the center of the narrative. FDR was intrigued with those aspects of Hamilton's character as a romantic aristocrat, but Hamilton's role in the crisis was that of the insider, the court schemer and power broker. Seen through the lens of his own belatedness, FDR portrayed both men as nationalists and planners and thus equally viable as models. Only Jefferson stood outside society to create a new institution, the mass political party, which under his leadership would save the ideals of the revolution.

Thus Roosevelt in the Commonwealth speech focused upon the "revolution of 1800" as his framework for a new social contract. But if Jefferson provided FDR with a model from which he could approach his own poetic opportunity, he also stood as an obstacle. Roosevelt had already modified Jefferson to fit his poetic imagination. Jefferson was a nationalist, a visionary leader who mobilized a sleeping people to save the Republic. But FDR knew that by rescuing Jefferson from the derogation of progressive reform, he also risked placing himself in the shadow of the third president. Was his task in 1932 a mere replication of Jefferson's? In his Concert of Interest address FDR had shown how Jefferson's colossal task was incomplete. Generations of great leaders after him had been unable to create a permanent "shared public life," which was imminent in Jefferson's project. The third American president had employed two fundamental rights, "personal competency" (freedom of speech) and property, to beat back an attempt to capture the federal government in 1800. Here comes FDR's revision: "But even Jefferson realized that the exercise of the property rights might so interfere with the rights of the individual that the government, without whose assistance the property rights could not exist, must intervene, not to destroy individualism, but to protect it." In its place, Roosevelt promises a "new social contract" to secure the "apparent Utopia which Jefferson imagined for us." "Every man has the right to make a comfortable living" is the new Jeffersonian right.[34]

In the language of the belated poet, FDR said, "This is the way Jefferson would have turned in order to achieve a full transformation (if he were the greatest poet)." Lincoln's belated frustrations were projected upon "new reapers"; Roosevelt's upon European monarchs and American captains of industry. In the Lyceum address, Lincoln submerged his threat to Washington by proposing an oath not to "trample on the blood of his father." Roosevelt too proposed a new social contract, one that Jefferson *would* have written. That Jefferson would have swerved is based on a (mis)reading of his work as a democratic nationalist. But the fact that Jefferson did not, permits FDR to overcome Jefferson and initiate an exceptional presidency. Lincoln overcame Jefferson by treating his Declaration as containing an "embalmed" truth that was his monumental task to bring to life; FDR must rescue Jefferson from the dead in order to surpass him.

FDR underscored the colossal nature of his own project by reviewing the efforts of previous great presidents to meet the terms of the Jeffersonian contract in light of the consequences of the ruthlessness of the captains of industry. "Clear-sighted men," said Roosevelt, "saw with fear the danger that opportunity would no longer be equal; that the growing corporation, like the feudal baron of old, might threaten the economic freedom of individuals to earn a living." Theodore Roosevelt, "the first great Republican Progressive," identified these men as "malefactors of great wealth." TR, however, attempted "to turn the clock back, to destroy the large combinations and to return to the time when every man owns his individual small business." "This was impossible," concluded FDR, and TR was "forced to work out a difference between 'good' and 'bad' trusts." Woodrow Wilson, however, saw the problem "more clearly." He knew that "Jefferson had feared the encroachment of political power on the lives of individuals" and that the "new political power was financial." "He saw, in the highly centralized economic system, the despot of the twentieth century, on whom great masses of individuals relied for their safety and their livelihood, and whose irresponsibility and greed (if they were not controlled) would reduce them to starvation and penury." The war in Europe, however, forced Wilson "to abandon his study of this issue."[35]

Roosevelt did not say explicitly that these great men failed, but his final paragraph noted "our common failure" and concluded that "failure is not an American habit." Most notably, Berle had ended the speech with the statement that the new social contract would be fulfilled as was "the apparent Utopia which Jefferson imagined for us" in 1776 and "brought to realization" by "Washington, Jefferson, Madison and Jackson." FDR excised all these names save Jefferson and added instead Theodore Roosevelt and Woodrow Wilson. In place of "brought to realization" he placed "sought to bring to realization."[36]

These revisions and others tell a great deal about FDR's own social contract with Berle. In earlier drafts of the speech, Wilson formed the center of the argument for a new social contract. Wilson was a great liberal whose cry for a new freedom was doomed because "facts were against him, American life had become corporate not individual . . . his eyes were too strongly blinded by the nineteenth century to see the hand writing of the twentieth." Why, might ask the belated president, had Roosevelt not only shifted his focus from Wilson's failures but moved the entire address away from Wilson and to Jefferson? In the final draft, FDR had actually inverted the positions of TR and Wilson on the question of the trusts, at least from the perspective of the 1912 election. TR had eventually learned that the clock could not be turned back, but he is identified as a trust buster. Wilson, who actually used Jefferson as a club against TR, is the man who saw the concentration of corporate power "more clearly." Moreover, Wilson's economic project is portrayed as untried. The war arrived and Wilson was "forced to abandon the study of the issue." The belated president is puzzled by this rearrangement until he undertakes the working hypothesis that FDR had decided to make his statement as "protagonist of an outstanding public policy" exclusively in terms of Jefferson. Berle originally portrayed Wilson as the last of a line of liberal statesman from which FDR would depart. To Berle, the centering of Jefferson must have seemed like a retreat from the founding of an enlightened administration. But FDR's rearrangement shows that he is going after bigger game. Berle had provided a framework for an outstanding public policy that abandoned Jefferson through a rejection of Wilson. FDR, however, altered the line that read Jefferson-Wilson as a completed experiment with FDR initiating another one which read Jefferson-FDR, with TR and Wilson great men who were unable to revise Jefferson under modern conditions. Hence Roosevelt's alteration of "brought to realization" to "sought to bring to realization" and the deletion of all figures but Jefferson and his twentieth-century manqués.

But in the ominous months before the inauguration, even FDR's amended Jeffersonianism seemed hopelessly utopian. His inaugural address, in fact, borrowed much more heavily on Lincoln, with its martial rhetoric (Americans must pledge "a sacred obligation with a unity hitherto invoked only in time of armed strife") and intimations of the possibility of temporary dictatorship.

Following the inaugural, however, FDR returned to his new Jeffersonianism as outlined in the campaign. At the Naval Academy, he reminded graduates that while "esprit de corps, pride of profession is a delightful element in the making of a good officer," it is not an appropriate ethos for "a citizen of a democratic society." "Avoid an exclusive relationship to your own clan" was Roosevelt's advice. "Remember to cultivate the friendship of people, not alone your own class or profession, but the average run of folks, the same folks you would have known and liked and affiliated with had you not chosen to enter and to graduate from a highly specialized institution of higher education." Think of the people you serve, continued FDR, "not as an abstract mass, but as one hundred and twenty millions of men and women and children in forty-eight states—on sea coast, on plain and among mountains; in city, in village, and on the farm; rich people, people of moderate means, poor people; people employed and people out of jobs."[37] At Vassar College, another elite institution, the new president introduced the symbol of neighborliness as a national ethic. Let's begin "extending to our national life the old principle of local community, the principle that no individual man, woman or child, has a right to do things that hurt his neighbors." The New Deal would apply the "old precept" that "what is good for my neighbors is good for me, too."[38] At an extemporaneous speech at Washington College, FDR used the metaphor of pioneering to explain the direction he hoped the nation would move. He criticized a previous speaker who spoke of the pioneers in individualist terms: "It is true that the pioneer was an individualist; but at the same time, there was a pioneer spirit of cooperation and understanding of the need of building up, not a class, but a whole community."[39] Before the National Conference of Catholic Charities, he combined the two themes: "We have recaptured and rekindled our pioneering spirit . . . A democracy, the right kind of democracy, is bound together by the ties of neighborliness."[40] Throughout these addresses Roosevelt urged a reevaluation of existing institutions by urging the nation to ask a "new question in an old form": "Is this practice, is this custom, something which is done at the expense of the many?" For "the many" are our "neighbors."[41]

When the belated president studies these addresses he happily concludes that FDR was certainly no Jefferson. There are aspects of Jeffersonian republicanism in these formulations: the celebration of neighborliness as a reading of Jefferson's localism; the opposition to elitism as a reading of Jefferson's monocrats; a willingness to experiment with new political forms as a reading of Jefferson's belief that the earth belongs to the living. But the belated president delights in the fact that Roosevelt is not a reembodiment of the American Enlightenment. He is, after all, a very pleasant man who is now president. Just then he remembers that it is precisely this geniality which he was determined to resist. If FDR were no Jefferson, the man behind the mask was at least a happy one and no real harm was done. Thus the belated president learns, this time unhappily, that his reaction is the intended one. Dispirited but still driven by his belatedness, the imaginary president reminds himself that FDR is not the pleasant man playing at Jefferson but a belated figure determined to surpass his model.

What then, beyond the comfortable appeals to the Jeffersonian sentiment in American political culture, is involved in these reiterations especially in the context of the Depression and the enormous poetic opportunity it afforded FDR? The belated president rereads Jefferson and then rereads Roosevelt. He detects in Jefferson a central ambiguity that FDR and his New Deal bureaucrats seem to be exploring.

Crucial to Jefferson's philosophy was the concept of the purpose of government as an agency to promote the "pursuit of happiness." Jefferson's understanding of happiness was itself systematically ambiguous. Was happiness the pursuit and satisfaction of private desire or the creation and maintenance of a just political order? Sometimes Jefferson clearly spoke of happiness in the former terms and sometimes in the later. The belated president studies Jefferson's interpreters on this point. Hannah Arendt, for example, argues that Jefferson himself was not "very sure in his own mind what happiness meant."[42] She does, however, note that he brooded over the absence of arenas for the pursuit of public happiness after the Revolution. Arendt herself notes that while in America spontaneously created forums of direct political participation were not crushed by dictatorship as was the case in later revolutions, the founders, in their desire to solve the problem of the political stability of republican government, chose to substitute representation for direct political action. Jefferson "knew, however dimly, that the Revolution, while it had given freedom to the people, had failed to provide a space where this freedom could be exercised."[43] The failure of the founders to incorporate the township and the town meeting into the constitution was to be remedied by Jefferson through his proposal to sub-divide the country into wards. Here a citizen would be a "participator in the government of affairs, not merely at an election one day in the year, but every day." To Arendt, "the basic assumption of the ward system, whether Jefferson knew it or not, was that no one was happy without his share of public happi-ness, that no one could be called either happy or free without participating, and having a share, in public happiness."[44]

To the belated president, FDR seemed to have appreciated the same sort of insight in his insistence that the dialectic of the Jeffersonian-Hamiltonian debate could never be transcended until permanent structures of public par-ticipation were built. Unlike Jefferson, FDR saw the location of these struc-tures in national terms. Was it possible that Roosevelt was attempting to cre-ate the functional equivalent to wards at the federal level? Were the concepts of "pioneering" and "neighborliness" and his insistence that New Dealers ex-amine "all kinds of human relationships" an effort to found nationalized insti-tutions of public happiness? Was the appeal to Jefferson less an opportunistic manipulation at traditional American symbols or lack of imagination on the part of a mediocre politician and more FDR's way of conveying his revolution-ary grasp of the openings created by the Depression, openings revealed by his quest against belatedness? After all, according to Arendt, the emergence of centers of public happiness in a revolution were largely historically invisible since they were ignored or crushed by the acknowledged great leaders of revo-lution. That FDR was not a Lenin was readily accepted but was he not a Kerensky but a Luxembourg?

The belated president ponders these questions, but when he studies the new government agencies created in the early days of the New Deal, he wonders if FDR had even a less clear idea than Jefferson of new forms of public happiness. What the belated president sees when he examines the "alphabet agencies"—the NRA, AAA, WPA, FERA, CCC, TVA, and others—is Hamiltonian-in-spired structures designed to stabilize the economy and provide temporary re-lief to both desperate workers and capitalists, each managed by enlightened administration. He notes the lack of institutions of democratic participation in these structures, the vaguely militarist élan in others (NRA, CCC), and the authority of policy entrepreneurs in their administration. Later generations would name the system "corporate liberalism" and argue that the New Deal entailed more an implementation of Hoover's vision of corporate-governmental cooperation than any Jeffersonian experimentation.[45]

Ready to either give up his hypothesis that FDR sought to complete the Jeffersonian vision of new institutions of public-happiness or count Roosevelt as a failure, the belated president searches for some confirmation of his assumption. He studies the various public-works agencies and is impressed at the sheer scope and size of their activities. The PWA (Public Works Administration) and the WPA "changed the face of the land."[46] The NYA built tuberculosis isolation huts in Arizona, raised a milking barn at Texas A&M, landscaped a park in Cheboygan, Michigan, renovated a school house in North Dakota. The CCC, the longest-lived New Deal relief agency, enrolled over 2.5 million youths in its existence, working in reforestation, soil conservation, and parks projects. The Federal Arts Project of the WPA included in its final report that it had created 15,666 murals, 17,744 pieces of sculpture, 108,099 paintings, 240,000 copies of original designs.[47]

There is a severe contradiction between FDR himself and Congress and the middle-level administrators and participants themselves regarding the theoretical justification of these programs. The relief projects were regarded as a necessary expedient by New Deal supporters. Hopkins himself complained about criticism that the New Deal had created a nation of "leaf-rakers" by arguing that many seemed to prefer direct relief. "Let these fellows . . . sit home and get a basket of groceries, that is what a lot of people want."[48] Roosevelt too defended the projects as the only way to avoid the "narcotic" of receiving relief. "Usefulness" was usually the strongest defense of the projects. But participants tended to see these efforts in broader terms. A CCC member pointed out the "big trees you see along the highways" and recalls planting them in an atmosphere that taught people that "everybody here was equal." Another looks at the Children's Zoo in Central Park: "This was built during the Depression by WPA workers. Its an absolutely lovely place. I go to the park often. And I cannot help remembering—look, this came out of the Depression. Because men were out of work, because they were given a way to earn money, good things were created."[49] The unemployed were engaged in public projects in a deeper sense than the New Dealers chose to speak. They were creating projects designed to promote happiness-public and in an inchoate way were participants in a new arena of public freedom.

Is it possible that FDR in his imitation of Jefferson and his project to nationalize his vision had inadvertently created a Jeffersonian spirit in the very structures of which he was so suspicious? Much the same conclusion could be reached, ponders the belated president, about the NRA, the most Hamiltonian of all New Deal efforts. It is in the areas of the arts that one sees the clearest articulation of the idea of happiness-public both because of the nature of the activity and the creativity of its several directors. Here again Hopkins tended to be aggressively utilitarian. Responding to criticism of the Federal Arts Project, he replied, "Hell! They (artists) have to eat just like other people."[50] But directors such as Hallie Flanagan (theater), Holger Cahill (art), and Nikolai

Sokoff (music) advanced the concept of "cultural democracy" as a theme for work-relief projects.

The directors and their participants pursued Jeffersonian ideas in several ways. First, they argued that in democratic societies support for the arts tended to be limited to "legacies from rich men's houses" and that the bulk of the population was alienated from its own heritage. Thus, under Flanagan the Federal Theater Project was conceived in terms of "people's theater" in which the stage as a place "where sophisticated secrets are whispered to the blase initiate" would be abandoned and replaced by a theater that was accessible and devoted to American themes and history. In Flanagan's mind, people's theater required new experimental techniques in order to break away from the elitist tradition. Arthur Arendt's documentary theater, the "Living Newspaper," was one example of this attempt. Flanagan herself had proposed dramatizing the WPA guides. The New Deal cooperative ethic of "neighborliness" was pursued in a number of original plays, much to the concern of the House UnAmerican Activities Committee in its 1937 investigation. One play, *The Revolt of the Beavers*, was designed to teach children "never to be selfish"; another, *Power*, explored the case for public ownership of utilities. Staff members attempted to attract as wide an audience as possible by encouraging block ticket purchase for union locals and WPA workers. Cahill helped create community art centers for the employment of artists in small cities and for training for amateur artists. In an effort to provide "a work of art for every American home" the Federal Arts Project sold graphics for as little as $2.50.[51]

Second, the directors took very seriously the belief that a national art was foremost a regional one. Perhaps in no other set of New Deal programs was the effort to invigorate Jeffersonian principles of localism through federal support more successful. Everything American was the goal of all the project directors, and American meant the rediscovery of regional and vernacular art forms. The music project, perhaps the most traditional of the programs, transcribed traditional folk music. The artists who worked on the Index of American Design copied quilts, stoneware jugs, dolls, carvings, weather vanes, ironwork, all reminders of America's "true artistic past."[52]

Perhaps the most enduring legacy of the arts projects is the mural commissions, especially the post office murals created under the direction of Edward Bruce in the Treasury Department. Walter Quirt, a WPA/FAP artist from 1935 to 1943, complained that the American muralist was denied the "common ideology in the form of religion" that the Renaissance artist enjoyed. Nor did he have the common ideology of revolution to convey "simply and clearly in murals for an illiterate population" as had the Mexican artist. This was an important restriction in a medium whose "first task" was "ideological."[53] Yet the WPA muralists, led by a committed "Section" board, did develop its own ideology. Every region of the country had its own history portrayed. New England muralists attempted to capture the revolutionary experience, mid-Atlantic artists, the rise of industry. Southern muralists, who were especially handicapped by the special history of the region, focused upon the relationship between work

and a bucolic culture, while the midwestern and western artists sought to portray the interaction between human beings and the vastness of the prairie. In
all these works, the famous are conspicuously absent. The theme of the muralist was a people's history. Folk heroes made their appearances. Arthur Covey
painted three panels of the life of John Brown; a mural depicting Molly Pitcher
was commissioned for Freehold, New Jersey. Foremost, however, are murals
illustrating collective activity of anonymous Americans: Saul Levine's *Ipswich
Tax Resistance*, Gerald Foster's pictorial account of the battle of Milburn Bridge,
Mary Earley's *Down-Rent War*, Anton Reffreiger's *Sand Lot Riots*. Every region
of the country celebrated its pioneers, from Leopold Scholz's pioneer woman
defending her family against bears in Angola, New York, to Edward Chavez's
Building a Sod House in Geneva, Nebraska, to Anton Reffreiger's *The Donner
Party* in San Francisco.[54]

The New Deal symbols of neighborliness and pioneering were thus given an
artistic rendering for America's ubiquitous post offices and courthouses. When
muralists were not depicting the people's struggle against authority and the
elements, they interpreted the collective and social nature of American life.
FDR had insisted that pioneering involved a "spirit of cooperation and understanding," and these murals prominently display an American Geist that cel-
ebrates work as a collective activity. Every conceivable form of work is promoted
on these terms. There may be bosses in the foreground or background, but it is
the communal and creative nature of the enterprises of lettuce picking, peach
growing, cypress logging, mining, cotton picking, paper making, threshing, and
building that the artists attempt to capture. Leisure too is given a collective
interpretation. Simple socializing is a very common theme. Street themes in
cities and small towns show groups of people conversing. Peppino Mangravit's
Family Recreations in Atlantic City is a panel celebrating the most basic forms
of leisure (biking and horseback riding, swimming, dancing, sun bathing, chat-
ting on park benches). Lee Allen's mural depicting fishing and hunting even
manages to achieve a collective aspect.

FDR's reliance upon Jefferson was based on the assumption that Jefferson
could be "nationalized," that a reinterpretation of localism and self-government
would reveal an inner unity (public happiness) among Americans making the
Lincoln alternative unnecessary and exploding the elitist cast of the Hamilto-
nians. At a cultural level the arts projects achieved just that. There is an Arcadic
element in the most industrial of the murals, a sense of industrial discipline in
all the depictions of farm activity. Doris Lee's *General Store and Post Office*
portrays all the myths of rural sociality, the chatty store owner, the community
of women engaged in shopping, the men around the cracker barrel. Kinred
McLeary's panel, *The Lower East Side*, shows tenements in the background and
conspicuously depicts different ethnic and racial groups, but its essence is the
same as Lee's. Children peer appreciatively into a baby carriage, men talk over
their newspapers, street vendors are tiny points of momentary conversations.
Work itself is transformed. As we noted, the most regional and specialized economic activities are the subjects, but in all the murals, work is stripped of its

alienating character. As communal effort it becomes, as Thoreau once remarked on seeing the boatmen, stone masons, and lumberers along the Merrimack River, "less like toil and more like a game of chess."

The mural projects, and in a more blatant ideological way, the Federal Theater, articulated the utopian aspects of the New Deal. Here were images of public happiness, drawn from but scaling far beyond reality, that were not portrayed as temporary measures. They were, as critics charged, agitprop for the New Deal, but at the same time they stood as utopian criticisms of an administration committed to the principles of neighborliness and pioneering for more limited purposes or—to put the point more kindly—for more immediate objectives. In what directions would the New Deal have had to proceed in order to politically and bureaucratically capture the visions of the federal artists? This is a question that does not appear to have been asked beyond the confines of the section apparatchik, and it may be that no political-administrative structure could capture the idealized nationalized Jeffersonianism of the various projects. But the point the belated president grasps is that these temporary and utilitarian efforts brought forth efforts to conceive new kinds of public space intuited from American experience.

The belated president wonders if he has placed too much emphasis on the New Deal effort to reform culture. Perhaps one would expect to find utopian fantasy in this sector once Roosevelt had unleashed their imagination with his tropes of neighborliness and pioneering. When he surveys other New Deal programs, however, he sees similar experiments. He is surprised to find the utopian impulse in Tugwell's administration of the "greenbelt" towns. Tugwell's reaction to FDR's musing, "Suppose one were to offer these [unemployed] men opportunity to go on the land, to provide a house and a few acres in the country and a little money and tools to put in small crops," was dismissive, yet he did bravely attempt to found a series of new cities in an effort to modernize the family farm. The TVA had long been a progressive dream, but FDR's several administrators competitively attempted to bring it in line with the revised Jeffersonian vision. David Lilienthal's slogan "decentralized administration of centralized authority," borrowed from Tocqueville, hid the Hamiltonian structure of the experiment more than New Dealers would ever admit, but he did manage to fit it into the Jeffersonian project that FDR had outlined.[55]

As a final effort, the belated president decides to test his hypothesis against one of the most nationalist of New Deal programs, the NRA. If there was any effort which seemed to contradict the thesis that FDR attempted to complete the Jeffersonian project, it would be this agency, which was arguably modeled along the lines of the new Italian corporate state. The NRA slogan "We Do Our Part," with the blue eagle insignia that FDR himself compared to the "bright badge" worn by soldiers at night to distinguish friend from foe, became a ubiquitous federal presence in every Jeffersonian hamlet. But here again the belated president discovers unanticipated features of a plan that seemed to fit the Plan. Many NRA administrators regarded this attempt to create a whole new economic infrastructure for America as one in which labor unions would become largely irrelevant. Hugh S. Johnson once told a cabinet member that "when this crisis is over . . . there won't be any need for a Department of Labor or a Department of Commerce"[56] But imbedded in the NIRA was what was to become the famous section 7a, which included the clause that every business which subscribed to the NRA code must permit its employees to "organize and bargain collectively through representations of their own choosing . . . free from the interference, restraint, or coercion of employers." From this small concession on the part of corporativists, the modern labor union movement was born. The AFL gained 500,000 new members in 1933 and nearly doubled its membership a year later. In 1935 the CIO represented the first successful attempt to organize an industrial union. FDR's attitude toward this development was largely one of bemusement, despite the fact that organizers used the argument that "the President wants you to join the union" in their registration drives.

The NRA was soon discarded for both constitutional and political reasons. But section 7a was to be given a new statutory home with the passage of the Wagner Act. The belated president notes FDR's complex relationship with the new union movement and his later antagonism with some of its leadership. Yet he is impressed with this creation of a whole new structure of public happiness awakened and then wrestled from the president's corporate experiment. The connection between the labor movement and the belated president's hypothesis about FDR is a weak one and he attempts to examine it more closely. He returns to the dilemma posed in the Commonwealth Club speech, which was veiled but nevertheless partially exposed by Roosevelt. Certainly the NIRA was an example of the alternative of enlightened administration. Was it possible that FDR was vaguely concerned that this routinization of the economy implied a threat to his own poetic intent? If so, the emergence of the unions might have represented a mixed blessing in his quest to alleviate belatedness. The volatility of the movement represented a threat to his own secret plan of poetic greatness but it also suggested openings for the achievement of monumental tasks unavailable in a corporate state. Would awakened labor provide the core for a permanently realigned Democratic Party, placing the forces of reaction clearly on one side and liberal sentiment on the other? The belated president knows that this was precisely FDR's project in 1938, and while he is not willing to conclude that he had waited for that moment to initiate this monumental task, he wonders if the blasé abandonment of the NRA, which many biographers have noted, was the result of his own secret hope that it would indeed fail.

THE JACKSON MASK

The belated president rests. He is convinced he has discovered and substantiated Franklin Roosevelt's poetic intent. FDR sought to overcome belatedness by identifying Jefferson's project to overcome aristocratic challenge through the creation of a party system with his own yearnings for poetic greatness. He sought to surpass Jefferson's monumental achievement by altering his conception of democratic reform. FDR would nationalize Jefferson, preserving the spirit of the democratic impulse in the American demos who were villagers by cultural tradition by redirecting its goals. Thus altered, FDR could break the historical pattern of democratic assertion followed by somnolence as the people awaited a new leader to redefine democracy under new conditions. "The spirit of the frontier husking bee is found today in carefully-drafted statutes," Roosevelt told the American people in 1938 and he hoped, according to the belated president, to become the "first" to place institutions of public happiness on a permanent footing and at a national level. The belated president is comforted that FDR did not have a detailed plan to nationalize Jefferson, that he experimented with a whole a range of structures leaving his newly formed apparat to intuit the bureaucratic forms encapsulizing the meanings of neighborliness and pioneering that he provided. He is also not a little bit amused when he studies FDR's secret effort to avoid his own routinization or, in the framework of Jeffersonianism, his effort to avoid the Hamiltonianization of the New Deal. The belated president is, however, admiring of the monumental task Roosevelt set for himself given the enormous risks entailed in its implementation under the crisis conditions of the Depression and the almost universal denigration of the Jefferson exemplar among the elites he was forced to rely upon for his project.

Just as the belated president is about to survey his own alternatives in overcoming FDR, he notes a change in Roosevelt's direction in 1935. At first, he dismisses his unease. He studies the 1937 Farm Tenancy Act. He concludes it is one of the most clearly Jeffersonian-inspired pieces of legislation produced by the New Deal. But there is some shift in FDR's persona in 1935. Roosevelt is decidedly more aggressive in his attacks on business. The Jeffersonian premise of the New Deal required the derogation of business elites as party to a new social contract, but it was one thing to speak of a "small group of men" whose outlook "deserves the adjectives selfish and opportunist" in 1932 and another to refer to business as the "resolute enemy" who required "weeding out" in 1935. In his 1936 Annual Message to Congress, FDR raised the question of whether "reforming in a piecemeal fashion" was enough for a "population suffering from the old inequalities." FDR's inaugural contained the famous phrase that the American people had nothing to fear but fear itself. Now he gave that fear a specific source. The people had been subjected to "a synthetic, manufactured, poisonous fear that is being spread subtly, expensively, and cleverly." Business elites were poised to "steal the livery of great constitutional ideals to serve discredited special interest."[57]

The belated president learns that FDR was in a "stew of indecision" throughout 1934 and seems to have considered whether a "breathing spell" was necessary to reassure "frightened" businessmen. Yet two months later the president told his speech writers that he wanted a "fighting speech" to deliver before Congress in his annual message.[58] The result was the most sustained, impassioned attack on business ever made by an American president. The belated president tries to reassure himself that the Jefferson exemplar contained antibusiness symbolism in terms of its agrarian perspective that divided the political economy into producers and nonproducers. John Taylor of Caroline, a Republican more strident than the third president, for example, warned of a new "capitalist aristocracy" and "idle" capitalists. Thus the belated president tries to convince himself that the "left turn" of the president is simply a form of heightened Jeffersonianism.

Yet there is a tone in this shift that continues to disconcert the belated president. To a doubtful Raymond Moley, FDR snapped, "There is one issue in this campaign. It's myself, and the people must be either for me or against me." The Jeffersonian approach certainly made room for heroic acts. This aspect of the Jeffersonian project is what so excited the young Roosevelt when he read Bowers's book. But Jefferson's poetic achievement was premised upon the activization of a sleeping people through what FDR had redefined as a concert of interests. The belated president understands the shift thusly: Jefferson (FDR) forms a party coalition that beats back elitist designs to one that now reads Jackson (FDR) battles elites. In the later rendering, the president becomes the personification of all the aspirations of the people and, more centrally, all the fears of his opponents. In the campaign, Roosevelt announced, "They are unanimous in their hate for me" and "I welcome their hatred."[59]

As the belated president ponders the nature of this now twice revised Jeffersonianism (the attempt to permanently complete Jefferson's aim and the new attempt to personify Jefferson's project), he is surprised to discover the systematic addition of a new exemplar on FDR's part. Five days after the 1936 annual message, Roosevelt presented an analysis of Andrew Jackson. To FDR, Jackson was a man who the "average American deeply and fundamentally understood." The people "loved him well because they understood him well." Yet Jackson seemed to be hated by everyone. He was hated by the "great media," by "haughty and sterile" intellectuals, by "musty" reactionaries, by "hollow and outworn" traditionalists. Indeed, it "seemed that all were against him—all but the people of the United States."[60] In June at Little Rock, Arkansas, FDR added the theme of youthful vigor to the image of passionate devotion to Jackson. He reminded his audience that it was Jefferson who had "the courage, the backbone" to purchase the Louisiana Territory so that it might be peopled by "hardy pioneers." But it was from their "contemporary and counselor" Jackson that Arkansans understood that their "fellow frontiersman" made "possible the first truly democratic Administration in our history." Arkansas became a state in the last year of Jackson's presidency and Arkansas represented a westward expansion that flowed "with the vigor of a living stream" through the "stagnant marshes" of a seaboard oligarchy. Prior to this movement west, power in America with rare exception rested "in the hands of men who, by birth or education, belonged to a comparatively small group." Jackson, as the epitome of the frontier spirit that brought men into the "Arkansas wilderness," inaugurated "an era of truer democracy," much to the "widespread apprehension" of the "so-called guardians of the Republic."[61]

The belated president now begins to wonder if FDR has simply begun the pursuit of a heightened Jeffersonianism. It is true, he notes, that Roosevelt still honored Jefferson and contended that Jackson was "like Jefferson" and Jackson followed the "fundamentals of Jefferson" by pursuing a "broad philosophy" of democratic empowerment. But FDR's remarks implied that the Jeffersonian project died before Jackson's presidency. America was, after all, in the grip of a "comparatively small group" of men. Then there is the peroration on the nature of Jackson's hold on the people. Jefferson represented many things to the American people—the author of its revolutionary document, the paradigm of the American Enlightenment, the spokesperson of republican agrarianism—but he was not a figure who brought forth feelings of a passion like love. FDR's analysis of Jackson's relationship with the people actually emphasized everything that Jefferson was not. Foremost, of course, was Roosevelt's stress on Jackson's passion and not his intellect. The "average American" could "understand" Jackson; "his purposes and character were an open book." "Red-blooded"-ness was also a common theme in FDR's Jackson. For the "man on the street" and the "man on the farm" Jackson was loved because he was "two-fisted," "rugged and fearless." This emphasis on Jackson's masculinity as a replacement for intellect was for Roosevelt the key to his adoration, and the repeated trope of the youth and vigor of the western man that Jackson represented underscored his reading. Not least, as well, was FDR's attention to the hatred and fear that Jackson created that came as much from his actions as from his character.

The belated president is now convinced that the attention to Jackson represented the employment of a new exemplar on FDR's part. This new mask was not wholly different from the old one. There were strong historical connections between the Jeffersonian and Jacksonian movements. Both sought to bring a risorgimento to America through mass political action and both centered their appeals as protests against commercial elites who had captured the national government. Moreover, the Jacksonians aggressively appropriated the symbol of Jefferson "by squirting Jefferson's opinions" in the eyes of their opponents.[62] But the belated president is astonished by FDR's grasp of the difference between the two exemplars. Jefferson, the tidewater aristocrat and diplomat, is far removed from Jackson, the frontier parvenu and military commander. Their respective personal designations, the "Sage of Monticello" and "Old Hickory," capture this difference between intellect and passion, philosophe and man of action. He is awed by the ease with which Roosevelt has slipped from the Jeffersonian persona of reassurance and cosmopolitanism to the angry populist who provocatively welcomes the hatred of his opponents. Opponents of Jackson tended to see his ascendance as a kind of delayed Bonapartism that it seemed the American revolution now had not avoided. Landon reacted similarly to FDR. "We have seen," he warned, how in "nation after nation . . . democracies fall and dictatorships rise." We have seen how the belief in a "all-powerful executive" destroys liberty as authoritarian leaders like FDR first "ridicule" constitutions and "then, section by section" throw them away.[63] FDR, like Jackson, threw back these concerns with ever sharper attacks on elites who would "gang up" on the peoples' liberties and "regiment people, their labor and their property" through their poisonous propaganda. Fear is the glue of the Jacksonian coalition, not some Enlightenment-inspired concert of interests.

The belated president wonders if Roosevelt's Jacksonian mask was designed to avoid the routinization of charisma that might threaten his monumental ambitions. As a Jeffersonian, FDR might have kept the business of enlightened administration veering toward incoherence through his insistence upon experimentation and the serendipitous invention of Jeffersonian structures, but the Jacksonian variation held out even greater possibilities. In 1934 he told his vice-president that "the more I learn about old Andy Jackson the more I love him."[64] Certainly, Roosevelt had immediate models of charismatic leaders in the Jacksonian populist model. In fact, in the early thirties they seemed to emerge in tandem. Each—Father Couglin, Huey Long, Francis Townsend—offered critiques of elites and employed the passions more vividly even than did FDR. Most important, their heroic plans to end the Depression, each spewed forth in the pared down discourse of anger and resentment (Destroy finance capital! Tax the rich! Give pensions to the elderly!), completely avoided the threat of enlightened administration. Commentators have always emphasized how FDR cunningly borrowed from these men, how FDR coopted their simple populist plans and built a complex welfare state.[65] From the standpoint of the belated president, however, this assessment is a typical one offered from the perspective of an apparatchik. The notion that FDR, for political advantage, of course, imaginatively shepherded the crackpot schemes of demagogues into statutes drafted by talented New Deal lawyers assumes that enlightened administration was his primary goal. But what if enlightened administration was a poetic veil, or at least less a goal than a means to overcome belatedness? What if FDR's goal, much to the surprise of some of his critics, was not more government per se but heroically led government? If such were the case, so thinks the belated president, then what FDR learned from Jackson and the great demagogues on his left/right was not so much programs that the people wanted. What he learned from them was the politics of fear designed to create a personal bond with the people.

Throughout the 1936 campaign FDR presented the American people with images of the Republic imperiled by a conscious design on the part of elites. He spoke of "forces of selfishness," "enemies of peace," autocrats, "economic royalists," "aliens to the spirit of democracy," "new mercenaries." They lied when they had said that Jackson planned to "surrender American democracy to the dictatorship of the frontier mob" and they lied now when they charged the president with dictatorship. In the logic of the Jacksonian risorgimento, the greater the criticism of the president, the greater was his heroic task. "I welcome their hatred," FDR told the frenzied crowd at Madison Garden. The president was psychologically egging on the American people to welcome this hatred. For the task of the spirited leader is to bifurcate the polity into (Jackson)(FDR)/elites as the victorious end of monumental historical struggle between elites and the people. FDR captured perfectly the apotheosis of the *resentiment* fantasy when he suggested that if capitalist elites could not or would not conform to the new order, "let them emigrate."

The belated president, however, knows that those who suffer from the same affliction as he seek to imitate men who have freed themselves from belatedness in order to free themselves. Thus FDR's imitation must at some level be a hostile one. Roosevelt's assertion that he was "like Jackson" must contain some means by which the president would overcome him, else he would become enveloped by Jackson's own achievements. It is clear to the belated president that FDR attempted to replicate the special psychological bond between the leader and the people forged by a common hatred of elites that Jackson first created. He discovers, however, that while Jackson appealed to the blood and sinew of the people to rise up against the "moneyed interest," as indeed did FDR, Old Hickory's political agenda was based on the dismantling of the national government. To Jackson, the federal government seemed to be by nature always open to capture by the "monied aristocracy" and hence must be under the watchful eye of presidential populism. No doubt there was an irony in Jacksonianism itself in its suspicion of centralized power *and* its willingness to read the president as the people's tribune but it was on the basis of this assessment that Jackson attacked the recharter of the national bank, opposed federal projects for "internal improvements," and sought to eliminate the national debt. The fact that each of these agendas represented an inversion of the Roosevelt program is not lost upon the belated president. In fact, he notes that the economic spirit of the Jacksonians was distinctly laissez-faire. "The World is Governed Too Much" was the slogan of the Jacksonian press, and the ideological dictums of the Democrats centered upon attacks on high taxes, government regulation, and demands for economy in government, rhetoric that the belated president also notes fit more with Hoover and Landon than with FDR.[66]

The belated president is clearly curious since he now knows that FDR must have (mis)read Jackson. He finds a key to this misreading when he surveys Tocqueville's contemporary interpretation of the Jacksonian movement. To Tocqueville, the narrow range of income differences in America produced a certain personality type. The predominance of "eager and apprehensive men of small property" who "still almost within the reach of poverty . . . see its privations near at hand and dread them; between poverty and themselves there is nothing but a scanty fortune, upon which they fix their apprehensions and hopes." Without the distinction of ranks in society and with the subdivision of hereditary property, "the love of well-being" became the "predominant taste of the nation . . . the great current of human passions runs in that channel and sweeps everything along its course."[67]

According to the belated president, Jackson appealed to the fragile position of this petit bourgeoisie, which, swollen enormously by European standards, assumed the status of a national condition. In regard to their apprehension, he spoke of the "monied aristocracy" who had, through their privileges and power, used government to so enrich themselves that they escaped from economic risk and also placed those below them in peril. In regard to their eagerness, he spoke of entrepreneurial opportunity once the "predatory portion of the community" was restrained. The Depression presented FDR with an opportunity to largely ignore bourgeois eagerness, and thus FDR used the Jacksonian persona to address an apprehensiveness that had reached a historical peak. To the belated president, Roosevelt spoke what was on every American's mind when he extemporaneously addressed a crowd in Poughkeepsie, New York. The Depression crystallized "two very definite thoughts on people's minds." One involved a decision to retain democratic government, according to FDR (which the belated president reads as FDR's recognition that the great American petit bourgeois had decided to keep a capitalist system). The other involved a decision "to eliminate . . . chances in life." "People in the past," said Roosevelt, "have gone along with the idea that they could do without a great many things, for instance, as security. Well, security means a kind of feeling within our individual selves that we have lacked all through the course of history. We have had to take our chance about old age in days past. We have had to take our chances with depressions and boom times. We have had to take our chances on our jobs. We have had to take chances on buying homes."[68] Thus FDR changed the Jacksonian slogan "The World is Governed Too Much" to "The World is Too Risky."

The belated president notes how prudently and delicately FDR altered Jackson's project despite the spiritedness of the Jacksonian persona. To a reporter in 1935 he listed the "social objective" of his administration as one that would "try to increase the security and happiness of a larger number of people in all occupations of life and in all parts of the country." He promised to give the people "more of the good things of life," to give them "places to go in the summertime—recreation; to give them assurance that they will not starve in their old age; to give honest business a chance to go ahead and make a reasonable profit, and to give everyone a chance to earn a living."[69] The belated president stops for a moment in his quest to alleviate his affliction to consider how moderate, indeed how meager are the aspirations of the petit bourgeoisie that lie behind its anger and its attraction to Jacksonian spiritness. He is forced to admire how perfectly FDR intuited that these were the apprehensive objectives standing behind their rancor and fear and observes how the programs of the "second hundred days" (social security, utility and banking legislation), which were the foundations of the American welfare state, were framed within the contours of a loss of nerve on the part of a once proud and eager bourgeoisie. The belated president reads William Leuchtenburg's assessment of the Social Security Act as "an astonishingly inept and conservative piece of legislation." "In no other welfare system in the world did the state shirk all responsibility for old age indigency and insist that funds be taken out of current earnings of workers," he concludes.[70] Medical care was not addressed, no national standard of unemployment compensation was created, nor were workers such as farmer laborers and domestics covered by the legislation. The belated president appreciates this evaluation, but he is more impressed with FDR's reading of the nature of the Jacksonian exemplar, requiring a satisfaction of bourgeois apprehension—and no more.

However, if FDR perfectly read the nature of Jackson's support and thus overcame Jackson by creating a welfare state on populist fears, he did nevertheless ultimately misread Jackson in a negative way after his landslide victory in 1936. In his second inaugural, Roosevelt layered the Jacksonian persona with the image of himself as a Moses standing on Mount Sinai. Viewing the nation from this height, FDR/Jackson/Moses engages in a series of "I see" descriptions of a nation in which one third are "ill-housed, ill-clad, ill-nourished." Demanding that the people meet the terms of a covenant that would wipe out "the line that divides the practical from the ideal," Roosevelt warned the American people not to "tarry" in following his lead.[71] But the belated president discovers that the people did tarry as FDR attempted to lead them in an assault against the court and a "purge" of reactionary elements from the Democratic Party. However clever FDR might have been in his "court-packing" plan and however persuasive he might be in his plea to realign the parties of the Republic to "liberal" forces on one side and reactionary ones on the other, the people did tarry. Victorious we are now, so seemed the great American bourgeoisie to say, but "who will save us except the courts?" should our own property be imperiled, and who would guard, despite the president's assertion that southern politicians were more committed to the protection of feudalism than democracy, our local prerogatives without our trusted folk? Popular arguments against the reorganization of the court were contradictory and often vague, but they did clearly express the same apprehensiveness that FDR rode to electoral victory. This nervousness on the part of the demos emboldened senators who had their own reasons to tarry.[72] And while Roosevelt may have thought that he was only repeating an axiom that he had proved by his own readings of Jefferson/Jackson when he repeated and repeated the remark that "we are thinking of all our problems in national terms," the old Jeffersonian reliance on local elites reasserted itself. Sometimes it reasserted itself in terms of racist fantasy, as when Cotton Ed warned South Carolinians that a vote against him would be "voting to let a big buck nigger sit next to your wife or daughter on a train," and sometimes it reasserted itself in the form of a republican affection for its demes, as when Senator Tydings exclaimed that "Maryland will not permit her star in the flag to be 'purged' from the constellation of the states."[73] FDR gamely fought back against these bourgeois symbols of legality and localism that he thought he had tamed and redirected. In 1939 he used the rhetorical device of calling Jackson on the phone. Old Hickory advised Roosevelt to fight on, not to get "scared . . . because you don't have majorities so big that you can go to sleep without sentries."

The belated president is pleased, very pleased. He is pleased to learn that this great president erred. And he is especially pleased for he knows the psychological humiliation which a belated president must have endured to have been forced to call back to a ghost he must have thought he had already exorcised.

THE LINCOLN MASK

FDR's smile might have remained broad and his geniality still intact, but the belated president thinks he knows how his comrade in affliction must have felt when he realized that he had played out his Jefferson/Jackson persona. But, of course, the belated president also knows that FDR won two more unprecedented terms in office despite the fact that the media had declared the New Deal dead and were openly speculating about new presidential aspirants in 1940. He has known for some time what he would find next in his belated narrative of the president, but he is still shocked, resentful, and awe-stricken as he observes how FDR picked up yet a new mask in 1938–39. He himself feels that he has discovered belatedness as the cause of Abraham Lincoln's achievements, but he nevertheless enters a state of disbelief when he contemplates the risk FDR undertook when he adopted the Lincoln persona.

The belated president had studied FDR's allusions to Lincoln in the 1932–33 crisis, but he noted how he had veered away from him and toward Jefferson. Now he watches Roosevelt circle Lincoln. In his Jacksonian turn, the president began to use Lincoln as a supplement to his newly read exemplar. In 1936 he began to emphasize Lincoln's modest class origins. Lincoln could not have come from "any class that did not know, through daily struggle, the grim realities of life." In his 1938 Jackson Day address, FDR spoke of Lincoln as a man "scorned for his uncouthness, his simplicity, his homely stories and his solicitude for the little man." Lincoln's enemies were the same as Jackson's (and by analogy to his own). "Gold speculators in Wall Street," a "minority unwilling to support people and their government unless the government would leave them free to pursue their private gains" were the declared enemies of Jackson/Lincoln/FDR. Had Lincoln lived, there would not have been the "uninspired commercial era" that followed the Civil War.

These references to Lincoln do not arouse the belated president. He knows that the populist Lincoln is part of the great obstacle that towers over his predecessors, but it is not the foundation upon which the Lincoln memory is based. The belated president is not even terribly disturbed when he finds FDR citing Lincoln in terms of the tests he passed. In 1938 Roosevelt also began comparing Lincoln's crisis in 1860 to his own in 1933. FDR said that the crisis he faced in 1933 was equivalent to Lincoln's. Both involved a threat to the nation. Roosevelt's comparisons were post factum, and the invocation of past crises neatly avoided the invitation to compare himself with Lincoln in terms of present conduct.

In fact, the belated president is confident that FDR, despite his affliction, will not undertake a direct hostile imitation of the Lincoln, whose monumental achievement as savior of the nation is so immense that it eclipsed Washington and led the eulogizing New England ministry to assign him biblical status. He has numerous reasons to be confident.

The belated president is, of course, intimately conversant with the critical

Lincoln tradition that makes any attempt at imitation a great risk. Thus FDR is faced with the prospect that he will be humiliated by a reaction that would ask in essence, "How can you possibly compare yourself with this great leader?" *or* the possibility that he would be asked, "So you intend to imitate this dangerous man?" He now learns that the existence of these two traditions with their many variations was complicated by the reevaluation that both Lincoln and the Civil War were undergoing in the Depression years. It is difficult to define a "Depression Lincoln" before FDR successfully appropriated his own version late in the decade. Yet most of the various reinterpretations that FDR confronted made his task an extremely difficult one.

Herbert Hoover attempted to close off any attempt to fashion a connection between the crisis of the Civil War and the Depression when in a radio broadcast on Lincoln's birthday he warned Americans who would use Lincoln as a justification for the creation of a "centralized government": "If Lincoln were living," he would seek solutions which provided "opportunity" for every person "to rise to that highest achievement of which he is capable" and oppose any policies which would lead to a "superstate where every man becomes the servant of the State and real liberty is lost."[74]

Hoover's Whig Lincoln, whose rise from humble beginnings epitomized policies of self-reliance, was given a different interpretation by both the progressive and Marxist scholarship that dominated the thirties. To men like Charles Beard, the Civil War was indeed a "second American revolution," but both its origins and result involved an "arrangement of the classes, and the accumulation and distribution of wealth." The war provided the avenue for the rise to power of "northern capitalists and free farmers."[75] Thus from the "realist" perspective of the progressive, Lincoln was an agent of the domination of capital. Marxists too tended to conceptualize the Civil War as an American instance of primitive accumulation but searched for revolutionary lessons. For Louis Hacker, the Civil War became a kind of American version of the Russian experience in 1905, with Southerners as "counter revolutionists." Hacker credited the North for its determination to engage in what Lincoln had called a "people's war." The pattern of postbellum economic growth also produced "the growth and discipline" of a working class that now stood poised to take power in the present "revolutionary situation." Both progressives and Marxists formally assigned little weight to individual acts in history, but some began explore the policies and personalities of those to the "left" of Lincoln, like Phillips, who connected chattel to wage slavery.[76]

Southern commentators kept the anti-Lincoln tradition alive during the Depression. The belated president is quite familiar with Edgar Lee Master's furiously negative biography of Lincoln. Now he finds southerners who reiterated Masters's themes. Frank L. Owsley's essay in the manifesto "I'll Take My Stand" described the legacy of the Civil War in terms of a northern impulse to consciously destroy southern culture and defiantly refused to accept the "self righteous Northern legend," asserted by Lincoln in his second inaugural, "which makes the South the war criminal."[77]

The rebuttals of the southerners might be dismissed had not so many prominent historians begun to undertake a skeptical assessment of the inevitability of the Civil War and Lincoln's missed opportunities as peacemaker. Berveridge's influential biography of Lincoln published in 1928 argued that the war was not inevitable. Emanuel Hertz argued in his 1931 biography that the lesson of Lincoln actually rested with his antiwar message: "If Lincoln were alive today and in a position of power, he would prevent the contamination of the United Sates by union with people who thrive on war, who pray for war, and whose business is war." Randall, writing on the eve of American participation in a war in Europe, urged Americans to reexamine the Civil War by ignoring the "splendor of battle flags" and focusing on war as "organized murder." Gilbert H. Barnes and Avery Crane portrayed abolitionist leaders as irresponsible and suggested that war guilt rested with their radical moralism. George Fort Milton's 1934 biography of Douglas attempted to rehabilitate Lincoln's famous opponent by contending that Lincoln adopted a "sectional" perspective while Douglas offered a "national" one.[78] Milton was careful not to directly attack Lincoln, but if Douglas was genuinely committed to avoiding war through reason and compromise, the reader was left to ask what role Lincoln had played.

The belated president knows, of course, that presidents do not imitate leadership exemplars on the basis of current historiography. But the Depression biographies and histories of Lincoln and the Civil War represented a continuation of a generational reexamination of Lincoln in American political culture. Radical Depression scholarship and the antecedent progressive assessments reflected and crystallized doubts about the viability of Lincoln as a model. Did he represent the triumph of capital under whose rule Americans were now suffering? Or was he, as Hoover argued, a beacon against those who would create a new tyranny through governmental regimentation? Was indeed Lincoln largely irrelevant compared to the enormous economic forces that determined the fate of nations? Did Lincoln work hard enough to avoid war? If FDR reached back to reconstruct a Lincoln to imitate, could he convince the American people that he deserved to be compared to the Black Easter Lincoln? How could the Civil War Lincoln be portrayed in the face of antiwar sentiment? Would even an adoption of the populist Lincoln center questions about race submerged by the New Deal coalition?

The belated president skips ahead to read the 1940 Jackson Day dinner. He learns that FDR announces that he intends to talk not only about Jackson but about Lincoln as well. Nothing new, the confident but nervous belated president mumbles. Then Roosevelt's subsequent comment strikes out at him with the force of electric shock: "Yes, the devil can quote past statesmen as readily as he can quote Scriptures." His purpose was to examine "the motives behind the leaders of the past" to see how they completed "the big job that their times demanded to be done." Had he again underestimated FDR? The belated president is raging now. Surely, he concludes, this is a clear statement of poetic intent. Behind that grin is a man of infinite guile. He even announces to an audience oblivious to his belatedness that he, like the devil, can and will misread

Lincoln and that his purpose is to overcome him by discovering their "motives" and examining their monumental achievements.

If the belated president had any doubts that FDR now intended to imitate the Black Easter Lincoln, Roosevelt dispelled them with his review of personal heroes. Jackson naturally was on the list and, of course, so was Jefferson. But the belated president stops reading to ponder the very untypical criticism of Jefferson. Jefferson was "a hero to me despite the fact that the theories of the French revolutionists overexcited his judgment." If Jefferson's radicalism was now negatively reviewed, Hamilton's conservatism was excused: "He was a hero because he did the job which then had to be done—to bring stability out of the chaos of currency and banking difficulties." Lincoln, of course, was now on the list since he preserved the union and made possible the "united country that we all live in today."

The belated president already thinks he knows that Lincoln's monumental achievement was a response to his own affliction of belatedness. Now he concludes that FDR is in possession of the same knowledge. Lincoln's grand strategy involved the "double cross," a misreading of presidential texts with the purpose of reordering them to make room for his own achievement. Roosevelt had already misread Jefferson through his assertion that Jefferson was overlooked as a nationalist. In 1936 he attacked the notion that Jefferson was infatuated with French radicalism as a figment of aristocratic fantasy. Now Jefferson is still retained as a hero despite his overexcitedness in regard to the French Revolution. Needless to say, Hamilton was the bête noire of FDR's Jeffersonian and Jacksonian phases. Now his nationalism, which was once attacked as aristocratic intrigue, is praised.

Jackson posed a bit of an immediate problem for FDR. Not only was he the most recent of his personas but his comparisons were the most forthright. Nevertheless, the belated president knows that Jackson must be dumped by FDR. The credibility of the Lincoln exemplar rested upon national unity and Jackson had been the most partisan of presidents. Moreover, not only had his Jacksonianism failed him in his court fight and attempted party purge but his misreading of Jackson as an appeal to middle-class apprehensiveness had badly eroded. Roosevelt found himself attacked from the right by the "new faces" in the Seventy-sixth Congress who were finding some success in turning this apprehensiveness back on Roosevelt himself. Thus FDR simply dropped Jackson. The 1940 Jackson Day speech was his last, and he never returned to Jackson, except briefly in the last days of the 1940 election and as part of a litany of "liberal" presidents who were implicitly equally weighted. Roosevelt, in effect, double-crossed his own misreadings by 1940. Gone were Jefferson/Jackson and in its place stood Lincoln, a diminished Jefferson, and a refurbished Hamilton.

The belated president has now come to the conclusion that FDR's strategy against belatedness does not necessitate a complete appropriation of the exemplars he has selected. This genial president operates on the assumption that a series of masks will do. He need not be Jefferson, even in his own misreading, but show only a Jeffersonian veil, for he knows that underneath he can show his apparent native joviality. Thus, on these terms, Roosevelt set out to replace his Jackson persona with a Lincoln one.

In 1939–40 FDR was willing to directly imitate the Black Easter Lincoln. Sandburg's second volume of his Lincoln biography, *The War Years*, was published in 1939. The work in many ways reflected a shift from the radical perspective in America. Shortly after its publication, Archibald MacLeish castigated the irresponsibility of a generation of intellectuals for focusing their energies on "revolt" rather than "acceptance and belief."[79] Sandburg's wartime Lincoln epitomized this change of focus. Lincoln represented the triumph of democratic will and the incredible burden of its translation into concerted action by a president: "To think incessantly of blood and steel, steel and blood . . . of a mystic cause carried aloft and sung on dripping and crimson bayonet points—to think so and thus across nights and months folding up into years, was a wearing and grinding that brought questions. What was this teaching and who learns from it and where does it lead?"[80]

When a group of students arrived for a meeting at the White House in the spring of 1940 to complain about the guns and butter problem, the president halted the barrage of criticism by asking one questioner, "Young man, I think you are very sincere. Have you read Carl Sandburg's Lincoln?" When the man answered negatively, Roosevelt responded thusly: "I think the impression was that Lincoln was a pretty sad man because he could not do all he wanted to do at one time, and I think you will find examples where Lincoln had to compromise to gain a little something. He had to compromise to make a few gains. Lincoln was one of the unfortunate people called a 'politician' but he was a politician who was practical enough to get a great many things for his country. He was sad because he could not get it all at once. And nobody can." Privately FDR referred to college pacifists as "shrimps"; publicly he took on the role as the suffering leader.[81]

Robert Sherwood, the author of the popular Broadway play *Abe Lincoln of Illinois*, was hired as a speech writer late in 1940. Viewing the film version of Sherwood's play, FDR requested copies of two of Lincoln's speeches from the debates with Douglas. Sherwood worked hard to extend the Lincoln exemplar to FDR. In fact, he highlighted Roosevelt's previous concessions to the isolationists (his accessions to Hearst's demands in regard to the League of Nations, his signing of the Neutrality Acts, his retreat from his 1937 quarantine speech) as actually paralleling Lincoln's career. Lincoln opposed the war with Mexico and was not publicly opposed to slavery until after the passage of the Kansas-Nebraska Act. Not until "Lincoln saw that the spirit of slavery was spreading" did he turn from an "appeaser into a fighter." In this respect, "Lincoln's attitude in the years before the Civil War paralleled the development of the attitude of the whole American people in the years before 1940."

On election eve, as part of a nationwide radio program, Carl Sandburg offered an emotional eulogy to Lincoln and closed with his support for Roosevelt. Sandburg implied that this election was much like the one in 1864, Lincoln was much like the prophet Samuel, and FDR was much like Lincoln. The Lincoln biographer spoke as an independent who belonged to "no political party, no faction, no political group open or secret," who recognized Franklin Roosevelt, as earlier generations recognized Lincoln, as "not a perfect man and yet more precious than gold." On election day Stephen Vincent Benét published a poem in the *New York Post* that spoke of leaders who knew "the tides and ways of the people / As Abe Lincoln knew the wind on the prairies." One was "A country squire from Hyde Park with a Harvard accent, / Who never once failed the people / And whom the people won't fail."[82]

After the 1940 election, in August, the president paused in the middle of a press conference. He again pulled out Sandburg's *Lincoln: The War Years* and read two passages. One, made in 1862, was a complaint that "the people have not yet made up their minds that we are at war with the South." The other was reported to take place a year later. It too was a complaint directed toward McClellan and his supporters: "They have no idea that the War is to be carried on and put through by hard, tough fighting, that it will hurt somebody; and no headway is going to be made while this delusion lasts." FDR noted what he called an "interesting parallel . . . Lincoln's belief that this country hadn't waked up to the fact that they had a war to win, and Lincoln saw what was going on." When a reporter asked how his lead ought to read, the president answered: "I'd say, 'President quotes Lincoln—And Draws Parallel.'"[83]

The belated president saw Lincoln's opposition to slavery as part of his quest to alleviate belatedness, and thus it involves the smallest of steps for him to conclude that FDR's opposition to fascism was derived from the same source. The adoption of the Lincoln persona with FDR now a man who faces agonizing "tests," tests which face the polity as a whole that he has refracted upon himself, he sees as part of a systematic pattern to imitate and then overcome Lincoln. And boy did Roosevelt play this new role of the anguished leader! complains the belated president. He reads, for example, FDR's statement in 1940 about how in other "troubled times" Lincoln "year after war-torn year . . . sheltered in his great heart the truest aspirations of his country."

Here was FDR's own "crisis" in 1940, according to the belated president. The problem that Lincoln and FDR both faced was in a broad sense a heritage of the Jeffersonian mind, a cultural disposition that both men were forced to honor publicly. Both slavery and Nazi conquest challenged American beliefs in pluralism. There was a widespread belief in antebellum America that slavery was wrong. The belief that fascism was an evil was even less contested. The question in both cases was how in terms of national policy could the evil be resisted. Roughly, Lincoln had used three lines of argument. He appealed to the self-interest of white citizens. He reminded his audience at Peoria that the opportunities in the territories would diminish with the spread of slavery: "Slave States are places for poor white people to remove from, not remove to. New free States are the places for poor people to go to, and better their condition."[84] He insisted that if slavery was a moral wrong, indifference was not a suitable policy. Douglas "could not say people have a right to do wrong." And finally, he argued that the major reason for the evil of slavery rested with the fact that it directly contradicted the moral base of the American regime. Lincoln found this base to rest with his (mis)reading of the Declaration of Independence. If slavery was accorded any status higher than necessity, the "first precept of our ancient faith" was repudiated. In his famous Springfield address, Lincoln concluded that conflict would not cease "until a crisis shall have been reached and passed." America could not "endure permanently half-slave and half-free."[85]

FDR employed not only Lincoln vocabulary but Lincolnian arguments in his third-term acceptance speech in Chicago. It was to a certain extent the ideological equivalent to Lincoln's Peoria address. FDR mentioned neither forgotten men nor economic royalists in 1940. New Deal legislation was described simply as the result of a "growing sense of human decency." This sense was "confined to no groups or class"; it was an "urge of humanity" that could "by no means be labelled a war of class against class." Rather it was a "war in which all classes are joining in the interest of a sound and enduring democracy."[86]

FDR claimed that much still needed to be done in terms of human decency, but now the task was entrusted to "poor and rich alike." There were still enemies. "Appeasers and fifth columnists" charged the president with "hysteria and war-mongering." But these were men and women who were unwilling to extend the principles of human decency to the democracies of the world. In the height of the Jacksonian period of the New Deal, Roosevelt declared that economic royalists were "aliens to the spirit of democracy." "Let them emigrate," he told crowds at Madison Square Garden in 1936. In 1940 he spoke of "selfish and greedy people" whose desires for money led them to "compromise with those who seek to destroy all democracies everywhere, including here."[87]

In 1861 Lincoln had asserted that the Civil War was a "people's contest." FDR did not in 1940 call for armed conflict, although he spoke of military readiness and he claimed Lincoln as the authority for the truth that democracy can thrive only when it enlists the devotion of the common people. More generally, all the basic principles of the Lincoln exemplar were in place. If human decency was a principle of America's national identity, "our credo—unshakable to the end," then indifference to "free peoples resisting . . . aggression" was not possible. People do not have a right to do wrong. The ethical choice was "moral decency versus the firing squad."[88]

In September, the president repeated Lincoln themes. He reiterated his pledge of no foreign wars except in cases of attack to a Teamsters Union Convention but reminded labor leaders that it was in their self-interest to "loyally cooperate" in the task of munitions making: "In country after country in other lands, labor unions have disappeared as the iron hand of the dictator has taken command. Only in free lands have free labor unions survived."[89] On registration day for selective service, he announced that "we cannot remain indifferent to the philosophy of force now rampant in the world." To the Jeffersonian-Jacksonian principles of "equal rights, equal privileges, equal opportunities," Roosevelt added "equal service": "Universal service will not only bring greater preparedness . . . but a wider distribution of tolerance and understanding." It would "bring an appreciation of each other's dignity as American citizens." In

October, drawing the first numbers for the draft, the president referred to "our democratic army." At the University of Pennsylvania, he reminded scholars of the fate of books under dictatorships as he also did at a dedication of three new schools in New York. In a letter read to the World's Fair on the seventy-fifth anniversary of the ratification of the Thirteenth Amendment, he noted the irony that in just three-quarters of a century there were now forces who would "return the human family to that state of slavery" from which Emancipation came through the Thirteenth Amendment.[90]

FDR repeated these arguments—self-interest, a people's war, the immorality of indifference—throughout the 1940 campaign. The belated president notes how readily the press and the American people seemed to accept FDR's new mask. Max Lerner, for example, was prepared to sympathetically ask in the *Nation*, "How much does Roosevelt have in him?" The skittishness which Americans began to feel with regard to their president after the court fight and the attempted purges seemed to fade almost in the same proportions as Roosevelt discarded his Jacksonian persona for his new Lincolnian one.

But FDR was nevertheless still to confront his own crisis in regard to his adoption of the Lincoln exemplar in 1940. He might have galvanized a cynical and pacifist-inclined American intelligentsia to his cause. He might have copied the Lincoln persona, shedding the angry Jackson for the long-suffering Lincoln. He might have copied Lincolnian arguments against slavery in his appeal to antifascist sentiment. But he still faced the dredging up of the anti-Lincoln tradition. Perhaps, observes the belated president, few persons save the scattered but earnest detractors of Lincoln and subsequent other belated presidents "knew" Lincoln as he did. Perhaps FDR's opponent in the 1940 election, Wendell Willkie, did not suffer from belatedness, nor was he part of this remnant of his critics. But Willkie did intuit the liabilities of the Lincoln exemplar and pursued them so effectively against the president that he was forced in October to briefly remove the Lincolnian mask and pick up again the discarded Jacksonian one.

Willkie never took on the role of Douglas in the 1940 campaign, let alone one of the Vallandighams that FDR complained about after the contest. In fact, after the election Willkie immediately and aggressively assumed an internationalist position. But after a brief early attempt to portray Roosevelt as an appeaser, Willkie undertook the role of the peace candidate in 1940. The belated president is not sure that Willkie understood FDR's strategies against belatedness, but he does know that he resented Roosevelt's adoption of Lincoln and that when he cabled his wife about an earlier meeting with the president he began "CHARM EXAGGERATED." Willkie raised doubts about the president by raising doubts about the Black Easter Lincoln. He conflated two issues that troubled Americans, FDR's breaking of the Washingtonian rule against third terms and the prospect of American participation in another European war. In regard to both questions, he struck at the heart of the Lincoln persona. Were the "tests" that the president faced manufactured ones that were more connected with his own ambitions than with the international situation? The charge that FDR had created an executive branch run amuck was, of course, by now a hoary Republican tactic in regard to the New Deal. But heretofore FDR had responded by charging that such attacks were thinly disguised attempts at the restoration of class domination. To the extent to which Roosevelt was now acting on the basis of the Lincoln exemplar of unity, this response was not available.

Willkie's Coffeyville, Indiana, speech was, of course, part of the politician's traditional obeisance to the small town, one that both Hoover and Landon also enacted. Willkie too was attempting to capture the Jeffersonian mind for his campaign. But he gave a special cast to this strategy. Hoover had praised the morality of Main Street only to warn against nostalgia for its economic and political forms. Landon focused upon rural and small-town commitments to constitutionalism and free enterprise. For Willkie, the small town was the repository of "freedom," "equality," and "democracy." The philosophy of democracy was nurtured and taught and preserved across generations at this level: "Our mothers taught us to be honest, polite, to be pleasant and kind. . . our fathers to be brave." The New Dealers spoke in the language of democracy and portrayed themselves as "great 'defenders' of democracy," but they are all "cynics who scoff at our simple virtues . . . and govern us with catchphrases." They have used relief money to manipulate votes; they "terrorize" their opponents by leaking untruths to newspapers; they "purge and purge" those who try to be independent of the "New Deal machine." Because they do not trust in a philosophy of democracy, they "have concentrated power in their own hands." FDR "may not want dictatorship," but "in his hands our traditions are not safe." He had "declared forty emergencies in the past seven years."[91]

In Peoria, Willkie argued that whenever democracies existed in history—"the ancient Roman republic or Sparta, or Athens"—they fell when economic chaos came. So too in Germany when economic breakdown occurred, the people turned to a paper hanger because their democratic system would not work. Where was FDR when Germany fell? Willkie asked. He was attacking the Supreme Court: "He tore this country, this great united people to pieces when he might have exercised leadership." The policies of the New Deal set an example for the world, and Willkie contended that Blum modeled his policies on Roosevelt's and "took France to its wreckage."

Later in the campaign, Willkie suggested that not only had Roosevelt's policy failures promoted dictatorship abroad but also FDR himself was following a path toward dictatorship. Since he had been in office, he repeatedly declared emergencies (the count now was at 67) and "seized more power." "I will leave it to any student of our time whether this pattern I have described is not the pattern and the exact pattern of the decline in democracy in every country in the world where democracy has passed away." Now he was asking for more power, the violation of the "unwritten law" that prohibits a third term. This was a government that "treats our Constitution like a scrap of paper." This was a man who referred to an ambassador of the U.S. as "my ambassador." "Pretty soon it may be 'My Generals' . . . After a while it will be 'My People.'"[92]

While Roosevelt was trying to argue that the choice the American people faced was a commitment to a world of democracies versus dictatorships, Willkie was contending that perhaps the president was on the other side. FDR was casting himself as the "indispensable leader," a "tactic used by tyrants throughout history and the world today." Those who opposed the New Deal needed no such urging, but for those who had doubts, Willkie repeated the nine million unemployment figure as well as the suspicion that the current crisis in international affairs was, unlike the Depression, avoidable. Could the president be trusted? Willkie's Jeffersonian "philosophy of democracy" suggested that Americans rely on themselves rather than indispensable leaders.

FDR recoiled before this ideological assault. Opinion polls showed a marked movement toward Willkie. The belated president, who has suffered through observing victory after victory on Roosevelt's part, is delighted to now watch him squirm, for it seems as if the president is almost in a state of panic. FDR even wonders if Gallup might be tempted to doctor future poll results to give Willkie even more momentum. When the *New York Times* supported Willkie, he dashed off an angry letter to Josephus Daniels. In a note to Rosenman, he complained that those who "most loudly cried dictatorship against me would have been the first to justify the beginnings of dictatorship by somebody else." FDR planned five major campaign speeches between October 23 and November 2. For one, which was incorporated into his Cleveland address, he wrote notes for his writers to state why "FDR could not be a dictator, etc."[93] It would have been a fascinating debate had the president continued to pursue the Lincoln exemplar in the face of Willkie's Jeffersonian-inspired one. But FDR did not. Not only did he pledge that "your boys are not going to be sent into any foreign wars," but he largely, although temporarily, abandoned Lincoln to return to Jefferson and Jackson again. In Brooklyn, FDR returned to his 1936 response to his critics. His opponents had no conception of public happiness because they "measured prosperity only by the stock ticker," and in Cleveland, he repeated the domestic themes of his second inaugural and charged that those who criticized the New Deal hoped to "weaken democracy" and "destroy the free man's faith in his own cause."[94]

It pleases the belated president to learn that Roosevelt lost his nerve at exactly the point when he faced an electoral "test" of his Lincoln persona that was so centered upon meeting tests. He is nevertheless greatly impressed with the president's long-term steadfastness. For he concludes that in his post-election actions, FDR not only returned immediately to Lincoln but also articulated a new expression of the American presidency that radically enlarged even the Lincolnian conception of the institution as an office requiring monumental personal tests. Like Lincoln, FDR misread Jefferson, but exceeding Lincoln, FDR globalized his (mis)reading of the Declaration.

The December 29 fireside chat began with the assertion that it was not a speech on war, but on national security: "The purpose of your President is to keep you now, and your children later, and your grandchildren much later, out of a last-ditch war for the preservation of American independence." While Roosevelt admitted that there was a risk of war in making America "the great arsenal of democracy," the action was justified because "we and our children will be saved the agony and suffering of war which others have had to endure." He repeated his Boston campaign pledge: "There is no demand for sending an American expeditionary force outside our borders. There is no intention by any member of your government to send such a force. You can, therefore, nail any talk about sending armies to Europe as deliberate untruth."[95]

Yet despite these disavowals, the arsenal of democracy speech was very much the ideological equivalent of Lincoln's Springfield address. Lincoln had declared that the government "cannot endure permanently half-slave and half-free," that the discord in the nation would "not cease until a crisis shall have been reached and passed." FDR too spoke of crisis, one as great as that of 1860 (and 1932). Lincoln had argued that Douglas's "care not" policy could not maintain a status quo. Roosevelt stated the belief of some that "wars in Europe and in Asia are of no concern to us." He spoke of those "who want to see no evil and hear no evil, even though they knew in their hearts that evil exists." But the Nazi goal was world conquest. If Britain fell, Hitler would turn to this hemisphere. The United States "would be living at the point of a gun." "To survive in such a world we would have to convert ourselves permanently into a militaristic power on the basis of war economy. The U.S. was threatened with a modern form of slavery." The Axis proclamations were correct: "There can be no ultimate peace between their philosophy of government and our philosophy of government."[96]

A week later, in his annual message to Congress, the president repeated his argument in military-political terms. The threat of war facing the country was unlike any except the Civil War. FDR defended various American military actions in the past but admitted that even in World War I there was "only a small threat of danger to our own American future." But today "the future of all the American Republics is in danger." Without the protection of the British navy, the United States would not immediately be subject to invasion, but only because strategic bases would be required to facilitate troop landings. Thus the first phase of invasion would occur in Latin America through the activities of "secret agents and their dupes," just as it had already occurred in Norway. No negotiation is possible, despite those who "with sounding brass and tinkling cymbal preach the 'ism' of appeasement," for "no realistic American can expect from a dictator's peace international generosity."[97]

So imminent is the crisis that must be reached and passed in Roosevelt's image of the world situation that he also declared what amounted to war aims:

The first is freedom of speech and expression—everywhere in the world.
The second is freedom of every person to worship God in his own way—everywhere in the world.
The third is freedom from want . . . everywhere in the world.
The fourth is freedom from fear . . . everywhere in the world.[98]

The "four freedoms," included in the Atlantic charter and repeated throughout the war, are often interpreted as part of FDR's progressive heritage. The

president had "picked up Woodrow Wilson's fallen banner, fashioned new symbols and programs to realize old ideals of peace and democracy."[99] Indeed, FDR
had already begun to elaborate a defense of America's participation in the war
as part of his attack on the isolationists and the charge that America had been
drawn into the conflict by munitions dealers. But the belated president is convinced that four freedoms owed much to the Lincoln exemplar. In his debates
with Douglas, Lincoln had insisted that the principles of Jefferson's Declaration of Independence applied to African Americans over his opponent's objections that he was extending the meaning of the document. Roosevelt's
Jeffersonian-inspired freedoms were not only overlaid with New Deal understandings but also involved a globalization of the Declaration. "Everywhere in
the world" constituted FDR's expansion of the document. When the president
dictated the close of his annual message to his secretary, Rosenman was impressed with the way the "words seemed to roll off his tongue as though he had
rehearsed them many times over." Thus the belated president wonders how long
FDR had considered this dual (mis)reading of Jefferson/Lincoln. The first two
formulations were directly derived from Jefferson. The "American invention"
in 1776 was the key to understanding the current crisis of democracy.[100] "Freedom from want" entailed the New Deal reading of Jefferson that FDR offered
in his 1932 Commonwealth Club speech, and freedom from fear was a reiteration of his famous first inaugural injunction, which had been later overlapped
with a Jacksonian (mis)reading.

The two exemplars are poetically merged in the third inaugural. Lincoln, as
well as Washington, are presented as symbols of unity and order: "In
Washington's day the task of the people was to create and weld together a
Nation. In Lincoln's day the task of the people was to preserve the nation's from
"disruption from within." FDR announced that his task was to save the nation
from "disruption from without."[101]

Lincoln's great contribution to political thought, which the belated president thinks was derived from his own affliction, centered around his admonition, stated as early as the Lyceum address, that time was the great destroyer of
free government. The "jealousy, envy, and avarice, incident to our nature" are
only "smothered and rendered inactive" during a crisis. Only a conscious, rational rededication to the principles of the regime can defend against the "silent artillery of time."[102] From the perspective of a reading of Lincoln informed
by a knowledge of belatedness, these concerns also presented an opportunity
for monumental achievements. Thus Roosevelt too began to explore this theme
in his third-term campaign. "Remember 1932" was of course important as a
simple campaign slogan, but it also served as an occasion to remind Americans
that it is in the memory of crisis that a people prolong their freedom. And, of
course, Roosevelt was a central part of that memory. In the inaugural, the president declared that "the lives of nations are determined not by the count of years,
but by the lifetime of the human spirit." A man's life was "three score and ten;
a little more, a little less." But the life of a nation is determined by the "measure of its will to live."[103]

The central metaphor of the inaugural was the assertion that a nation was "like a person." The Lincolnian interpretation that a nation could not be divided on basic principles, that it could not remain "half-slave and half-free," was generally consistent with the claim that there are certain elements of a political system that cannot be subject to pluralism. Lincoln used the house-divided metaphor to both convey the nature of this unity and to attack putative healers who would avoid the crisis that the situation demanded be overcome. Roosevelt's formulation took on Hegelian tones. A nation, like a person, has a body that must be "fed and clothed and housed." A nation has a mind that "must know itself" and understand the "hopes and needs of its neighbors." but most of all a nation, like a person, has a soul, "something deeper, something more larger than the some of its parts." This aspect of a nation was the most important of the three and requires "the most sacred guarding of its present." A nation that loses its spirit loses its will to live, and FDR asserted that since the spirit of America was "born of the multitude of those who came from many lands" and represented the culmination of democratic struggle from the "ancient life or early peoples," it must speak to other nations—"the enslaved, as well as the free."[104]

The third inaugural claimed that the United States was, to use Hegelian language, a world historical nation. This of course was not a new assertion, and Lincoln raised it to poetic form in his Gettysburg Address. But now America as "novus ordo seculorum" was interpreted in global terms even more far reaching than the Wilsonian make the world safe for democracy. For, unless the spirit of America defeated the spirit of tyranny, the spirit of America would perish, although the nation's "body and mind" might live on for a while "constricted in an alien world." Here was a position as demanding and crisis-ridden as Lincoln's house-divided interpretation of the problem of slavery. But if the spirit of America must become absolute, the spirit itself was a spirit of localism, pluralism, political restraint, and freedom. The spirit was "written into the Magna Carta, the Mayflower Compact, the Declaration of Independence, the Constitution." The spirit of America spoke through "our daily lives, through the processes of governing in "the sovereignties of 48 states," through our "counties," "cities," "towns," and "villages." It is true, of course, that there are principles and practices that so affront the nature of a free people that they cannot be tolerated. If fascism (and chattel slavery in Lincoln's time) did not qualify as the outer limit of pluralism, then no principles and practices could. But one can still ask if in Roosevelt's formulation the American spirit that was to protect freedom had become so generalized and so absolute as to become detached from the actual life of a free society, which after all is one in which many voices speak. But the belated president understands the origin of this inconsistency for FDR's honoring Jefferson was derived from the same quest to avoid belatedness that led Lincoln to adopt the same strategy. Lincoln "honored" Jefferson by bringing to life a principle embalmed in a merely revolutionary document. FDR repeated the misreading by bringing the document to life internationally.

Presidents who successfully overcome belatedness eventually discard the exemplars they have hostilely imitated since they have now become an exemplar unto themselves. Such was the case with Washington as he closed up any future imitators in his Farewell Address, and such was the case with Lincoln, who let Washington's memory fade after his election. So too with FDR. Vallandighams were everywhere in 1941, but except for a brief moment in 1944, when it appeared that MacArthur might become his McClellan, FDR was afforded the great luxury of finishing his administration without anymore recourse to belated-inspired strategies. He was simply Franklin Delano Roosevelt, the man of monumental achievement who saved both America and the world from catastrophe.

The belated president does not know, of course, precisely how he will overcome FDR. But he experiences some relief from his belatedness since he now thinks that he has discovered his poetic intent and the nature and origins of his poetic achievements. Roosevelt's geniality, to him, was his supermask which disguised his poetic intent. His poetic achievement rested with his capacity to add to it multiple masks. For the belated president shudders when he concludes that if he could (mis)read Jefferson, Jackson, and Lincoln, he could thus become anyone. Thus it is upon his use of serial masks that Roosevelt's monumental achievements rest. And here too rests the key, perhaps, to overcoming Roosevelt. For a belated president, armed with the knowledge of FDR's poetic intent, must be able to copy and misread not only Jefferson/Jackson/Lincoln but also FDR himself. But the task of misreading FDR is too great for the belated president to initiate, and he therefore decides to construct still more narratives of poetic intent and achievement.

Part II

SPIRITED PRESIDENTS

. . . .

His thoughts are savage like a lions's, who follows only
his own great strength and his proud heart.

—*Iliad*

L et us be direct about spiritedness and spirited presidents. There are some men for whom desire seems to overtake their whole person. They are eager men, angry men, indignant men. Often they are impetuous men, and frequently they are violent men. The ancient Greeks, whom the belated president has learned knew a great deal about spiritedness, spoke of *thymos* as the seat of anger and rage and *thysis* as a kind of "boiling over" of the soul as character traits of spirited men.[1] He also has learned that the affliction of belatedness has driven many of these spirited ancients. He reads, for example, Plutarch's account of the young Alexander's outrage at his father's successes: "My father will forestall me in everything. There will be nothing great or spectacular . . . to show the world."[2] The belated president also surveys both the admiration and fear of spirited men in the ancient world. He studies Homer's treatment of Achilles and Socrates' attempt to restrain the spirited men of the guardian class. He ponders the Greek and Roman fascination with generals: Scipio, Achilles, Cyrus, Alexander, Caesar.

We have not given our belated president a spirited personality, but the belated president can nevertheless acutely understand spiritedness because he now understands his own generic affliction. To him the spirited man is so overcome by his sense of belatedness that he "boils over" in disgust and anger at his impotence. The belated president has, of course, experienced these emotions himself when he has examined the lives of other presidents. But he has also learned from other presidents how to veil his rage. What, however, if belatedness struck so massively that he could never hope to contain himself? Socrates does not speak in the language of belatedness, but his description of the intensity of the suffering of the spirited informs our president's point: "The nobler [a man] is, won't he be less capable of anger at suffering hunger, cold or anything else of the sort inflicted on him by one whom he supposes does so justly . . . ? [But] when a man believes he's being done injustice? Doesn't this spirit in this case boil and become harsh and form an alliance for battle with what seems just; and, even if it suffers in hunger, cold and everything of the sort, doesn't it stand firm and conquer, and not cease from its noble efforts before it has succeeded, or death intervenes?"[3] The belated president knows that those who share his affliction never accept the proposition that those who came before him justly deserve their fame. He knows, in other words, that the spirited suffer and boil until they succeed or until "death intervenes."

Everything the belated president knows about overcoming belatedness comes from his analysis of Washington, Lincoln, and FDR. He knows, then, that except for the young Washington's discernable spiritedness, which he was apparently able to overcome, success against belatedness seems to derive from the capacity to hide thymos. The belated president rarely feels empathy, but in this case a pang of pity rises up in him. How, he asks, are spirited men, men whom in his mind suffer from belatedness in a particularly violent way, ever able to find relief? Once his identification with the spirited subsides he is able to rephrase his question: How do spirited men, men apparently unable to hide their poetic intent, overcome belatedness?

He begins his attempt to answer this question by considering the dual fascination and repulsion that others experience in the face of the spirited. For the citizen, the spirited are admired for their singleness of purpose, their courage, their eagerness. The rage of the spirited he takes as a refusal to accept injustice. To him these are qualities which make men able guardians of the Republic. But this fearlessness troubles the citizen and he sleeps at night less well than he expects. For if the spirited are so ferocious against the enemies of the Republic, how might he behave if the objects of his anger somehow changed? It is, of course, this concern that the citizen expresses which represents an intuition on his part of poetic intent on the part of the spirited. The citizen still wonders just what is the source of this ferocity. The more spirited is the leader, the more the citizen wonders about the nature of his spiritedness. When he hears or reads narratives of the spirited, his anxiousness rises. Achilles withdrew from battle because his sense of justice was offended. Nothing would bring him back to the battle as Achilles' anger over the denial of what he regards as his due as a warrior spills over to anger at the human condition: "Stay at home or fight your hardest—your share will be the same. Coward and hero are honoured alike. Death does not distinguish do-nothing and do-all."[4] Only his anger at the death of Patroklos averts his rage against a world which can never truly offer honor. Achilles' grief is inconsolable and his desire for revenge is frightful. He swears to cut up Hector's body and eat his "flesh raw" and so defiles his opponent's body that Apollo remarks: "He had no decency in his heart, his mind cannot be turned in his breast, but his thoughts are savage like a lion's, who follows only his own strength and his proud heart, and goes to make his meal on the flocks that men keep."[5] The citizen knows that Achilles' thysis is contained by the intervention of Zeus, but can anyone who reads Homer's epic not cringe at the prospect of becoming the object of Achilles' anger? Achilles does not "eat" his rival but he threatens to, and Apollo himself speaks of Achilles in terms of such metaphors. The citizen cringes at another thought. Which is worse, he wonders, the possibility of becoming the object of the spirited's anger or the prospect that the spirited will cast his anger indiscriminately against the world in general?

Modern philosophers have been less concerned with restraining the spirited than with eliminating their emergence altogether. Far better to encourage the spirit of commerce and improvement of man's estate than to rely upon great-spirited men to effect justice. Far better, in Locke's words, to encourage the "industrious and rational." Thus the citizen is to be spared the anxiety of "being eaten" by spirited men. Yet even in the most liberal of regimes, not only do spirited men still emerge but some philosophers, notably Machiavelli, insist upon their usefulness. Thus spiritedness is transformed into "love of liberty," and Machiavelli writes it was the "love of liberty," defended "obstinately" and with "vigor," "fierceness," and "savagery," that maintained "abundant freedom" in the ancient world.[6] There is in Machiavelli's formulation a democratization of spiritedness in that it is a people at large who love liberty. Still, there are exemplars of freedom-lovers, "commanders of armies and rulers of republics," and thus the ancient problem of restraining the spirited emerges in another form.

The belated president thus sees how spirited presidents come to hide their affliction with belatedness despite the boiling over of their passions. If the thymos of the spirited can be expressed in the form "lover of liberty," he assumes the role of tribune, and who can question the singlemindedness of one devoted to freedom? How can a man driven by a defense of liberty be a threat to the liberty of the citizenry? The spirited man, then, still has his secrets, since he must hide his poetic intent, though not his thymos, from the worrisome citizen who in the back of his mind wonders about the prospect of his being eaten. This, of course, is not the spirited president's only problem, for the belated president knows, and so too do the greatly spirited, that he has only one weapon, his own rage, to overcome belatedness. He can study Washington's calculated abdication of power, Lincoln's double crosses, and FDR's multiple persona, but he knows that none of these strategies are really available to him. He knows too not only about the citizen's fear of being eaten but also that most of the citizenry are not really "lovers of liberty." They are "industrious and rational" women and men who, for the most part, do not crave freedom as much as comfort and security. Thus he must somehow learn to "move" the nation toward his projects without letting his rage overflow to those who are reluctant to follow with the same ferocity and vigor as he.

America, the most modern and most Lockean of all nations, has nevertheless produced spirited men, and the belated president has identified three spirited presidents: Andrew Jackson, Theodore Roosevelt, and John F. Kennedy. Jackson's spiritedness was so great that it consumed his whole persona. He was the "man of iron," a man of "indomitable perseverance and ceaseless activity." No narrative better illustrates Jackson's spiritedness than his famous duel with Charles Dickenson. Jackson knew that his opponent was the better marksman. Nevertheless, he waited until Dickenson fired. His bullet lodged in his chest,

Jackson cocked his pistol to fire. The gun jammed, but the rules of dueling permitted him another shot. Jackson recocked his pistol and fatally wounded Dickenson. Jackson left the field standing, and when one of his early biographers researched the incident, he learned that Jackson refused first aid because he did not want the dying man to have the satisfaction that his shot had hit his target.[7]

There is Achillean immoderation in this story, as there is in Theodore Roosevelt's life. When John D. Long pleaded with fatherly concern that TR not organize a calvary regiment in the war against Spain, he wrote in his dairy about Roosevelt's thymos: "His heart is right, and he means well but it is one of those cases of aberration-desertion-vain glory; of which he is utterly unaware."[8] Roosevelt fought bravely in Cuba, but one biographer noted that his gloating over the body of a dead soldier he had personally "doubled-up" involved a "desecration of the human spirit that will forever bar him from the immortality of Jefferson, Lincoln, and Wilson."[9] Louis Hartz once described TR as America's only Nietzschean president, but Norman Mailer found a will-to-power that lay just below JFK's cool persona.[10] The Kennedy mythmakers spoke in terms of his "grace under pressure," but more recent analyses emphasize his personal and political recklessness. The belated president collects and studies these narratives of spiritedness, for he is anxious to learn how the spirited became "great" presidents.

Chapter 4

ANDREW JACKSON: WILL

* *

When the belated president surveys Jackson's generation, he initially concludes that there could not have been a period more opposed or indifferent to the demands of a spirited leader. America was on the verge of an economic takeoff, perhaps in unanticipated consequence of the War of 1812. Forced to improvise as a result of import restrictions, American merchants brought the factory system to the country, much to the awe of men like Everett who struggled to connect this "great Arabian tale of real life" which caused the city of Lowell to rise as if a "beneficent genius . . . touched the soil with his wand" to the "wisdom and patriotism of our fathers." America had come into existence by "sacrifices and privations," and he was amazed how "all the voices of successful industry,—the abode of intelligent thousands" could come into almost immediate existence except through the "work of enchantment." The Americans whom Tocqueville met were an energetic, bustling people the likes of which the world had not yet seen. The United States in the 1820s and 1830s was embarking upon an experiment with a new kind of "newness," a newness that was all the more exhilarating because it had not yet become the definition of American character. James Kirke Pauling concluded that "the inventors of machinery have caused a greater revolution in the habits, opinions, and morals of mankind, than all the efforts of legislation. Machinery and steam engines have had more influence on the Christian world than Locke's metaphysics, Napoleon's code, or Jeremy Bentham's codification." To Daniel Webster, the present was "distinguished from every preceding age by a universal ardor of enterprise in arts and manufactures."[1]

Who could be more irrelevant in the dawn of America's first commercial age, wonders the belated president, than an aged military man who forthrightly defended dueling, still harbored open hatred of the British during the Revolutionary War, openly admired Napoleon, and once asserted that his reputation was worth more to him than his life? Yet the belated president knows that

Jackson's spiritedness so spoke to his generation that this period was named after him. What he learns is that Jackson's spiritedness conflated, inverted, transformed, and mutated the tropes of old/young in ways that made him an object of awe, adoration, and, yes, anxiety to a generation of Americans. The belated president decides to attempt to sort out these multiple interactions between old and new, for he sees in them the key to both Jackson's poetic intent and poetic achievement.

The belated president begins with the assumption that spirited men are not calculating men or, more accurately, do not acknowledge their calculations. He notes, for example, Theodore Roosevelt's response to a query about his presidential ambitions from Jacob Riis when he was police commissioner. TR complained that no true friend would raise such a question. Then he continued: "I am going to do great things here, hard things that require all the courage, ability, work that I am capable of. I must be wanting to be President. Every young man does. But I won't let myself think of it: I must not, because if I do, I will begin to work for it, I'll be careful, calculating, cautious in work and act, and so—I'll beat myself. See?"[2]

Jackson himself expressed similar sentiments slightly veiled. In 1806, he warned a fellow Tennessean that "when Great and sensible men form plans of operation, with deep design, the[y] always keep out of view their real object, until it is ripe for execution and unfold it to no one."[3] Jackson expressed his disdain and anger for this approach when he rejected the advice of Henry Dearborn a year later. He would never act "in the yankee stile of base duplicity, by smiling in the face of an enemy and plunging a dagger to his [heart]." Such actions were not worthy of a general in a "great and rising republik, whose principle pillars, is virtue candeur and truth."[4] Thus Jackson's success in directing the spirit of his age toward himself, concludes the belated president, must have been intuitive. He is aware of those scholars who insist that Jackson did not have a cohesive program, but he also faced this assessment in regard to FDR and discovered that his geniality was a mask for a consistent campaign against belatedness. Jackson's dilemma is at once the same one and quite different. Like FDR and his geniality, Jackson's spiritedness was both his great asset and liability in recovering from belatedness. But how could Jackson hide behind his spiritedness which would psychologically admit no subterfuge?

OLD/YOUNG

The belated president studies Jackson's early career, especially those aspects which became part of his contested persona in 1824 and 1828. He discovers the first uses of old/young tropes. Born on the Carolina frontier in 1767, his family suffered disastrously from the Revolution, which reached proportions of civil war in this part of the country. His father had died shortly before his birth. The young Andrew's older brother died from fever early in the war. He and his other brother were captured by the British; both were wounded by an insouciant British officer when they refused to shine his boots. Robert died from small-

pox and the young Andrew barely survived. His mother died from cholera attending two cousins interned on a British POW ship. Orphaned at fourteen,
the young Jackson later insisted that while he was "amply repaid by living under the mild administration of a republican government," he swore enmity to
the "tyranny of Britain" which had forced him to "struggle for our liberties" in
his early youth and took "everything that was dear to me."[5]

Jackson's traumatic youth thus formed a persona which was both old (he was
a youthful example of revolutionary sacrifice raised by an aunt who was the
model "Spartan mother") and new (he had no family, repeatedly announcing
that he had no living blood relative in America and without "any extrinsic
advantage to promote his advancement, he had to rely solely upon the intrin-
sic worth and decisiveness of character, to enable him to rise rapidly with a rising
people").[6] This interpretation of the content of old/new provided a combination of martial and acquisitive sentiment, expanded in theorized form as repub-
licanism/liberalism which would provide the foundation for Jackson's resolution for the great problem of the spirited. Indeed, his postrevolutionary activity continued to correspond to these themes. Like JFK, another spirited president, Jackson had a reckless youth. He quickly dissipated his small inheritance
before leaving for Tennessee. Jackson then took up law, married well, and in-
vested successfully in land and slaves. He was elected to the Senate in 1798 and
resigned two years later to assume a judgeship on the Tennessee Supreme Court,
which he vacated in 1804 to return to private practice and business ventures
as part of the Nashville parvenu planter aristocracy. Throughout this Lockean
period, however, Jackson remained a spirited figure, quick to anger and to resort to violence. "His displays to temper," concludes one recent biographer,
"were extreme even by southwestern standards."[7] A near-disastrous loss in real
estate speculation may have prompted his interest in the military. Jackson was
elected a major general in the militia in 1802 and aggressively sought to defend the Tennessee frontier from the Creeks and their allies, the British.

It was, of course, the Battle of New Orleans that established Jackson's reputation for spiritedness at the national level. Americans were so thrilled by the
victory that they joyously passed credit in many directions. They attributed the
victory to the sharp-shooting "Hunters of Old Kentucky," to the American
"democratic spirit," to the courage of the "western farmer," to American technology. But most of all they praised Jackson, the "king-breaker," the "man of
iron" who gave the "infant" Republic its manhood from colonial dependency
and humiliation. One nineteenth-century account of Jackson's entry into the
liberated city captures perfectly the equipoise of old/new as young/old that came
to form Jackson's persona: He "was a tall, gaunt man, of very erect carriage, with
the countenance full of stern anxiety. His complexion was sallow and unhealthy;
his hair was iron grey, and his body thin and emaciated . . . But the fierce glare
of his bright and hawk-like grey eye, betrayed a soul and a spirit which tri-
umphed over all the infirmities of the body."[8] Walker's metaphors of youth and
age are balanced ("gaunt," "stern," "sallow and unhealthy," "thin and emaciated," and "fierce," "bright," "hawk-like," with the metaphor of grayness used

to express both old/new. As John William Ward has more recently observed, to his admirers like Walker the more infirm became Jackson's body, the more visible became his iron will.[9]

Jackson's own account of the significance of the victory too theorized in terms of old/young. He used the multiethnic and racial composition of the American forces to give the battle a world historical significance which evened the score from centuries of British domination. To French soldiers, he spoke of the victory as one over "the hereditary, the eternal enemies of your ancient country." To the Spanish, he urged remembrance of past injury and "avenging the brutal injuries inflicted by men who dishonor the human race." He praised the heroism of "men of color" whom he had invited "to share in the perils" and now invited "to divide the glory of your white countrymen." To the regulars, he exclaimed: "This is the true military spirit! This is the true love of country!" Most telling of all to the belated president is Jackson's accolade to the people of New Orleans: "Inhabitants of an opulent and commercial town, you have by spontaneous effort shaken off the habits, which are created by wealth, and shewn that you have resolved to deserve the blessings of fortune by bravely defending them." Thus, in Jackson's mind, the people of New Orleans (and by implication, all Americans) were rejuvenated through the contagion of martial spirit. The city had become old and "weak," but this threat gave its inhabitants the knowledge that liberty is more dear than property, "dearer" even than "your wives and children."[10]

These were the meanings that Jackson attributed to the battle of New Orleans, and the belated president has to admire the snug fit Jackson had epitomized between his spiritedness and the nation's. But Jackson's spiritedness did not go unnoticed and he was forced early and often to respond to those who would make the American public worrisome. Jackson's own spiritedness gave his opponents plenty of ammunition. His unprecedented declaration of martial law in New Orleans later brought him before a federal court. In the Seminole campaign, Jackson raged through Florida as a renegade general seemingly uncontrollable by federal civilian authorities. His order to hang two British subjects for allegedly aiding the enemy and his attack upon a Spanish fort created an international incident and prompted a French governmental official to refer to Jackson as that "Napoleon des bois."[11] As Jackson's presidential ambitions became clear, his opponents began "building ardently upon incidents of his military past" and "managed almost to read into the records of history a legend of his rude violence and uncontrolled irascibility."[12]

Central to the argument that Jackson's spiritedness was so great that Americans were in danger of being eaten was the description of the general as a "military chieftain." Henry Clay made this claim with his characteristic eloquence after the Seminole campaign. Recall the "free nations which have gone before us" said Clay:

> Where are they now, and how have they lost their liberties? If we could transport ourselves back to the ages when Greece and Rome flourished in their greatest

prosperity, and mingling in the throng, ask a Grecian if he did not fear some daring military chieftain, covered with glory, some Philip or Alexander, would one day overthrow his liberties? No! No! the confident and indignant Grecian would exclaim, we have nothing to fear from our heroes; our liberties will be eternal. If a Roman citizen had been asked, if he did not fear the conqueror of Gaul might establish a throne upon the ruins of public liberty, he would instantly have repelled the unjust insinuation. The celebrated Madame de Stael, in her last and perhaps best work, has said, that in the very year, almost the very month, when the president of the Directory declared that monarchy would never more show its frightful head in France, Bonaparte, with his grenadiers, entered the palace of St. Cloud, and dispersing with his bayonet, the deputies of the people, deliberating on the affairs of state, laid the foundations of that vast fabric of despotism which overshadowed all Europe.[13]

Clay concluded his address with the warning that "Greece had her Alexander, Rome her Caesar, England her Cromwell, France her Bonaparte": "Beware how you give a fatal sanction, in this infant period of our republic, scarcely yet two score old, to a military insubordination." Thus Clay offered his own peroration on the old/new tropes of Jackson and his spiritedness. For he had asserted that spirited men were an old phenomenon which the great republics of the past had encountered, and it was the duty of this "infant" Republic to fashion a new response lest it repeat history.

The belated president notes that Jackson did not retreat from attacks such as these. His spiritedness drove him to rage. He attacked Clay as a hypocrite "in pretending his friendship to me, and endeavoring to crush the executive through me." "I despise the villain," said Jackson, and he swore he would "defeat these hellish machinations." Jackson was, in fact, so certain that Clay's charges would backfire that he urged his friends to print and circulate his House speech: "I hope the western people will appreciate his conduct accordingly. You will see him skinned here and hope you will roast him in the West." He attacked those in the cabinet who questioned his actions in Florida charging Crawford as a "miscreant" unfit to "fill any office in republican government" and complained that Monroe was insufficiently supportive. His rage even extended to John Quincy Adams, who had defended Jackson. When Adams told him that his support of his actions in Florida was based upon the great international lawyers, Grotius, Puffendorf, and Vattel, Jackson exclaimed to his horror: "Damn Grotius! Damn Puffendorf! Damn Vattel! This is a mere matter between Jim Monroe and myself."[14]

Jackson stormed Washington and had to be intercepted at the Capitol steps by a friend as the general sought to assault a member of the investigating committee. While the treaty with Spain ceding Florida and Jackson's obvious popularity with the general public defused the crisis, Monroe himself seemed unable to decide what to do with this spirited man. He considered offering Jackson an ambassadorship to Russia but was deterred when the aged Jefferson exclaimed, "Good God! He would breed you a quarrel before he had been there a month."

Jackson, even in his rage, did manage to construct an alternative narrative in the 1824 campaign to the challenge that he was a dangerous "military chieftain" by linking his martial persona to George Washington's. The press obliged by characterizing the election as one between the "second Washington versus the second Adams," and the Jacksonians staged an impressive media event during Lafayette's tour of the country conflating Jackson, Lafayette, and Washington. Still, friends warned him that "your enemies are very industrious, they have labored hard to produce an impression that you were a man governed by Passion and impulse." Jackson/Washington, moreover, was always an uneasy fit. Jackson did resolutely imitate the Washingtonian strategy of seeking power through its abdication. He resigned the governorship of Florida and feigned reluctance to enter the presidential race, insisting that his health and an objective assessment of his talent prevented his candidacy. But Jackson's persona of spiritedness was too widespread and too intense for a comparison. Adams, in fact, considered him at one point for his vice-president on the grounds that this was "a station in which the General could hang no one."[15]

Shortly after the House elected Adams, Jackson responded to the military chieftain charge once again. The belated president finds his response especially fascinating, for what could throw a spirited man into a more uncontrollable rage than the theft of the presidential chair through "secret enclaves" and "cabals entered into"? What he finds is a surprisingly calm Jackson, at least by the standards of the spirited. He pointed to the fact that ninety-nine electors had voted for him as proof of its inaccuracy. He admitted spiritedness in his youthful opposition to the "yoke of tyranny" during the Revolution and defense of western citizens against "savages" and concluded: "If this can constitute me as a "Military Chieftain I am one." He had been charged with "taking bold and high-handed measures," but none of them were designed for his "personal aggrandizement." Did the charge imply that "all our brave men in war, who go forth to defend their rights and the rights of their country . . . be termed Military Chieftains?" Under these definitions even Washington could be so considered, "because he dared to be a virtuous and successful soldier, an honest man, and a correct man." He might be a military chieftain but at least he had not been part of plans to "impair the pure principles of our Republican institutions" or to frustrate the people's will. Jackson concluded that "demagogues . . . had done more injury to the cause of freedom and the rights of man, than ever did a 'Military Chieftain.'" He had been "a soldier for the good of my country" and now he would retire again to his farm. He would never be a "hanger on upon office and power." "If this makes me so, I am a 'Military Chieftain.'"[16]

The belated president knows, of course, that Jackson could never shed his spiritedness. Jackson's public personality after 1825 does not undergo the same alteration that Washington's did the 1760s. But he sees in this letter and others to Samuel Swartwout, which were printed in newspapers, a transformation of Jackson's spiritedness. Central to this change, concludes the belated president, is Jackson's psychological acceptance of the charge of military chieftain and thus an acceptance of his own spiritedness. It is in this traumatic defeat, a defeat of enormous proportions for a spirited man, that Jackson acknowledges the charge and generalizes his spiritedness into a political ideology. Robert V. Remini notes the nature of this self-revelation in his assessment of Jackson: "The House election of 1825 that awarded the presidency to John Quincy Adams had a profound impact on Jackson's thinking. Unquestionably, it was *the* single event—if single events in history actually do determine actions by themselves— that converted him into a rabid democrat."[17]

INSPIRITING JEFFERSON

The belated president wonders what directions Jackson's spiritedness would have taken had the House elected him president in 1825, but he agrees with this biographer that Jackson's spiritedness was given a clear form after his defeat. Jackson in 1825 had no clear position on the great projects of his presidency—opposition to internal improvements and the Bank of the United States—but he had already divided the polity into the intrigues of demagogues and hangers-on and the will of the people, a theme that characterized his presidency. It was the people's will (of course as filtered through his own great spirited will) which had been "mutilated" by Clay, "the Judas of the West," who "sold himself and his influence to Mr. Adams."[18] After 1825 Jackson set out to awaken the will of the people in terms broader than military glory. The "majority is to govern," he announced in his inaugural, and "their will is absolute."

The day after Adams's own inauguration, Jackson began his first use of Jefferson as the legitimizing device of his presidential campaign. While Jackson continued to employ Washington as a general symbol, it was henceforth Jefferson that became the great weapon of the Democratic Party. "So tight" were the Jacksonian symbols of Jefferson, democracy, and the Democratic Party that "one scarcely existed in the public mind apart from the others and attempts to disengage them met with fleeting success." Democratic politicians developed with unerring accuracy the tactic of answering opponents "by squirting Jefferson's opinions in their eyes."[19] Jackson thus began his own "inauguration" when he compared Adams's "pomp and ceremony" to the swearing in twenty four years earlier: "When Mr. Jefferson was inducted into office, no such machinery was called in to give solemnity to the scene. He rode his own horse, and hitched him himself to the inclosure."[20]

The belated president makes two notes on Jackson's appropriation of Jefferson. He is by now intimately familiar with misreadings of the Sage of Monticello since he has already studied two monumental efforts to overcome Jefferson by Lincoln and FDR. Thus he is quick to note the gap between Jackson and his alleged mentor. It is true that Jefferson opposed the Bank of the United States as well as internal improvements, distrusted the courts, and campaigned on the postrevolutionary emergence of an aristocracy. It is also true, of course, that Jefferson would have never conceived the presidency as a tribune of the people, held the legislature in such low esteem, harbored hatred for Indians, nor adopted a nationalist ethos that reached its apogee in Jackson's nullification crisis. It hardly surprises him then to learn that Jackson's record as Jeffersonian was mixed since he knows that his appropriation was designed to disguise poetic intent rather than to simply imitate. What he does find arresting, however, is the general nature of Jackson's transformation of Jefferson. For Jackson had done nothing short of inspiriting Jefferson.

Jefferson's revolutionary credentials were, of course, impeccable. But not only was he not a general, he epitomized the Enlightenment man. His self-reported encounter with Hamilton on heroes perfectly expresses his differences from Jackson. According to Jefferson, Washington had asked the secretary of state to call together the heads of other executive departments to discuss some policy problems. During dinner, Hamilton asked who were the portraits on the wall. Jefferson replied that these were pictures of the greatest men humanity had ever produced—Bacon, Newton, and Locke. Hamilton hesitated and then responded that "the greatest man that ever lived was Julius Caesar." The remark horrified Jefferson and served as proof to him that Hamilton was a potential usurper. Jefferson's own remark, lately contested by historians, that Jackson was a "dangerous man" would certainly have been reenforced by Jackson's response had he been asked the same question.[21]

Yet Jackson's total lack of Jefferson's subtlety and cosmopolitanism, let alone his martial view of the world, did not prevent him from offering a reading in terms of his own spiritedness. Indeed, contained in the old/new tropes of Jackson's Jeffersonian risorgimento was a veiled acknowledgment of Jefferson's failure to rid America of a recidivous aristocracy. One member of a Kentucky Democratic nominating convention in 1830 reported delegates whose "old grey heads, and furrowed faces seemed young again . . . the doctrines announced 'fell upon their ears like music of other days'. . . . I could almost imagine that I was carried back by time to the days of Jefferson." Jackson's trusted advisor, Amos Kendall, noted implicitly that the Jeffersonian revival contained in it a determination that the Jacksonian revolution would succeed where the "revolution of 1800" had failed. There was a "general shaking . . . which was destined, after a long agony to separate parties on original principles, much better defined and understood than they were even in the days of Jefferson."[22]

But if Jackson invented a spirited Jefferson, the belated president also notes that this choice had a certain taming effect on Jackson himself. There is no doubt that Jackson's Jeffersonian spiritedness vastly increased the power of the presidency, but there is also no doubt that if Jackson's natural spiritedness took the form of a backwoods Napoleon, his adoption of a decentralized ideology produced a different kind of administration than the one for which so many later Democrats hoped. There was thus, in fact, very little military adventurism in the Jackson administrations and a definite decline in those governmental projects which form the structure for state building. In short, Jackson continued, and actually intensified, the Jeffersonian tradition of democratic protest in America along antistatist lines.

No project of Jackson better reveals the impact of a spirited Jeffersonianism than his war with the Bank of the United States. The BUS was the creation of

Hamilton, Jefferson's rival, and represented the antithesis of nearly every point in Jefferson's program. Its legal authority was considered constitutionally dubious; it constituted a semimonopoly granted by the federal government; its head, Nicholas Biddle, seemed beholden to no one; bank policies were alleged to favor the wealthy and the manufacturing class (which after all was Hamilton's intention). Still, the BUS survived the revolution of 1800 and was rechartered in 1816 by Congress. Jackson's description of his battle with the bank as one in which he asserted would only end when one killed the other was given symmetry by Biddle's own prediction: "When we begin, we shall crush [the Jacksonians] at once."[23] It is difficult today to appreciate the significance of Jackson's project to destroy the BUS. The bank was in a position to bring the nation to economic ruin when challenged (which Biddle attempted to do), and it was a national institution almost coterminous with the founding. The decision to destroy the bank was in many ways the liberal equivalent of the socialists' nationalization of property.

Thus few Whigs or Democrats originally took Jackson seriously, despite his criticism of the BUS in several annual messages. And while it is not clear whether Biddle requested an early date for recharter because he concluded that he could never reach a modus vivendi with Jackson or he moved quickly in an effort to politically embarrass the president at Clay's urging, the action began the war in earnest in what Biddle described as a "trial of strength." The July 1832 veto message, drafted by Jackson and his advisors, represents a culmination of Jackson's attempt to focus his spiritedness. Jackson's own health, always imperilled, was in such serious decline that Van Buren remembered him as a "spectre" close to death. But, as in the past, his physical frailty seemed to heighten his spiritedness. Shortly after the message he wrote Kendall to say that "Providence has had a hand in bringing forward the subject at this time" and he was determined to "preserve the republic from its thralldom and corrupting influence."[24] The message itself was a mélange of traditional Jeffersonian sentiment (that the bank was constitutional "I cannot assent," wrote the president) and Jacksonian's spirited nationalism (a large portion of the bank's stock was owned by the "foreign few" who would influence the "purity of our elections in peace and the independence of our country in war" when any bank should be "purely American").[25] But it was in the concluding argument that Jackson hit upon a remarkable connection between spiritedness and acquisitiveness:

> It is to be regretted that the rich and the powerful too often bend the acts of government to their selfish purposes. Distinctions in society will always exist under every just government. Equality of talents, of education, or of wealth can not be produced by human institutions. In the full employment of the gifts of Heaven and the fruits of superior industry, economy and virtue, every man is equally entitled to protection by law; but when the laws undertake to add to these natural and just advantages artificial distinctions, to grant titles, gratuities, and exclusive privileges, to make the rich richer and the potent more powerful, the humble members of society— the farmers, mechanics, and laborers—who have neither the time nor the means of

securing like favors to themselves, have a right to complain of the injustice of government. Its evils exist only in its abuses. If it would confine itself to equal protection, and as Heaven does its rains, shower its favors alike on high and the low, the rich and the poor, it would be an unqualified blessing. In the act before me there seems to be a wide and unnecessary departure from these just principles.[26]

The belated president ponders this portion of the veto message. Acquisitiveness has always been the enemy of the spirited, who regard the pursuit of material wealth as a goal for small men unable to fix their sights on glory. Jackson himself responded during the Bank War to panicked business people by swearing that he would "not bow down to the golden calf." But here his opposition to the bank is framed in terms of its role in blocking the pursuit of wealth. The "true strength" of the federal government lies in "leaving individuals and States as much as possible to themselves."[27] Thus Jackson told the American people how they could be both spirited ("revive that devoted patriotism . . . which distinguished the sages of the Revolution and attack the rich who would make themselves "richer by act of Congress") *and* acquisitive (confine the government to equal protection, do not expect equal wealth which "can not be produced by human institutions" but receive the "fruits of superior industry" as Heaven "showers its favors alike on the high and the low").

Spirited men take risks, and Jackson, unlike his genial imitator, FDR, did in his own war against the court, outflanked his opposition by undertaking the veto under conditions which "leave the Subject open for the decision of the people in the next Election." Jackson won reelection handily with about the same margin of victory as in 1828. Although he privately felt that he deserved even greater support, Jackson broke the inaugural tradition of nonpartisanship by including a veiled attack on the BUS in his speech. In a bold effort in forestall any congressional attempt to recharter the bank, he announced his intention to withdraw federal funds from the BUS as a logical extension of his recharter veto, which was "sustained by a just people" in his reelection.[28] The decision was made over strong objections from members of his cabinet and extremely skittish congressional Democrats. This action, which both critics and his supporters immediately saw as a momentous extension of presidential power, initiated a second battle in the Bank War which was even more acrimonious than the first. Biddle too responded boldly by tightening credit and sending the already jittery economy into a recession. Jackson, however, seemed to welcome the maneuver, relishing the prospect of drawing from him and the bank "every tooth and then the stumps" until Biddle and the BUS were "quiet and harmless as a lamb."[29] He wrote his son of the incomparable satisfaction which this latest battle against the "corrupting monster" gave him and urged him to save all records: "The history of my administration will be read with interest after I am dead."[30] He would not budge when a delegation of terrified businessmen pleaded with him. Jackson responded, "I am not in any Panic." "Were all the worshippers of the Golden Calf to memorialize me and request a restoration of Deposits, I would cut my right hand from my body before I would do such an act," he said. If business needed relief, Jackson told them: "Go to the monster. Go to Nicholas Biddle."[31]

The belated president studies Jackson's description of the BUS as a monster ("monster of corruption," "monster of Chestnut Street," "hydra of corruption" were several of his variations) and the way this designation focused all of his spiritedness upon a single object. It was this great-spirited battle, the belated president concludes, which would provide Jackson with relief from his own affliction of belatedness. Both Clay and Webster found tyrannical thymos in Jackson's spiritedness. "The premonitory symptoms of despotism are upon us," Clay told the House, and Webster found ominous similarities between Jackson's defence of his action and those of Cromwell and Napoleon. Webster in particular was appalled by Jackson's argument that the presidency was the primary defender of the people's liberties. The entire history of the "spirit of liberty" was devoted to restraining executive prerogative, not expanding it. "Crowned heads have been compelled to submit to the restraints of law, and the PEOPLE, with that intelligence and that spirit which make their voice resistless, have been able to say to prerogative, 'Thus far shalt thou come and no farther.'"[32]

The belated president, however, knows that this spirited assertion of presidential prerogative against the monster bank had more to do with Jackson's own spirit of liberty than the people's. For Jackson seemed to feel that he was now free of belatedness. Even his "Protest" against censure by the Senate, which literally boiled over with rage, included a sense of peace against his real monster, belatedness: "In the history of conquerors and usurpers, never in the fire of youth nor in the vigor of manhood could I find an inducement to commence their career of ambition when grey hairs and a decaying frame, instead of inviting toil and battle, call me to the contemplation of other worlds, where conquerors cease to be honored and usurpers expiate their crimes."[33] To Jackson, his conscience was clear. He would be remembered as one who thwarted the formation of a "splendid government supported by powerful monopolies and aristocratical establishments" and returned to the people unimpaired "a plain system, void of pomp, protecting all and granting favors to none, dispensing its blessings, like the dews of Heaven, unseen and unfelt save in the freshness and beauty they contribute to produce."[34] Read in terms of belatedness, the tropes of old/new were finally united in this reiteration. Jackson, the spirited man whose will fought against the weakness of his own body and an array of the powerful, would now be refreshed by the dews of Heaven.

Although the belated president does not usually think in these terms, it occurs to him that a case can be made for the position that Jackson's adoption of the Jeffersonian exemplar formed a useful contract on all sides. Jackson's spiritedness was tamed, if a "rabid" focus upon democratic principle deserves to be so described, and the American people received a spirited version of their beloved Jefferson.

Chapter 5

THEODORE ROOSEVELT: ENERGY

◆ ◆

W hen the belated president reviews two other spirited presidents, he immediately sees the same restlessness, the same propensity to the use of force, the same anger. But in Theodore Roosevelt and John F. Kennedy he discerns a variation on the theme of spiritedness. Here are "young" presidents, young personally and young, of course, in terms of their sense of belatedness. Jackson's persona represented an artful antithesis between his bodily age and the youthful vigor of his will. To men like TR and JFK, a dichotomy such as this was unavailable. They could not "lean" upon their age to both create awe for the youthfulness of their thymos nor employ their agedness as source of reassurance. Youthfulness filled the Roosevelt and Kennedy personas. Indeed, they were nothing without their youth. How then, asks the belated president to himself, can men such as these achieve monumental acts to relieve their belatedness since it is axiomatic that spirited men cannot hide their poetic intent? The belated president has been studying spiritedness so intensely that he reacts like the spirited and answers his question quickly and directly. If I were young and spirited and unwilling and unable to decorously hide my poetic intent, I would fashion a strategy of overcoming belatedness by so "vigorously" pursuing the goals of my predecessors that I would exceed their projects and become exceptional. As with all battles against belatedness, this ephebian strategy carries risks. The advertisement of one's youthful status emphasizes impetuosity and immaturity if self-imposed tests are not passed. But those afflicted with belatedness must attack their condition, and spirited men are especially attracted to such challenges.

The ephebian strategy, of course, has its own modes of reassurance. Both TR and JFK exuded a boyish charm that could disarm many potential interpreters of their poetic intent, for there is contained in the trope of youthfulness an intimation of innocence and openness. Being in TR's presence could be intimidating, indeed, frightening. Here was a man little over five feet eight inches but who seemed "palpably massive," with an enormous head, a frame of pure muscle, and shining teeth and glasses that cartoonists would employ alone to indicate his persona. When he spoke, one contemporary could think of nothing but "a man biting ten penny nails." But still his admirers reminded the public of his boyishness. "You must remember, said TR's friend Sir Cecil Spring-Rice, "that the President is about six." Thus the citizenry was reassured sending him hundreds upon hundreds of teddy bears. There were others, however, who did manage to see poetic intent behind this allegedly boyish energy. To Mark Twain, the president was "clearly insane"; to Woodrow Wilson he was "the most dangerous man of the age." The Speaker of the House, Joe Cannon, a man not adverse to the use of power, complained through the use of another boyish trope: "Roosevelt's all right but he's got no more use for the constitution than a tom cat has for a marriage license."[1]

EPHEBIAN BIOGRAPHER

The young Roosevelt's pre-presidential writings seethe with frustration over belatedness. In a review of a determinist historical account, Roosevelt contended that pessimism was the attitude of both the "weakling" and "very strong men." The former uses the philosophy to explain why he "cannot struggle with his fellow-men and with the conditions that surround him." The latter, particularly "if of a morose and dyspeptic temper," are "apt to rail at the present, and to praise the past simply because they do not live in it."[2] Roosevelt clearly identified with the dilemma of the very strong man but challenged the belief that "the great poems have all been written, that the days of the drama and epic are past."[3]

TR wrote three biographies, two of which appeared in a period in which he fought against belatedness in literary terms. "I should like to write a book that would really take rank in the very first class, but I suppose this is a mere dream," he confessed to a friend.[4] The belated president surveys Roosevelt's biographical choices: Governeur Morris, an aristocratic supporter of the Revolution; Thomas Hart Benton, Tennessee senator and uncompromising Jackson supporter; Oliver Cromwell, Puritan commander in the English civil war. Undoubtedly, concludes the belated president, these are each spirited men, but he also notes that they are also men who failed to focus their spiritedness. Is, he asks, TR attempting in these biographies, which are also part of his own effort to overcome belatedness, to learn from the failures of men like him? The belated president finds this assessment at the close of the Morris biography:

> There has never been an American statesman of keener intellect or more brilliant genius. Had he possessed but more steadiness and self-control he would have stood among the two or three very foremost. He was gallant and fearless. He was absolutely upright and truthful; the least suggestion of falsehood was abhorrent to him. His extreme, aggressive frankness, joined a certain imperiousness of disposition, made it difficult for him to get along well with many of the men with whom he was thrown in

contact. In politics he was too much of a free-lance ever to stand very high as a leader. He was very generous and hospitable; he was witty and humorous, a charming companion, and extremely fond of good living. He had a proud, almost hasty temper, and was quick to resent an insult. He was strictly just; and he made open war on all traits that displeased him, especially meanness and hypocrisy. He was essentially a strong man, and he was an American through and through.[5]

"And he was a failure," adds the belated president in what he sees as an acute examination on Roosevelt's part of Morris's inability to confront his spiritedness.

If Gouverneur Morris represented an examination of the limits of an aristocratic version of spiritedness with which TR partially shared, Thomas Hart Benton represented something of a template for Roosevelt's own persona of spiritedness. Indeed, TR told Henry Cabot Lodge that he was "evolving him from my inner consciousness," and one biographer describes the biography as one in which "Roosevelt gleefully discovers many points of common identity with his subject, and in describing them, describes himself."[6]

TR left New York for the Dakota Territory in 1884 to start a life as a rancher when both his wife and mother died within hours of each other. The migration had the most positive impact on Roosevelt. "He had gone West sickly, foppish, and racked with personal despair; during his time there he had built a massive body, repaired his soul, and learned to live on equal terms with men poorer and rougher than himself." In *Thomas Hart Benton*, TR found similar transformations, indeed, he discovered the transformation of an entire "race." He saw the creation of the "young" West in terms quite different than other migrations, such as California or Australia, which "were suddenly filled up by the promiscuous overflow of a civilized population, which had practically no fear of any resistance from the stunted and scanty native races." The western expansion was "far more closely akin to the tribe movements of the Germanic peoples in time past." Here were spirited men and women, "valiant warriors" and "hardy pioneers," "men of stern stuff, who from the very beginning formed a most warlike race." Benton was an exemplar of this spiritedness: "He was a faithful friend and a bitter foe; he was vain, proud, utterly fearless, and quite unable to comprehend such emotions as are expressed by the terms despondency and yielding. Without being a great orator or writer, or even an original thinker, he yet possessed marked ability; and his abounding energy and industry, and his tenacious persistency and personal courage, all combined to give him a position and influence such as few American statesmen have ever held."[7]

Roosevelt, nevertheless, had some misgivings about Benton's character. He was able to examine the underside of Benton's spiritedness and admitted that he was "sometimes narrow-minded, and always willful and passionate."[8] He was especially critical of Benton's support of slavery, which Roosevelt described as a "grossly anachronistic and un-American form of evil," especially in terms of his failure to see how the institution was "interwoven with the disunionist movement."[9] TR, however, had the most difficulty coming to terms with Benton as Jacksonian Democrat and in particular his role as point man in the Senate for the president in the Bank War. He was at pains to praise Benton's loyalty to the president but regarded opposition to the BUS as a cause "apt to be popular in a Democratic republic, partly on account of the vague fear with which the poorer and more ignorant voters regard a powerful institution whose workings they do not understand and partly on account of the jealousy they feel toward those who are better off than themselves."[10] Thus TR was uncharacteristically ambivalent toward a major American historical event. He was, of course, much taken with the earnestness and courage of both Benton and Jackson and praised both for educating the people about the virtues of sound money. On the other hand, he was offended by Benton's "pure demagogic pyrotechnics" and his "extreme Jeffersonian doctrinaire views."

TR's summary finally veered in a derisive direction: "Jackson and Benton solemnly thought that they were taking part in a great act of justice, and were amusingly unable to see the comic side of their acts. They probably really believed most of their own denunciations of the Bank, and very possibly thought that the wickedness of its followers might tempt them to do any desperate deed. At any rate they enjoyed posing alike to themselves and to the public as persons of antique virtue, who had risked both life and reputation in a hazardous but successful attempt to save the liberties of the people from the vast and hostile forces of the aristocratic 'money power.'" Roosevelt then dismissed Benton's heroism as one "little elevated above the character of a contemptible farce."[11]

Roosevelt's last biography was written even more hurriedly than the others. His spirited military exploits in Cuba had so captured the public imagination that he was elected governor of New York in 1898 and he was being promoted as a presidential candidate in 1900 and under consideration by McKinley for the secretary of war. TR knew that the prize was within his grasp, and thus the belated president finds his examination of Oliver Cromwell particularly intriguing. Reviews of this biography were clearly not as positive as those of Morris and Benton, since the book contained no original research but the belated president finds in TR's conclusion a noteworthy examination of roads this spirited man decided he would not take. Roosevelt concluded that the English civil war included both medieval and modern elements, and though the revolution failed, it "laid the groundwork for all subsequent movements." He drew parallels between England's struggle and America's in both 1776 and 1860. As to Cromwell, Roosevelt concluded that he was "not only one of the greatest generals of all time" but also "a great statesman who on the whole did marvelous work." He failed because he "lacked the power of self-repression possessed by Washington and Lincoln." "The more I have studied Cromwell," concluded TR, "the more I admire him, and yet the more I have felt that his making of himself a dictator was unnecessary and destroyed the possibility of making the effect of that particular revolution permanent."[12]

The belated president learns a great deal about Roosevelt from these three biographies of spirited men and he concludes that so did TR. He learns, as TR did, that aristocratic spiritedness must be expanded and modified in a Republic which was rapidly losing its landed base. Proof of the extremes which Morris's frustration could take was his proposal that the West "be governed as provinces, and allowed no voice in our councils" and his part in aligning with the "forces of disorder" in the Hartford convention.[13] He learns, too, as TR did, of the farcical directions which American politics can take and how Benton deluded himself in his spirited support of democracy that he was exemplifying ancient republican virtue. And he learns, as TR did, that the wresting of political power in the form of dictatorship which is so natural to spirited men like Cromwell actually destroys the opportunity to alleviate belatedness.

The belated president thus now sees the nature of the dilemma that his studies in spiritedness revealed to TR. If men like Morris, Benton, and Cromwell were useful to study as exemplars of failure, Roosevelt could turn to them only in inverse imitation. Unlike other belated presidents, TR refused to refashion Jefferson to his needs. The mere mention of Jefferson set TR in fits of rage. It was not simply Jefferson's states' rights positions that enraged Roosevelt. To him, Jefferson, "miscalled the great," was the epitome of unspiritedness. His was the most "helpless" of presidencies, and Jefferson delivered a "terrible blow" to the nation's development when he sought to defend America with tiny gunboats and intrigued against Washington when he was secretary of state. Most of all, Jefferson was unmanly. He was "scholarly, timid and shifty" and "doctrinaire." TR could understand Benton's support of Jackson since he was a "man who never feared anything," but he was mystified by Benton's attraction to Jefferson, whose beliefs lead him to think in terms "foolish and illogical."[14]

In a series of essays published as *American Ideals*, Roosevelt attempted to resolve the dilemma that his spiritedness placed him by refusing as an act of will to succumb to the tendency to regretfully recall the past by positing a heroic project possible only to the sons of the founders. The generations of the Revolution and the Civil War bequeathed to the present a "great nation" instead of "a cluster of jangling little communities." The "noble deeds and noble words" of Washington and Lincoln (sans Jefferson, the belated president observes) constitute an "incalculable debt" owed by later generations. TR's focus, however, rests upon the nature of the inheritance provided by Washington and Lincoln. He notes the economic advantages provided by the success of the founding and the Civil War but concludes: "Each of us who reads the Gettysburg speech or the second inaugural address of the greatest American of the nineteenth century and the lofty statesmanship of that other American who was even greater, cannot but feel with him that lift toward things higher and nobler which can never be bestowed by the enjoyment of mere material prosperity."[15] As a result of the valor of these men and the men of their generations, "we have in us nobler capacities for what is great and good because of the infinite woe and suffering, and because of the splendid ultimate triumph."[16]

Read as a response to belatedness, Roosevelt's analysis contends that as a result of previous deeds, the current generation, under the "immense . . . moral influence" of precursors, is now capable of actions greater than their forebears. The notion that the more that one comes under the influence of Washington and Lincoln the greater his capacity "for what is great and good" is a central poetic act uniting both spiritedness and cunning for TR's goal is to overcome this influence. In the ephebian turn, greatness is measured by the capacity of youth to "honor" the fathers to such an extent that they are finally surpassed.

THE SLAIN PRESIDENCY

Throughout his career the young Roosevelt searched for opportunities to heroically replicate the deeds of his acknowledged fathers. TR thought that the "crowded hour" for which he had awaited arrived when he received the order to charge San Juan Hill in the Cuban campaign.[17] Such a moment of greater import came with the assassination of President McKinley. Roosevelt's estimates of McKinley were always polite, but it had also always been clear that he regarded the president as an unspirited and mediocre man. Nevertheless, TR in his first annual message to Congress as president compared the fallen president to Lincoln and praised McKinley for "the grand heroism with which he met his death." The slaying of McKinley represented an attack not only on "this President, but all Presidents," even "the very symbol of government." McKinley had so embodied the will of the people that the assassination was as if an entire New England town meeting had been stuck down.[18]

Roosevelt's magnification of the murder, however, also contained a characterization of McKinley that was decidedly feminine. The dead president had "kindly eyes," was free of "the bitter animosities incident to public life," and exhibited "sweetness and gentleness of character." The murder illustrated that the risk to life was now a part of the presidency, and Roosevelt concluded that future presidents would be very un-McKinley-like. Read as a confrontation with belatedness, Roosevelt spoke of a "new" kind of president, one which emerged from the slain presidents (Lincoln, McKinley) poetically transferred as *the* slain presidency. He was on these terms "first" since "the office would more and more come to be filled by men of spirit which would make them resolute and merciless."[19]

As president, Roosevelt found that outlets for spiritedness were limited. He criticized both the "speculator" and the "demagogue" as social types and noted that the spirit of class was the downfall of republics in the past. He expressed his determination that America would become neither a "government by a plutocracy" nor a "government by a mob." Roosevelt regarded both labor and capital as lacking in discipline and vision. Capitalists could show a "hard indifference to suffering," a "greedy disregard of every moral restraint which interferes with the accumulation of wealth, and cold-blooded exploitation of the weak." Laborers were prone to "laziness, of sullen envy of the more fortunate, and of willingness to perform deeds of murderous violence." In the poetic narrative which defeats belatedness, Roosevelt assumes the image of an Augustus Caesar, savior of the Republic.[20] Both labor and capital are unable to place "moral chains upon their own appetites" and Roosevelt called for a reinvigoration of citizenship as an alternative. What "really counts" is not class division but a division among the honest and dishonest. It is a man's "moral quality, his attitude toward the great questions which concern humanity, his cleanliness of life, his power to do his duty toward himself and toward others" which determines the success of self-government.[21]

But the very notion of a via media suggests a tending to governmental institutions rather than heroic deeds. Roosevelt often noted that the newness of his mission rested in part on managing the "delicate" nature of modern capitalism. Both the corporation and the union "has come to stay," and the task of government was to check them where each "acts against law and justice." Moreover, Roosevelt's exemplification of martial virtues of citizenship were encased within the parameters of a commercial Republic. His annual messages to Congress began with the report that the people enjoyed prosperity. "Manly qualities" there must be, but Roosevelt was confronted with the fact that Americans seemed more interested in restraining appetitive drives than transcending them.

Only in the area of foreign policy was TR able to directly confront belatedness, and it is here that he was able to propose his most exceptional (mis)reading. The greatness of the presidencies of Washington and Lincoln had not rested upon a conception of America as a hegemonic power, and thus Roosevelt could be the "first" to explore the nature of America's "international police duty." Roosevelt repeatedly recommended Washington's Farewell Address as a documentation of America's purpose, but he was challenged by Washington's "great rule of conduct," which proposed extensive commerce but as "little political communication as possible" with foreign governments. In his pre-presidential years Roosevelt discovered a "forgotten maxim" in Washington's counsel. "To be prepared for war is the most effectual means to promote peace" was a maxim with which Americans gave "lip loyalty . . . to Washington's words" but which "has never sunk deeply into our hearts."[22] The Farewell Address includes the argument that a policy of neutrality was essential to "diffusing and diversifying" the "streams of commerce."[23] By reading the "great rule" in martial terms, Roosevelt's reading inverted Washington's advice. "A rich banker may be a valuable and useful citizen, but not a thousand rich bankers can leave the country such a heritage as Farragut left . . . the people of a given section of our country may be better off because a shrewd and wealthy man has built up therein a great manufacturing business . . . but the whole nation is better, the whole nation is braver, because Cushing pushed his little torpedo boat through the darkness to sink beside the sinking Albermerle." Washington's counsel was based upon the belief that the spirit of faction in republican governments could be inflamed and enlarged through identification with other nations. Roosevelt, in remembering Washington's "forgotten maxim," argues that an aggressive foreign policy is a source of national cohesion. "The memory of every triumph won by Americans, by just so much helps to make each American nobler and better," concluded Roosevelt. The happiness of the commercial Republic of which Washington spoke and which was threatened by the "current of the passions" is replaced by the passions of valor. "The fight well fought, the life honorable lived, the death bravely met—those count for more in building a high and fine type of temper in a nation than any possible success in the stock market, than any possible prosperity in commerce or manufactures."[24]

Washington did argue that should his counsel be followed there would be a time "in a period not far off" when Americans would have the strength to "defy material injury" from foreign powers. To Roosevelt, America had emerged from this period of infancy, under which Washington was handicapped, to the strength of youth.[25] In 1903 he compared America's new international role to its own westward expansion. As Americans had "tread the rugged ways that lead to honor and success" as pioneers, they now stood on the verge of becoming one of the "great expanding nations" in world history.[26] The power and authority of all such nations were eventually destined to decline, but the opportunity now existed for Americans to leave "indelibly their impress on the centuries."

Here was the euphoria of the poet freed. Roosevelt had connected his own youth, with all its associations of indeterminacy and vigor, with the heroic projects of a youthful nation as it stood to remake the world. Only "a small body of shrill eunuchs" could object to embarking upon "the greatest of its opportunities." Roosevelt acted swiftly and repeatedly throughout his administrations to assert American hegemony. He solidified colonial control of the Philippines, fomented revolution in Columbia in order to obtain rights to build the Panama Canal, intervened in the Dominican Republic, pledged U.S. support of the Open Door policy in China, mediated an end to the Russo-Japanese War (for which he became the first American to receive the Nobel Peace Prize). In his 1913 *Autobiography*, TR described his action sending an American fleet around the world as his greatest achievement in foreign policy. He was certain that this decision was "essential" for "our own people especially, but also by other peoples, that the Pacific was as much our home waters as the Atlantic, and that our fleet could and would at will pass from one to the other of the two great oceans."[27]

However talented the president-poet might be, his projects are, nevertheless, connected to Machiavellian fate. Belatedness kept rushing back to confront Roosevelt. It is difficult to imagine reasons why TR decided to seek the nomination of the Republican Party in 1912 independent of his spiritedness and his affliction with belatedness. One of his biographers writes: "Had Theodore Roosevelt been not quite so ambitious, or even a shade less self-righteous, the history of twentieth century politics must surely have been different." TR should have waited out the election and prepared for 1916 if president again he must be. But William Harbaugh captures the dilemma the upcoming election held for a spirited man: "Could he avoid stumbling over himself? Could he for five years do and say the contradictory things necessary to the preservation of his hold on both the right and left? Could he accept the inevitable even after he had convinced himself that Taft's nomination in 1912 was in fact inevitable?"[28] Still, Harbaugh concludes that Roosevelt did not act until he was reasonably certain that he could win renomination by his party. The belated president agrees that these are very difficult maneuvers for a spirited man, but he wonders when exactly Roosevelt himself knew he simply could not or would not undertake them. He does know that Roosevelt's estimation of Taft cascaded in a matter of months from one which concluded that he was not a "bad President," and certainly a better one than McKinley, to the assessment that he was a "flub-dub with a streak of the second rate and the common in him." The belated president notes that on close examination the two estimations are not that far apart in an objective sense. What changed was Roosevelt's willingness to accept a second term for Taft.

These evaluations of TR's decision in 1912 do not, however, satisfy the belated president. He is used to veils and he is suspicious that Roosevelt's policy differences with Taft over foreign policy and the trusts and even his general spirited eagerness do not fully account for Roosevelt's actions. He returns to TR's decision not to seek reelection in 1908 and finds that Roosevelt sought an imitation of his two exemplars: "I regard the memories of Washington and Lincoln as priceless heritages for our people, just because they are the memories of strong men, of men who cannot be accused of weakness or timidity . . . who, nevertheless, led careers marked by disinterestedness just as much as by strength."[29] Four years later, he revised his position. The danger to the Republic rested with a president who sought three consecutive terms. A man "who had been in office eight years and may be thought to have solidified his power by patronage, contracts and the like, using that power to perpetuate himself" represented the kind of threat he had had in mind.[30] In 1908 the colonel was satisfied that a renunciation of a third term was an act of disinterestedness which befitted a strong man. When he reneged on his own assessment, he had redefined the problem in much more banal terms. The danger to seeking a third term came not from the threat of the strong but, in the language of the spirited, from the weak. Presidents in power seek to perpetuate themselves through petty rewards like patronage and contracts. These were never temptations for a spirited man like TR. The belated president returns to Roosevelt's original renunciation and discovers an additional comment: "It is a very unhealthy thing that any man should be considered necessary to the people as a whole, save in the way of meeting some crisis."[31]

"Save in the way of meeting some crisis": this is a phrase which captures the belated president's attention for he knows that from the standpoint of those afflicted with belatedness the invocation of crisis constitutes a reference to internal need. What, he asks, so troubled Roosevelt in 1912? He considers a possibility which could have been the cause for this unexpected "crisis" which accounted for TR's recurrence of belatedness. One involves an estimation on Roosevelt's part that the domestic agenda he fashioned in his two terms was on the verge of moving toward a dramatically different level. Most students of TR emphasize his radical ambivalence toward progressive reformers. From his spirited perspective, capital represented decidedly unheroic projects and labor was incapable of fashioning any. On the other hand, the reformers were somehow unmanly in a different way. In his famous attack on reformers in 1906, Roosevelt used Bunyan's narrative of the Man with the Muck-rake in *Pilgrim's Progress* to criticize those who were so preoccupied with the "filth on the floor" that they were unable to see that which was "lofty" and "spiritual" around them.

To TR the man with the muck-rake was a threat to society because his frame of mind led to a "moral color-blindness" implicating every single individual in the system.[32] The address is often offered as proof of Roosevelt's conservatism, but the belated president sees the attack in terms of TR's spiritedness as a kind of Nietzschean warning against the nihilistic motives of the priests who would forever destroy the capacity of the strong to make history.

Is it possible, wonders the belated president, that Roosevelt revised this assessment in 1912 and concluded that progressive reform was capable of heroic projects? Certainly Roosevelt felt that men such as La Follette and Pinchot were incapable of undertaking them and he had already concluded that the Republican Party regulars were too steeped in materialism to even envision them. We are on the "verge of an economic revolution," declared Roosevelt in 1912.[33] Here was the "crisis," concludes the belated president, and he confirms his assessment when he reads TR's Columbus speech in February in which he affirmed the progressive agenda with a such vigor that he literally snapped any strained relationship with moderates and conservatives. Not only did Roosevelt support control of monopoly prices and initiative, referendum and recall, but he took on that great trump of the grand bourgeoisie, the courts. As a result, the speech was described as a "charter of demagoguery" and "the craziest proposal" that ever came from Roosevelt "or from any other statesman."[34] Roosevelt subsequently insisted that he had always "had a natural tendency to become a Progressive, anyhow," and he framed his "confession of faith" at the Progressive Party convention so earnestly and so vigorously that men like William Allen White said: "I put his heel on my neck and I became his man."

Roosevelt lost, and his loss was all the more infuriating because he not only fared less well in his adopted West as he expected but he was defeated in part by Wilson's adept use of Jefferson, his bête noire, as a weapon against his "New Nationalism." Historians have credited his quixotic campaign with invigorating the Democratic Party as an agent of reform, but to the belated president his defeat must have been an inconsolable misery. TR immediately set out to write his autobiography. Serialized in *Outlook,* his remembrances portrayed himself as a lifelong progressive without mentioning the campaign. He had no interest in the party he spiritedly formed and left his supporters to themselves.

The belated president, however, is impressed with the continued spiritedness of this defeated man as he reads his "History as Literature" address before the American Historical Association in 1913. The lecture contains the same spiritedness, this time directed against historians rather than capital or politicians or reformers, in his attack upon those who lack the vision of "great architects" which even the "most competent mason" could not do without. But the central subject of the address was the indispensability of the lyric in historical studies. It takes the belated president no more than a moment to conclude that Roosevelt's plea to "embody old ghosts" and to "make dead men living before our eyes" is a slightly veiled plea for history to remember the lyric in TR himself. The very best historians, said Roosevelt, were poets as Shakespeare had been in his treatment of Richard III and Keats with Balboa. Years before the colonel had described his adventure in Cuba as his "crowded hour," and now he urged the professionals in his audience not to neglect the extraordinary and the spectacular out of the pursuit of scientific objectivity or cynicism. "There are hours," he pled, "so fraught with weighty achievement, with triumph or defeat, with joy or sorrow, that each such hour may determine all . . . that are to come thereafter."[35] The belated president's heart now softens toward TR, no doubt because he examines him under conditions of his defeat. Nevertheless, he is struck by not only the poignancy of the remarks but by the brave act of self-realization they entailed. "Remember me!" he reads under the veil as he surveys Roosevelt's analysis. "Remember me as a spirited president!"

In a very short time, Roosevelt realized that the opportunity to lead America in war, a project that is essential to any spirited man, was now available to others. Again, belatedness rushed back to attack him. It is the belated poet once again speaking when TR criticized Wilson as another Buchanan knowing that he could never be another Lincoln.[36] Shortly before Roosevelt's death, Edgar Lee Masters (who was especially adroit at lifting poetic veils) was nonetheless so shaken by his visit to the president that he wrote a poem, a portion of which the belated president sits and ponders. He concludes that it is the kind of tribute TR might have hoped for in his spirited quest against belatedness:

> The talk begins.
> He's dressed in canvas khaki, flannel shirt,
> Laced boots for farming, chopping tress, perhaps,
> A stocky frame, curtains of skin on cheeks
> Drained lightly of their fat; gash on the neck
> Where pus was emptied lately; one eye dim,
> And growing dimmer; almost blind in that.
> And when he walks a little like
> A man whose youth is fading, like a cart
> That rolls when springs are old. He is a moose,
> Scarred, battered from the hunters, thickets, stones;
> Some finest tips of antlers broken off,
> And eyes where images of ancient things
> Flit back and forth across them, keeping still
> A certain slumberous indifference
> Or wisdom, it may be.
>
> But then the talk!
> Bronze dolphins in a fountain cannot spout
> More streams at once. Of course the war, the emperor,
> America in the war, his sons in France,
> The dangers, separation, let them go!
> The fate has been appointed—to our task,
> Live full our lives with duty, go to sleep!
> For I say, he exclaims, the man who fears
> To die should not be born, nor left to live.[37]

Chapter 6

JOHN F. KENNEDY: PROMISE

· ·

T he belated president abruptly closes Masters's book of poems. It is precisely this kind of sentimentality that encases my own affliction, he says
to himself. The belated president is determined to move on looking for
other spirited men. He stops for a moment at Harry Truman's presidency. He
already knows that Truman is widely quoted by later presidents as the modern
epitome of spiritedness. The young John Kennedy told an audience that Democrats "have always loved the happy warriors" and compared him to TR's biographical subject, Senator Thomas Hart Benton. Although the president had
never shot anyone as Benton did, "at least anybody we know of," he continued, "nevertheless he has been dueling with heavy artillery at even closer range
for most of his life."[1] Even the genial Republican Reagan spoke fondly of
Truman's spiritedness and enjoyed moments when members of the audience
would shout, "Give 'em Hell!"[2] He does not doubt the president's "plain speaking," his quickness to anger, his irascibility, but he wonders if Truman had ever
been struck by belatedness. Was he too much in the shadow of FDR to even
contemplate his own exceptionalism? The belated president is willing to grant
Truman a certain spiritedness but concludes that it was of a minor sort, the kind
which, to paraphrase the young Lincoln, led him to be more than content with
the presidential chair itself. Perhaps it is this version of spiritedness sans belatedness that makes Truman such an attractive figure to later presidents. Truman
is feisty and salty and a formidable opponent in party wars but really not the
kind of man one has to worry about devouring you.

He comes across Kennedy. While he stops for a moment to ponder the
president's youthful persona and the eagerness with which he attempted to
symbolize the end of what some regarded as the somnolence of the Eisenhower
years, he initially rejects the characterization of spiritedness. He sees Kennedy
as an above-average politician who used his personal attractiveness and family
fortune to grasp the presidency in the name of moderate reform. He was, the

belated president initially thinks, the modern Democratic equivalent to William H. Harrison. That is, JFK represented a deft strategic attempt to break the threat of Republican hegemony through the nomination of a young representative of a new generation unburdened by prewar liberalism. Besides, continues the belated president musing upon the Harrison comparison, here too was a "short" presidency. How could a presidency of a thousand days overcome belatedness? As soon as these words enter his thoughts, the belated president feels the panic that is a typical feature of his affliction. He immediately asks, "If this presidency was so short why the repeated, seemingly endless, examinations of JFK?" No other short presidency, expanded to include single terms, receives this kind of attention, he thinks. He quickly pages through the evaluations of Kennedy from early studies by "Kennedy men" (the large collection of JFK's political, academic and journalistic admirers) to the first revisionists like William G. Carleton, George Kateb, and Henry Pachter, to the another wave of revisionists (Gary Wills, Henry Fairle, Nancy Gager Clinch), to another wave of admirers (Doris Kearns Goodwin, Herbert S. Parmet, Wofford), and still another wave of revisionists (Reeves, Nigel Hamilton).[3] And then there is the truly enormous number of volumes on the assassination, a subject that has received more attention than any other aspect of the Kennedy presidency, including the Cuban missile crisis. He concludes that the "Kennedy myth" is a rolling enterprise, sometimes dialectical and sometimes simply eclectically additive like a snowball that picks up volume in its tumble. Despite these inexorable disclosures, invariably portrayed in the most iconoclastic and sensationalist terms, about JFK's personal amorality, the pathology of his family, connections with organized crime, and the nefarious legacy of his policies, his approval ratings by the public soar.[4] The thought of this ceaselessly moving myth, often expressed in terms of cycles of hope and skepticism or cynicism, and frequently characterized by a raw, insatiable desire to recover something, whatever its essence might be, about the man and this short presidency, terrifies the belated president. That he has experienced this terror before in the face of Washington, Lincoln, and FDR is his only consolation, for he knows now that somehow Kennedy was a "great" president who stands as yet another obstacle to his own greatness.

COOL/HOT

He sets out once again to discover JFK's own sense of belatedness, to look for poetic intent and poetic veils. Since he is now prepared to acknowledge Kennedy's greatness, he totes up a preliminary list of his firsts: the first Catholic president, the youngest elected president, the first president to bring the nation to the brink of nuclear war. Excepting for the truly colossal import of the last item, the belated president is at a loss to find monumental achievements. He finds Kennedy's domestic agenda an imaginative but moderate one that left few immediate achievements of any kind: a tax cut, an upward revision of the minimum wage, a housing act, and a few pilot programs designed to help the poor. The "second reconstruction," which began in Kennedy's administration, certainly qualified as a major historical event, but the president's leadership here was hardly courageous or spirited. In foreign policy, the belated president finds Kennedy careening from crisis to crisis from inaction in the face of the construction of the Berlin Wall to the failure at the Bay of Pigs and ad hoc reaction to communism in Indochina.

The belated president concludes that he faces a unique challenge in overcoming the Kennedy presidency. In respect to other presidents, he acknowledged monumental achievements and then sought to find how belated presidents engineered them through hostile imitations of their predecessors. Here he cannot grasp the achievement in order to locate the poetic intent behind the veil. Is it possible, he considers, that Kennedy's greatness lies primarily in what he *was* rather than what he *did?* Such a possibility deeply troubles the belated president for the proposition, if true, suggests not only a major revision in his definition of monumental achievement but a new obstacle in his own effort to overcome belatedness. Still, the belated president is determined to find the source of JFK's greatness, no matter what in direction it takes him. How else can he relieve this affliction? He thus begins with this hypothesis: Kennedy's monumental achievement rests with his "promise." The "promise" has protean forms, hence the rolling Kennedy myth. The "promise" is in its essence the promise of youth and entails the glorification of vigor and eagerness, the unboundedness of future projects, and the potential for personal development. These qualities represent, of course, the nature of the positive side of spiritedness, qualities which Jackson encapsulated in his iron will and Theodore Roosevelt in his ceaseless energy. The key here for the belated president is that age eventually overtook Jackson's will as it did with TR, as so beautifully captured in Masters's poetry. Spirited men are able to carry their vigor well into their chronological lives (Jackson was even reputed to have said during his last days that he was dying as fast as he could), but the citizen cannot fail to see the aged frames which encase spiritedness even if, as was the case with Jackson, they highlight thymos. Nor can they fail to evaluate the monumental achievements of the spirited. With Kennedy, however, his youth is frozen. As William G. Carleton noted in 1964, Kennedy's spiritedness became after his assassination mixed with the "mystic, the tragic." His death had in it "the touch of the religious epic, of man pitted against fate." Kennedy was "surely one favored by the gods, one possessed of power, wealth, youth, the aura of manly war heroism, zest for living, personal charm and beauty, glamour, imagination, keen insight, intelligence, immense popularity, the adoring love of family and friends." But he was also one "cut down in a flash" in the "fullness of his strength."[5] There is no thought here, hence the beauty of the tragedy, of a gray, paunchy, cigar-addicted former president, conniving behind the scenes to advance epigone of his patriarchy and struggling to come to terms with postmodern culture and post–Cold War politics.

The belated president is willing to accept Kennedy's exceptional status as one related to "The Promise," as he now calls it, but he is determined to unearth the relationship between The Promise and JFK's spiritedness and hopefully his attempts to overcome belatedness. He now knows that Kennedy's achievements are not monumental in themselves but somehow tethered to The Promise through the spiritedness the president exuded. Yet he is puzzled by the nature of JFK's spirited persona. It is true, of course, that Kennedy's youthful persona captured a sense of eagerness and energy, but he knows that the defining characteristic of spirited men is that they are quick to anger and especially prone to violence in word if not deed. But all of Kennedy's commentators emphasize his detachment and restraint. Arthur Schlesinger Jr., for example, described JFK's youthful essay, "Why England Slept," as "so cool and clinical . . . so skeptical of the notion that the individual could affect events."[6] And Norman Mailer, who succeeded perhaps more than others in capturing the nature of the Kennedy's spiritedness, noted his "aloofness," "detachment," and "elusiveness" at press conferences.[7] The belated president begins to doubt his categorization of Kennedy as a spirited one. But he reads more of Mailer's description of JFK:

> His personal quality had a subtle, not quite describable intensity, a suggestion of dry pent heat perhaps, his eyes large, the pupils grey, the whites prominent, almost shocking, his most forceful feature; he had the eyes of a mountaineer. His appearance changed with his mood, strikingly so, and this made him always more interesting than what he was saying. He would seem at one moment older than his age, forty-eight or fifty, a tall, slim, sunburned professor with a pleasant weathered face, not even particularly handsome; five minutes later, talking at a press conference on his lawn, three microphones before him, a television camera turning, his appearance would have gone through a metamorphosis, he would look again like a movie star, his coloring vivid, his manner rich, his gestures strong and quick, alive with that concentration of vitality a successful actor always seems to radiate.[8]

The belated president compares this description to the one he had studied of Jackson in New Orleans. He is, of course struck by the incongruity between the circumstances in the descriptions. Jackson was a triumphant general on horseback and Kennedy an aspiring presidential candidate before microphones. Still there is that same sense of awe before a spirited man as Mailer witnesses Kennedy, whose persona he concludes is "conquistadorial," and there is the same perception of will beneath the physical exterior. In this case, it is Kennedy's middle-agedness which clashes with his youthful glamour. But while this hero reportage supports his inclination to view Kennedy in terms of spiritedness, he is most struck by a phrase in the earlier portion of the description of Mailer: "A suggestion of dry pent heat perhaps." The belated president is reminded of a dichotomy offered by the controversial media theorist of the period, Marshall McLuhan. It was common in the Kennedy era to note the impact of television on presidential politics, and Kennedy became known as the first electronic president. McLuhan himself concluded that in the 1960 television debates Kennedy appeared the "shy young sheriff" and Nixon the "railway lawyer."

Kennedy was nonchalant, slightly blurred—"cool"—and hence ideal for the new medium.[9] Was, the belated president wonders, Kennedy a spirited man whose persona took on the form of "cool" rather the traditional "hot" of Jackson and Theodore Roosevelt?

The belated president is not particularly interested in McLuhan's theories and his emendations on hot and cool, but he is fascinated with the relationship between the two tropes on the question of Kennedy's spiritedness. He first examines hot and cool as forms of spiritedness. Mailer offered one connection in his suggestion that JFK's detachment indicated a "dry pent heat." He thinks of a line from Whitman, "the love in the heart long pent, now loose, now at last tumultuously bursting," and sees coolness as a form of thysis. To Mailer, JFK's detachment was the shape his spiritedness took. Kennedy's battle with U.S. Steel was hardly equivalent as a monumental achievement to Jackson's Bank War, but the belated president does think it illustrates the relationship between cool and hot in Kennedy's own mind. To the president the big steel's announcement that it would raise prices was equivalent to a "cold, deliberate fucking." "They fucked us, and we've got to try to fuck them," he told Ben Bradlee. This is a classic example of thysis, an immediate "hot" response to insult. In his April new conference, Kennedy described the action in more polite but still hot terms. While Americans were risking their lives abroad and union members were sacrificing wages, a "tiny handful of steel executives whose pursuit of private power and profit exceeds their sense of public responsibility . . . show . . . utter contempt for the interests of 185 million Americans." But the description of steel's action also reveals Kennedy's own conception of cool. The corporation had engaged in a "cool, deliberate fucking" and he would return this calculated act of sodomy in the same terms. To Kennedy, cool and hot, rationality and domination, were interconnected and, hence, Bradlee thought he learned from the episode the secret of JFK's coolness. He loved James Bond novels for "the cool, the sex and the brutality."[10]

It is this cool version of spiritedness which could threaten a belated president's projects even more than the more common hot variation since it entails a Nietzschean obliviousness and objectivization of those who come across the spirited one's path should it be fully exposed. Hence Midge Dexter was moved to conclude that the style of "Kennedyism" emanated from "the assertion of the right" to rule on the part of superior men. Even Mailer wondered, despite his sympathetic portrait of Kennedy's detached "conquistadorial" style, if this young man should make "the national psyche . . . shiver in its sleep" at night.[11]

The Promise blocked off any systematic assessment of this sort, however, since, so the mythical narrative reads, Kennedy's ruthlessness was worn away by his experience as he "grew" in office. The belated president does, however, note another aspect of the cool/hot thematic. This one advanced Kennedy's battle against belatedness. No president, particularly no Democratic president, could help but be stricken with a sense of belatedness whenever he had the courage to stand poetically before FDR. Kennedy's own case was heightened by the fact that his father, himself once stricken with presidential aspiration, had fallen before Roosevelt. The youthful Kennedy was a dutiful son of the New Deal in domestic programs, energetically supporting national medical care and other liberal causes while he seemed to carve out positions on what had become the right of even Cold War liberalism in foreign policy. As a congressman he criticized the Yalta agreement (negotiated by a "sick Roosevelt") and voted to limit presidential terms, legislation which every American knew was itself a belated attempt to rein in FDR. Russia was a "slave state . . . embarked upon a program of world domination." Kennedy supported the "get tough with Russia policy . . . most vigorously."[12] His general relationship with the liberal wing of the party was correct but cool. He politely rejected Eleanor Roosevelt's assertion that he was too much under his father's control. Generally hesitant to call himself a liberal, a word whose current definition had been created by Roosevelt, he offered this explanation, an unusual combination of guile and frankness, in 1956 in response to a questioner who had spoken of the "somewhat emotionless quality" of his liberalism: "In 1946 I really knew nothing about these things. I had no background particularly; in my family we were interested not so much in the ideas of politics as in the mechanics of the whole process. Then I found myself in Congress representing the poorest district in Massachusetts. Naturally, the interests of my constituents let me to take the liberal line; all the pressures converged to that end."[13] That his family (read his father) had only been interested in the "mechanics" of politics and not the figure of FDR is equivocation bordering on dishonesty. That he "found himself in Congress" continues the veiled answer. Any reputed liberalism on his part must be taken in terms of his representative functions.

Necessity forced JFK to honor the name of Roosevelt when he became a presidential candidate in 1960. But the standard speech he offered to party activists is easily decoded by the belated president. Kennedy remembered how at Franklin Field in 1936 FDR had fallen down, got up, and delivered "one of his most buoyant, winning speeches." In the language of belatedness: FDR was disabled; I am young and as "buoyant" as his speeches were. The remembered address itself spoke of the fact that governments and presidents can err but "the immortal Dante tells us that divine justice weighs the sins of the cold-blooded and the sins of the warm-hearted in different scales. Better the occasional faults of a government that lives in a spirit of charity than the omissions of a Government frozen in the ice of indifference." In the language of belatedness: FDR made mistakes.

The belated president too notes the opposition of cool/hot in the speech JFK chose to remember. Throughout the primaries, the campaign and his administration, Kennedy repeatedly contrasted the "hot" ideology of the New Deal with the "cool" approach of the New Frontier. Hot/cool served several functions in Kennedy's terminology. Sometimes it meant rational rather than emotional: It was the task of Democrats "to use the impulses of liberalism without creating an impulsive party." Sometimes it meant effective rather than simply morally right. To James MacGregor Burns in 1960, Kennedy's cool liberalism should be given a chance. This "liberalism without tears" came from a man who was not "in love with lost causes" but with political effectiveness.[14] Sometimes it even meant masculine rather than feminine. In response to Eleanor Roosevelt's charge that he was reckless, Kennedy wondered aloud about her candidate's sexual preference. "He must be a switcher," JFK told a friend.[15] It was Arthur Schlesinger Jr., however, who theorized a distinctiveness to the New Frontier that separated it from the New Deal. New Frontiersmen disdained moralism and reflected instead a coolness that was derived from a belief that things must be done because they are "national and necessary" rather than because they are "just and right."[16] If Kennedy's liberalism represented a "politics of modernity," what did Roosevelt's entail? Clearly from the vantage point of JFK's belatedness, FDR's politics, hot or cool, were a precursor to his own. In 1961, Kennedy told the president of Harvard: "When Franklin had this job, it was a cinch. He didn't have all these world problems. He had only to cope with poverty in the United States, but look what I've got."[17]

Kennedy's surpassing of FDR, like all of his achievements, is tied to The Promise. But the belated president can determine the outlines of his more general strategy against belatedness by surveying other exceptional men who stood in his path. Part of JFK's persona rested with his establishment of an intimate familiarity with the nation's past leaders. *Profiles in Courage,* published in 1955, was conceived as part of a strategy which would position him for the presidency. In the mythic narrative, a young leader, temporarily in medical exile and privately courageously confronting pain, reflects upon the public courage of the nation's great leaders—among them John Quincy Adams, Daniel Webster, Thomas Hart Benton, Sam Houston. Here is JFK, biographer and the young man of intellect, who very much like his fellow spirited president, Theodore Roosevelt, searches history for the "inspiration" it can provide.[18]

Questions about the authorship of the volume plagued Kennedy throughout his life.[19] The belated president, however, is less interested in JFK's role as researcher than his conceptualization of the project which most participants and biographers acknowledge to be Kennedy's. Every contributor to the book offered his own favorite man of courage. Kennedy seemed most intrigued with John Quincy Adams; Arthur Krock suggested Robert Taft; Sorenson, George Norris. The individual narratives show the touch of knowledgeable historians, and certainly the overall style reflected Sorenson's efforts. The general theme of the project, however, intrigues the belated president. Sorenson acknowledges that the Kennedy influence was strongest in the first and last chapters. It is in these chapters that the belated president detects, in a veiled way to be sure, Kennedy's struggle with belatedness.

The introduction to the volume leans heavily upon autobiographical experience. Every politician, Kennedy included, faces enormous pressures to discard his principles. He must learn to "get along" with his colleagues; he must be concerned about reelection; he faces constituency pressures in the form of public opinion and interest groups; he must accept the leadership of his political party. While Kennedy is careful to acknowledge the authority of each of these pressures ("We should not be too hasty in condemning all compromises as bad morals" and "the legislator has some responsibility to conciliate these opposing forces"), the belated president sees the lament of one who suffers from the same affliction as he. "Where else," JFK complains, "but in the political profession is the individual expected to sacrifice all—including his own career—for the national good? . . . In no other occupation but politics is it expected that a man will sacrifice honors, prestige and his chosen career on a single issue." Lawyers, businessmen, teachers, doctors face difficult decisions, but "few if any, face the same dread finality of decision that confronts a Senator facing an important role call." Senator Kennedy concludes by describing a mythical constituent "perched on his desk" like "the Raven in Poe's poem . . . croaking, 'Nevermore'" as he casts his vote. To the belated all manner of forces contrive to confine those afflicted and Kennedy adds that even his hero John Quincy Adams was not confronted with the restrictions of modern politics—public relations men and a Cold War which encouraged "rigid ideological conformity and orthodox patterns of thought."[20]

The belated president is aware that, like Theodore Roosevelt's, Kennedy's objects of biographical study are failures, at least in terms of any success in the relief of belatedness. Houston, Webster, and Taft were never able to seize the presidential chair, and Adams's act of courage did not prevent his later eclipse in the face of Jackson nor, in Kennedy's words, his complicity in his elevation through the "schemes of Henry Clay." Unlike Roosevelt, however, Kennedy does not study these courageous men as exemplars of failure (although the fact that none held monumental achievements that the Senator must surpass makes his project a more simple one) for he conflates the actions of each into a single recognizable achievement, the exhibition of "the most admirable of human virtues." Courageousness, for Kennedy, is a virtue that cannot be taught. His "stories make clear" that courage requires "no exceptional qualifications, no magic formula, no special combination of time, place and circumstance."[21]

The belated president sees similarities in *Profiles in Courage* to Lincoln's Lyceum speech. The object of Lincoln's struggle against belatedness was the great founding leaders of the Republic who stood before him as barriers to monumental projects. He cast out these ghosts by detecting a love of fame in their achievements and creating a monumental project for himself by asserting that the pillars they had erected were in decay. The object of the young Kennedy's frustration are not great men but the "sea of popular rule." The stories he told were stories of men "who accomplished good in the face of cruel calumnies from the public." The Senator was careful to keep the veil over his poetic intent: "This book is not intended to disparage democratic government or popular rule." We cannot solve the problems of "independence and responsibility by abolishing or curtailing democracy," he insisted. But he reminded his audience that a democracy which fails to acknowledge courageous men "is not worthy to bear the name."[22]

Profiles in Courage reflected Kennedy's cool spiritedness. None of his courageous men were "fanatics and extremists" (although it is hard not to place

Calhoun in that category) and each was "shadowed by a veil which cannot be torn away." Nevertheless, the volume is an extended argument that mass democracies make room for the spirited. The concluding chapter is a rumination on the sources of courage. Senator Kennedy describes what the ancients knew as thymos. Kennedy rejects the notion that each of these courageous men "wholly forgot about himself in his dedication to higher principles" as "hero-worship." He argues that courageous men so act not "because they love the public better than themselves": "On the contrary, it was precisely because they did *love themselves*—because each one's need to maintain his own respect for himself was more important to him than his popularity with others—because his desire to win or maintain a reputation for integrity and courage was stronger than his desire to maintain his office—because his conscience, his personal standard of ethics, his integrity or morality, call it what you will—was stronger than the pressures of public approval because his faith that *his* course was the best one, and ultimately be vindicated, outweighed his fear of public reprisal."[23] Kennedy quoted John Adams in support of his theory, which fit neatly with New England rectitude, and has led some observers to conclude that *Profiles* was a restatement of conservative Whig philosophy, but the belated president knows that the quote could have been uttered by Homer's Achilles or Socrates' guardian warrior or even Nietzsche's true aristocrat. Perhaps only the belated could detect the dual acknowledgment in *Profiles*, the acknowledgment on the young Kennedy's part of his own spiritedness and his demand that it be accorded respect by the mass public despite the fact that Kennedy's own career to date gave no indication how he actually deserved to be included among his profiles. Yet the work did seem to have this effect, since, as always, any such claim was tethered to The Promise. Kennedy "was thought to be a deep thinker, an important writer, a champion of principle, a conqueror of adversity, and a politician of the highest promise." *Profiles in Courage* celebrated this image, and the Democratic National convention was only a few months away.[24]

If from the standpoint of belatedness *Profiles in Courage* established Kennedy as a spirited man, a "conqueror of adversity," what directions could his cool thymos take? Kennedy's early speeches reveal a restlessness characteristic of the spirited. A 1949 address on Columbus Day illustrates the young Kennedy's eagerness. A tribute to Columbus was, of course, de rigueur for a congressman representing a district with a large Italian American constituency. But the young JFK's appraisal of Columbus was so effusive that it gives the belated president some pause. Kennedy compared the explorer to Christ. As Jesus sought to inform the world about the Kingdom of God, Columbus sought a new land, realizing "the time had come for the emancipation of humanity." "God always has in training some commanding genius for the control of great crises in the affairs of nations and peoples," and the young Kennedy expressed his awe for Columbus. He was no king, but a "proud beggar" who had demanded aristocratic standing as the payment for his adventures. He admired his "daring spirits" and his "picturesque figure." Columbus possessed the "zeal of Peter the Hermit, the courage of CID, and the imagination of Dante."[25]

The youthful Kennedy also showed great interest in other adventurers and spirited aristocrats: T. E. Lawrence (who said in his *Seven Pillars of Wisdom* that "Blood was always on our hands; we were licensed to kill"), John Buchan (who wrote of his friend in JFK's favorite book, *Pilgrim's Way*, "He disliked emotion not because he felt lightly but because he felt deeply"), and Lord Melbourne. In subsequent years, Kennedy expressed admiration for Shakespeare's young Prince Hal and the spirited Henry V, who spoke of his troops at St. Crispin as "we few, we happy few, we band of brothers" and declared that later men would "think themselves accurs'd they were not there."[26] Then, of course, there were the press references to the young King Arthur of Camelot, which were further magnified by the media in the most maudlin ways and encouraged by the Kennedy family after his death as the "brief shining moment" of The Promise.

The belated president is hardly surprised by these identifications with daring young men with their allusions to aristocratic élan. This is certainly the stuff the spirited feed upon, he says. What initially puzzles him, however, is Kennedy's general neglect of the spirited American presidents and his treatment of the monumental ones who faced crises like Henry V's. From his early speeches to presidential addresses, Kennedy made ongoing, plentiful dutiful references to these exemplars, as the belated president had noted in regard to FDR, but the commentary was rarely extended and always quickly folded into the ephebian charge. For example, in his 1963 televised civil rights address, Kennedy noted that Lincoln had freed slaves one hundred years ago, "yet their heirs, their grandsons, are not fully free." Jefferson, not FDR, Washington, or Lincoln, was Kennedy's most frequently cited presidential exemplar. Kennedy was fond of citing the Declaration of Independence as a "revolutionary document" with international significance. It was a "trumpet call" to freedom which would provide a foundation for America's "leadership in that world-wide movement for independence to any nation or society committed to systematic human suppression."[27]

Jackson and TR had remade Jefferson and Washington into spirited presidents respectively in order to engage in their ephebian projects, but Kennedy seems to have engaged in no such effort. Thus the belated president draws a schema of the relationship between the mythical figures which so excited Kennedy's imagination and the presidents he cited. There were, so Kennedy said under poetic veil, youthful, spirited men who arrived at various points of history, men of vigor and daring with aristocratic heritage who could energize a nation. The references to monumental historical figures of youth served to confirm Kennedy's persona as a "thoughtful" politician, but to the belated president this aspect of the Kennedy intellect was a veil to hide poetic intent. He thus finds the president's reference to the Greek practice of honoring a young victor returning home from the Olympic games by ripping a hole in the town's wall as symbolic assurance that "any polis possessed of such a hero had no need of a wall to defend it" as poetically significant.[28] Men like Columbus and Lawrence stood on the outside of the political system, as did spirited aristocrats who, like Prince Hal and Melbourne, enjoyed what only seemed like the dissipation of youth until called for their moment of glory by the elders who would honor them for their talent and bravery. Hence Kennedy's perpetual calls for "service" could serve as a poetic project, the trumpet summoning rededication in the form of an ephebian charge in the name of America's exceptional presidents taken as a composite, and as a veil for poetic intent.

COLD WAR/HOT WAR

But where, as the belated president, does a man of such spirited vision find heroic acts to perform in America of the 1960s? The president-elect exhibited the restlessness characteristic of the spirited when he spoke before the Massachusetts state legislature the week before his inauguration. The address firmly encased Kennedy's president project within the New England tradition of service, but the belated president notes the spirited reading Kennedy offered of the Puritan experiment. Citation of Winthrop's "city on the hill" speech aboard the *Arbella* is a standard of American political discourse, but the young president-elect enspirited the address. Winthrop quoted Isaiah as part of a plea that the settlement could only be a success if its participants "delight in each other, make others conditions our own, rejoice together, mourn together, labor and suffer together, always having before our eyes our community as members of the same body." Kennedy took from the city on the hill a pledge for heroic action on the part of an elite, "aware of their grave trust and their great responsibilities," who possessed "courage, judgment, integrity, dedication" as they approached a "perilous frontier."[29]

A sluggish economy might provide some outlet, and Kennedy did pledge to "get America moving again." But without capital in disarray and national fear intense and widespread as it was in 1932, JFK could find no occasion for the wall to be ripped open, nor did he seem to have the taste to precipitate an economic crisis in the Jacksonian manner, even though the steel crisis afforded him an opportunity.

The race question was clearly a crack in the wall, but Kennedy chose not to make an opening. During the 1960 presidential campaign, JFK deftly worked the civil rights issue. He supported a strong pledge in the party platform, although he complained to Sorenson later that it raised "unwarranted hopes."[30] His effort to gain the release of Martin Luther King from a Georgia prison sentence, which gained him enormous support in the black community, was undertaken with extreme caution. His selection of LBJ was undertaken over objections from the party's Left. The unique aspect of his campaign was his emphasis on the contribution which a "strong" president could make to civil rights through moral persuasion, legislative proposal, and executive order. The later option particularly attracted activists who were disappointed when Kennedy delayed not only legislative proposals but also a housing order. What they had left was a president who granted more access and gave clearer moral support but also could be testy when challenged about his commitments. During a meeting with Father Theodore Hesburgh shortly after his inauguration, the president corrected him on several minor points regarding segregation. When Hesburgh complained that there were no Negroes in the Alabama National Guard, Kennedy replied: "I may have to send the Alabama National Guard to Berlin tomorrow and I don't want to do it in the middle of a revolution at home."[31] It is true, notes the belated president, that Kennedy's June 1963 speech represented a major departure on race since it recommended to Congress sweeping change in ending segregation and securing voting rights. Kennedy spoke eloquently (and all the more impressively because portions of the address were adlibbed) of the morality of the cause. Yet again, there was the tether to the Cold War and its consequences for maintaining a martial ethics, this time one which required action: "When Americans are sent to Viet Nam or West Berlin, we do not ask for whites only."[32]

No, concludes the belated president, the prize that Kennedy eyed was contained somewhere in the endless Cold War, which had been conducted now for almost fifteen years without victory in sight. He cites, as just one example, Kennedy's tirade in the company of Richard Nixon after the Bay of Pigs: "It really is true that foreign affairs is the only important issue for a President to handle, isn't it? I mean, who gives a shit if the minimum wage is $1.15 or $1.25 in comparison to something like this?"[33]

The youthful Kennedy was always fascinated with the Cold War and searched for openings from which victory could be seized. Cold War rhetoric was always hyperbolic, but Kennedy's certainly kept up with the most strident. He spoke of the Soviet Union as a "slave state" and warned of the "storm troops of the new totalitarianism," and described the upcoming "crisis" and the "darkening scene" of a hot war. He declaimed the "loss of China" (which was generally a Republican gloss) "saved" by "our young men" and "frittered away" by the president and his diplomats and discovered a submarine gap between the United States and the Soviet Union.[34]

The new president's pledge in his inaugural that America would "pay any price, bear any burden, meet any hardship" in the cause of American freedom initiated an administration restless and eager to bring the Cold War to some kind of resolution. Thus the belated president sees Kennedy commanding a global "great battlefield" careening from one international crisis to another, heating up the arms race, encouraging citizen fallout shelters, and forming policy outside existing bureaucratic structures. The focus of the un-routinization of the Cold War soon settled on Cuba, which became in the minds of this president and his band of brothers the equivalent of a Carthage. The belated president wonders if the liberation of Cuba might have been the heroic act which Kennedy thought might bring his poetically inspired city to knock down the wall for him. The campaign to destabilize Cuba is now well known. There were assassination attempts, including clandestine governmental contracts with organized crime, and the recruitment and training of an exile army on American soil. How humiliating! How galling must have been the debacle at the Bay of Pigs, if the president had set his eyes on Cuba as his prize and relief from belatedness! concludes the belated president.[35]

The belated president now studies two narratives of Cuba, Kennedy and The Promise. One emphasizes the invasion as an Eisenhower project, a replication of the Guatemala venture, and notes the insight Kennedy gained from the failure. To Sorenson, for example, the Bay of Pigs showed that Kennedy's "luck and his judgment had human limitations," and the experience "taught him invaluable lessons for the future."[36] Proof of the maturity lies in the Cuban missile crisis a year and a half later in which the president "dazzled the world" with his "combination of toughness and restraint, of will, nerve and wisdom, so brilliantly controlled, so matchlessly calibrated."[37] Thus the Bay of Pigs had been a small price to pay for the leadership that emerged in the second crisis. Another speaks of the recklessness of Operation Mongoose and asserts that Kennedy "learned nothing from the first crisis."[38] It was, so this narrative reads, counterinsurgency in Cuba which propelled the Soviets to install missiles. Here the critical narrative takes two turns. One describes Kennedy's recklessness in the second crisis, setting deadlines for Soviet responses and making public demands, rather than exercising diplomacy. Thus Gary Wills writes in support of the first turn in his discussion of Kennedy's refusal to accept a simple trade of Cuban for Turkish missiles:

> [JFK] wanted to remove the missiles provided he did not appear forced to bargain with the Soviets to accomplish this. He must deliver the ultimatum, make demands that made Russia act submissively. He would not, as he put it, let Khrushchev rub his nose in the dirt. Which meant that he had to rub Khrushchev's nose in the dirt; and that Khrushchev had to put up with it. Kennedy would even risk nuclear war rather than admit that a trade of useless missiles near each other's countries was eminently fair. The restraint, then, was not shown by Kennedy, but by Khrushchev. He was the one who had to back down, admit his maneuver failed, take the heat from internal critics for his policy.[39]

Another concludes that despite all the bravado, JFK got the worst part of the bargain as he had done at the Bay of Pigs, in Berlin and in Laos. The second turn emphasizes what Kennedy "lost" in the missile crisis. The pledge to never invade Cuba placed the island in the communist orbit for the foreseeable future and Khrushchev received private assurances that the missiles in Turkey, which symbolically "crowded" the Soviets (as he had illustrated to the Americans by his Cuban initiative) would be removed as well. Robert Smith Thompson thus reaches this conclusion based upon assessments like the above: "The more appropriate lesson of the missile crisis might be in the ancient idea of hubris, pride, arrogance, and that these qualities lead to a fall. As sure that they could control the Caribbean and indeed the world as they controlled their own campaign, the Kennedys found themselves, in the end, faced down by that stubby little peasant, Nikita Khrushchev."[40]

The belated president ponders these narratives. He knows, of course, that these assessments involve weighing contradictory and incomplete evidence. Was the installation of the missiles, for example, primarily a response to a threat of invasion (as the Soviets now insist) or was it an attempt to gain a quick and cheap parity with Kennedy's nuclear buildup, using Cuban frightfulness as an opportunity?[41] If the later was the case, then Kennedy appears the "winner," since the withdrawal of the weapons would be more significant than the continued existence of a communist Cuba. What interests the belated president more, however, is how each narrative of the crisis is also a narrative of Kennedy's spiritedness and The Promise. The first becomes an exemplary example of JFK's coolness. The president carefully weighs alternatives, rejects the irresponsible advice of both "hawks" and "doves," undertakes imaginative decision-making procedures (Excom), policies (the blockade), and channels of communication (the Scali connection, RFK's meetings with Dobrynin, and the response to Khrushchev's first letter), and permits his opponent room to maneuver. Here, concludes the belated president, is a description of the attraction of spiritedness. Only a spirited man would possess the nerves and resolve to bring such a crisis to a peaceful conclusion. Here it is (cool) spiritedness which saves America and the world from nuclear war. Thus, if the president had accepted the counsel of Senators Fulbright and Russell or segments of the military establishment, America would have invaded Cuba and perhaps precipitated a nuclear holocaust. If the president had accepted Stevenson's counsel, America would have suffered ignominious defeat by negotiating with nuclear blackmailers. Kennedy himself offered his own version of this narrative lesson when he remarked to Bradlee "without vindictiveness that he felt the country was lucky that Nixon had not been president during the Cuban missile crisis."[42]

On the second narrative, however, the underbelly of spiritedness emerges. Kennedy the (cool) spirited becomes Kennedy the (hot) reckless. The crisis itself is precipitated by Kennedy's own recklessness in regard to Cuba, and the president so structures his response as to force Khrushchev to "blink." Or perhaps, so suggests the other version of the critical narrative, the crisis reveals Kennedy's youthful immaturity. Kennedy's "indecisiveness and lack of experience was never more clearly evident," concludes one critic. One participant complained about the "high school thought" exhibited by the president and his brother during the ExComm meetings and the administration's systematic downgrading of the ragged details of the postcrisis period (the insistence that the Turkish missiles were obsolete and the secrecy about the agreement to dismantle them; the failure to force UN supervision of removal of missiles in Cuba).[43]

The belated president observes how each of these narratives of spiritedness (spiritedness as courageous resolve, spiritedness as recklessness and spiritedness as immaturity) makes its way to The Promise. In the first, Kennedy surely overcomes belatedness. He is the *only* president to face a direct confrontation with the Soviets in the Cold War and he is the *only* president to have faced the imminent possibility of nuclear war. Even Lincoln and FDR never faced a crisis so colossal as this. In fact, the missile crisis was described as "the Gettysburg of the Cold War" and the "greatest personal diplomatic victory of any President in our history."[44] Moreover, The Promise tells us that Kennedy singlehandedly altered the direction of the Cold War by confronting the Cold War apparat and, as is suggested in his American University speech, laying a foundation for its end. Had Kennedy lived, so says this version of The Promise, there would never have been a Vietnam. The belated president is now an expert in detecting how presidents enclose their achievements so that no successor can overcome them and now he seethes with resentment at the prospect of succeeding a man with such accomplishments. The substance of Kennedy's speech before the nation on October 22 reiterated the same application of the Munich model that had been offered by three previous presidents ("The 1930s taught us a clear lesson: aggressive conduct, if allowed to go unchecked and unchallenged, ultimately leads to war") and repeated America's resolve as he had done in his inaugural ("We will not prematurely or unnecessarily risk the costs of world-wide nuclear war in which the fruits of victory would be ashes in our mouth, but neither will we shrink from the risk at any time it must be faced").[45] But the president delivered these words after cabinet members had been given passes to fallout shelters, nuclear missiles and submarines worldwide were on ready alert, SAC nuclear bombers were airborne, the U.S. Army's First Armored Division and other combat units were poised to invade Cuba, and 180 navy ships roamed the Caribbean.

The belated president receives, of course, some solace from the other narratives, narratives which suggest that Kennedy left a legacy of recklessness or even inadequacy. "For three decades . . . the 'lesson' of the Cuban missile crisis has persisted in the textbooks of our minds," says one critic. "When confronted by aggression, you hang tough, stay cool, show flexibility over minor points, but never yield major ones . . . keep the bludgeon nearby."[46] But the belated president knows these intimations of The Promise are the narratives of a minority, and his anger rises.

He is now in a state of panic as he surveys the assassination literature. That day in Dallas became the defining political event for a generation of Americans who found that the loss of the their young leader "killed at the height of his powers" left them in a state of grief with physical ailments and clinical symptoms of depression.[47] For the next generation the assassination grew into a narrative that seemed to overwhelm the Kennedy presidency itself as it took on the Shakespearean status of telling "sad stories of kings." The belated president especially notes that every assassination theory involves a connection to Kennedy's spiritedness and The Promise. For those who believe that Oswald acted alone, Kennedy's death symbolized the capriciousness of the human condition. The slain president might have escaped had not a thousand acts of fate intervened. For those who refuse to accept the lone assassin theory, the death of the president is sometimes traced to the first narrative: The courageous young president had decided to radically alter the course of the Cold War, for which he was killed by his own Cold War apparat. Sometimes it is traced to the second: The reckless young president who had unroutinized the Cold War was brought down by his own intended assassination target (Castro) or by those dark forces he had awakened (anti-Castro operatives/organized crime forces acting separately or in concert).[48]

The belated president is shaken by his study of spirited presidents. He now knows that even these eager, restless men, men unable to hide their poetic intent, are still capable of poetic achievements. To date none has quite gained parity with the monumental poet-presidents, but Americans reserve a special affection for spirited men even in (or perhaps because of) their residual fear of them. On the other hand, the belated president knows that while he may not be himself a spirited one, he has learned from FDR's imitation of Jackson that the possibility exists for the creation of a spirited moment. Thus he considers the replicability (and, of course, the surpassing) of Jackson's moment against the Bank of the United States, TR's foreign policy adventures, and JFK's moment in the Cuban missile crisis. He knows that the likelihood of reproducing the latter, particularly in light of the narrative richness and inventiveness of The Promise, is probably beyond his reach. His affliction flares when he ponders this conclusion, but he consoles himself that perhaps a series of spirited moments might compensate.

These musings hardly produce a placidity on the belated president's part. He finds himself quite jittery when he admits to himself the chances of successfully producing a string of spirited moments. As always, he concludes that his only relief lies in further study.

Part III

MINOR AND FAILED PRESIDENTS

. . . .

Glendower: I can call spirits from the vasty deep.
Hotspur: Why so can I, or so can any man;
But will they come when you do call them?

—*Henry IV, Part I*

• •

The belated president now has studied six great presidents—Washington, Lincoln, FDR, Jackson, Theodore Roosevelt, Kennedy—and divided them into monumental and spirited ones. He has examined their various strategies to overcome belatedness: Washington's creation of an aegis, Lincoln's double crosses, FDR's geniality, and the struggles of Jackson, TR, and JFK to present their spiritedness in benevolent terms. He poses a question for himself: Do I need to analyze more presidents? He knows that not all presidents are afflicted with belatedness, and then the thought occurs to him that not all belated presidents are successful in overcoming their affliction. Two possibilities strike him: are there belated presidents who partially overcome belatedness? Are there belated presidents who struggle mightily but are unable to overcome their affliction? These two prospects excite the suffering president, not simply because he feels he can examine men who do not strike terror in his belated heart but because he feels that an examination of what he has just named minor poets and failed poets might complete his process of self-medication.

What, asks the belated president, makes a minor poet? Is not the status of subordinate, subordinate even if to the monumental, a failure? Should not minor poets be conflated into the category of failed ones? Is not the overcoming of belatedness a zero-sum game and is it not this aspect that makes belatedness so sublime an affliction? The belated president considers these questions he has posed for himself and is ready to conclude that the status of minor poet is a kind of failure. But he is also ready to conclude that there is something lacking in the resolution of the question as expressed in those presidential performance polls that rate presidents as "near great" or "above average." A minor poet is still a poet nevertheless, in a way that a failed poet is a poet. For him, the language of belatedness marks off rather clearly dutiful and competent presidents and presidents who were conventional flops from poets of any poetic status. Thus a 1962 poll rated Cleveland, Adams, Jackson, and Theodore Roosevelt as "above average" and a 1982 poll rated Nixon and Harding as "failures."[1] To the belated president there is a world of poetic difference between Cleveland and Jackson and Nixon and Harding. Thus the belated president discards the language of good or above-average and failed presidencies for poetically incomplete or flawed ones and is willing to grant a certain fluidity in regard to the latter categories. He is even willing to consider the proposition that from the standard of belatedness there may be a striking inversion of the conventional rating system; that is, a failed poet-president might be more "successful" than a minor one.

The belated president's research strategy now must be slightly revised. Heretofore, his task of identification had been a simple one. He declared: These are the monumental ones and these are the spirited ones. As he sets out to study minor poets, he finds that he requires a somewhat different theoretical framework. He could never ignore a monumental president on the grounds that he had studied one of them. Uncovering Washington's poetic intent would not suffice passing over Lincoln. But minor poets do not fully overcome belatedness since they do not fully surpass the influence of their "fathers." However "near great" Truman, John Adams, Polk, and LBJ might be in regard to the achievements of their administrations, it is difficult to speak of any of them without reference to FDR, Washington, Jackson, or JFK. Thus the incompleteness of the poetic project which characterizes the minor poet forms a narrative less closed than those of both the monumental president and the monumentally failed one. The belated president is therefore even willing to consider spirited presidents as minor poets, as presidential raters are wont to do, but on his own grounds. Although their eagerness is never satiated, he himself believes that the phenomenon of spiritedness is a sui generis that deserves its own categorization. Does the fact that the minor poet "just misses" relieving belatedness place him in a realm of regret and vexation in which he must come to complete his project in his own mind? The belated president wonders if this makes his affliction ever more intense or if the minor poet can ever come to terms with his contention. Is, for example, the conclusion offered by John Ashbery, the poet proper, that the belated still have the liberty to heal themselves by walking away, a poetic veil concealing failure or true self-consolation?

It is on the basis of these reflections that the belated president selects two minor poets, presidents whose stature is less than monumental but excruciatingly close. He believes that while the presidencies of Thomas Jefferson and Ronald Reagan may not exhaust the category of minor poetry and that narratives of incomplete poetics might be extended to other presidencies, they are reliable exemplars. The belated president is not concerned with substantive similarities between these minor poets, their common aversion to government and what their critics called their addiction to popular acclaim. What strikes him about these two men is the nature of their common effort to relieve belatedness. Both Jefferson and Reagan described their administrations in revolutionary terms. Jefferson repeatedly referred to his presidency as a "second American revolution," and the leader of the "Reagan revolution" proclaimed his administration altered the "tide of history." Both men saw their movement as one which awakened a sleeping people. Jefferson hoped to "awake and snap the Lilliputian chords" that entrapped Americans, and Reagan hoped to "capture the imagination of the American people." Whose principles were both men attempting to overturn? For Jefferson, Washington was the central figure in the attempt to create "an Anglican monarchical, and aristocratical party" after the first revolution, and for Reagan it was FDR who led a movement which used "fascism" as its policy model. For both, then, their poetic intent was shockingly clear. Jefferson hoped to overturn Washington *and* the monumental achievements of 1788–96, and Reagan, FDR and 1932–45. Both described their revolutions in a reactionary republican sense. Jefferson's goals involved a return to the principles of 1776 before the financial and political corruption in the "ministry" of Washington-Hamilton and Adams, a characterization which the creator of the Reagan revolution would surely endorse in regard to FDR and his liberal followers. But despite the openness of their poetic intent, both Jefferson's and Reagan's relationship with their adversaries was an extremely complex one. Both fought belatedness with the language of betrayal and both were systematically ambiguous concerning precisely how they had been betrayed and what role their fathers played in the subversion of the liberties they sought to recover. The belated president understands this paradigm of betrayal as a poetic veil, and he is, of course, correct. The refusal to point their fingers directly at their sources of belatedness is characteristic of all afflicted presidents. But betrayal assumes a particularly close tie between its subjects, one which drew the belated back to their affliction. Thus the aegis between Hamilton and Washington, never fully exposed by Jefferson, and FDR's geniality, scrupulously imitated by Reagan, permitted both Jefferson and Reagan some space from which they could hide their respective poetic intent, but both also left their predecessors room to protect their own monumental stature. When the "revolution of 1800" came to be celebrated for its moderation, as did the "Reagan revolution," the figures of Washington and FDR reemerged to assert their firstness and Jefferson and Reagan fell to the status of minor poets.

Chapter 7

THOMAS JEFFERSON: THE DOUBLING EFFECT

• •

The belated president realizes the irony of studying Jefferson, America's greatest poet, as a minor poet when he is universally recognized by belated presidents as a central obstacle requiring (mis)reading. But Jefferson's monumental status is not derived from his presidency. To his sympathizers, the Jefferson presidency enhanced his already monumental persona. To his critics, it was proof of at least some of his republican delusions. This notion of two Jeffersons, Jefferson the philosopher, champion of liberty, and apostle of Americanism and Jefferson the politician and man of affairs lays bifurcated for subsequent presidents to examine and (mis)read. Merill D. Peterson has described this division of Jefferson's poetic achievement as a doubling effect. "For just as Jefferson multiplied himself through the range and variety of his interests," says Peterson, "he doubled, quite unconsciously of course, his political usefulness to the generations, simultaneously posing in himself the dilemmas they must face, by seeming to recommend one thing in theory and another thing in practice."[1] Thus Jackson acted as if the second Jefferson simply did not exist. Careful not to announce that the "revolution of 1800" was a failure, he nevertheless acted as if Jefferson the president never happened as he took on the (enspirited) role of a Jefferson presidency in 1828. Lincoln used the first Jefferson to double-cross the founders and transferred the moment of protecting America as the "world's best hope" from 1800 to 1863. Only FDR explicitly drew upon the second Jefferson, telescoping his monumental achievements to the formation of a party system and the purchase of Louisiana, two monumental acts about which Jefferson was often ambiguous. This division of two Jeffersons, of course, did not make the task of subsequent belated presidents by any means an easy one, but it did permit men like Jackson, Lincoln, and Franklin Roosevelt to elide past his presidency. Imagine, wonders the belated president, if the two Jeffersons had been more firmly connected or formed as one then the belated must confront the inventor of America's more natural political dialect, the "apostle of Americanism" in Gilbert Chinard's apt phrase, and the monumental leader of the revolution of 1800!

WASHINGTON'S SONS: HAMILTON, JEFFERSON

To the belated president, the key to Jefferson's status as minor poet rested with his relationship with Washington. John Adams showed flashes of belatedness in regard to Washington, complaining that the veneration of his persona bordered on the "Romish," especially considering the fact that this republican paragon was "illiterate, unlearned, unread for his station,"[2] and late in his life Jefferson gave indirect expressions of resentment. "His mind was great and powerful," he told Walter Jones, "but not of the first order" and "slow in operation." Still, although it was unimaginative, he could be "sure in conclusion."[3] Unlike Adams, however, and especially unlike Hamilton, Jefferson's relationship to Washington was colored by attitudes of subservience and reverence that he could never quite discard.

Any belated president struggles with such emotions. He is overwhelmed by his predecessor and so both loves and hates him as he struggles to make room for his own monumental achievement. For how could he not love greatness if he too is to become great? There is no doubt that Jefferson was confronted with a difficult decision in regard to Washington: Was he Hamilton's aegis or was Hamilton his aegis? The poetic veil which Jefferson finally cast for himself entailed the former, and from the standpoint of belatedness it mattered not which decision he had reached, for Jefferson could leave it to his Republican Party cohorts to raise the latter conclusion (which they did). But Jefferson seemed to be obsessed with reaching a decision in his own mind. The conversations which he recorded in *The Anas* show an excruciatingly painful attempt on his part to uncover Washington's true poetic intent. Washington's responses to his entreaties both direct and indirect are icily remote. Should not, Jefferson asked, the State Department be made responsible for the posts since the Treasury "possessed already such an influence as to swallow up the whole Executive powers"? To this Washington considered and responded the next day that he put his request in writing. When he drew a picture of Hamilton's efforts to create a Walpole constitution in America, Washington asked for specifics. When Jefferson spoke of designs to create an American monarchy, Washington said there might be some "desires" but no "designs." Yet Washington *seemed* to wish Jefferson to remain in his administration. On the other hand, had Washington shown disrespect for Jefferson by hiring L'Enfant to design an imperial capital? The difference between L'Enfant's plans and Jefferson's revealed two very different worlds of America's future, one grand and imposing and the other modest and republican. Washington had pronounced Jefferson's as serviceable and of "moderate expense." Jefferson watched the president anxiously in regard to his attitude toward developments in the French Revolution. Why had Washington so little faith in the people of France? Perhaps his attitudes had been colored by the dispatches of Governeur Morris who was a "a high flying monarchy man." But then why had Washington appointed Morris to the post?[4]

This confusion reached a conclusion with the publication of the Philip Mazzei letter in 1796. Jefferson had written about the emergence of "an Anglican monarchical aristocratical party" in America whose "avowed object is to draw over us the substance, as they have already done the forms, of the British government." This observation alone constituted a direct attack on Washington since the first president had already been epitomized as the founder of the Constitution as he himself asserted in his the Farewell Address he had prepared.[5] But Jefferson continued: "It would give you a fever were I to name to you the apostates who have gone over to these heresies, men who were Samsons in the field and Solomons in the council, but who have had their heads shorn by the harlot England."[6] Although Jefferson did not mention Washington by name and his heretics were in the plural, the designations Samson and Solomon left no doubt to the readers of the letter that his reference was to the president. Who else received such descriptions? Jefferson remained silent while the Federalists waged war over Jefferson's "assassination" of the president. But the president's anger showed when he learned of a ruse on the part of Republicans to elicit monarchical sentiments from him. Jefferson had no part in the plan, and so told Washington, but his relationship with his secretary of state became even more distant. The two men did not meet or correspond after Washington's retirement.

Had Jefferson "slain" Washington on his own way to overcoming belatedness? If the belated president who cures himself is indifferent or casually gracious to the men he had defeated, such was not the case with Jefferson. His taunts of the president as he retired from his cabinet, his assertions that he had loved him more than Hamilton, his complaints about his remoteness ("His heart was not warm in its affections") have led numerous historians to assert that he never recovered from the belief that he was the less favored son to Hamilton.[7]

The belated president wonders if Jefferson's regret is that Washington would not act as *his* aegis. The closest that Jefferson came, and it was quite close indeed, in acknowledgment that Washington employed Hamilton as his aegis is to be found in his 1814 valedictory sketch. Jefferson's assessment of Washington's abilities was, as the belated president noted, poetically ambivalent. His assessment of Washington's commitment to republicanism, however, is quite damning. To Jefferson, Washington believed that the practicality of republican government was an open question which he was determined to give a "fair trial." But Washington's distrust of human nature led him to believe that "we must at length end in something like a British constitution." This belief, Jefferson concluded, was the reason Washington adopted so many "levees, birthdays, pompous meetings with Congress. These ceremonies were "calculated to prepare us for a change which he believed possible, and to let it come on with as little shock as might be to the public mind." "Federal monarchists" had poisoned Washington's mind against him, and Jefferson notes that "to this he listened the more easily." The belated president finds these conjectures remarkable, and he is even more astounded that Jefferson should have concluded that he "felt on his death, with my countrymen, that 'verily a great man hath fallen this day in Israel.'"[8]

The belated president lays out Jefferson's attitudes toward Washington, expressed publicly and privately: Washington was a republican hero "entitled" to "first place in his country's love"; Washington became the aegis of Hamilton, who planned to implant the British constitution in America; Washington had serious doubts about the viability of republican government and therefore planned a peaceful transition to the British model as a contingency; Washington was himself a "monocrat," an apostate of the Revolution, who hid his beliefs through Hamilton. Surely, concludes the belated president, Jefferson's first assessment is a poetic veil, a prudent acknowledgment of Washington's firstness. And likewise this systematic ambiguity reflected in the four assessments taken together gave Jefferson poetic openings necessary to overcome his belatedness, but it also made the "revolution of 1800" systematically ambiguous. Was Jefferson carrying on the work of "our first and greatest revolutionary character"? Was Jefferson overturning the project of the evil son Hamilton? Was Jefferson closing off the British alternative that Washington had only considered but "monocrats" were intent upon implementing? Was Jefferson saving the Republic from twelve years of executive administration and finally putting the nation on the "republican tack"? Only the last interpretation of the revolution of 1800 would with certainty place Jefferson beyond the reach of belatedness, and it is an interpretation that historians have generally not accepted, in part, concludes the belated president, because Jefferson so invited the other three. He wonders if the elusive Washington who thwarted Jefferson's project to make him his aegis is not responsible for his status as minor poet. In any case, Jefferson in early 1797 seemed to have accepted the wall of support that surrounded the Washington persona and thus accepted some sort of poetic retreat if not poetic defeat. "Such is the popularity of the President," he told Archibald Stuart, "that the people will support him in whatever he will or will not do, without appealing to their own reason or to anything but their feelings toward him."[9] He would thus try to "soothe" the monumental president "by flattery" if he thought his own measures had a chance of success and remain silent in other instances.

Jefferson's poetic ambiguity in regard to Washington led nineteenth-century historians to accuse Jefferson the President of both duplicity and cunning and extravagant idealism. Henry Lee's *Observations on the Writings of Thomas Jefferson* is certainly the most venomous of anti-Jefferson assessments, provoked by what Lee regarded as the Jeffersonian's own attacks on his family's name. But Lee offered an interpretation of Jefferson that had been made less maliciously by others. The author of *Observations* systematically reviewed the Jefferson correspondence and charged that Jefferson experienced a sense of guilt about his own motives which created a "chameleon order" of mind. To Lee, Jefferson possessed an uncanny ability to discern the basest desires in others and a power "to instill, under guise of disapproving—to stimulate, while pretending to dissuade, to urge on, while appearing to check,—and, a skillful rider of men as he was, to make the bridle perform the office of spur." Thus from Lee's perspective he had uncovered the precise form of Jefferson's poetic intent, which, if applied to his relationship with Washington, involved a systematic project to awaken doubts about the first president (based on his own psychic deformity) and at the same time appear to oppose and disapprove of the antagonistic expressions when they surfaced. Only in the Mazzei letter had Jefferson let down his guard, and Lee treated this assessment as central proof for his argument.[10]

Lee's analysis certainly provided an explanation of Jefferson's ambiguity toward Washington by uncovering systematically hostile and vindictive motives. Henry Adams's *History of the United States During the Administrations of Jefferson and Madison* is widely regarded as a magistral work, but his attitude toward Jefferson was not appreciably different from Lee's. Certainly Adams's view of Jefferson was more scholarly and more complex, especially in terms of his examination of the conflict between the democratic and republican aspects of Jefferson's personality, but his antagonism to Jefferson was quite clear and he set out in his multivolume work to ridicule him. To Adams, Jefferson may not have been the theoretic Jacobin that Federalists described, but he "seemed during his entire life to breathe with perfect satisfaction nowhere except in the literary, and scientific air of Paris in 1789." Thus to Adams, Jefferson possessed the naïveté to reject the principles of Washington's Farewell Address. Everything that Jefferson touched illustrated the futility of his efforts: "Facts, not theories, were all that survived the wreck of Mr. Jefferson's administration." Even his great triumph, the Louisiana Purchase, required a military system to protect it and internal improvements to secure it. The grand failure of this departure from the father of the country was the Embargo Act, which overturned all the "achievements" of his first administration. The act "opened up the sluice-gates of corruption" in government which Jefferson had pledged to remove. Adams was wrong, of course, at least in the long run, that "upon the shock of these discoveries" Jefferson's vast popularity vanished.[11]

The belated president knows, of course, that the anti-Jefferson forces enjoyed an enormous head start in the histories of his administration, and he is aware of defenses on the part of George Tucker and Henry S. Randall, both of whom insisted that if the threat of monarchy was not a real one, then Jefferson was a "cold-blooded demagogue," a description which neither man could accept.[12] But he is nevertheless impressed with these two samples, for they encapsulate two critical versions of Jefferson's status as poet in regard to Washington. Lee's is an account of the bad son, the very opposite of Jefferson's own feelings, and Adams's is an account of the errant but well-meaning one.

JEFFERSON'S SECOND REVOLUTION

Armed with these interpretations and his own knowledge of Jefferson's complex relationship to Washington, the belated president sets out to study the poetry of the revolution of 1800. His first discovery gives him some pause, for he notes that the constitutional crisis of February 1801 certainly contained the potential for a revolution conventionally defined. The election produced a tie between Jefferson and his vice-presidential candidate, Burr, in the Electoral College. Federalists had thoughts of making a deal with Burr and depriving Jefferson of the presidency and, barring this, preventing the election of any candidate by inauguration day and devolving the selection of a president by a Federalist Senate. After the crisis was over, both parties insisted that no other outcome was ever really considered, but there is considerable evidence to suggest that Jefferson was prepared to resist the possibility of "usurpation." Writing Monroe and anticipating victory two days before he was elected by the House on the thirty-sixth ballot, Jefferson said that had the Federalists declared an interregnum, "the middle states would arm, and that no such usurpation, even if for a single day, should be submitted to." His trump card, as he saw it, however, was the threat of a constitutional convention. "The very word convention gives them the horrors," he told Monroe, "as in the present democratical spirit of America, they fear they should lose some of the favorite morsels of the Constitution."[13]

Even the most hostile historians focus upon the conciliatory sentiments of Jefferson's inaugural as the apotheosis of the revolution of 1800, but the belated president will not let go the Jefferson of February 15. He sees a Jefferson poised for the possibility of a "real" revolution, and he cannot fail to note the remove from which he regards the Constitution itself. "A convention, invited by the republican members of Congress, with the virtual President and Vice-President, would have been on the ground in eight weeks," he told Priestly in March.[14] Thus Jefferson intimates the flawed nature of the great document containing as it does the "favorite morsels" of the "monocrats." Nor does the belated president fail to notice the irony of Jefferson's suggestion that the Constitution is at least the partial possession of the others given his fears about Washington's own commitments.

It is revolutionary flashes such as this on the part of Jefferson, which appear sporadically throughout his administration, that intrigues so the belated president. The minor poet always shows hints and instances of poetic autonomy and greatness and in Jefferson's presidency there are many. Although they never add up to a whole, and it is possible to regard them as wrecked theories as Henry Adams did, their brilliance and monumental possibilities are undeniable. Excitedly, he searches for more of them.

Few contemporaries failed to note the conciliatory tone of Jefferson's first inaugural, and indeed it is this apparent moderation that is the basis for the judgment of later generations that Jefferson should be accorded poetic status for defusing partisan antagonism in a young Republic, which could have led to civil war, and that quickly came to be seen as a poetic moment of American self-congratulation. Indeed, Jefferson favorably compared this transfer of power to the "throes and convulsions of the ancient world" and the violence of the French Revolution, which had even reached "this distant and peaceful shore."[15]

John Marshall, however, saw the dual messages in the inaugural. After praising the speech as "conciliatory" and "giving the lie to the violent party declamation which has elected him," he noted that "it is strongly characteristic of the general cast of his political theory," which he had negatively described as one of a group of "speculative theorists" in the Republican Party.[16] Indeed, Jefferson's later comment that his administration constituted a revolution though not by the "sword" was a belated effort on his part to center the radicalism of his efforts.

Thus when the belated president reads the first inaugural he sees how circumscribed are the gestures of conciliation. Jefferson does note that the authority of the majority rests upon its reasonableness and respect for the rights of the minority (although later he speaks of the need for their "absolute acquiescence in the decisions of the majority") and that "every difference of opinion is not a difference of principle."[17] The poetic phrase for which he is most remembered, however, has a narrower meaning than was later attributed to it. "We are all Republicans, we are Federalists" did not contain the capitalization that later editors and Americans in general gave it. One current scholar has read the phrase as a statement of Jefferson's political theory that America constituted a *federal* union and a *republican* government.[18]

But even more revision can be read in the sentence. One of Jefferson's favorite pastimes was classification of Federalists. Three days after his inaugural, he noted that some federalists were so frightened by the events in February that they had "come over" due to their "timidity of constitution." "I always exclude their leaders," he told Monroe. A few weeks later, he spoke of those Federalists who were monarchists "in theory only." Others were "more ardent for introduction of monarchy, eager for armies, making noise for a great naval establishment." This later class "ought to be tolerated but not trusted." In July he urged cooperation with "the federal sect of republicans . . . to a certain degree" while "we must strip of all the means of influence the Essex junto" and "their associate monocrats in every part of the Union." In the later category he placed Adams as well as Hamilton. By the end of the summer of 1801, Jefferson announced his delight with a report that "republican federalists" were "still coming into the union." As to the others, they were "incurables, to be taken care of in a mad house, if necessary."[19]

The belated president thus concludes that "we are all republicans, we are all federalists" was a category he had layered over Republicans and Federalists, and his policy of "deliberation" and "consolidation" would thus silence most Federalists. Those Federalists who acquiesced to his agenda would become federalists. Jefferson's own agenda was fully presented in the inaugural address. The pledges to create a "wise and frugal government," to rely upon a "well-disciplined militia" for defense, to support state governments as "the surest bulwarks against antirepublican tendencies," to encourage agriculture, and commerce "as its handmaid," were all pledges of the Republican Party in 1799. It is certainly true that Jefferson believed that the vast majority of Federalists were or would become federalists, and thus he had not placed himself in the position of

Robespierre or Lenin, but the belated president concludes that this poetry of conciliation had terms which were left unstated by later generations.

The belated president firmly believes that Jefferson's statement that "the revolution of 1800 . . . was as real a revolution in the principles of our government as that of 1776 was in its form"[20] is a clear statement of what he regarded as his poetic achievement. Although his ambiguity in regard to Washington muddled his own poetic intent, Jefferson's project could be stated thusly: "I will be the first *republican* president." In the first days of euphoria after his election by the House, Jefferson clearly expressed his intent in these terms. The belated president has observed the ecstacy of the poet freed before, and when he reads that Jefferson announced two days after the inaugural that he would put the Republic back "on her republican tack," he recognizes the moment immediately. Jefferson is overjoyed with the prospect of his project. Twice he focuses upon immortality. He speaks of the "joy" he expects in "the mansions of the blessed, when received with the embraces of our forefathers, we shall be welcomed with their blessing as having done our part not unworthily of them." He closes by expressing the "satisfaction" he receives from "the contemplation of the benevolent effects of our efforts." "I shall have the happiness of living and dying" in refuting the tenets of the Federalists, he tells Dickinson.[21] Since it would be an understatement to say that Jefferson's faith in the immortality of the soul was a weak one, the belated president takes these musings as expressions of the prospect of freedom from belatedness.

By the end of March, Jefferson's sentiments turned sober. He considered "how difficult it is to move or inflect the great machine of society, how impossible to advance the notions of a whole people suddenly to ideal right."[22] But despite these remarks the belated president is not surprised to find that Jefferson's model is the monumental reformer Solon, and he speaks of the "wisdom" of the Athenian's remark that "no more good must be attempted than the nation can bear."

Was Jefferson an American Solon? A year after his allusion, Jefferson himself reviewed his own agenda thusly:

The first session of Congress convened since republicanism has recovered its ascendancy, is now drawing to a close. They will pretty completely fulfil the desires of the people. They have reduced the army and navy to what is barely necessary. They are disarming executive patronage and preponderance, by putting down one-half the offices of the United States, which are no longer necessary. These economies have enabled them to suppress all the internal taxes, and still to make provision for the payment of their public debt as to discharge that in eighteen years. They have lopped off a parasite limb, planted by their predecessors on their judiciary body for party purposes; they are opening the doors of hospitality to fugitives from the oppressions of other countries; and we have suppressed all those public forms and ceremonies which tend to familiarize the public eye to the harbingers of another form of government. The people are nearly all united; their quondam leaders, infuriated with the sense of their impotence, will soon be seen or heard only in newspapers, which serve as chimneys to carry off noxious vapors and smoke, and all is now tranquil, form and well, as it should be.[23]

The belated president knows, of course, that the Jeffersonian revolution in toto, particularly in regard to the judiciary, would not be as effortless as the president described here. But he also notes that the ease with which Jefferson describes the achievements of his first year in office is emblematic of a poetically independent president. Jefferson had always believed that the natural course of American development was the republican tack which Washington's popularity had delayed as the Republic had lain on its "oars" when Washington was "at the helm." He had frequently expressed doubts, doubts about how deeply the Hamiltonian apparat had dug itself into the polity, doubts about his ability to awaken republican sentiments in the people, and doubts about how far he could take his revolution. These vexations had disappeared in 1802. Jefferson and his party had rationalized the "artificial and mysterious" Hamiltonian budget, reduced the debt, eliminated nearly all federal domestic taxes, cut appropriations for the navy (the institution Jefferson perhaps feared the most after the courts), virtually wiped out the traces of the terror of '98 (repealing those portions of the Alien and Sedition Acts which had not expired and pardoning those convicted), and scrapped the courtly practices of the presidency.

It is certainly true that each of these achievements was negative in character, lending to the charge once made by John Quincy Adams that Jefferson's talents were of the destructive sort ("he could demolish, deface, and cast down; he could not build up or preserve").[24] But events, partly fortuitous and partly the result of Jefferson's poetic vision, would shortly alter even this description. It was an axiom of Jeffersonian republicanism that the political economy imposed upon the nation by Washington-Hamilton threatened to make America "old" before its time by introducing a system of finance capital and manufacture. Jefferson's commitment to this scenario of classical republicanism, which posited a state of inevitable decline and corruption as societies moved from an agricultural to commercial base, varied across his career, but in the 1790s it formed a major theoretical base of the Republican opposition. In his *Notes on the State of Virginia* he advanced the exceptionalist argument that this "natural" process might be "retarded" by the vast land that lay to America's west.

The belated president, of course, knows well the poetic rendering of the Louisiana Purchase. Jefferson, a president suspicious of the presidency, nevertheless acted boldly and independently in securing a tract of land for America from the world's most feared leader, Napoleon, which doubled its size overnight. This classic act of executive power, both swift and daring, "at first dazzled and then delighted the American people."[25] No belated president could fail to be elated by the success of this project. When Jefferson learned that Louisiana was retroceded to France from Spain, he was stuck with the prospect of unavoidably carrying out the Federalist program: "The day that France takes possession of New Orleans . . . we must marry ourselves to the British fleet and nation." As Jefferson ruminated on the possible scenarios of a French empire in the West, one which he concluded had "produced more uneasy sensations through the body of the nation" than any "since the revolutionary war," he considered the option of French secession to the United States as an alternative.[26] Less than two years later, celebrations of the formal transfer of authority in New Orleans began. The *National Intelligencer* announced that "an assemblage so numerous, to celebrate an event, at once so glorious and so happy, may not occur again for centuries to come." Federalists derisively referred to the banquets as the "Louisiana jubilee," but to the great majority of the nation this was as great a cause for celebration as the adoption of the Constitution. The Jefferson administration "had acquired almost a whole new world, and had laid the foundation of the happiness of millions unborn!"[27]

Yet Jefferson even in his triumph against belatedness was not quite so happy. The prospect of an "empire of liberty" (and from the belated president's standpoint his own founding role in the enterprise) thrilled him. Some Federalists opportunistically appropriated old antifederalist arguments concerning large territory and republican government. "Now, by adding an unmeasured world beyond that river," warned Fisher Ames, "we rush like a comet into infinite space."[28] On this point Jefferson had no worries. He saw the Louisiana Purchase as his final blow to the Hamiltonian project of making the nation old before its time. He had given America youth, and in the language of republican political economy, he had given America as close to eternal youth as any nation could hope: "By enlarging the empire of liberty we multiply its auxiliaries, and provide new sources of renovation, should its principles, at any time, degenerate, in those portions of the country which gave them birth."[29]

Still there was something in this poetic achievement that nagged at the president. From the first moment of its success, Jefferson felt the "gagging conviction" that his action had exceeded the limits of the Constitution.[30] Every person he consulted about the constitutionality of the action, from his secretary of treasury, Gallatin, to Levi Lincoln, his attorney general, to Republican Party stalwart Breckenridge to even the international radical Thomas Paine, assured him there were no difficulties, but Jefferson, seemingly alone, persisted. When he learned of the signing in July, he drafted a constitutional amendment which he intended to submit to Congress along with the treaty and later he wrote new drafts. The international situation was still a fluid one, however. The president worried about the possibility of reneging on Napoleon's part and finally submitted the treaty to Congress "in silence" regarding any constitutional amendment. By August he had reached a personal philosophical accommodation concerning his action, which he now described as one which involved the "executive seizing the fugitive occurrence." Admitting that he had engaged in an act "beyond the constitution" and that so too would the Congress in its ratification, both parties would have to present their deed to future generations:

> The Legislature in casting behind them metaphysical subtleties, and risking themselves like faithful servants, must ratify and pay for it, and throw themselves on their country for doing them unauthorized, what we know they would have done for

themselves had they been in a situation to do it. In the case of the guardian, investing the money of his ward in purchasing an important adjacent territory; and saying to him when of age, I did this for your good; I pretend to no right to bind you; you may disavow me, and I must get out of the scrape as I can; I thought it my duty to risk myself for you. But we shall not be disavowed by the nation, and their act of indemnity will confirm and not weaken the Constitution, by more strongly marking out its lines.[31]

The belated president ponders Jefferson's personal resolution. His own belatedness prevents him from acknowledging that Jefferson has a conscience, and thus he tries to arrive at an interpretation that accords with poetic intent. He notes that Jefferson apparently believes that there is something shameful in the deed he committed, despite the fact that he believes that the action "so much advances the good of their country." The phrase "their country" reverberates in the belated president's thoughts, for he recognizes that Jefferson has now separated himself from the nation, seen in his apologia as composed of present and future generations. He remembers that Washington too employed the same language of separation as he spoke to forthcoming generations in his Farewell Address. Jefferson had acted as a father, as did Washington, but rather than demanding obedience to his acts (that is, to the Constitution from which he claimed poetic authorship), Jefferson almost asks for forgiveness. The belated president repeats Jefferson's words: "I did this for your own good; I pretend to no right to bind you; you may disavow me, and I must get out of the scrape as I can; I thought it my duty to risk myself for you." Jefferson even told Breckenridge that later developments might lead to secession: "If they see their interest in separation, why should we take side with our Atlantic rather than our Mississippi descendants? It is the elder and younger son differing."[32]

A thought strikes the belated president as he continues to ponder the phrase "You may disavow me." The purchase was a monumental act that would authorize a firstness to Jefferson in terms of his project to retrieve a youthful economy from the Federalists, and it certainly dwarfed Washington's efforts to secure western boundaries in Pinckney's Treaty. But the purchase itself nevertheless awoke the ghost of Washington's presidency with its assertions of presidential authority and independence and broad interpretations of constitutional power. Even the dreaded levees and parades returned much to Jefferson's lament. One contemporary biographer concludes thusly about the constitutional impact of Jefferson's deed: "A revolution in the American Union became, perforce, a revolution in the Constitution. A momentous act of Jeffersonian statesmanship unhinged the Jeffersonian dogmas and opened, so far as precedent might control, the boundless field of power so much feared."[33] Yet Jefferson was prepared in 1803 to be disavowed in a poetic sense. Throughout his life he was reluctant to take much credit for his action and omitted the deed from his epitaph. The belated president wonders if Jefferson had feared whether the consequences of his deed might have destroyed his own project. Had he placed his own presidency in the shadow of Washington's? If so, was Jefferson saying in poetic form that he meant not to bind future generations in terms of accepting presidential power or even the empire of liberty itself? His accommodation, which he announced to Breckenridge, was addressed to future generations. But to the belated president it was also poetically framed to himself as the discovered poetic solace that he is free to walk away.

The Louisiana Purchase expressed perfectly Jefferson's doubling effect as minor presidential poet. Indeed, for Peterson it represented the "most striking instance of this curious doubling."[34] To his belated champions, the deed was an illustration of the indispensability of farsighted executive statesmanship; to his belated opponents, it was proof that iron necessity always defeats theory. Neither conclusion would have been pleasing to Jefferson as belated president. But as is always the case with Jefferson, any poetic assessment must be withheld at this point for he was always able to suggest in the most tantalizing form a poetic rendering that indicates, if not an alleviation of his own belatedness, at least the intimation of one. In this instance, the deed is given a poetic indeterminacy by Jefferson's designation "empire of liberty."

Immediately the Louisiana Purchase seemed to pose the classic dilemmas of empire. How were the new Americans to be governed? How could the nation assimilate a territory as large as itself? How could a Protestant country assimilate a Catholic population? How should a liberal nation treat a culture with a Spanish and French feudal heritage? Would slave trade be permitted in a region already teeming with servitude? Jefferson, of course, confronted all these issues. At first he moved slowly on these questions, asserting that the inhabitants "are as yet as incapable of self-government as children." Pressures from all directions (international, partisan, and local), however, forced him to drastically speed up his timetable for republicanism and Americanization, and the nation was able to avoid the kind of cultural bifurcation that plagued other nations.[35]

Throughout this process, however, Jefferson's occasional elucidation of the "empire of liberty" seemed to soar poetically far above the bureaucratic-political question of colonial administration. Sometimes he spoke of it in terms of westward expansion "advancing compactly as we multiply." He also referred to a future hemisphere of "sister republics" that suggested a republican version of what later became known as soviets. In 1786 he noted that "our confederacy must be viewed as the nest from which all America, North and South is to be peopled." To Monroe in 1801 he fantasized a system, covering North and South America, "with a people speaking the same language, governed in similar forms, and by similar laws."[36]

The belated president notes how gloriously poetic is Jefferson's language when he speaks of an empire of liberty, how enchanted Jefferson could become when he spoke of its forms, so much so that John Quincy Adams grumbled that the West overexcited Jefferson's "itch for telling prodigies." His poetic passion reached one of its heights in the first inaugural, when Jefferson spoke of "a rising nation, spread over a wide and fruitful land, traversing all the seas with the rich productions of their industry, engaged in commerce with nations who feel power and forget right, advancing rapidly to destinies beyond the reach of the mortal eye." When the new president took to "contemplate these transcendent objects," he would "shrink from the contemplation, and humble myself before the magnitude of the undertaking."[37]

In moments such as these, Jefferson would discard republican pessimism about the mortality of even the most glorious political systems and ignore his own advise that "more blest is that nation whose silent course of happiness furnishes nothing for history to say."[38] Moments of enchantment such as these led Julian Boyd to argue that Jefferson's empire of liberty lay primarily in the "realm of the mind and spirit of man, freely and inexorably transcending political boundaries, incapable of being restrained, and holding imperial sway not by arms or political power but by the sheer majesty of ideas and ideals."[39]

From the perspective of the doubling effect, the empire of liberty is another bifurcation in Jefferson's poetry. Is his empire a poetic act of ideological self-deception for American hegemony? Is his empire a poetic dream of the American Enlightenment, a possibility not yet seen? Is his empire an attempt on Jefferson's part to construct poetically an alternative to the Hamiltonian-Washingtonian conception of a commercial-military world power? The belated president, of course, opts for the latter interpretation and sees the empire of liberty as a poetic escape from belatedness, an attempt to transcend the "fugitive occurrence" that would retrace his achievement back to Washington through a poetic projection of futuristic transcendence. From his perspective the other two options are the result of the doubling effect. But as a belated president he, too, is intrigued with the poetic power of the empire of liberty and is determined to offer his own misreading, should fate permit.

THE EMBARGO, WARDS, AND OTHER POETIC FRAGMENTS

Jefferson's first term was, and is, regarded as a remarkable one. Forrest McDonald concludes that its achievements rivaled those of Washington's and that "they would never be matched again, not by Jackson, by Lincoln, or by either Roosevelt."[40] Here, of course, notes the belated president, comes another instance of the doubling effect, for McDonald suggests that the second term stands in dialectical relation to the first. "Had history ended" in 1804, the nation would not have suffered from the consequences of military budget cuts and the slashing of taxes. Jefferson dismantled America's defense when the world was at war, and the elimination of internal taxes made the nation's revenues dependent upon the wills of Napoleon and the ministry of George III. As a result, the disastrous embargo of the second term can be seen as the ideological outcome of the first. Unprepared to defend itself and dependent upon foreign trade, Jefferson attempted to avoid war and ended by "levying war on his own citizens."

Taken by itself the embargo is monumental evidence of Jefferson as failed poet. To Henry Adams the embargo brought upon Jefferson "mortification such

as no other President suffered." Even worse, the embargo was final proof of the
delusional basis of his American exceptionalism: "America began slowly to
struggle under the consciousness of pain, toward a conviction that she must bear
the common burdens of humanity, and fight with the weapons of other races
in the same bloody arena; that she could not much longer delude herself with
hopes of evading laws of Nature and instincts of life; and that her new statesmanship which made peace a passion could lead to no better result than had
been reached by the barbarous system which made war a duty."[41] Such was the
assessment of a nineteenth-century Washingtonian, but later-day Jeffersonians
drew equally negative lessons. Albert Jay Nock, for one, called the act "the most
arbitrary, inquisitorial, and confiscatory measure formulated in American legislation up to the Civil War."[42] Thus as the doubling effect had in Jefferson's
first administration produced a bifurcated Jefferson as subject for admiration,
the Embargo Act in the second produced dual lessons of failure. To both Adams
and Nock, Jefferson had misread America. On Adams's part, Jefferson had failed
to recognize the brute facts of the international struggle for survival and on
Nock's part, he had failed to recognize that centralized democratic accountabil-
ity had the same impact as more surreptitious forms of finance capital and judicial power.

The idea of the embargo itself began modestly as an action designed to protect the nation from immediate war and not as the philosophical experiment
in "peaceable coercion" that Jefferson later defended. Very quickly, however,
Jefferson requested a series of supplemental acts designed to close legislative and
administrative loopholes and soon found himself to be the "commissar of the
nation's economy" personally licensing shipping and confronting problems such
as the amount of flour permitted in the cargo holds of vessels. "I do not wish a
single citizen to be deprived of bread," wrote the suspicious president, "but I
set down the exercise of commerce, merely for profit, as nothing when it carries with it the danger of defeating the objects of the embargo."[43] Jefferson, who
was critical of Washington's action in the Whiskey Rebellion, now declared
the Champlain region in a state of insurrection.

The belated president surveys these developments. While he is always prideful of executive determination and places Federalist exclamations of presidential usurpation in partisan context, he detects intimations of a revolutionary
spirit in Jefferson's rapid and dedicated exercise of power. In fact, Jefferson
hinted that the emergency raised the question of possible need of dictatorship
as the "universal resource," comparing the enforcement of the Embargo Act to
the extralegal character of the Revolution: "Should we have ever gained our
Revolution, if only we had bound our hands by manacles of the law, not only
in the beginning but in any part of the revolutionary conflict?"[44] It seems to the
belated president that the embargo became entwined with Jefferson's affliction
of belatedness in ever broader circles of significance. One contemporary historian has noted that his policies became "dominated by a problem of theory" and
that there was no doubt that his great desire to demonstrate the effectiveness
of his experiment was connected with its power as future exemplar.[45] Dumas

Malone wonders why "he minimized the impatience of men with hampering restrictions to which they were unaccustomed" and "underrated both the extent and potency of private greed."[46] Indeed, Jefferson knew of the havoc his administration of the embargo was producing on his party and yet still spoke of "unprincipled adventurers" who used the legitimate needs of citizens as "a cover for their crimes" and of the desire for "unlawful profits of the most worthless part of society." Federalists wondered aloud whether the real purpose of the embargo was a Lycurgian attempt, revolutionary in its scope, to return America to a Spartan republic which forbade commerce and manufacture. One partisan charged that Jefferson planned a "Chinese" approach to political economy, shutting off America to foreign commerce in the mistaken belief that the nation would "enjoy an eternal rusticity and live, forever, thus apathized and vulgar."[47]

Was the embargo an act pursued on Jefferson's part as an opportunity to overcome belatedness through the enunciation of a policy of "peaceful coercion" which later presidents would be forced to imitate or was it an aegis for a plan to convert America permanently to the status of an agricultural republic? The repeal of the act, legislated by Congress, took effect the day he left the presidency. Jefferson did not resist the measure in part because of the threat of secession on the part of New England, but he continued to defend the act in retirement.[48] But the belated president wonders whether Jefferson in his belatedness considered either or both these strategies and whether such projects account for the verve with which he pursued them.

The belated president is about to leave Jefferson when he notes a series of letters he wrote in his retirement about the Constitution and its radical reformation. The keystone in these musings is his notion of a ward republic. Perhaps no idea of Jefferson's has stimulated the imagination of later American radicals more than his proposal for a ward system, and it is this knowledge that stimulates the belated president. He knows that Jefferson's support for the Constitution in its particulars was always tepid. In his 1799 "platform" he complained that the "elective principle" was in danger of being "wormed out" of the federal Constitution. In a letter to John Taylor in 1816, he defined a republic in terms of its provisions for political participation: "The further departure from direct and constant control by the citizens, the less has the government of the ingredient of republicanism." The House of Representative exemplified the "purest republican feature" in our Constitution. The Senate was less so, and the executive still less. The judiciary was "seriously anti-republican."[49] One of the purposes of the formation of the Republican Party was to arrest the formation of any more antirepublican practices. Jefferson did not seem to have appreciated party activity itself as more than a temporary remedy for participation. Nor did he generally look to the democratization of the federal Constitution (direct election of Senators; obsolescence of the electoral college) as a solution.

Late in his life, however, the belated president learns that Jefferson seemed to have become more and more convinced that some new structure needed to be invented in order to promote direct political participation. In letters to friends he recommended the formation of wards through a subdivision of counties.[50] Each ward would have its own school, justice of the peace, constable, and militia captain. Most significant, however, the citizens of each ward, or "hundred," would meet regularly. Jefferson felt that the attachment to republican government would be much stronger among citizens who regularly directly participated in their own affairs. The citizen of a "ward-republic" will "let his heart be torn out of his body sooner than his power be wrested from him by a Caesar or a Bonaparte." The belated president takes particular notice of Jefferson's self-effacing substantiation of his point. He himself felt the "foundations of government shaken under my feet" when the participants of the New England town meetings rose in opposition to his embargo policy when he was president.

Although he still insists upon the designation of "minor poet" for Jefferson, with all its affinity to failure, the belated president is struck with a new sense of dread as he surveys the plan for a ward republic on the part of the retired "failed" president. For if this is the work of a *minor* poet, what are my chances? Here is a belated president who reflects upon the causes of his own failure and constructs, for all posterity to consider, a plan for Constitutional revision that not only shows the unmistakable marks of his authorship but that if ever implemented would thwart the aims of future American Caesars and Bonapartes as indeed it did in a minor way his own projects. The belated president is quite used to confronting presidents from their graves, which he understands is after all the basis for his affliction, but he is unprepared for a confrontation in retirement after their moment to issue monumental obstacles had passed and a president is at his most powerless. He concludes that however remote in terms of immediate implementation is the Jefferson idea of a ward system, it stands as a time bomb planted by this "minor" poet.

Chapter 8

RONALD REAGAN: NEW DEAL SHARDS

◆　◆　◆　◆　◆　◆　◆　◆　◆　◆　◆　◆　◆　◆　◆　◆　◆　◆　◆　◆

The monumental status of FDR has stood as an obstacle to all postwar presidents and presidential aspirants. For Democrats, his successors found that a contemporary liberal "measures politicians by the memory of Franklin Roosevelt" as they attempted to formulate policies for their generation. Political necessity required obeisance to FDR's New Deal, but, as John Kennedy once complained, 1933 is not 1963 and "what was fine for Roosevelt simply would not work today."[1] For Republicans, however, FDR's achievements (from the creation of the American welfare state to U.S. participation in the United Nations) have been centrally contested. Eisenhower, for example, wrote in his memoirs that he hoped that his administration would be remembered as "the first break with the political philosophy of the decades beginning in 1933."[2] Nevertheless, Republican presidents have often been forced to reach accommodations with "New Deal socialism" and to reinterpret FDR's internationalism.

The belated president has discovered that the notable exception to this pattern of hostile accommodation is Ronald Reagan. More than any post-Roosevelt president, Reagan successfully challenged the authority of FDR and initiated his own "revolution" in American politics. Yet the achievements of the Reagan revolution were constructed from unusual elements. Reagan always referred to Roosevelt as his "idol." His "Time for Choosing" speech, however, connected the New Deal to Karl Marx, and later he contended that New Dealers used fascism as their policy model.[3] This paralleling of strident critiques of the New Deal and imitative gestures toward FDR characterized Reagan's entire presidency. Reagan repeatedly and readily admitted that he was a Roosevelt supporter *and* portrayed the New Deal in the satanic mode of the new American Right.

Certainly Reagan's relationship to FDR bears resemblances to Jefferson's relationship with Washington, concludes the belated president. Reagan attacks the Roosevelt "ministry," but, like Jefferson, is unable or unwilling to extend the critique to the monumental figure who was responsible for it. Unlike Jefferson, however, there is no evidence of the agony that Jefferson underwent in attempting to determine the president's motives. While it is true that the Washington-Jefferson connection was a personal one, the belated president knows that belatedness can form intimacies that cross graves, so he pauses to consider the form of the Reagan-FDR association. The Jefferson of *The Anas* was continually struck by Washington's remoteness. Reagan, on the other hand, who never knew FDR personally, fondly captures Roosevelt's casual geniality. Indeed he appropriates the persona for himself and sometimes seems closer to the dead president than Jefferson was to the live one.

MAKING ORAL HISTORY

Central to Reagan's strategy was acknowledgment of his youthful status under the influence of FDR. So powerful was the presence of Roosevelt surrounding the Depression and World War II, the last remembered crises in American history, that to the extent to which Roosevelt's successors recognized these events autobiographically they were touched with the problem of belatedness. Reagan, however, gave these remembrances a central place in his own persona as he created his own oral history of FDR.[4] In his "memory clusters," he recalled Roosevelt's election, his father's jobs in New Deal relief programs, FDR's speeches and personal appearances. Reagan's remembrances of the Depression and FDR's heroic actions are quite vivid. The Depression hit his boyhood town of Dixon "like a cyclone": "One of its first casualties was my father's dream." The Depression "had such an oppressive effect that it cast a dreary pall over everything." In these "cheerless, desperate days," Reagan remembered the "strong, gentle, confident voice" of FDR, who "brought comfort and resilience to a nation caught up in a storm and reassured us that we could lick any problem. I shall never forget him for that."[5]

This seemingly frank and fond oral history provided the foundation for Reagan's strategy. But leaning conceptually on these memory clusters, as well as partially hidden from them, was an alternate narrative. Reagan tells the story of his father's job as New Deal relief administrator and then as local head of the WPA. Although Ronald Reagan described the WPA as "one of the most productive elements of FDR's alphabet soup agencies," he notes that his father had difficulty signing up participants. Jack Reagan later found that relief administrators were discouraging able-bodied men from applying. Reagan the son concludes: "I wasn't sophisticated enough to realize what I learned later: The first rule of bureaucracy is to protect bureaucracy. If the people running the welfare program had let their clientele find other ways of making a living, that would have reduced their importance and their budget."[6] The young Reagan, however, was unaware of this danger. He was a "very emotional New Dealer" and a "near-hopeless hemophiliac liberal" who was "blinded" by the brilliance of the president and "blindly" joined any organization that "would guarantee to save the world."[7] These two narratives, one of affectionate youthful remembrance and one of youthful indiscretion and conversion, form part of a general generational ambivalence to the thirties which Reagan captured as a personal odyssey in which FDR was a monumental figure.

No events in Reagan's youth were evoked more positively than the American experience in World War II. In a 1981 interview he reminisced about FDR's 1937 "quarantine" speech. "I remember when Hitler was arming and had built himself up—no one has created quite the military that the Soviet Union has, but comparatively he was in that way," he told Walter Cronkite. "Franklin Delano Roosevelt made a speech in Chicago at the dedication of a bridge over the Chicago River. In that speech, he called on the free world to quarantine Nazi Germany, to stop all communications, all trade, all relations with them until they gave up that militaristic course and agreed to join with the free nations of the world in a search for peace." Reagan continued to remember that "the funny thing was he was attacked so here in our own country for having said such a thing. Can we honestly look back now and say World War II would have taken place if we had done what he wanted us to do back in 1938?"[8]

Conventional Republican assessments of New Deal foreign policy centered upon the "treason" at Yalta, but Reagan generally interpreted the conference as evidence of Soviet betrayal. To him, FDR was "a great war leader." Under his leadership, "there were less of the tragic blunders that have characterized many wars in the past."[9] Reagan was especially generous in his accounts of the efficiency of the American war effort. FDR had taken a nation completely unprepared for war and in the forty-four months after Pearl Harbor, produced an awesome war machine. "We truly were an arsenal of democracy," he told one interviewer, as he noted that FDR was criticized for asking for fifty thousand planes a year.[10] The massive military budget increases in the 1980s were thus broadly justified by what Reagan regarded as FDR's own success in preparing against a hostile power despite the pessimism of his critics.

As was the case with his New Deal assessments, Reagan employed autobiographical remembrance to support his wartime assessment. Although his own tour of duty never took him out of California, Reagan insisted that the officers in his unit had a direct and "heightened" appreciation of combat since they watched unedited film footage. Reagan himself narrated a simulation of an aerial Tokyo for pilots. He marveled that the product was so "authentic" that "the film would always look exactly the way the target would appear to the crews going on the next run."[11] As president, Reagan's memories of the war focused upon the battlefield valor and the autobiographical remembrances of those who participated in the war effort. The centerpiece of his remarks at the Omaha Beach commemoration was the narrative of a daughter of one of the participants in the invasion.[12]

Reagan's memory of when he parted with the New Deal was systematically evasive. In many speeches he mentioned Al Smith's break with the administration in 1936, when the former governor charged that FDR was taking the "party of Jefferson, Jackson and Cleveland down the road under the banners of Marx, Lenin, and Stalin." In others he identifies strongly and warmly with the Lincolnesque wartime Roosevelt, although he once contended that the "first crack in my liberalism appeared in the last year and a half of my military career." Sometimes he identified with the pre–New Deal FDR. In his 1984 acceptance speech Reagan proudly noted that he cast his first vote for Roosevelt and referred to FDR's 1932 pledge to reduce the cost of government. In other autobiographical remembrances Reagan identified his departure at the time of his resignation from HICCASP (Hollywood Independent Citizens Committee of the Arts, Sciences and Professions) when he learned it was a communist front group. His postwar years as president of the Screen Actors Guild had been "eye-opening" ones, for he had repudiated the "orthodox liberal view" that Communists were "liberals who were temporarily off track."[13] Still he had remained a Democrat until 1962, when he finally registered as a Republican. Although Reagan's deep attachment to Whittaker Chambers, reiterated throughout many speeches, contains several meanings, one core significance involves Reagan's belief that he, like, Chambers, personally "witnessed" two great faiths of his time.[14]

What exactly were the achievements of FDR that made him Reagan's idol? asks the belated president. No New Deal program received unqualified endorsement and most were subject to severe criticism, including the TVA and social security. In his post-presidential autobiography, Reagan attempted an assessment. The appraisal consists of a series of positive and negative conclusions. After noting that Roosevelt brought hope to a despondent nation in 1932–33, he offered another conclusion to his legacy: "FDR in many ways set in motion the forces that later sought to create big government and bring a veiled form of socialism in America." He remembered, however, FDR's early pledge to cut government spending and speculates that "if he had not been distracted by war, I think he would have resisted the relentless expansion of the federal government that followed him." Quoting one of his sons for support, Reagan concludes that FDR intended his programs to be only "emergency, stopgap measures to cope with a crisis, not the seeds of what others tried to turn into a permanent welfare state." On a final note, he expresses more doubts: "As smart as he was though, I suspect even FDR didn't realize that once you created a bureaucracy, it took on a life of its own."[15]

Reagan's selective memory split FDR's policies and the New Deal legacy into ideological shards, but the authenticity of an autobiographical narrative protected Reagan against charges of misrepresentation. Here were the portions of the Roosevelt persona that were privileged to him, and the autobiographer is licensed to select those parts of events that are personally meaningful. Reagan's Roosevelt was composed of an autobiographical memory that was now tempered by his own maturity. His idolization of the president remained, but it was bracketed by FDR's failings, not the least of which was the New Deal creation of a federal apparat. About the only surviving element were the memories he kept of national unity and personal sacrifice that were formed through the Depression and war years. Peggy Noonan, a Reagan speech writer, captures the core of this remnant when she insists that Reagan's Roosevelt was derived from a scene in the 1942 *Yankee Doodle Dandy*. An actor playing FDR gives a presidential medal to George M. Cohan (played by Jimmy Cagney). Cohan/Cagney is rendered speechless by Roosevelt's comments about love of country as the president awards the medal for his authorship of "Over There" and "Grand Old Flag."[16]

As dismissive as Reagan would be of New Deal programs ("government is not the solution; government is the problem"), he picked the shard that FDR emphasized throughout his first term. "We have nothing to fear but fear itself" was a core portion of both Roosevelt's solution to the Depression crisis and Reagan's oral history. When asked by a reporter what he thought of FDR's speech exhorting confidence, Reagan replied, "Where do you think I got the idea?"[17] This sense of supreme self-assurance became a central aspect of FDR's persona that Reagan openly imitated, but it was highly distilled through Reagan's own oral history and thus extracted from Roosevelt's own project. The multiple narratives of when Reagan ceased to be a New Deal Democrat were actually exemplary departures of his generation at large. Those Americans, like Al Smith or Raymond Moley, who left the New Deal in 1936 could identify with Reagan's account, as could those who left the slow unraveling of the New Deal coalition at various later dates.

ROOSEVELT/JACKSON/REAGAN

Having shattered FDR into a series of autobiographical pieces, Reagan "repaired" the president through a selective reinterpretation of Roosevelt's own policy swerves and turns. Reagan may have frequently identified with Al Smith's critique of the New Deal, but the central thrust of his own revolution rested with an identification with the populism of the second-term FDR that so infuriated Smith. In order to appreciate Reagan's connection with FDR on this point, the belated president feels that it is necessary to briefly review the nature of Roosevelt's own revolution in 1935–36.

He recalls that until 1936 FDR largely justified New Deal programs through a nationalized interpretation of Jefferson. After a brief period in which he seemed ideologically immobilized, FDR turned ferociously against American corporate capital. Expressly employing the symbols of Jackson and Jacksonian democracy, FDR attacked "economic royalists" who were trying to "gang up against the people's liberties." These were the same kind of men who had also once attacked Jackson, but the people "loved him for the enemies he made." Roosevelt too "welcome(d) their hatred." Roosevelt constructed the welfare state on Jackson's antipathy to finance capital.[18]

The belated president remembers how FDR had engaged in significant misreading of Jacksonian democracy.[19] For while it was true that the western-based Democrats angrily spoke against the "exclusive privileges" of the "moneyed interests," it was the Whigs who attempted to convince the American populace of the value of the national idea and universal benefits which were derived from internal improvements. Thus Webster asked in his famous debate with Hayne: "Can there be nothing in government except for the exercise of mere control? Can nothing be done without corruption . . . ? What is positively beneficent, whatever is actively good, whatever opens channels of intercourse, augments population, enhances the value of property, and diffuses knowledge— must all this be rejected and reprobated as an obnoxious policy?"[20]

He notes too how Tocqueville's analysis captured the ambiguity of the Jacksonian as capitalist/anticapitalist when he spoke of the narrow range of property differences in the United States and the predominance of "eager and apprehensive men of small property" in America. These men are "still almost within reach of property, they see its privations near at hand and dread them; between poverty and themselves there is nothing but a scanty fortune, upon which they fix their apprehensions and hopes." Without the distinction of ranks and with the subdivision of hereditary property, "the love of well-being" becomes the predominant taste of the nation . . . the great current of human passions runs in that channel and sweeps everything in its course."[21] To the Jacksonian, the moneyed interests were attempting through the "monster bank" to close off economic opportunity. FDR played on this apprehensiveness when he drew a distinction between "static' and "dynamic" wealth. The former involved the "perpetuation of great and undesirable concentration of control in a relatively few individuals."[22] The Jacksonians generally sought protection through the dismantling of the governmental apparatus, which they saw as controlled by elites. For FDR, only the federal government could protect the people against rapacious capital. There is a "school of thought in this country that would have us believe that those vast numbers of average citizens who do not get to the top of the economic ladder do not deserve the security which government alone can give."[23]

The Great Depression, of course, highly magnified middle America's focus upon apprehensiveness, and thus FDR needed only to play lip service to "dynamic" capital. But in the post–New Deal era "eagerness" reemerged as a central desire of the mass of Americans, and Reagan's genius lies in rereading Roosevelt's revision of Jacksonianism. As FDR focused his attack on economic elites as those who would "gang up" against the people's liberties, Reagan focused his attack upon governmental elites who had the same ambitions. "Every businessman has his own tale of harassment," said Reagan in his 1964 speech. Roosevelt had demanded that everyone be given "a chance to make a living," travel, obtain a "better job," and "a chance to get ahead." Reagan spoke of the "heroes" who "every day" go "in and out of factory gates" and their "right to heroic dreams."[24] The theme of a hardworking, virtuous people whose aspirations and achievements are blocked by elites was a Jacksonian trope that Roosevelt (mis)read from Jackson and Reagan (mis)read from Roosevelt. In a sense, Reagan had found FDR and FDR had found Jackson much as Marx had found Hegel. Both predecessors were standing on their heads and needed to be turned right side up.

By breaking off the object of FDR's populism from its subject and substituting a new one, Reagan was freed to repiece the remaining pieces into his own "revolution." The decades of reluctant accommodation by Republicans with FDR and the New Deal were thus concluded as Reagan declared his own "rendezvous with destiny." One of the basic features of the New Deal was its use of a "brains trust" to implement FDR's ideological transformation and Reagan too attracted a generation of experts from the academy. At a Conservative Political Action Conference in 1985, Reagan claimed that as FDR once had "ideas that were new" and "captured the imagination of the American people," now he led a movement that no longer was "diffuse and scattered" but which had its own agenda. "We became the party of the most brilliant and dynamic of young minds"; we are "not the defenders of the status quo but creators of the future."[25]

Reagan's apparent affection for FDR angered and puzzled both his critics and supporters. Jimmy Carter charged that Reagan was in no position to quote Roosevelt when he and his party were staging "an attack on almost every achievement in social justice and decency we have won in the last 60 years—since Franklin Roosevelt's first term."[26] In 1982 the *National Review* charged that any formal remembrance of FDR (a planned celebration of the centennial of his birth which Reagan supported) should be "bureaucratic, Cabinet-rank, unconstitutional, more expensive than any before and perpetual so that our children can help pay for it a hundred years from now" for it "to be truly in the FDR mold."[27] Yet these criticisms of the use of Roosevelt missed the nature of Reagan's project. The belated president notes that the Left and Right were outraged because Reagan ignored the agenda of the New Deal. But it was this aspect of FDR that Reagan had repeatedly rejected as he reconstructed his own FDR. Reagan could applaud Roosevelt as "an American giant" and as "one of history's truly monumental figures" because he had broken FDR and his legacy into pieces both manageable enough for him to imitate and independent of his own agenda.[28]

To Reagan as aspiring poet, the lasting achievement of FDR was broken up and reduced to the fragment of confident leadership and an articulation of a unified, vibrant America. The other aspects of the New Deal and wartime policy Reagan treated as missing pieces antithetical or unrelated to his essential Roosevelt. When Reagan repieced the Roosevelt legacy, he was ingenious enough to substitute the leadership shard with another fragment of FDR's own text. Roosevelt's Jacksonianism involved an extremely talented reading of American political culture. FDR grasped how this populist sentiment which had appeared regularly in American politics (and indeed was emerging as a critique of the New Deal itself on the part of men like Long and Coughlin) could be reformed in the context of the Great Depression. Reagan applied this new Jacksonianism against the New Deal itself.

The belated president is appropriately awed by Reagan's strategy to overcome belatedness. He wonders, however, if Reagan had permanently shattered FDR the way that Lincoln had double-crossed the founders and FDR himself glided past them with his multiple masks. He considers the relationship between the Reagan revolution and the revolution of 1800. It is not, he thinks, that the Reagan revolution unraveled with the Iran crisis in his second term as some commentators argued that Jefferson's did with the embargo. To the belated president, the diversion of funds showed the same kind of poetic intent as did peaceable coercion. The Reagan executive-centered foreign policy apparat sought victory in its own fashion, as did Jefferson's with regard to the British. The Reagan doctrine and peaceable coercion might be miles away from each other in terms of the role of force, but both policies considered as poetic strategies sought to dramatically alter the world order as both men found it. Even the exercise of executive power in Reagan's case was less recognized in terms of the doubling effect than Jefferson's, since Reagan had long made military strength a central part of his own poetic project and insisted that it was one which FDR also shared.

No, continues the belated president, there was something missing in the Reagan revolution that made it significant but less than monumental. The belated president returns to his analysis of FDR and remembers his own conclusion that perhaps Roosevelt's adoption of the Jacksonian persona involved less an opportunistic strategy to rationalize power than an opportunity to save it from enlightened administration. It is true that Reagan brilliantly captured the other half of the Tocquevillian dialectic, substituting eagerness for apprehensiveness, but had he grasped the nature of FDR's poetic intent? For FDR, Jackson represented an opportunity to avoid the poetically disadvantageous possibilities of a nationalized Jefferson, and he found that he could also discard the Old Hickory persona when it was blocked and exhausted. But next to Reagan/Jackson there was no Lincoln (although there would be claims of monumental achievement in the fact that he occupied the chair in the last years of the Soviet empire). Thus the belated president concludes that while Reagan had imitated FDR's genial casualness masterfully and donned one of FDR's masks in order to shred one of his poetic projects, he had not left the shards in such a state that they were irrevocably broken. The belated president concludes that while FDR/Jefferson/Jackson/Lincoln became FDR alone, Reagan remained the man who genially tore off one of these masks. He was, in short, a president who challenged successfully one of FDR's poetic strategies by reversing, at least temporarily, the enlightened administration of America's first welfare state much as Jefferson had reversed the Washington-Hamilton ministry. During his address to the 1992 Republican presidential convention, Reagan's persona easily overwhelmed George Bush, but when he chided the young Clinton by exclaiming, "You are no Jefferson, I knew Jefferson," he epitomized his minor poetic achievement. It was certainly an intriguing and apt phrasing, at once an act of self-effacement and self-promotion. But had Reagan been more poetically direct and offered the line, "You are no FDR, I knew FDR," his still-belated relationship to Roosevelt could be discerned. His liberal detractors had long said that he was no FDR in an attempt to challenge his poetic project on ideological terms. To these criticisms, as the belated president saw, Reagan could be casually dismissive. But could he be as casual to the poetic assessment that he was no FDR?

Chapter 9

WILSON/HOOVER/NIXON: THE GREAT FALL

◆ ◆

The belated president concludes that these brief reviews of two minor poets have been extremely helpful in his quest to alleviate his condition, for they illustrate how extraordinarily difficult it is to fully overcome predecessors. There is no doubt in his mind that Jefferson and Reagan were poet-presidents as there is no doubt in his mind that they could not quite avoid the poetic assessment that they remained under the influence of Washington and FDR. It is this analysis of failure that leads him to undertake his final project in overcoming his own belatedness. For if Jefferson and Reagan were minor poets, they were by definition failed poets. But their failures were as incomplete as their efforts to achieve monumental status. His thoughts race to what he sees as the next logical course of his study. If there are monumental successes and incomplete successes/failures, there must then be monumental failures. He is uncomfortably aware that the history of the American presidency is strewn with failures: failures to achieve monumental status as well as failures to confront belatedness. Even in the hagiology of the presidency, in which poetic intent is completely disguised from view, narratives draw upon the confrontation with monumental crises, all of which contain the possibility, even the likelihood, of failure. There are also, discovers the belated president, presidents in which failure is so profound, so striking that they become defined in terms of their failure. They are in effect monumental failures. Naturally, not every feature of such a presidency deserves this characterization, just as not every feature of a monumentally successful presidency is one of achievement. But as in the case of monumental success, monumental failure captures the presidency and magnifies and informs all other elements. The belated president considers three such presidencies that came to be defined in these terms, and he links them with their narratives of monumental failure: Woodrow Wilson and the failed peace, Herbert Hoover and the Depression, Richard Nixon and Watergate.

FAILURE NARRATIVES

The belated president is immediately intrigued by his discovery that there are those who link these three presidencies and their narratives of monumental failure to one another. He studies James David Barber's categorization of the active-negative president. The active-negative character, one which includes strong impulses toward the denial of self-gratification and a struggle to contain aggressive impulses, produces a bellicose personality. Here are energetic presidents, "first extraordinarily capable and then extraordinarily rigid," whose characters seem programmed for failure. The belated president notes that each of his own selections of monumental failure are examples of active-negative presidents, presidents which Barber conflates into "a set of dynamically connected behavioral and psychological reactions to recurrent situations."[1]

He next reviews Gary Wills's assessment in *Nixon Agonistes*, written at the height of Nixon's power. While Barber links Wilson/Hoover/Nixon in terms of common character, Wills studies Nixon as part of a common ideology. Occupying a world view that was composed of markets—moral, economic, intellectual, and political—Nixon was the archetypical liberal. It was liberalism, from Wills perspective, which constituted the core explanation for Nixon's failure. Liberalism was Nixon's agon, and Wills placed Wilson, and to a lesser extent Hoover, as the exemplar of a "moldering system" that Nixon struggled to bring to back to life. "It is no wonder then," concludes Wills, "that Nixon—identifying so with Woodrow Wilson—should blunder as Wilson did."[2]

The belated president finds these analyses helpful as narratives of monumental failure, but he is much more impressed with the linkages constructed by these presidents themselves. Herbert Hoover had a number of subcabinet responsibilities in the Wilson administration. After he completed his series of justificatory memoirs and numerous political analyses, he began a book-length manuscript of another monumental poetic failure when he was in his eighties. As we shall see, Hoover's analysis of Wilson was not without strong hostile elements. On the whole, however, Hoover drew a poignant portrait of Wilson, whom he compared to the slain Greek warriors memorialized by Pericles. Hoover was not interested in Wilson's entire life, or even his whole presidency, but only in the period of Wilson's agon: "The purpose of this book is solely to unfold the President's plans, his obstacles, his methods, his successes and the causes of the tragedy which came to him in his efforts to bring lasting peace to the world."[3] Nixon never devoted a book to Wilson, but he certainly frequently expressed his poetic affinities. Wilson's was the only Democratic president's portrait hung in the Nixon White House. Nixon compared his religious and personal background to Wilson's and thought he was the best president of this century. Like Hoover, Nixon too was not uncritical of his self-proclaimed exemplar. Wilson "had the greatest vision of America's world role. But he wasn't practical enough."[4]

The belated president wonders what is the fascination that monumental failures hold for another monumental failure. Hoover's ruin was established beyond doubt when he wrote his biography of Wilson's "ordeal," and while Nixon's Great Fall was some years away, no president was more conversant with failure than he. In his subsequent introductions to *Six Crises*, which was occasioned by his failure to win election in 1960, Nixon spoke of his life in terms of an "exquisite agony" and recommended his work as "the record of one man's experience in meeting crises—including both his failures and successes."[5] Indeed, the opening lines of the original volume showed how intertwined was success/failure for Nixon. He had beat Hiss, but the victory was the reason why he failed to become president in 1960. On the other hand, had he not defeated Hiss, he would not have been vice-president nor a presidential candidate. Why did these failed men then so publicly identify with a failure? To Barber and Wills, who present a hagiography of failure, psychological and ideological, Hoover and Nixon were destined to reenact the Great Fall. But to the belated president this kind of analysis is the dialectical reverse of the success narrative. As the explanations of Washington's or Lincoln's or FDR's monumental successes could be traced backward to youthful moments of dedication and character formation indicating the inevitability of their greatness, so too can the Wilson/Hoover/Nixon failures be deterministically traced.

The belated president's illness makes him ruthless in his examination of past presidents, and thus he will not avert his eyes from such a conclusion, even if there exists the possibility that such an analysis applies to him. He may be terrorized by the prospect that he is destined to be a Wilson/Hoover/Nixon, but suffering from his affliction is worse. At the very worst, he might conclude, I could be a monumental failure, which, after all, is a mark of distinction that the belated cannot claim. So it is not timidity that makes him doubt the Barber-Wills approach but, rather, a dissatisfaction with their narratives of failure. If the mark of the active-negative is pursuit of policies that any rational person could see were failures, then Washington, Jackson, Lincoln, FDR, and others could be designated active-negatives. After all, Washington pursued the rebellious farmers in western Pennsylvania when it was apparent that there was no evidence of any real threat. The belated president, who has just studied Jefferson, could easily place him as an active-negative in terms of his pursuit of the embargo when it was clear that the policy was destined to failure. And what of Jackson's obsession with the Bank of the United States, Lincoln's pursuit of victory, and FDR's battle with the court? These dogged pursuits of policies are regarded as errant strategies in the hands of other strong presidents (Washington, Jefferson, FDR) or signs of monumental courage (Jackson, Lincoln). Similarly, the insistence that redeeming features be reclaimed from dead or dying ideologies is not necessarily a mark of programmed failure, else FDR would have been so designated (for what ideological system could have been more discredited in 1932 than liberalism?).

Instead, the belated president rejects the centrality of the failure narrative as a model for studying failed poet-presidents in the same manner that he rejected the success narrative in the cases of monumental and spirited presidents.

Hoover/Nixon sought Wilson as their poetic inspiration not because they were attracted to his Great Fall as a basis for their own programmed failure, even subconsciously, or even as their own justification of failure. It is true, thinks the belated president, that Hoover/Nixon focused upon Wilson's Great Fall, but their poetic intent may have centered upon their attempts to surpass Wilson by succeeding where he failed. It is also true, concludes the belated president, that when Hoover/Nixon experienced their own Great Fall, respectively, the success/failure narrative of Wilson intertwined and they did embrace the con-nection somewhat along the lines outlined by Barber-Wills. That is, Hoover/Wilson accepted the poetic status as monumental failure and compared their agon to Wilson's. Thus there are two narratives in the Hoover/Nixon exten-sion of the Wilson Great Fall narrative: failure (Wilson)/success (Hoover, Nixon) and failure (Wilson, Hoover, Nixon). In the former, poetic intent is revealed thusly: I will achieve poetic independence (and hence an end to be-latedness) by succeeding monumentally where another failed monumentally.

WILSON'S MONUMENTAL GAMBLE

What, asks the belated president, was the nature of Wilson's failed poetic project that Hoover/Nixon felt they could extract and recover as monumental success? Wilson's postwar poetic vision, of course, submerges the full range of his po-etic intent as well as his poetry. Wilson struggled as only a monumental poet can to interpret the world in order to alter it. His studies were "in keeping with my whole mental make-up" and "in obedience to a true instinct." Even Aristotle's efforts were not satisfactory in terms of his own ambition "to pen-etrate" a polity's "essential character."[6] In *Congressional Government* he an-nounced his discovery of what could be said to be the praxis for the realization of his poetic intent. If a president "rightly interpret the national thought and boldly insist upon it, he is irresistible."[7] The 1912 election represented a per-fect application of this method, for Wilson had correctly interpreted the public's reluctance to shed Jefferson and he attacked Theodore Roosevelt on precisely this point. Although his own hostility to Jefferson was not much less marked than TR's, Wilson stated his own "ever renewed admiration" for the president, praised Jefferson "more often and ardently than at any other time in his life and cast the election as an analogue to the struggles of the 1790s."[8]

Wilson's use of Jefferson in 1912 was thus reluctant and opportunistic, even for a belated president. He confided to Colonel House that he judged Hamilton the ablest man in the early days of the Republic. But Wilson eventually found a way to "honor" him in the context of his greatest poetic project. In 1916 he declared that the "immortality" of Jefferson rested with none of his achieve-ments "but in his attitude toward mankind and the conception which he sought to realize in action of the service allowed by America to the rest of the world." The *only* way, then, to "honor" him was to follow this universalizing spirit in demanding "concerted action for the rights of men, first in America and then by America's example everywhere in the world." This, said, Wilson, is "the thing that interested Jefferson" and "is the *only* thing that ought to interest me."[9] The belated president is struck by how visible here is Wilson's poetic intent. Jefferson's spirit is important not his achievements and the spirit is the "only thing" that *interest(s)* Wilson.

The belated president knows, as, of course, did Wilson, of Jefferson's hostility to relationships with Europe. Jefferson, in fact, referred to Europe as a "mad house" during the embargo. But he also discovered in the Hegelian fashion of interpretation that was his strategy against belatedness that Jefferson's spirit also intimated an eventual American hegemony. Thus Jefferson's belief in American exceptionalism, which did constitute his central poetic vision, or his "spirit" as Wilson called it, was both a source of a turning away from a contaminated preliberal world and an intimation encompassing it as a world historical nation. Such, believes the belated president, was in outline Wilson's great poetic project, and the Great War in Europe provided him with the opportunity. Wilson knew, of course, that Theodore Roosevelt had reached similar conclusions about international politics and poetic achievement. Roosevelt's vision, however, was very much a spirited one, and his references to Wilson as "only another Buchanan" could be taken as the agonies of belatedness.

Wilson's project, however, rested upon an intuitive grasp of Jefferson's poetic vision. In 1916 he observed that the progressive movement had discovered a national unity and spirit of cooperation in the antagonisms caused by industrialization. America stood now poised to bring unity to a world torn by aggression. When peace comes, Wilson told his audience, we "shall stand for the just conceptions and bases of peace, for the competitions of merit alone, and for the generous rivalry of liberty."[10] After America entered the war, Wilson attempted to Americanize the world at Versailles through his famous Fourteen Points and then through his vision of the League of Nations. One current analyst cogently states the nature of Wilson's project as one in which "a Wilsonian America was to be the historical agent of the world's transformation from chaos and imperialism to orderly liberal rationality." America "both participated in and yet, at the same time, transcended the existing system of international politics. America thus interacted as a nation-state with others in the 'Hobbesian' realm of world politics and shifting alliances, while America was simultaneously the carrier of values seeking to rationalize and to pacify that very political universe."[11]

There are, of course, several variations of the failure narrative in regard to this monumental poetic vision. One focuses upon the resistance at Versailles to the vision. Clemenceau and George were unmoved by Wilson's poetry, which was proof of Wilson's delusions or Europe's own lack of poetic vision. Others focus upon America's failure to join the league, which was the result of Wilson's moral self-righteousness, a reemergent American isolationism, or fate (Wilson's stroke prevented the success of taking his poetry to the people). In all these variations, Wilson experiences the Great Fall. He is struck down by petty men (George et al. and Lodge), American postwar loss of nerve, his own hubris, or Fate. Many students of Wilson are thus able to see the possibility of a success scenario in these failure narratives. Wilson should have relied more on his staff at Versailles, he should have seen Lodge's opposition as partisan and personal baiting, he should have compromised on the reservations, he should not have driven himself so hard. Is it possible, though, asks the belated president, that Wilson undertook a monumental poetic risk in his personal diplomacy at Versailles, in his insistence on maintaining the purity of the covenant, on endangering his health? Was it possible, in other words, that Wilson's actions were less programmed failures, personal or ideological, than a momentous bet which, if it had succeeded, would have transformed national boundaries in Europe along liberal lines of self-determination and transformed the international system into an extension of America? If this were the case, or more properly, if other presidents had grasped Wilson's monumental gamble, then he can see why others should make this monumental failure their exemplar to be surpassed. If other presidents secretly say to themselves, "I will succeed, where Wilson failed," then he will be in a position to study the repetition of these great bets.

HOOVER: RAISING THE ANTE

Did Hoover make such a monumental bet? In order to answer this question the belated president must first peel away the failure narrative that has enveloped the Hoover presidency. He must reject for the moment the story of poetic invention that he was a morally stubborn "cold hearted" man, "totally devoid of heart, inept, or actionless in the face of the Great Depression," a man who was "constitutionally gloomy," a man who covered his lack of feeling with his "mastery of information," a man who paid for his "obeisance to Mammon" as he must reject the story that he was a prisoner of nineteenth-century liberalism whose "policies as Secretary of Commerce, then as President contributed substantially and directly to the Great Depression."[12] The belated president notes that both of these critiques contain personal and ideological attributes that actually formed part of a success narrative until 1932. In 1928 he was known as the "Great Engineer," and the *New York Times* said his "office looked more like a machine shop than a room in whose mind commanded all experience and whose wave of hand organized fleets of rescue vessels and millions of contributions."[13] During the Depression the word "Hoover" became a description of any number of failures (Hoovervilles, Hoover gardens). During the war, however, "to Hooverize" meant to conserve for victory, and because of his successful activities as administrator of relief in Europe after World War I, his technical expertise and policy innovation had come "to mean food for the starving and medicine for the sick." The campaigner, who in 1932 was said to have a face that would wither a flower, was four years earlier "an idealist representing enlightened individualism, humanitarianism, harmony, liberty." To one of Hoover's biographers, "the great engineer and humanitarian still lived beneath the new mantle of the Great Depression president."[14] But as with all Great Fall presidencies, the former was solidly hidden.

Let me assume then, says the belated president, that Hoover had monumental potential and monumental ambition and attempt to discern how his Great Fall might be connected to his success rather than some narrative of failure. He studies historians who have examined both the pre- and post-Depression Hoover. Martin Fausold has concluded that the commerce secretary was "the more liberal and progressive candidate in 1928."[15] He received the support of Jane Addams, the Chicago reformer who voted for Debs in 1920 and LaFollette in 1924. She endorsed his farm policy, his positions on collective bargaining (Hoover had gone on record favoring the curtailment of "excessive use" of injunctions in labor disputes), his concern for the poor. Some historians believe they have detected in Hoover a political philosophy of considerable innovation that was neither liberal nor conservative. William Appleman Williams described Hoover as "the keystone in the arch that leads from Mark Hanna and Herbert Croly to such later figures as Nelson Rockefeller and Adolph Berle." For Williams it was Hoover who was one of the first American leaders to see that the competitive capitalism that characterized much of American history was operationally obsolete and needed to be replaced by a cooperative system of both labor and capital led by a "class conscious industrial gentry."[16] Ellis Hawley, a historian of both the "New Era" period and the New Deal, has taken Williams's observation one step further. Hawley calls Hoover's philosophy "corporativism." He is careful to point out that Hoover was not influenced by the "fascist perversion of the corporate ideal" but that like his counterparts in Europe he was concerned about the "destructive competition" and "social anarchy" in capitalism and envisioned a new order through "scientific coordination and moral regeneration." Hawley concludes, then, that the dividing line between Hoover and FDR is not one between a laissez-faire and a managed economy as proposed by those who see Hoover as a conservative, but "one attempt at management, through informal private and public cooperation to other more formal and coercive yet also limited attempts."[17] Murray N. Rothbard, the libertarian economist, concurs with this assessment. In his *America's Great Depression* he argues that in Hoover's programs like the Reconstruction Finance Corporation, which provided loans to banks and businesses, "laissez-faire was boldly thrown overboard and every governmental weapon thrown into the breach" and rejects, much to his own ideological regret, that Hoover did not hold steadfastly to nineteenth-century liberalism in order to weather the Depression.[18]

Was Hoover, who refused to use the full weight of government to deal with social and economic problems, a believer in laissez-faire? Was he really a progressive caught in the storm of the Depression? Was he a "corporativist" seeking new kinds of partnership between government and business? Did he, in fact, improvise when confronted with the Depression? The belated president turns to Hoover's major theoretical work, *American Individualism*, to judge for himself if Hoover was a man of poetic intent and vision.

He finds that *American Individualism*, published in 1922 when Hoover was secretary of commerce in the Harding administration, is a remarkable book. Hoover begins his essay by outlining his understanding of American exceptionalism. In his seven years of service overseas he had seen nations "burned in revolution." These ideologies may be "clothed by the demagogue" in "the terms of political idealism," but they have unleashed the "bestial instincts of hate, murder and destruction." America too had an ideology, one in which "partisans of some of these other schemes" insist is exhausted. Hoover defines this ideology as "individualism" but insists that "our individualism differs form all others" and is "not the individualism of other countries."[19] The remainder of the book involves an attempt on Hoover's part to define the historical development of this ideology in America and to explain how much it contributes to America's political stability and economic well-being.

Hoover, who describes himself as an "unashamed individualist," divides his discussion of individualism into four aspects: philosophical, spiritual, economic, and political. The philosophical grounding of individualism is based upon the recognition of two basic instincts, selfishness and altruism. For Hoover, the dominant human instincts are selfish and "the problem of the world is to restrain the destructive instincts while strengthening and enlarging those of altruistic character and constructive impulse." The "will-o'-the wisp of all breeds of socialism" is that it asserts "motivation of human animals by altruism alone." In order to achieve a surface resemblance to other-regarding behavior, socialists find that they must create a "bureaucracy of the entire population." Similarly, autocracies, in which Hoover includes all forms of class rule—even unrestrained capitalism—suppose that "the good Lord endowed a special few with all the divine attributes." Autocrats treat others only as means. The proof of the futility of this idea lay with the "grim failure of Germany" and those in America "who have sought economic domination."

To date, Americans had rejected both of these faulty conceptions of human nature. They had rejected the "clap-trap of the French Revolution" and they had rejected the ideas of a "frozen strata of classes." As proof of the latter, Hoover cites the twelve men comprising the presidency, vice-presidency, and cabinet, nine of which "earned their own way in life without economic inheritance, and eight of them started with manual labor."

The second aspect of individualism, the spiritual, assumes that there is a "divine spark" that can "be awakened in every heart." Hoover notes the impact of the religious origins of America in maintaining this idea, but it is in this section that he outlines his conception of what can best be called service individualism as the key element in the America individualism that "differs from all other." Proof of this spiritual spark is the "vast multiplication of voluntary organizations for altruistic purposes" in America. He continues:

> These associations for the advancement of public welfare improvements, morals, charity, public opinion, health, the clubs and societies for recreation and intellectual advancement, represent something moving at a far greater depth than "joining." They represent the widespread aspiration for mutual advancement, self expression, and neighborly helpfulness.[20]

The essence of American individualism, then, was service. Hoover asked, "When we rehearse our own individual memories of success, we find that none gives us such comfort as the memory of service given. Do we not refer to our veterans as service men? Do not merchants and business men pride themselves in something of service given beyond the price of their goods?" In his section on economic aspects of individualism Hoover completed his designation of the businessperson as one engaged in the provision of a service. The principle "every man for himself and the devil take the hindmost" may have been a code of conduct in the American past, but "our development of individualism shows an increasing tendency to regard right of property not as an object in itself but in light of a useful and necessary instrument in stimulation of initiative to the individual." The goal of economic activity, then, was not "the acquisition and preservation of private property—the selfish snatching and hoarding of the common product." As a form of "self expression" it was an activity designed to produce "a high and growing standard of living for all the people, not for a single class." Hoover listed the "comforts" (electric lights, plumbing, telephones, gramophones, automobiles) that had begun as luxuries and now had become so commonplace that 70 or 80 percent of the population could afford them.

Hoover admitted that when private property became concentrated in the hands of the few, "the individual begins to feel capital as an oppressor." But American individualism had devised a variety of mechanisms to prevent this occurrence. One was the "American demand for equality of opportunity" as "a constant militant check upon capital." Hoover cited the income tax as a means by which the "surplus" from profits could be shared. He also supported regulation to prevent economic domination and unfair practices. In his chapter on political aspects of American individualism, Hoover discussed the faults in the American system. He is careful to point out that the achievements far outweigh the shortcomings, but nevertheless his list is not a short one: "The spirit of lawlessness; the uncertainty of unemployment in some callings; the deadening effect of certain repetitive processes of manufacture; the twelve hour day in a few industries; unequal voice in bargaining for wage in some employment; arrogant domination by some employers and some labor leaders; child labor in some states; inadequate instruction in some areas; unfair competition in some industries; some fortunes excessive far beyond the needs of stimulation to initiative; survivals of religious intolerance; political debauchery of some cities;weakness in our governmental structure."[21]

The belated president can see how commentators can draw different conclusions from Hoover's political philosophy. An emphasis on his interpretation of American exceptionalism serves to underline the limits to governmental intervention in the economy. Hoover was so impressed by the failure of European governments and so impressed with the success of the American system that any measure that borrowed from socialism was to be rejected. There is a "deadline between our system and socialism," he wrote in *American Individualism*. "Regulation to prevent domination and unfair practices, yet preserving rightful initiative are in keeping with our social foundations. Nationalization of industry or business is their negation."[22]

Yet despite Hoover's profession of having discovered the essence of the

American system in the concept of individualism, there is clearly a collectivist strain in his thought. He warmly embraced the corporation as a new form of economic organization that was more efficient, more rational, more innovative, and even more public spirited than the small farm or firm. In 1928, for instance, he told the residents of his home town of West Branch, Iowa, that despite the bravery and kindness of the early settlers, we "must avoid becoming homesick for the ways of those self-contained farm houses of 40 years ago." These yeomen had "lower standards of living, greater toil, less opportunity for leisure and recreation, less of the comforts of home, less of the joy of living." Besides, there was no way to go back to simpler times. It was no more possible to "revive those old conditions than it was to summon back the relatives in the cemetery yonder." Farming was now a business with 80 percent of production for market use. Once self-sufficiency was transcended through improved feed and livestock and a "long list of mechanical inventions for saving labor," the economy of scale changed and the farmer joined an "economic system vastly more intricate and delicately adjusted than before."[23]

Hoover's model, then, envisioned groups of farmers, labor unions, corporations, chambers of commerce, bankers, all nationally organized and motivated, as he had said in *American Individualism,* by a mixture of self-interest and altruism. In Hegelian fashion, the former was declining and the latter rising. The government would foster the conditions for their cooperation. In this aspect, one can see the elements of progressivism in Hoover's political thought. He never advocated a "greed is good" ideology. In fact, his central defense of capitalism was always based upon its ability as a system to promote a sense of service to the community. He mirrored the progressive's commitment to discovering ways to promote the public good through a rational approach to solving social problems. For Hoover, no fault in the American system was potentially irremediable. Even poverty could be abolished through the general increase in the standard of living and the volunteer efforts of communities. The list of social problems he drew up in 1922 were "becoming steadily more local . . . That they are recognized and condemned is a long way on the road to progress."

Of course, Hoover's synthesis was short-lived. He barely had a moment to implement his ideas when the Crash and the Great Depression smashed the American system as he understood it. The very aspects of his thought that had seemed so irresistible in 1928 seemed limited and inflexible by 1930. Despite Hoover's famous dictum after the Crash that the economy was fundamentally sound, he expressed belief that the downturn would be a long, hard one. He refused to accept his treasury secretary's view that the Crash provided social Darwinist opportunities for the elimination of inefficient business and the liquidation of unnecessary labor. Wages must remain stable and the unemployed provided for, according to Hoover. Business must accept some of the responsibility for the Depression because of "over-optimism as to profits."

Hoover believed that the cause of the Depression rested with the unstable economies of Europe, and hence to copy measures undertaken in Germany, France, or England would only compound America's problems. His approach to relief for the unemployed paralleled his approach as relief administrator after World War I. In both cases, he saw the government's role as one in which private relief funds were coordinated. When a Democratic Congress demanded direct relief monies for the unemployed, he admitted that the impulse came from a "natural anxiety for the people of their states" but insisted that direct appropriations would "break down" the "sense of responsibility and mutual help." The issue was not one of financial integrity but that the "cost of a few score millions" would create "an abyss of reliance in the future upon charity in some form or another." Only the mobilization and organization of "the infinite number of agencies of self help in the community" could be the basis of "successful relief in national distress."[24] In 1932, however, Hoover acted more boldly (as Rothbard emphasizes) in dealing with what he called "the temporary mobilization of timid capital." The Reconstruction Finance Corporation, initially capitalized at $500 million by the federal government, was created to lend funds to railroads, banks, insurance companies, and building and loan associations. But the administration of the program tended to be overly cautious in its lending policies, at least in terms of the emergency at hand, and the public at large began to perceive the program as money spent on "plutocrats." By late spring, Hoover seemed to have almost given up on the plan.

The belated president understands that the problem with Hoover's American system was that, after 1929, its major premises no longer seemed operational. Local communities and volunteer organizations had nothing more to give. The prosperity that Hoover guaranteed would be the inevitable result of the growth of the corporation vanished to a memory. The divine spark seemed to have flickered and gone out. Still, Hoover believed that the country would have pulled out of the crisis had not European banks defaulted in 1931. Then he blamed the persistence of the Depression on Franklin Roosevelt's policies. In fact, in spite of his unpopularity, the former president continued throughout the 1930s to advance his belief in the verities of the American system.

The belated president wonders, then, if Hoover was not a nineteenth-century liberal; indeed, if he was in some sense a collectivist (and one more consistently so than FDR), and even a policy innovator in the face of the Depression, why did his presidency become so enveloped in failure? There is, of course, an answer that centers the role of fate in the Hoover presidency. No matter how innovative Hoover might have been, given the intractability of the economic crisis, voters would have cast out the incumbent. But the failure narrative itself rejects this simple formulation, arguing instead that Hoover drew a needless line between relief and grants and community and public aid much as Wilson had done in regard to Senate reservations and interpretations to the League of Nations and thus actively participated in his Great Fall.

He turns to Hoover's analysis of Wilson for an answer. To Hoover, Wilson was not an "obstinate" man. In fact, while he may have made errors of judgment in failing to compromise with the U.S. Senate, his refusal was based on the fact that he had compromised so much at Versailles. The European leaders were "cynical" men who hated Wilson for his ideals. Although the people they allegedly represented were either starving, "economically exhausted," or "desperate," they fed them hatred. "In the blood of many delegations at Versailles were the genes of a thousand years of hate and distrust, bred of religious and racial persecution and domination by other races."[25] Wilson gave in on each of his Fourteen Points, compromising to the point of surrender on Shantung, the Saar, reparations, and the blockade. Wilson acceded "along the line" in order "to rescue the League."[26] Regardless of American ratification, Wilson's bet, sacrificing his Fourteen Points "rather than lose the League," "sowed the whole earth with dragon's teeth." When the Depression broke, Hoover saw the economic chaos that Europe brought on itself as not only a vindication of Wilson's original project, which was so cynically rejected, but as a threat to the Europeanization of America.

In 1932 (and for the rest of his life) Hoover insisted that the Depression's source was in Europe (contrary to FDR, who Americanized the catastrophe as a result of the failure of home-grown economic elites) and saw any willingness to employ European policies as complicity in the creation of a Versailles II. Europe was a place of "disease and starvation" after the war, a place of "poisoned springs" after the armistice treaties, which produced "fear and hate" in their armament races and "enlarged" government spending in which everywhere power was centralized through the declaration of economic emergencies. In this sense, FDR was the Wilson of the Great Fall, since he incorrectly believed he could "experiment" with the economy and compromise with other economic theories as Wilson believed he could compromise on peace terms, and Hoover was the Wilson before the Great Fall, who envisioned the poetic project of pax Americana and developed a strategy of weathering the "violent shocks" that reached American shores with "hurricane force." Had Hoover won his bet, he would be in a position to abolish poverty in America and preside over the Hegelian rationalization of the new corporate economy as Europe sunk deeper in chaos until it was ready to accept salvation. The belated president concludes that Hoover's bet was a long shot but that it was not an irrational or unimaginative strategy. Most important to him, Hoover's bet involved a wager designed to overcome belatedness, for he would have succeeded where Wilson had failed. After the Great Fall, however, Hoover's identification with Wilson (in which poetic intent is, of course, veiled) appears to be neatly congruent with the failure narrative. Hoover was a monumental failure who admired Wilson, another monumental failure.

NIXON'S SECRET WAGER

The belated president hesitates as he approaches Richard Nixon, for Nixon employed so frequently and dramatically the failure narrative throughout his career that his entire persona seems to be mapped by sharp turns of failure/success. There are, to highlight: Eisenhower's intention to drop him from the 1956 ticket, the 1960 defeat, his defeat by Pat Brown, and, of course, the Great Fall—Watergate and resignation. In each of these cases Nixon advertised his con-

frontation with failure. It is certainly true that, except for the last monumental failure, Nixon's career was studded with successes: his successful campaigns
against Jerry Voorhis and Helen Douglas, his selection as a young man as
Eisenhower's vice-president, his landslide victory in 1972, the SALT agreement
with the Soviets, the opening to China. Yet Nixon dwelt upon his defeats, if
only to magnify his subsequent successes. Thus there was always a "new" Nixon
who emerged after he himself admitted that the press would not have him available to kick around anymore, after he was designated a "chronic campaigner."
Even in his success, Nixon held the failure narrative at its poetic center, as when
he told the press in 1973 after the signing of the peace agreement with North
Vietnam, which he described as "peace with honor," "I know it gags some of
you to write that phrase, but its true, and most Americans realize it is true."
Then, too, there were those dramatic gestures—gestures in which the American people seemed to see the man nearly unravel in alternate expressions of
desperation, self-pity, and anger—Nixon always undertook as he faced failure:
the Checkers speech, the "last press conference" in 1962, the late night trip to
the Lincoln memorial, and, of course, his resignation "address." The belated
president is so impressed with this autobiographical narrative of failure that he
is tempted to agree with the psychoanalytic observers who describe the president as "self-loathing," "compulsive obsessive," "paranoid." He was, so concludes
one such analyst, "his own executioner. He punished himself by arranging his
own failures."[27] Yet he knows these are anxieties that every belated president
experiences, although they are hidden behind poetic veils. Interestingly, Nixon
often expressed an affection for a spirited president, Theodore Roosevelt, who
too had difficulty hiding poetic intent, although in a very different way. He
concludes that Nixon's failure narratives are themselves poetic veils, perhaps
not always very effectively employed, but effective enough to disguise his own
poetic ambition. Thus even his admirers and opponents often admitted their
own failure to discern the "real" Nixon. Upon his election in 1968, Tom Wicker
confessed that the "career and personality of Richard Nixon defy confident
analysis."[28] Gary Wills, who hoped to capture Nixon as the last liberal and hence
a captive of ideology, admitted that he was "the least authentic man alive,"
always in the process of creation and re-creation. He "survived by keeping all
sides off balance—which makes it hard for a consensus to be reached among
people so often inspired and disgusted by his acts (often in quick succession)."[29]
H. R. Haldeman, William Safire, and Bryce Harlow often spoke of the impen-
etrability of the man. This remoteness and imperviousness, notes the belated
president, is a characteristic of successful poet-presidents like Washington,
Lincoln, and FDR.

The belated president concludes that he need not find the "real" Nixon, as
he did not need to discover the "real" Lincoln or the "real" FDR, beyond the
assumption that Nixon suffered from belatedness and that he coped with his
affliction in his own case history through the creation of failure narratives. He
makes a great effort to reject, for the moment, that the failure narrative itself
was Nixon's monumental project and that he sought in some psychologically

dense fashion his own monumental demise. He knows the poetically inclined Nixon was deft at employing these failure tropes, but he thinks that Nixon's poetic intent was like all other belated presidents. Nixon yearned for monumental success. He created his failure narratives either in order to remain positioned for poetic contention or to highlight his intended monumental achievements.

The belated president turns to Nixon's Wilson for some clue to his quest to alleviate belatedness. When Gary Wills interviewed him in 1968, Nixon spoke of his admiration for Wilson and added the conventional aspiring poet's caveat: "Wilson had the greatest vision of America's world role. But he wasn't practical enough. Take his 'open agreements openly arrived at.' That is no way diplomacy is conducted. The Vietnamese war, for instance, will be settled at secret high level negotiations."[30] It is a standard assessment of Nixon that his poetic ambition lay not in the domestic arena. Although he could be inventive enough to unbalance critics and even symbolized his policies in terms of Disraeli's, Nixon cast his poetic role as a "white revolutionary" (one who employs "radical" means for conservative ends) foremost in international terms.[31] The belated president notes that Wilson's international vision contained a strong central, although suppressed, agenda of containing revolutionary socialism as well as conventional great power imperialism, but he is most struck with Nixon's secrecy critique of Wilson. At the very heart of the Wilsonian project was openness. Once international antagonisms were submitted to world scrutiny, great power machinations would be restrained and forced to cope with standards of justice and reason. Nixon's rejection of the first of the Fourteen Points thus actually entailed a hostile reading of Wilson, and his substitution of secrecy showed the nature of his own poetic revision.

In 1971, when Nixon's strategy for ending the war "with honor" was in serious danger of failure, he turned to Wilson again. The *Chicago Sun-Times* had expressed its frustration with the administration's Vietnam policy and warned that as quarterback Nixon faced a "3rd and 20" situation. During his remarks at the dedication of the Woodrow Wilson Center, he reviewed Wilson's agon. Wilson had failed to reverse isolationist sentiment and died a broken man. Later generations, however, realized that Wilson had been correct and had they accepted his leadership, World War I might indeed been the "war to end all wars." Nixon noted that since Wilson's failure "every wartime president . . . had been tempted to describe the current war as the war to end wars . . . But they have not done so because of the derision that the phrase evoked, a reminder . . . of hopes that were raised and dashed." Nixon announced his poetic intent, the completion of the Wilsonian poetic vision that no subsequent president had dared to even state: "What I am striving for above all else . . . is something that America has never experienced in this century: a full generation of peace."[32]

In 1971 Nixon had already applied his poetic revision to the war in Vietnam. He had secretly corresponded with Ho Chi Minh; Henry Kissinger had entered secret negotiations with North Vietnamese officials; he had secretly bombed Cambodia. He had already initiated a series of covert actions designed to prevent leaks of his secret diplomacy and prosecution of the war. In essence, he had extended the doctrine of secrecy to the war at home. Nixon was a desperate president in 1971. He was determined "not to go out wimpering." The following year he blockaded Vietnamese ports and mined harbors and played his "hole card," the Christmas bombing of North Vietnam, "one of the most brutal examples of force in history."[33]

The belated president notes the parallel between Nixon's war against his own citizens and Jefferson's during the embargo. Both policies ended in failure and both presidents pursued their policies so ruthlessly because they regarded them as crucial to their poetic vision. But Nixon was not attempting to overcome Jefferson but Wilson, and the secrecy that so characterized his efforts, unlike Jefferson's, rested upon his revision of Wilson's poetic project. To Nixon, the war in Vietnam had to be brought to a conclusion "honorably" so that he could engage in his own surpassing of Wilson (and hence all his successors). His belief that it could be done so through the un-Wilsonian route of secrecy, which he was so confident about in 1968, failed. Indeed, it produced ever more secret projects against his opponents at home, which ultimately led to the Watergate crisis and his monumental failure.

But what, asks the belated president, was the poetic vision of which the Vietnam dilemma proved to be such a recalcitrant part? Even Nixon's most severe critics acknowledge a certain vision, if not poetic achievement, in his foreign policy. Nixon had set America on a "wholly new course in its foreign relations. These policies, irreversible in many areas, marked a most momentous shift in America's posture toward allies and adversaries alike. Basic relationships were realigned, and progressively new truths were recognized."[34] The belated president finds that secrecy too so shrouded even Nixon's project in this regard that it is difficult to even discern its character. What was his "Grand Design" to end war? "Was the Grand Design an intellectual construct Nixon had envisioned prior to, or early in his term as president? Did it take that framework and then seek to take the steps necessary for its full implementation? Or, did the Grand Design emerge piecemeal, as a result of accumulated small steps (e.g., the Nixon Doctrine, linkage, detente)? Did the pieces come first and the framework later as an afterthought? Were the pieces developed to fit the mold, or vice versa?"[35]

Whatever was Nixon's Grand Design, the belated president knows that it was quite different from Wilson's failed Covenant. On the other hand, the belated president feels that he knows Nixon's poetic intent and thus is convinced that the design entailed a grand vision of America's international role, one which Wilson had envisaged but was not "practical enough" to implement. He also knows that Nixon was intimately familiar with the character of the international system from which he had fashioned his entire political career. For any president-aspirant, particularly a Republican who could not campaign on the protection or expansion of the welfare state, the Cold War was an arena for monumental achievement abroad (Who can stand up to the Soviets?) and political survival at home (Who can fight domestic communism?). Nixon too knew that the Cold War had already undergone a process of routinization, particularly after the JFK bravado in Cuba, hence, lessening opportunities for achievement. No politician, however poetic in ambition, thought any longer of actually gaining fame from "winning" the Cold War. In fact, the experience in Vietnam and other international developments seemed to suggest a relative decline in American power, a point which Nixon was loathe to publicly admit but which his Nixon Doctrine seemed to recognize. America thus seemed poised for a return to some version of isolationism and any dedicated internationalist seemed a likely candidate to experience Wilson's fate. Nixon's wager, then, involved the formation and implementation of a project which would transform the international system, thinks the belated president. He would achieve monumental status by reversing Wilson's failure through a project that was Wilson's—the creation of a new international order more stable than before and one in which America played the central role.

Scholars who recognize Nixon's poetic intent are divided as to what kind of new international order he tried to construct.[36] Was it a return to a balance of power or a revived concert system? A balance of power system is generally theorized as one composed of at least five actors. An astute analyst could discern the breakup of communism as a monolithic network of client states as he could see the rise of new powers in Europe and the Pacific Rim. Balance of power also assumes an international arena relatively free of ideological and domestic constraints in order for powers to adjust to challenges from a hegemonic initiatives. Nixon's anticommunist credentials were an ideal protection against charges of appeasement, and, of course, his poetic commitment to secrecy was part of his Wilsonian revision. The system also required some recognition of the parameters of international competition, which Nixon attempted to institute with his demands for "linkage" and the policy of detente. Skeptics of Nixon's project pointed out the incomplete character of each of these features (the relative military and/or economic weakness of China, Japan, Germany as global powers; the still-potent role of ideology and the interpenetration of domestic and foreign policy in democracies; the recalcitrance of the Soviets). But to the belated president these are major obstacles which any belated president might be willing to undertake to alleviate his affliction.

The concert model gains some plausibility as a Nixon project because of Henry Kissinger's stated attraction to Metternick and Nixon's reputation as a white revolutionary. The Concert of Europe was very much a result of the great powers' effort to reconstitute stability in the wake of the Napoleonic wars and to regularize colonialism. The Cold War too had its own slow but calamitous effect on superpower budgets and politics, which became quite apparent in the 1980s and 1990s. Was Nixon attempting to create some version of a concert through his policies of detente and his opening to China? Was the Nixon Doctrine an attempt to regularize spheres of influence? Were the SALT agreements an effort to lower costly defense budgets on both sides?

His oft-quoted remark in 1972 ("I think it would be a safer world . . . if we can have a strong, healthy United States, Europe, Soviet Union, China, Japan, each balancing the other, not playing one against the other, an even balance") can be taken in support of either system, depending upon the emphasis placed on "each balancing the other" or "not playing one against the other."[37] To the belated president, it matters not which system Nixon poetically envisioned or even if he conceived, in his characteristic secrecy, some new imaginative combination. What matters is his recognition of the fact that Nixon's obsession with Vietnam was tied to the success of his vision and whether Nixon had waged a bet that he could succeed where Wilson failed. The inkling that despite Vietnam and Watergate Nixon might not be a monumental failure or that his failure deserves some asterisk of success or that his failure was poetically grand is the thread that the post-presidential Nixon used to offer his poetry. In 1991 he wrote that while Americans "instinctively agree" with President Wilson's famous call for "open covenants, openly arrived at" secrecy remains "indispensable to success," even in a "one superpower world" in which America has the opportunity to "seize the moment." For "only if this becomes a better world for others will it be a better world for us, and only when we participate in a cause greater than ourselves can we be truly true to ourselves."[38] Better to be a failed poet than no poet at all, thinks the belated president, who is certain that Richard Nixon would agree with him.

CONCLUSION

* *

T he imaginary belated president rests. He has completed his examination of strong presidents. To him there are eleven presidents who succeeded in overcoming their belatedness (in whole or in part, in monumental achievement or monumental failure).

BELATEDNESS'S VICTIMS

When he began his studies, the belated president swore that he would not study
those crushed by belatedness. Why, he thought, should I further depress myself by analyzing these failures, except those who were defeated in spectacular
ways? Why too should I study those unafflicted with belatedness for what can
they tell me? Only the belated speak to me in their graves. Now, however, in
this moment of theoretical victory, the belated president indulges himself. He
sits back and looks briefly at presidents crushed by belatedness and the unbelated
presidents.

His first reaction, which gives him a start, is how impossibly difficult is the
situation of the president who succeeds those who overcame belatedness. He
does not know for certain if John Adams, Madison, Van Buren, Andrew
Johnson, Taft, Harry S. Truman, Lyndon Johnson, and George Bush were
struck, and then defeated by, belatedness or if they were never even afflicted.
Yet he sees the symptoms of belatedness in many of these presidents—the fears
of catastrophic failure, the obsession with their "strong" predecessors (not always even poetically veiled), the recognition of their imprisonment as their own
projects disintegrate before the influence of those so recently and gloriously freed
from their own belatedness. It is the latter symptom, of course, that most distinguishes those presidents struck by but unable to alleviate belatedness.

As he continues, the belated president is not surprised to learn that those
crushed by belatedness succumb in different ways. He holds a certain admira-

tion for John Adams, who during and after the Revolution expressed his resentment in regard to Washington quite forthrightly. "I have been distressed," he told the Congress in 1777, during a debate over whether Washington should be given authority to select his major-generals, "to see some of our members disposed to idolize an image which in their own hands have molten. I speak here of the superstitious veneration which is paid to General Washington. Although I honor him for his good qualities, yet in this house I feel myself superior." Even while he was making his own inaugural address, the crowd, according to Adams, seem to be tearfully focused on the man who sat next to him; it was to Washington they flocked when ceremonies ended.[1]

Adams did have his own grand project, which was animated by his loss of faith in revolutionary élan as a foundation for nation building, and he hoped to "awake" Americans from "their golden dreams."[2] But during his presidency Adams was dogged by Washington's aegis Hamilton, and suffered many humiliations, not the least was his party's attempt to bring back Washington once again as military commander and then to conspire to make Hamilton his aide. Surely, thinks the belated president, this was at least a mythic coup d'état to which Adams in retirement responded with justifiable monumental resentment. The Federalists had killed themselves and the president with one shot, he bitterly complained years later, and then "maliciously indicted me for the murder."[3] When Adams finally broke with what had to be called the cabinet of Washington-Hamilton and sought peace with France on his own, he achieved some measure of independence (which moved some presidential raters many generations later to honor him), though no relief from belatedness.[4] His comment to a senator captures his presidency and the victory of belatedness: "I was no more at liberty than a man in prison chained to the floor and bound hand and foot."[5]

The imaginary president skips Madison as a victim of belatedness since he entered the office under the conditions of the enormously unpopular second-term of Jefferson. Other presidents would surely feel the heavy weight of Jefferson, but in 1805 Madison confronted only a president whose poetic intent had nearly carried him to the brink of monumental failure. He remembers, though, that there was, even in Adams's protestations, a certain stoicism that may have much later given him some strength and retrieved some measure of dignity. This is not so with other presidents crushed by belatedness. Did Martin Van Buren harbor ambitions of belatedness? asks the imaginary president.[6] It is possible, he thinks, that Van Buren had concluded that spiritedness had run its course as a mode of governing (he was the first president elected without any role in the Revolution) and that government by persuasion and cunning would provide a refreshing (and belated transcending) substitute. He was, after all, called the "Little Magician" when he took office in 1837. Van Buren, one of the most talented politicians America had yet produced and exuding the kind of confidence such skills produce, was overwhelmed by the economic legacies of his predecessor, charged first by the Whigs as running a "footsteps administration" and then called an effeminate aristocrat in 1840 and harassed and thrown aside by the spirited Jackson, who denied him his party's nomination in 1844.

Whether belated or not, Van Buren's stature reached such a point of invisibility that it is impossible to tell whether he ever did confront belatedness. Traces of belatedness do, however, remain in the presidency of James K. Polk, whom the young Lincoln thought he spotted as a late Jackson Recidivus. Polk exhibited all the elements of the ephebian strategy the belated president studied in Part II. As "Young Hickory" he set out with all the vigor of youth (Polk was America's youngest president in 1846) to reaffirm (read belatedly as: surpass) Jackson. In fact, his relatively high ranking among some presidential raters is derived almost exclusively from his youthful braggadocio to George Bancroft at his inauguration. According to Bancroft, Polk "raised his hand in the air and bringing it down with force on his thigh" announced four great measures for his administration: tariff reduction, an independent treasury, settlement of the Oregon boundaries, and the acquisition of California.[7] Since he completed each—and more, in terms of territory—why, asks the imaginary president, is Polk's name so forsaken as a national icon? Three years later, when the boast was reality, however, the young Polk was complaining frequently about disloyalty in his cabinet, saw his own party being pulled apart by the consequences of his policies in regard to the slavery question, witnessed the rise of his generals as national Whig presidential timber, and found himself caught on his own one-term pledge. As significant as his four-point project was his diary entry, "With me, it is emphatically true that the Presidency is no bed of roses."[8] Polk, thinks the belated president, had captured the energy of youth, but he was unable to surpass Jackson because he was unable to (mis)read his predecessor, a task urgently necessary because, as one who stood in another presidential time, he needed to innovate (and betray poetically) the "Old Hickory" while he ostensibly honored him. Spirited was Polk, and capable of poetic intent as well, but the "Young Hickory," while maybe not in his heart a loyal son, was nonetheless without the poetic imagination to surpass his father.[9]

The imaginary president next turns to one of the most scorned of presidents, Andrew Johnson. It was not as if the name of Andrew Johnson constituted monumental failure, or even failure without any magnificent proportions, for Johnson's agenda held sway and it was for generations the project of his sworn enemies, the Radical Republicans, which received the designation of a failed experiment. Rather, it is mean-spiritedness, so different from spiritedness proper as a force for poetic intent, which characterizes Johnson, that so nicely juxtaposes with the magnanimity of Lincoln (poetically symbolized in the second inaugural's "with malice toward none") in the later chapters of his poetic narrative.

Yet in many ways Johnson's career was a replica of Lincoln's. The vice-president was raised in a border state in very modest circumstances. He was economically a self-made man and taught himself to read as a adult. But there were an essential differences between Johnson and Lincoln, aside from different political and intellectual talents and psychological proclivities. Lincoln had become a Whig and later a Republican. Johnson's party ideology was derived from a more conventional route, given his economic background. He was a Jacksonian Democrat.

Lincoln's choice placed him among the affluent elites of antebellum America. His ability to create ideological bridges between the men and women of his origins and the agenda of the Whigs was part of his genius as a politician and his charm as poet-president. Johnson, on the other hand, nurtured his own personal class resentments. Early in his career he announced his goal: "Some day I will show up the stuck-up aristocrats who are running this country."[10] But class anger was not the only source of difference between Lincoln and Johnson. As a Democrat, Johnson accepted fully the Jacksonian vision of America as an egalitarian society of yeoman farmers and small business people who were betrayed by the efforts of the "money power" who used the government to take the fruits of their labor.

The outbreak of the Civil War made Johnson an ideal vice-presidential choice. Lincoln had complained in 1858 that "much of the plain old Democracy is with us, while nearly all the old exclusive silk-stocking Whiggery is against us," and when he approached his second term he sought to solidify this new base. When Tennessee joined the Confederate States of America (CSA), Johnson refused to give up his Senate seat and remained in the Union. In 1862 Lincoln appointed him military governor of the state. Johnson had such a hatred of the southern aristocracy, which he saw as a force that had a political and economic stranglehold on the small farmer, that some Republicans eagerly looked forward to his leadership after Lincoln's assassination.

Johnson's plan for Reconstruction included an amnesty for those who took an oath of allegiance to the Union, as did Lincoln's proposal. But Johnson's plan also included an important revision. Confederates who owned property worth more than twenty thousand dollars were ineligible for amnesty. Johnson explained to a Virginia delegation that the exceptioned class could appeal individually for special pardons to the president, but he reminded them that "you know full well it was the wealthy men of the South who dragooned the people into secession."[11]

When various states began to hold constitutional conventions, however, voters elected members of the planter aristocracy that Johnson so detested as delegates. His dream of a restored yeoman South shattered, Johnson seemed to move toward another ideological position. If the small farmers were unable or unwilling to wrest political control of their states from the old landed aristocracy, he would be certain that his beloved farmer would not be forced to share power and status with black Americans. He swiftly granted numerous pardons to the planter class. When the new state governments enacted the Black Codes, which restricted freedmens' movements without the permission of their employers and provided for imprisonment for blacks who quit work before the expiration of their contracts, and when numerous terrorist groups emerged in the South, including the Klan, Johnson refused to act, precipitating congressional attempts at Reconstruction.

An acrimonious exchange between Frederick Douglass and Johnson in 1866 illustrates the president's position. Douglass appealed to Johnson to support measures to give black Americans the right to vote in light of recent events in the former CSA. Johnson replied that slavery had been abolished with a "great national guarantee." He asked Douglass if it was not true that as a black slave he looked upon "a large family, struggling hard upon a poor piece of land" with less esteem than the large slave-owning planter. This in itself was a cruel question to ask a former slave, but Douglass politely but emphatically disagreed. Johnson, insisting that the affirmative was the case in his experience in Tennessee, continued:

> The colored man went into this rebellion a slave; by the operation of the rebellion he came out a freeman . . . The non-slaveholder who was forced into the rebellion, who was as loyal as those that lived beyond the limits of the State, but was carried into it, lost his property, and in a number of instances the lives of such were sacrificed, and he who has survived has come out of it with nothing gained, but a great deal lost. Now, upon what principle of justice, should they be placed in a condition different from what they were before? On the one hand, one has gained a great deal; on the other hand, one had lost a great deal, and in a political point of view, scarcely stands where he did before.

Douglass attempted to argue that the small white farmer and the new black freedman could use the ballot to overturn the plantation aristocrat, but Johnson found this scenario inconceivable and ended the exchange.[12]

To northern Republican representatives in Congress and some former abolitionists it seemed as if Hinton Helper had become president. The outcome of this reaction, impeachment—which had so long been treated as the unremovable blot on the presidency as an institution of which Johnson was judged responsible and constituted a claim for monumental failure—has been somewhat diminished by the historically variable reputation of the Radical Republicans, revisionist accounts of the actual circumstances of the proceedings, and congressional reaction to Watergate in which the Nixon resignation in the face of impeachment constituted an even more compelling narrative of poetic failure. But what so interests the imaginary president is the proposition that Johnson's overwhelming mean-spiritedness could be a reaction to belatedness. There was clearly no poetry that arose from Johnson's bile, but was there poetic intent? Certainly to his opponents in the Republican Party there was plenty of evidence that Johnson was striking at the heart of Lincoln's reading of the Declaration of Independence, if not Lincoln's own postwar implementation of it. And there was that characteristic expression of resentment and self-pity that is typical of presidents crushed by belatedness. In the summer of 1869 Johnson asked, "Caesar had a party, and Pompey and Crassius had a party," so why should his party "not take me up?"[13] But poetic intent, which, of course, originates in intolerable feelings of resentment, nevertheless requires some measure of their control. Johnson had none. The Will of Jackson certainly was evident, and it made itself felt in the most ugly proportions. And look at this racist inversion of the poetry at Gettysburg, says the imaginary president to himself: "This is a coun-try for white men, and by God, as long as I am president, it shall be a govern-ment for white men."[14] But in the end, Johnson's utterances expressed no more than his monumental resentment.

The imaginary president does not take very long in his glance at Taft, so overwhelmed was the twentieth-seventh president by the spirited Roosevelt that if there was any possible poetic intent, it seems to have been obliterated. As Jackson denied Van Buren reelection in 1844, so did Roosevelt Taft in 1912 in his own attempt to retrieve unquenched desires to overcome belatedness. So too does Harry S. Truman move rapidly across his field of vision since he had considered, and rejected, Truman's claims to spiritedness in Part II.

The figure of Lyndon Johnson, however, clearly attracts his attention, for not only had Johnson suffered the fate of all post-Depression/postwar presidents in regard to FDR but he was confronted with the monumental influence of the young, spirited, and slain John F. Kennedy. It is this simultaneous struggle against these *two* obstacles to exceptionalism that fascinates the imaginary president. The young Johnson played the role of dutiful son to FDR and, later, the defeated elder to Kennedy. Machiavellian Fate placed him in a position in which he could avenge both. Johnson's strategy was a brilliant one, concludes the imaginary president. He would with one stroke gain exceptionalism by completing the projects of both. To Johnson, FDR was never the country squire and he readily acknowledged his monumental poetic status. But Roosevelt had, despite his famous remarks about fear in his first inaugural, himself made people fearful. He was critical of the demagoguery in his Jackson turn and thought FDR made an irreversible strategic error in his court battle by so openly confront-ing such a central American political institution. But, as a result, the monu-mental FDR had left his protégé (the "perfect Roosevelt man") an opening. After JFK's assassination, Johnson told his advisors that "every issue that is on my desk tonight was on my desk when I came to Congress in 1937."[15] LBJ's Great Society thus was conceived as a monumental project which would su-persede the New Deal because it was based on tactics (consolidation and per-suasion) that FDR did not employ and because it was itself far more ambitious.[16] Not even the great Roosevelt, mired in the crisis of the Depression, could prom-ise—and deliver—a "total victory" over poverty. Johnson even confidently promised that he would defeat "hard core" poverty: "The people I want to help are the ones who've never held real jobs and aren't able to handle them. Most never had enough money and don't know how to spend it. They were born to parents who gave up hoping long ago. They have no motivation to reach for something better because the sum total of their lives is losing."[17]

If the Great Society would alleviate belatedness in regard to FDR, Johnson's civil rights initiative and prosecution of the war in Vietnam would defeat the slain Kennedy. He had urged Sorenson in 1963 to tell "your president" to "pull out the cannon" as a solution to the civil rights crisis. "You let him be on all the TV networks just speaking from his conscience . . . I know the risks are great and it might cost the South, but those sorts of states may be lost anyway."[18] Kennedy would soon follow Johnson's tactic, although it is less certain that he accepted his advice. When Johnson took office he "shoved his stack of chips in the pot" and not only vigorously supported civil rights legislation in 1964, completing the Kennedy commitment (and probably costing him the loss of five southern states in the election), but more audaciously proposed more legislation in 1965 by repeating what had already become the protest anthem, "We Shall Overcome," before Congress and the American public.

It is true that his increasing commitments in Vietnam never attracted LBJ's poetic imagination the way the war on poverty and civil rights did, nor was it the central strategy behind his poetic intent, but Johnson was determined to meet this pledge *and* his domestic agenda. Johnson was well aware of FDR's move right in World War II (he had fallen in right beside him), and he expressed his concern that should Vietnam be lost, Robert Kennedy would come charging at him in his brother's name from the right.[19] "I believe that we can continue the Great Society while we fight in Vietnam," he told a joyous Congress in 1966, and, at this point in the poetic narrative, thinks the imaginary president, who could not think he couldn't do both?

As his victories piled up, the ever-emboldened Johnson began to count his parallels to FDR/JFK and count the ways he had superseded them. His landslide in 1964 had surpassed FDR's in 1936. His hundred days in 1965 were more glorious than Roosevelt's and were dwarfed by Kennedy's limited successes. He had broken the unholy alliance with the party's southern wing, which neither FDR nor JFK had dared to do. He was providing "guns *and* butter." Yet just has quickly as the opportunities for the poetic narrative that Johnson had created had opened, they closed, and the two dead men, FDR and JFK, came back to life and rushed in upon him. Despite Johnson's monumental gamble (which to the imaginary president is an especially important one since it shows that it is possible for one who immediately succeeds a monumentally strong president to heroically resist belatedness), the civil rights movement that the spirited Kennedy regarded so prudently detached itself from his leadership. When the commitment in Vietnam grew larger and larger and merged with the rising domestic critique, Johnson found himself standing before the greatest cultural division that America had experienced since the Civil War. In regard to FDR, belatedness reemerged. Johnson had the insider's skills of the great president but not those of him as war leader, so now said presidential poetic critics; compared to JFK he was uncouth, they said as well. In fact, when LBJ sought to justify his "real" war, he could reach for FDR/Jackson/Jefferson but not FDR/Lincoln. His Johns Hopkins speech had its Lincolnian gloss, but it was its global Jacksonian/Jeffersonianism that predominated. Should the North Vietnamese listen to reason, there was the promise of programs that would "dwarf our TVA."[20] To critics, this professed humanitarianism in the face of this brutal war was not even comical, it was obscene.

To the imaginary president, though, there is a sad grandeur of the belated in this last great promise of economic aid. Much soul searching, resentment, and charges of ungratefulness marked Johnson's last days as president and his short life thereafter. Johnson dreamed that he was drowning, that he was para- lyzed. (When he woke up from this nightmare, he found it soothing to stroke Woodrow Wilson's portrait). But he finds no better belated epiphany than the revised poetic narrative of defeat that he offered to Doris Kearns Goodwin:

> I felt that I was being chased on all sides by a giant stampede coming at me from all directions. On the one side, the American people were stampeding me to do something about Vietnam. On the other side, the inflationary economy was booming out of control. Up ahead were dozens of danger signs pointing to another summer of riots in the cities. I was being forced over the edge by rioting blacks, demonstrating students, marching welfare mothers, and hysterical reporters. And then the final straw. The thing I feared from the first day of my Presidency was actually coming true. Robert Kennedy had openly announced his decision to reclaim the throne in the name of his brother. And the American people, swayed by the magic of the name, were dancing in the streets. The whole situation was unbearable to me.[21]

The imaginary president finally considers the presidency of George Bush. Noted for his fragmented syntax and extended nonage in service of strong presi- dents, Bush seems the most unlikely of poet-presidents. Indeed, most students of belatedness would even likely see him as part of the safe army of the unbelated. But to the belated president, there are some signs of belatedness in his confusion. He reminds himself that those crushed by belatedness need not all be victimized in precisely the same manner, although the results are uni- form. The "tragedy" of LBJ, in which both monumental success and monumen- tal failure just eluded him, is not the predominant narrative of belatedness's victims. There is then in Bush's very choices of professed exemplars some traces of poetic intent. Overtly, the very essence of the Bush presidency involved imitating Reagan. In esoteric terms, the belated president finds a frenzied pur- suit of a presidential ideal as inchoate as his announcements about the "vision thing" and his intentions to be remembered as the "Education President" and the "Environmental President." Bush once compared himself to Lincoln but only in a limited way (both were thinkers faced with "new facts").[22] Truman's name began to appear late in administration. The imaginary president sees this imitation as one more conventionally opportunistic and unrelated to belated- ness. Both men tried to transpose their failures on Congress, and both men, succeeding popular strong presidents, were underestimated. It is the identifi- cation with Theodore Roosevelt, expressed by Bush early in his term, that in- trigues the belated president the most.[23] It was TR's aristocratic bearing that gave this identification some resonance, and even more revealing, it was this presidency that could permit Bush some poetic fantasy since Roosevelt suc- ceeded a slain president. But most important, it was TR who searched for an American world role when none was available.

Bush could be shockingly nonchalant about the postwar world's greatest events, which occurred during his presidency. Imagine JFK's poetic reaction if the Berlin Wall had fallen during his watch, or even Eisenhower's if the iron curtain had been drawn back during his! But to Bush, these may have been monumental events for which he could never take credit and poetically memorialize. It was only after the Berlin Wall fell and the Soviet Union disintegrated that Bush reached for parallels in the Persian Gulf War, which, if he did suffer from belatedness, was surely his exceptionalist moment. World War II metaphors cascaded from the president's addresses and remarks. He pointedly told reporters that he had been reading Martin Gilbert's *Second World War*, which he described as "a great, big, thick book of history" which showed that Churchill was correct in asserting that Hitler should have been stopped at the Rhine in 1936. The Iraqi tanks "stormed in blitzkrieg fashion" in Kuwait. Saddam was the "brutal dictator" of the 1930s reborn: "A half century ago, our nation and the world paid dearly for appeasing an aggressor who should, and could, have been stopped. We are not going to make that mistake again." He told David Frost in January that there had been no event of such moral significance since World War II. [24] The belated president is impressed with Bush's ingenuity, for he portrays himself as the first Roosevelt of the post–Cold War era and the first capable of erasing the "Vietnam syndrome" from the American psyche.

It is certainly excusable that the success of the allied effort in Iran would have led Bush to assume that his reelection was assured and, perhaps, that horizons were visible in regard to overcoming belatedness. In the aftermath of his defeat in 1992, could the defeated president have concluded that the war, despite his own heroism in elaborately piecing together an international coalition and the individual acts of service men and women, was too quickly won to erase the memory of Vietnam? Easy, little wars have a habit of diminishing presidents in the long run or ending in a wash in terms of belatedness, as TR found in Cuba and Reagan in Grenada (since this effort had no major relationship to his success). Or was it the ragged ending of the war (Saddam remained and the Kurds continued to suffer from his tyranny) that lead to its irrelevance? If Bush were a belated president, he could have defended himself by insisting that the way he concluded hostilities was connected to larger perspectives in the building of his "New World Order" in which reasons of state forbade the dismemberment of Iraq. In any case, Americans, while undoubtedly grateful for the quickness of the fight, focused on other standards in the evaluation of the Bush presidency, and the Persian Gulf War did not develop into a poetic narrative that carried it to reelection, let alone exceptionalism. As a result, inchoateness remained the defining characteristic of the Bush presidency, and it is this fragmentation, which signifies the inability to create poetic narrative, that was the form that his belated victimization took.

The imaginary president now knows that those presidents crushed by belatedness may have struggled heroically before their defeats (LBJ) or more weakly (Bush). They may accept their vanquishing with some measure of grace (Adams) or with bad character (Andrew Johnson), and the cruel god of belatedness may even deny to them some measure of insight (Van Buren, Polk). Thus he feels a different kind of jealousy when he ponders the lives of nearly half the presidencies, the unbelated occupants. How sweet must their tenures of office have been! Some were quite talented and others less so. Some were good, decent men and others rogues. Some served the nation well and others not so ably. He even wonders if even among this group there were brief moments when feelings of belatedness cropped up but were quickly struck down by the ghosts of the strong ones or by limited imagination. But this moment of regret on the part of the imaginary president is fleeting. Here were men who won the prize but not the Prize because they apparently never sought it. Who, in later generations, he asks, struggles against the achievements of Grover Cleveland, Calvin Coolidge, or Gerald Ford, and who seeks to study their poetry that memorializes their deeds? No, he exclaims, I would rather suffer in order to excel than be tranquil in order to imitate, and in his belated state, he is certain that the American people would support his choice.

Of course, he tells himself, I cannot know the circumstances under which I will become president, nor the opportunities which might appear when I am president. I do not know, he continues, the precise structural arrangements of the international order or the specific state of the economy. I cannot anticipate the exact period in "political time"[25] under which I shall appear, nor can I predict the issues of the moment or the "crises" upon which I will wage my war against belatedness. Lest he risk becoming overwhelmed by historical contingency, the belated president pauses to remind himself of the knowledge he does possess in his battle against belatedness. If he cannot forecast opportunity or the form it might take, he believes he does have in hand the means to address his motive. He knows that he will lead a large powerful nation with citizens who are suspicious of authority but who also value, even love, strong presidents. He knows intimately what kind of men are strong presidents and how they imitated and then excelled their strong predecessors. He knows now he need not simply be like Washington or Lincoln except in terms of their poetic intent. There are other personas available to him from which he can select, mix, and match, and there are other poetic strategies untried and thus untested. He knows there will moments of frustration and despondency as he struggles to create his own poetic narrative, but his heart rises when he lets himself consider occupying the *first* presidency of the twenty-first century.

"FARE THEE WELL, GREAT HEART!"

We leave the imaginary belated president to his revelry, recognizing that should fate permit him to fill the office, his battle against belatedness must be confronted in practice however many times he successfully maps his victories in his mind. Instead we move to reconsider the questions we asked in a preliminary way at the close of chapter 2 (What did the belated president learn and what do we learn about the strong president?), for these questions provide an opportunity for assessing the plausibility and consequences of our theoretical account of strong presidents.

Let us review the belated theory of executive leadership with a view toward narrowing the focus to its most central features. Although the terms *poetic achievement*, *poetic persona*, and *poetic narrative* are theory-specific in a technical sense, descriptions of the American presidency which lean upon the strong president as the prototype employ analogous terminology. Thus Clinton Rossiter writes of the presidency as the "breeding ground for indestructible myth," Erwin Hargrove speaks of an "heroic model" of the presidency, and Michael Nelson the "savior model."[26] Each of these designations conceive of the strong president in terms so monumental that a special vocabulary, a poetic one, is necessary to convey the "reassurance, inspiration, power and hope" that characterizes the person, his agon and his achievements.[27] What the perspective of the belated president reveals is how central are these narratives and achievements, stated in poetic terms, to the formation of strong presidencies. Edward Corwin contended that it was the "stamp of personality and crisis" imprinted by TR, Wilson, and FDR which characterized the twentieth-century presidency,[28] but this conjunction of poetic persona with the agon he carries through crisis to poetic achievement is a feature of all strong presidencies, and prototypes extend back to Jackson and Lincoln. Without the creation of a poetic personage and the formulation of a narrative conveyed poetically, strong presidencies cannot be formed. Just read the source of these poetic encounters of strong presidents in their most condensed forms: Washington = Founder; Lincoln = Civil War; FDR = Depression/War; Jackson = BUS; TR = World Power; JFK = Missile Crisis; Jefferson = Revolution of 1800; Reagan = Reagan Revolution; Wilson/Hoover/Nixon = Failure. Each of these poetic signs contain narratives of monumental achievements (and failures) told in terms of will making history. Each sign unfolds in narrative form until it reveals the strong president's poetic persona as the central motif, for the narrative cannot be told without the reluctant Washington, the suffering Lincoln, the genial FDR, or the determined Jackson at its center. It is true, of course, that even without introducing the belated president's alternate narratives, these monumental stories contain absences and ellipses. Washington's firstness would have been enhanced if he had put down a truly formidable rebellion among Pennsylvania farmers, Theodore Roosevelt's if he had the opportunity to lead America in war, Roosevelt's if his policies provoked extraconstitutional opposition. Moreover, even strong presidents most of the time operate in an arena in which they are simply *in authority* rather than *the authority* of the achievement narrative. Washington's strategy of the aegis nearly collapsed at the end of his second term and Congress reasserted itself at some points in all the strong presidencies. Even after poetic crises, Congress challenged Lincoln's plans for Reconstruction as it blocked FDR's "court-packing" proposal.

These kinds of queries are, of course, the quibbles of the poetic critic. More importantly, they raise questions which continue to promote the achievement narrative. For it is the highlighting of the closeness of catastrophe, encased as it is in particular periods in a strong presidency, that gives the narrative its poetic form. Thus the citizen is able to imagine possible collapsed foundings, reactionary seizures of power, dismemberment, lost wars, and nuclear holocaust which stand behind the persona of the strong president. He is also able to imagine, as a discernable subtext, the closeness to which a particular strong president stood to the full seizure of power for himself. It is thus the opportunities for Caesarism and its rejection (opportunities never even considered except by the poetic reader) that is so thrilling in the poetic narratives of strong presidents.

The concept of poetic intent brings this second kind of closeness to the forefront of the poetic narrative and uses it to construct its alternate. We have personified and magnified this attribution of an intense desire to surpass other strong presidents as the single motivation of a strong president in the form of an imaginary belated aspirant's study of the office and its occupants. But it was Hamilton who first recommended the presidency on precisely these terms. "The love of fame, the ruling passion of the noblest minds," he wrote in the *Federalist*, leads "a man to plan and undertake extensive and arduous enterprises."[29] What we have called poetic intent and alternate poetic narratives are not unrecognized in presidential scholarship and have certainly been asserted by opponents of every specific strong president. Especially in his second term, Republicans, not the least of whom was, as we discussed, Thomas Jefferson, openly questioned Washington's motives. Charges of Caesarism have followed strong presidents ever since. Jefferson was accused of secretly promoting a Lycurgian project for Americans during the enforcement of the Embargo Act. The early charge of "military chieftain" followed Jackson throughout his presidency. Lincoln's assumption of emergency power in 1861 was resisted as tyrannical measures by peace Democrats. FDR was openly compared to European dictators in 1936 and 1940. The flutter of evaluations of the office as a "constitutional dictatorship" in the 1930s and 1940s and the new "imperial presidency" in the 1970s recognized, sometimes obliquely, what we have called poetic intent in their assessments of presidential power.[30]

Poetic intent, then, exists in both narratives of strong presidents, as an imagined possibility in the achievement narrative and as a real motivation in its alternate. Thus we need to review what theoretical insights have emerged when it was centered by the personification of an imaginary belated president. As we noted in the introduction, presidential discourse conceptualized as a genre has been subject to numerous categorizations. From the standpoint of belatedness and the efforts of strong presidents to overcome this affliction, we found, employing the model of the imaginary president, four basic features: closed texts, (mis)readings, (re)orderings, esoteric messages.

The central feature of the great texts of strong presidents are their closedness. Washington's admonitions in his Farewell Address created monumental obstacles to later presidents, even strong ones as, did Lincoln's readings. Jackson reminded his audience in his own farewell that he had slain the monster bank and demanded that future generations adhere to the principles of a frugal and simple government. Theodore Roosevelt announced the end of the "kindly" presidency with the death of McKinley. In FDR's first inaugural lay the closed text of the narrative of economic recovery with the subsequent challenge of one hundred days to match it. If JFK's missile crisis speech was the "Gettysburg of the Cold War," no future strong president could follow with a greater achievement. Subsequent belated presidents even attempted to "open up" Wilson's Great Fall with projects intended to reverse his monumental failure.

So too has the belated president shown that a major preoccupation of strong presidents involves reading and (mis)reading other strong presidents. Sometimes this process is achieved through selected emphasis in the poetic narrative (FDR's focus upon the Jefferson's formation of a political party and the Louisiana Purchase). Sometimes it involves a veiled derogation of an achievement (Lincoln's reading of the Declaration of Independence as "embalmed"). Sometimes it involves a (mis)reading of a poetic persona (Jackson's enspiriting of Jefferson; Reagan's oral history of FDR). Sometimes it involves the heroic expansion of a great project (Theodore Roosevelt's revision of Washington's admonition; FDR's globalization of Lincoln). Sometimes there are inversions of a strong president's poetic encounters (FDR's Jacksonian turn). Sometimes it involves wagers in reversing poetic failure (Hoover's and Nixon's revision of Wilson's narrative). Sometimes there are (mis)readings by omission (Washington's silence in regard to the Declaration in his Farewell Address).

Each of these (mis)readings, when successful, produce a (re)ordering of presidential greatness which not only elevates a president to the level of strong presidents but also juggles his status among these select few. These (re)orderings are formed on the basis of a revision of the challenging president's reading of the poetic narrative or poetic persona in complex ways. The most monumental of (re)orderings on the basis of (mis)reading is, of course, Lincoln's achievement in regard to Washington. Lincoln's new firstness is achieved through his revision of Jefferson's achievement narrative (of which Washington was silent), so that (re)ordered, Washington-Jefferson (a pairing which contained many antagonisms, given the mutual hostility that emerged between both men) becomes Lincoln-Jefferson-Washington in an unfolding rather than suppressed-conflict poetic narrative. According to Lincoln's (mis)readings, the revolution of 1800, with all its submerged hostility in regard to Washington's presidential founding, is erased and Lincoln brings to life the Declaration (Jefferson) and saves the Republic under circumstances more harrowing than those which faced Washington. Jackson's enspiriting of Jefferson, too, had its own erasures. Jefferson, the poet yet failed president, was redeemed but placed poetically behind Jackson and his successful revolution. Reagan attempts to (re)order FDR through his (mis)reading of Jackson. Thus his (mis)readings pierce FDR's Jacksonian persona, and he is able to employ his own version of FDR's happy casualness, to produce Reagan-Jackson instead of FDR-Jackson. JFK's task of (mis)reading FDR was all the more delicate because of his own party affiliation. Kennedy used his own "coolness" and his youth to mark off a liberalism more "modern" and more complex than the "simple" impulses which FDR channeled.

These (mis)readings and (re)orderings are, from the perspective of a belated president, constructed esoterically. An esoteric reading of presidential texts has long been accepted as a method for uncovering partisan intent and/or psycho-

logical disposition. Political theorists and presidential scholars have also recognized that certain texts, such as Lincoln's Lyceum address, require esoteric
analysis. A belated perspective centers this practice and extends it beyond
immediate political advantage or personal perspective to include poetic intent.
In each of the strong presidencies, an esoteric reading uncovers complex strategies to relieve belatedness. In an exoteric reading, when a strong president
speaks, he expresses his resolve to initiate a major project, and his (mis)readings
of past presidents and the (re)ordering which follows are treated as incidental.
An esoteric reading, which places poetic intent as a possible key to interpretation, seeks to discover and follow strategic patterns across the presidential genre.
A distinct poetic persona thus emerges in each of the strong presidents which
is connected to a strategy for overcoming belatedness. Washington's great reluctance to accept power, which animates every act of his career, becomes the
defining feature of his personal discourse. So too is Lincoln's mournfulness,
which personified his sense of national tragedy and providential testing and
redemption. FDR's geniality exuded a self-confidence which suffused all his
speeches. The spirited presidents portray a sense of excitement and energy that
is captured in their discourse. Each of these poetic personas epitomizes the many
forms in which strength can be exhibited: the strength to refuse power; the
strength to confront and make meaningful tragedy; the strength to maintain
confidence under adverse conditions; the strength to confront tirelessly complex problems head-on.

But while the poetic persona which emerges from the reading of presidential texts is exoterically a sign meant to convey strength, it is also a poetic veil
covering poetic intent. The model of an imaginary belated president who reads
belatedly assumes that these poetic personas function as mechanisms to clear
the way for the creation of poetic narratives on the part of strong presidents.
Washington's great refusals formed the basis for his "firstness" by conveying the
symbol of a new republican leader who rejected open opportunities for assuming concentrated power. His use of the aegis was a perfect mechanism for his
strategy. Hamilton became the focus of critiques based upon exposure of poetic intent, not he. Even Jefferson could never quite determine who was behind the shield. In regard to Lincoln, if America was destined to pursue a tragic
path which could lead to national redemption and he was its agent, other strong
presidents must be (re)ordered (Washington) and leaders in other scenarios
(Clay, Douglas) pushed aside. Lincoln employed a strategy of "double cross,"
actually (mis)reading the great texts of the Republic esoterically so as to make
a monumental role for himself which excluded or (re)ordered others. All of his
great texts, from the Lyceum and Temperance addresses to the house-divided
speech and the Gettysburg Address and the inaugurals, involve esoteric readings on Lincoln's part in which he discovers secret agendas (Caesarist-inclined
politicians emerging in the third generation of the Republic; temperance reformers who really stand for other agendas and alcoholics who epitomize certain virtues in flawed ways; slave conspiracies; "embalmed" texts) that invite
their own esoteric readings sans poetic intent. So too did FDR's geniality, which

promoted self-confidence (and a disarming benevolence), enable him to imitate the most diverse group of strong presidents (Jefferson, Jackson, Lincoln) without alarming most citizens and in the process make the case that the imitation of so many poetic personas suggested that he was the exemplary strong president.

As we noted, spirited presidents face a difficult task, since while the public loves them for their energy and will, their persona lies so close to the impetuosity of the tyrant that they risk exposure of poetic intent. But if their thymos can be conveyed in terms of their love of liberty and hatred of tyranny, foreign or domestic, the veil is preserved. Esoteric readings of Jackson, TR, and JFK illustrate the attempts to place recklessness and animosity in this light. Minor and failed poet-presidents, of course, present personas more incompletely, though not necessarily without completely uncovering poetic veils. Jefferson's "double effect" captured his poetic persona as the president of the American Enlightenment, but it also opened up the poetic critique of a chasm between practice and theory in his administrations. The genial Reagan expertly imitated the genial FDR and, as our esoteric reading attempted to show, sliced through the inconsistencies of the New Deal as FDR's project against belatedness preserving only the FDR persona while rejecting his mission. Esoterica suggests that the strong presidents who experienced great falls were high rollers rather than severely flawed leaders.

What can we learn from the theory of belatedness and the model of the imaginary belated president about strong presidents? The imaginary belated president began with the assumption that strong presidents are driven by the simple desire to overcome or transcend their strong predecessors. He thus began with the same assumption as did Hamilton when he recommended the presidency as an institution in the second founding as an outlet for those driven by "love of fame." Hamilton's description, however, that the "extensive and arduous enterprises" promoted by this "ruling passion of the noblest minds," included the assertion that they would be undertaken "for the public benefit." It is certainly possible to expand or relax the premise of the belated president and make "for the public benefit" the central feature of poetic intent rather than resentment. Yet even if we place public benefit as the passion, a strong president would soon find that other strong presidents block his agenda, if only because he must find a way to construct a poetic narrative sufficiently powerful to enable him to initiate and complete his own projects, some of which do substantively block his own projects. The addendum which Hamilton noted in his argument against rotation in office indirectly supports this assessment. Should ineligibility for reelection be part of the Constitution, former presidents would be "wandering among the people like discontented ghosts." Projects left incomplete, so intimates Hamilton, would leave the ruling passion unsatisfied and presumably unloosened "from the public benefit." Thus the "love of fame" will find an outlet, whether it is connected with the public benefit or whether it is not, a point that the young Lincoln grasped in his first battles against belatedness.

We leave aside the question of whether the planning of projects for the public good as an outlet for the love of fame is itself a poetic veil on Hamilton's own part and pose the question which Hamilton, certainly one of the most avid supporters of the strong presidency, raised: "Are strong presidents 'for the public benefit'"? It is the model of the imaginary belated president which helps us focus upon this question, for it permits us to consider an answer based on the most unflattering assumptions. If strong presidents are driven by poetic intent conceived in its most Nietzschean terms, are their presidencies for the public benefit?

Since would-be strong presidents speak to an audience in a way with which the citizenry is largely unaware, are these conversations with dead men a threat to the democratic polity? To the extent to which past strong presidents have come to represent core dispositions in American political culture, are these (mis)readings threats to consensus? Is the strong president an unraveler of consensus who seeks to alter and destroy the received wisdom of the polity? Is the strong president fundamentally an irrational actor who is willing to place whole populations at risk in his search to reduce and eliminate his personal anxieties over influence?

The theoretical construct of the "textbook presidency" and its variants have attempted to confront the consequences of this rebellious confrontation with belatedness, but the concept itself can be interpreted in light of these patterns as poetic trope that both disguises and illuminates the task of the occupant.[31] For if the idealized conception of the office itself transforms the holder into "the most powerful person in the world," then the poetic achievement is assured with election. He has, in the words of a presidential advisor, been "transported across an infinite flight of time and duty" to "that place called the presidency."[32] On the other hand, this poetic transformation immediately places him in the realm of the great poet-presidents with whom he must struggle to claim a place. An abandonment of the "textbook presidency" or the "rhetorical presidency," however, risks further disguising and heightening confrontations with belatedness. By asserting that the age of the heroic presidency has ended or was never an accurate description of "real presidencies," future occupants will be driven to recapture distinctions denied to them.

Another alternative to belatedness deserves consideration. It leans upon Hamilton's justification of the office in *Federalist* we have just quoted. Even though Hamilton's discussion may itself be a mask for his own ambition since his conception of the power of the office exceeded the constitutional arrangements he defended, his observation that the presidency was a safe outlet for "the love of fame, the ruling passion of the noblest minds" recognized the need for a republic to provide room for poetic ambition, although he shrewdly tied it to the "public benefit." The assertion that self-interested behavior could be harnessed for the public good was itself part of the revisionist project of the founders, but Hamilton also can be read in terms of an institutionalization of a more complex process.

Let us return to the student of belatedness who contends that the entire struggle of a generation of English poets is a narrative writ small of a larger cultural dilemma. Bate identified a broad cultural challenge in the confrontation of the English neoclassical poets with their predecessors. The task of the artist is to confront two processes "crazily split down the middle by two opposing demands." On the one hand, he is required to learn from the "great examples that, from childhood up, are viewed as prototypes." Having engaged in this exercise which is a "natural response of the human heart" until it is "gradually absorbed into the conscience and the blood stream," he is confronted with a "second injunction": "You are forbidden to be very closely like these examples." The poet is thus enjoined to "admire and at the same time to try, at all costs, not to follow closely what you admire." To Bate, the agony of the poet mirrors the problem of culture itself—"How to use a heritage . . . and how to acquire our own identities"—and those who overcome it, do so by defying the taboo of imitation.[33]

The confrontation with belatedness, then, is similar to the presidential demand to imitate and excel. His anxiety of influence is in part so acute because his rebellion is focused upon texts that were themselves confrontations with belatedness and thus designed to be "closed" to future poet-presidents. Confronted with texts that are themselves (mis)readings intended as foundations for imitation, his anxiety and struggle is a personification of culture itself. The president who succumbs to the challenge is thus a president who does not succumb to culture but who "forgets" his predecessors and thus fails to participate in community.

That the project of confronting anxiety and overcoming belatedness is a dangerous one is indisputable. Yet the "closeness" with which strong presidents come to destroying culture in their poetic narratives of salvation also illustrates how always close a culture in general is to the threat of disintegration. Thus the hazards may lie more in the tendency of the American public to ignore this struggle rather than to regard itself as a common participant. Citizens who themselves do not confront belatedness, who do not search for heroic opportunity in the public realm, are citizens who are ultimately unable to even judge the poet-president. When belatedness ceases to be an obstacle and cause for anxiety and every president can easily regard himself as first, (mis)readings will no longer be necessary.

We have awarded the center of this essay to the imaginary belated president, and it is thus fitting at the close to give some small space to an imaginary citizen, one who, in this case, not only has read the poetic narratives of strong presidents but also is familiar with the analyses of his own imaginary counterpart. After recovering from the shock of reading such sustained resentment and after accepting at least some of his esoteric readings of strong presidents, he may conclude something like the following: I know that you are driven by belated desires, but I also know that these desires to excel can have beneficial consequences. Washington's conceptualization of his firstness gave the young Republic some accommodation between the need for a Rousseauean legislator and its justifiable suspicion of executive power. Lincoln's great poetic drama against belatedness forced Americans to confront, if only for a historical moment, a feature of American exceptionalism that was horrific, a Republic which contained the institution of slavery on its soil. FDR's challenge to Jefferson, stated esoterically, opened up democratic possibilities never imagined in America. So too for other strong presidents who have set forth "arduous enterprises" that have revitalized the Republic. I thus commend your desire to excel, so says the imaginary citizen. But he adds a codicil: I shall be watching you! I will honor you as you have "honored" your strong predecessors. Sometimes I will reject you and sometimes I will abandon you. You will, of course, insist that you cannot engage in poetic achievements on these terms and that, after all, it is the citizen who places upon him the contradictory demands of imitation and exceptionalism. But those are the terms of the contract that other strong presidents risked, even though they may not have been stated within the theory of belatedness. Imagine, if you will, how sweet it will be to excel under these most demanding conditions. "Fare thee well, great heart"!

NOTES

* *

Introduction

1. *New York Times,* Jan. 20, 1993.
2. *RN: The Memoirs of Richard Nixon* (New York: Grosset & Dunlop, 1978), 1088.
3. Harold Bloom, *The Anxiety of Influence: A Theory of Poetry* (New York: Oxford Univ. Press, 1973), 5–13; Harold Bloom, *A Map of Misreading* (New York: Oxford Univ. Press, 1975), 18–19.
4. Robert Weisbuch, *Atlantic Double-Cross: American and British Literature in the Age of Emerson* (Chicago: Univ. of Chicago Press, 1986).
5. W. Jackson Bate, *The Burden of the Past and the English Poet* (Cambridge: Harvard Univ. Press, 1970), 133–34.
6. Niccolo Machiavelli, *The Prince and Discourses* (New York: Modern Library, 1940), 19–20.
7. Clinton Rossiter, ed., *The Federalist Papers* (New York: New American Library, 1961), 437.
8. See Ralph Ketcham, *Presidents Above Party: The First American Presidency, 1789–1829* (Chapel Hill: Univ. of North Carolina, 1984).
9. Bert Rockman, *The Leadership Question* (New York: Praeger, 1984), 43–59. Also see Richard Ellis and Aaron Wildavsky, *Dilemmas of Presidential Leadership* (New Brunswick, N.J.: Transaction Books, 1989) for a valuable analysis of presidential struggles to accommodate cultural predispositions.
10. Clinton Rossiter, *The American Presidency* (New York: Harcourt, Brace and World, 1960), 257.
11. Bloom, *Map of Misreading,* 19.
12. Rossiter, *American Presidency,* 108.
13. The uniqueness of presidential discourse has been examined by many students of the presidency. I have found Karlyn Kohrs Campbell and Kathleen Hall Jamieson, *Deeds Done in Words: Presidential Rhertoric and the Genres of Governance* (Chicago: Univ. of Chicago Press, 1990) to be the most informative.
14. The most theoretically focused example of this position is Jeffrey Tulis, *The Rhe-*

torical Presidency (Princeton, N.J.: Princeton Univ. Press, 1987). Also see Roderick P. Hart, *The Sound of Leadership* (Chicago: Univ. of Chicago Press, 1987).

15. Tulis, *Rhetorical Presidency*, 177. Also see Hart, *Sound of Leadership*, 210–14.

16. Karlyn Kohrs Campbell and Kathleen Hall Jamieson make a forceful argument along these general lines in *Deeds Done in Words*, 9–13. Also see Philip Abbott, "Do Presidents Talk Too Much?" *Presidential Studies Quarterly* 18 (Spring 1988): 347–62.

17. David Gergen to Paul D. Erikson in Paul D. Erikson, *Reagan Speaks* (New York: New York Univ. Press, 1985), 8.

18. Harvey Mansfield Jr. argues that the predominance of executive power is derived from its capacity for sudden execution which Machiavelli recognized and centered in his analyses of the *ad uno tratto* aspect of executive action. *Taming the Prince: The Ambivalence of Executive Power* (New York: Free Press, 1989), 142–44.

19. Richard Pious ably catalogues presidential expansive rules of construction in *The American Presidency* (New York: Basic Books, 1979), 42–44.

20. *Public Papers of the Presidents of the United States: Lyndon Baines Johnson.* 2 vols. (Washington, D.C.: Government Printing Office, 1968), 1:483.

21. Bate, *Burden of the Past*, 6.

22. Leo Strauss, *Persecution and the Art of Writing* (Glencoe, Ill.: Free Press, 1952), 22–37.

23. Ibid., 24–25.

24. Ibid., 34, 36.

25. Roy P. Basler, ed., *The Collected Works of Abraham Lincoln* (New Brunswick, N.J.: Rutgers Univ. Press, 1953), 3:376 (hereafter cited as *CW*).

26. Franklin Delano Roosevelt, *The Public Papers and Addresses of Franklin D. Roosevelt*, 13 vols. (New York: Macmillan, 1938–50), *1928–32*: 628–29, 639–40.

27. See Bloom, *Anxiety of Influence*, 14–16. Bloom expands and revises his "ratios" throughout his criticism, which includes *A Map of Misreading, The Breaking of the Vessels* (Chicago: Univ. of Chicago Press, 1982), and *Agon: Towards a Theory of Revisionism* (New York: Oxford Univ. Press, 1982).

28. Bloom, *Map of Misreading*, 9, 19.

29. Ibid., 199; Bloom, *Anxiety of Influence*, 153.

30. Weisbuch, *Atlantic Double-Cross*, 3, 4, 32.

31. Ibid., 24.

32. Bate, *Burden of the Past*, 27.

33. Noble E. Cunningham Jr., *Popular Images of the Presidency* (Columbia: Univ. of Missouri Press, 1991), 25–89.

34. I borrow here loosely from Weisbuch's description of belated strategy in regard to American writers.

PART I. MONUMENTAL PRESIDENTS

1. E. E. Stoll, "Shakespeare's Presentation of a Contemporary Hero," in *Shakespeare: Henry V*, ed. Michael Quinn (London: Macmillan, 1969), 101.

2. Gary Taylor, ed., *Henry V* (Oxford: Oxford Univ. Press, 1982), 4.3.230.

3. Ibid., 1.2.113.

4. Ibid., 4.7.247.

5. Fluellen makes the point that Alexander's actions were often undertaken in

anger and drunkenness while Henry's are cold-blooded. The discussion turns to a comparison of Alexander's murder of his best friend, Cleitus, to Henry's renunciation of Falstaff. In a peroration on fame, Shakespeare has Fluellen forget the name of "the fat knight." Shakespeare confronted the moral ambiguity in Henry's act despite his effort to write of Henry as the "mirror of all Christian kings." It is not clear that Henry is aware of French atrocities when he gives the order. In fact, Gary Taylor insists that he is not (33). In any case, most productions of *Henry V* are squeamish enough to move the slaughter offstage, despite the fact that the Q version of the text has the instruction for Pistol to "coup la gorge" after the order.

6. Taylor, ed., *Henry V*, 4.1.214.
7. Ibid., 1.2.104.
8. W. B. Yeats, *Essays and Introductions* (London: Macmillan, 1961); Mark Van Doren, *Shakespeare* (New York: Holt, Rinehart and Winston, 1967); Alvin B. Kernan, "'The Henriad': Shakespeare's Major History Plays," in *William Shakespeare: Histories and Poems*, ed. Harold Bloom (New York: Chelsea House, 1986), 220–28.

Chapter 1. George Washington: The First

1. See Catherine L. Albanese, *Sons of the Fathers: The Civil Religion of the American Revolution* (Philadelphia: Temple Univ. Press, 1976), chap. 5; Barry Schwartz, *George Washington: The Making of an American Symbol* (Ithaca, N.Y.: Cornell Univ. Press, 1987); Robert P. Hay, "George Washington: American Moses," *American Quarterly* 21 (1969): 780–91 for extensive reviews of these comparisons.
2. Ebenezer Marsh, *An Oration, Delivered at Wethersfield . . . on the Death of General George Washington* (Hartford, Conn.: Hudson and Goodwin, 1800), 8.
3. George Will, *Cincinnatus: George Washington and the Enlightenment* (Garden City: Doubleday, 1984), 3.
4. Ralph Louis Ketchum, *Presidents Above Party: The First American Presidency, 1789–1829* (Chapel Hill: Univ. of North Carolina Press, 1984), 92.
5. John E. Ferling, *The First of Men: A Life of George Washington* (Knoxville: Univ. of Tennessee Press, 1988), 7.
6. Ibid., 10.
7. Washington to John Augustine Washington, May 31, 1754, in Saxe Commins, ed., *Basic Writings of George Washington* (New York: Random House, 1948), 26.
8. Ferling, *First of Men*, 29.
9. Washington to John Augustine Washington, June 28, 1755, in W. W. Abbott et al., eds., *The Papers of George Washington* (Charlottesville: Univ. Press of Virginia, 1983), vol. 1:318.
10. Ibid.
11. Don Higginbotham, *George Washington and the American Military Tradition* (Athens: Univ. of Georgia Press, 1985), 37, 38.
12. Marcus Cunliffe, *George Washington: Man and Monument* (Boston: Little, Brown, 1958), 45, 50.
13. Higginbotham, *George Washington and the American Military Tradition*, 39.
14. Cunliffe, *George Washington*, 50.
15. Robert F. Jones, *George Washington* (New York: Fordham Univ. Press, 1986), 35.

16. Washington to Bryan Fairfax, Aug. 24, 1774, in W. B. Allen, ed., *George Washington: A Collection* (Indianapolis: Liberty Classics, 1988), 39 (hereafter cited as GW).

17. Ferling, *First of Men*, 476–78.

18. Jones, *George Washington*, 40.

19. "To the President of the Second Continental Congress," GW, 40.

20. Washington to Warner Lewis, Aug. 14, 1755, in Commins, ed., *Basic Writings*, 42–43.

21. Cunliffe, *George Washington*, 72.

22. Jones, *George Washington*, 47.

23. Washington to Nathaniel Greene, in Commins, ed., *Basic Writings*, 453.

24. Charles Royster, *A Revolutionary People at War: The Continental Army and American Character, 1775–1783* (Chapel Hill: Univ. of North Carolina Press, 1979), 331.

25. See the following for examinations of the centrality of the standing army controversy in colonial American culture: John Phillip Reid, *In Defiance of the Law: The Standing Army Controversy, the Two Constitutions, and the Coming of the American Revolution* (Chapel Hill: Univ. of North Carolina Press, 1981); Royster, *Revolutionary People at War*, chap. 1; John Todd White, "Standing Armies in Time of War: Republican Theory and Military Practice during the American Revolution" (Ph.D. diss., George Washington Univ., 1978).

26. Royster, *Revolutionary People at War*, 26.

27. George Washington, "To the President of Congress," GW, 79.

28. Washington to John Bannister, Apr. 21, 1778, GW, 102–3.

29. George Washington, "Circular to the States," Oct. 18, 1780, GW 168.

30. Washington to Joseph Reed, Dec. 15, 1775, GW, 54.

31. George Washington, "To the President of Congress," Sept. 24, 1776, GW, 75.

32. Washington to John Banister, Apr. 21, 1778, GW, 99.

33. Washington, "To the President of Congress," Sept. 24, 1776, GW, 80.

34. George Washington, "To the President of Congress," Feb. 9, 1776, GW, 63.

35. George Washington, "General Orders, January 1, 1776" and "To the President of Congress," Feb. 9, 1776, GW, 56.

36. Washington to Joseph Reed, Feb. 10, 1776, GW, 66; Washington, "To the President of Congress," Feb. 9, 1776, GW, 63.

37. Washington, "To the President of Congress," Sept. 24, 1776, GW, 81, 76.

38. GW, 76.

39. Royster, *Revolutionary People at War*, 87.

40. Washington to Governor Dinwiddie, Mar. 20, 1754, in Commins, ed., *Basic Writings*, 13.

41. Washington to Alexander Hamilton, Mar. 4, 1783, GW, 212.

42. Washington to Governeur Morris, May 8, 1779, GW, 130.

43. Washington to Hamilton, Mar. 4, 1783, GW, 211.

44. Richard H. Kohn, *Eagle and Sword: The Beginnings of the Military Establishment in America* (New York: Free Press, 1975), 29–30.

45. Richard H. Kohn has been instrumental in refocusing attention on the Newburgh conspiracy. See his "The Inside History of the Newburgh Conspiracy: America and the Coup d'Etat," *William and Mary Quarterly*, 3d ser., 27 (1970): 187–200, which offers a bolder interpretation than his subsequent book. Also see Paul David

Nelson, "Horation Gates at Newburgh," *William and Mary Quarterly*, 3d ser., 29 (1972): 143–58 and C. Edward Skeen, "The Newburgh Conspiracy Reconsidered," *William and Mary Quarterly*, 3d ser., 31 (1974): 273–98 for rebuttals and comments by Kohn.

46. George Washington, "Speech to the Officers of the Army," Mar. 15, 1783, GW, 217–18.
47. Douglas Southall Freeman, *George Washington* (Boston: Scribner's, 1948–57), 5:435.
48. Kohn, *Eagle and Sword*, 32.
49. George Washington, "Circular to the States," GW, 239.
50. William Tudor, "An Oration Delivered March 5, 1779 . . ." (Boston, 1779).
51. Washington, "Circular to the States," GW, 247.
52. Ibid., 226.
53. Washington to Marquis de Lafayette, Feb. 3, 1784, GW, 280.
54. Ferling, *First of Men*, 333.
55. Washington to Marquis de Lafayette, Feb. 1, 1784, and Washington to John Jay, Aug. 15, 1786, GW, 280, 334.
56. Washington to Henry Knox, Dec. 26, 1786, and Washington to David Humphreys, Dec. 26, 1786, GW, 348–49, 351. In December, Washington was uncertain whether the rebellion was being orchestrated by "men of consequence and abilities behind the curtain" (351).
57. Washington to John Jay, Mar. 10, 1787, GW, 358.
58. Freeman, *George Washington* 6:83.
59. Ferling, *First of Men*, 354.
60. Washington to Jay, Mar. 10, 1787, GW, 358.
61. Wills, *Cincinnatus*, 153.
62. Washington to Henry Knox, Mar. 8, 1787, GW, 357.
63. See Glenn A. Phelps, *George Washington and American Constitutionalism* (Lawrence: Univ. Press of Kansas, 1933), chap. 4 for a revealing discussion of Washington's active participation in the debates despite his role as the "silent delegate" from Virginia.
64. Cunliffe, "The Presidential Elections of 1789 and 1792," in *In Search of America: Transatlantic Essays, 1951–1990*, by Marcus Cunliffe (Westport, Conn.: Greenwood Press, 1991), 85.
65. Washington to Hamilton, Oct. 3, 1788, GW, 423.
66. Forrest MacDonald, *The Presidency of George Washington* (Lawrence: Univ. Press of Kansas, 1974), 185.
67. Ibid., 186.
68. Michael P. Riccards, *A Republic If You Can Keep It: The Foundation of the American Presidency, 1700–1800* (Westport, Conn.: Greenwood Press, 1987), 166.
69. Kohn, *Eagle and Sword*, chap. 8 concludes that the incident was the result of a concerted effort in the Washington administration to demonstrate the need for federal force.
70. George Washington, "Farewell Address," GW, 512–13.
71. Ibid., 514.
72. Ibid., 521.
73. Ibid., 518.
74. Marsh, *Oration, Delivered at Wetherfield*, 13.

Chapter 2. Abraham Lincoln: The Double Cross

1. Marcus Cunliffe, "The Doubled Images of Washington and Lincoln" in Cunliffe, ed., *In Search of America*, 202–3.
2. Michael Davis, *The Image of Lincoln in the South* (Knoxville: Univ. of Tennessee Press, 1971), 125.
3. Edgar Lee Masters, *Lincoln, the Man* (New York: Dodd, Mead, 1931); Edmund Wilson, *Patriotic Gore* (New York: Oxford Univ. Press, 1962), xvi–xviii; M. E. Bradford, *Remembering Who We Are* (Athens: Univ. of Georgia Press, 1985), 155. Don E. Fehrenbacher unsympathetically reviews the anti-Lincoln tradition, which he concludes "persists in lonely splendor" in *Lincoln in Text and Context* (Stanford, Calif.: Stanford Univ. Press, 1987), chap. 15.
4. Masters, *Lincoln the Man*, 491; Wilson, *Patriotic Gore*, 108, 102; Bradford, *Remembering Who We Are*, 155.
5. George B. Forgie, *Patricide in the House Divided* (New York: W. W. Norton, 1979).
6. Dwight G. Anderson, *Abraham Lincoln: The Quest for Immortality* (New York: Knopf, 1982).
7. Freud first advanced what he called his "fantastic hypothesis" in *Totem and Taboo* (New York: Random House, 1918), 182 and returned to reconsider it throughout his writings. See *Group Psychology and the Analysis of the Ego* (New York: Liveright, 1949) and *Moses and Monotheism* (New York: Knopf, 1947).
8. CW 3:111.
9. CW 3:108.
10. CW 3:113.
11. CW 3:114.
12. CW 3:112.
13. Harry Jaffa, *The Crisis of the House Divided* (New York: Doubleday, 1959), 214. Defenders of Lincoln make various concessions to his poetic intent in the Lyceum speech. Robert V. Bruce contends that "we all have our daydreams and playing Napoleon might have been among those of an ambitious young political leader." Lincoln may have had a "vagrant fantasy" of assuming the role of a Caesar but not a "serious game plan." "Commentary on 'Quest for Immortality,'" in Gabor S. Borit and Norman O. Forness, eds., *The Historian's Lincoln* (Urbana: Univ. of Illinois Press, 1988), 276. Gary Wills argues that Lincoln's target was a conventional partisan one (Andrew Jackson), as does Marcus Cunliffe (though more tentatively than Wills). *Lincoln at Gettysburg* (New York: Simon and Schuster, 1992), 82 and Borit and Forness, eds., *Historian's Lincoln*, 281.
14. Wilson, *Patriotic Gore*, 108.
15. CW 1:115.
16. Jaffa, *Crisis of the House Divided*, 270.
17. Anderson, *The Quest for Immortality*, 107.
18. CW 1:275.
19. CW 1:273–74.
20. CW 1:279.
21. CW 4:439.
22. CW 3:522.
23. CW 3:376.
24. CW 2:499.
25. Bradford, *Remembering Who We Are*, 144.

26. CW 4:240.
27. CW 4:434, 439, 438.
28. Thaddeus Stevens cited in James M. Macpherson, "Abraham Lincoln and the Second American Revolution," in *Abraham Lincoln and the American Political Tradition*, ed. John L. Thomas (Amherst: Univ. of Massachusetts Press, 1986), 146.
29. CW 5:346, 350.
30. For a review of the initial ambiguous status of Lincoln among northern radicals, see Lloyd Lewis, *Myths After Lincoln* (New York: Readers Club, 1941).
31. CW 8:333.
32. The characterizations are Jaffa's and Simon's. Jaffa, *Crisis of the House Divided*, 185 and Paul Simon, *Lincoln's Preparation for Greatness: The Illinois Legislative Years* (Norman: Univ. of Oklahoma Press, 1965), 292.
33. CW 1:178.
34. CW 1:439.
35. CW 1:447.
36. CW 1:457.
37. Democratic Party cohesion frayed as well. Van Burenites remained loyal to the war effort until 1847 and would eventually form the Liberty Party. "Calhoun Democrats" drifted from the party as well. See John H. Schroeder, *Mr. Polk's War: American Opposition and Dissent, 1846–1848* (Madison: Univ. of Wisconsin Press, 1973), 26–32; 131–33.
38. Gansevoort Melville (June 1844) in Charles Sellars, *James K. Polk: Continentalist 1843–1846* (Princeton, N.J.: Princeton Univ. Press, 1966), 140–41.
39. James K. Polk, "Inaugural Address," in *Messages and Papers of the Presidents*, ed. James Richardson (New York: Bureau of National Literature, 1897), vol. 4:29, 32.
40. CW 1:438, 441–42.
41. CW 1:439.
42. Ibid.
43. Michael P. Riccards, *The Ferocious Engine of Democracy: A History of the American Presidency* (Lanham, Md.: Rowman and Littlefield, 1994), 200–201.
44. CW 3:334.
45. CW 1:508.
46. CW 2:85.
47. CW 2:89.
48. CW 3:303, 304.
49. CW 2:519.
50. CW 1:347.
51. CW 2:125.
52. CW 2:122.
53. Daniel Walker Howe, *The Political Culture of the American Whigs* (Chicago: Univ. of Chicago Pres, 1979), 275.
54. Don. E. Fehrenbacher, *Prelude to Greatness: Lincoln in the 1850s* (New York: McGraw-Hill, 1964), 96, 161.
55. Jaffa, *Crisis of the House Divided*, 408.
56. Forgie, *Patricide in the House Divided*, 247, 250.
57. Anderson, *The Quest for Immortality*, 119.
58. CW 2:136.
59. CW 3:9.

60. Robert W. Johannsen, *Stephen A. Douglas* (New York: Oxford Univ. Press, 1973), 31, 130, 139.
61. Ibid., 381.
62. CW 3:54, 55.
63. Fehrenbacher, *Prelude to Greatness*, 95; Wills, *Lincoln at Gettysburg*, 169. For a significant exception, see Charles B. Strozier's thoughtful analysis. *Lincoln's Quest for Union* (New York: Basic Books, 1982), 179–81.
64. Matthew 12:25–28.
65. Matthew 12:33–35.
66. CW 2:465–66.
67. CW 3:22.
68. Ibid.
69. John Nicholay and John Hay noted the story in their biography. *Abraham Lincoln: A History*, 10 vols. (New York: Century, 1917), 3:326–27. J. G. Randall, however, treats the incident skeptically. *Lincoln the President* (New York: Dodd, Mead, 1956), 1:295.
70. CW 4:191, 204.
71. CW 4:240.
72. Cited in Forgie, *Patricide in the House Divided*, 209.
73. Willmoore Kendall and George W. Carey, *The Basic Symbols of the American Political Tradition* (Baton Rouge: Louisiana State Univ. Press, 1970), 88, 94.
74. Stephen Skrowenek, *The Politics Presidents Make* (Cambridge: Harvard Univ. Press, 1993), 226.
75. Richard Reeves, *President Kennedy: Profile of Power* (New York: Simon and Schuster, 1993), 20.

Chapter 3. Franklin D. Roosevelt: Genial Masks

1. Tugwell, *Democratic Roosevelt*, 11.
2. See Fred I. Greenstein's discussion of FDR and the transformation of the presidency into its "modern" form. "In Search of the Modern Presidency," in *Leadership in the Modern Presidency*, ed. Fred I. Greenstein (Cambridge: Harvard Univ. Press, 1988), 296–352.
3. Roosevelt, *Public Papers and Addresses: 1944–45*: 29.
4. *New York Herald Tribune*, Apr. 28, 1932.
5. George Creel, *Rebel at Large* (New York: Putnam, 1947), 270.
6. Marquis Childs, "They Hate Roosevelt," *Harpers*, May 1936, 634–42.
7. Elliot A. Rosen, *Hoover, Roosevelt, and the Brains Trust* (New York: Columbia Univ. Press, 1977), 97.
8. Howard Zinn, "The New Left Views the New Deal," in *The New Deal: Analysis and Interpretation*, ed. Alonzo L. Hamby (New York: Weybright and Talley, 1969), 235–36.
9. Arthur Schlesinger Jr., *The Age of Roosevelt: The Politics of Upheaval* (Boston: Houghton Mifflin, 1960), 653.
10. James MacGregor Burns, *Roosevelt: The Lion and the Fox* (New York: Harcourt, Brace and World, 1956), 404.
11. *New York Times*, Sept. 17, 1940.
12. Elliot Roosevelt, ed., *FDR: His Personal Letters, 1928–45* (New York: Duell, Sloan and Pearce, 1950), vol. 1:669–70.

13. Burns, *Roosevelt: The Lion and the Fox,* 404.
14. John T. Flynn, *The Roosevelt Myth* (New York: Devin-Adair, 1948), 278.
15. Franklin Delano Roosevelt, "Is There a Jefferson on the Horizon?" *New York Evening World,* Dec. 3, 1925.
16. Herbert Croly, "The Great Jefferson Joke," *New Republic,* June 9, 1926.
17. See Arthur Ekirch Jr., *Ideologies and Utopias: The Impact of the New Deal on American Thought* (Chicago: Univ. of Chicago Press, 1969), chap. 2; Philip Abbott, *Political Thought in America: Conversations and Debates* (Itasca, Ill.: F. E. Peacock, 1991), chap. 7.
18. Roosevelt, *Public Papers and Addresses: 1928–32:* 628–29, 639–40.
19. Raymond Moley, *After Seven Years* (New York: Harper, 1939), 332ff.
20. Seth Ames, ed., *The Works of Fisher Ames* (New York: Lennox Hill, 1971).
21. Roosevelt, *Public Papers and Addresses: 1928–32:* 646–47, 648–50, 746–48.
22. Tugwell, *Democratic Roosevelt,* 246.
23. See Schlesinger, *The Crisis of the Old Order* (Boston: Houghton Mifflin, 1957), 426.
24. Joseph P. Lash, *Dealers and Dreamers: A New Look at the New Deal* (New York: Doubleday, 1988); Jordan A. Schwarz, *Liberal: Adolph A. Berle and the Vision of an American Era* (New York: Free Press, 1987), 62.
25. Beatrice Bishop Berle and Travis Beal Jacobs, eds., *Navigating the Rapids, 1918–1971: From the Papers of Adoplf A. Berle* (New York: Harcourt, Brace, Jovanovich, 1973), 57.
26. Ibid., 59.
27. Schwarz, *Liberal,* 106.
28. Roosevelt, *Public Papers and Addresses: 1928–32:* 744–45, 747–48.
29. Ibid., 750.
30. Ibid., 752, 755.
31. Adolph Berle, "The Social Economics of the New Deal," *New York Times Magazine,* Oct. 29, 1933, 19.
32. John Locke, *Of Civil Government: Second Treatise* (Chicago: Regnery, 1971), 89–91.
33. Walter Lippman, "On Planned Planning" (Apr. 26, 1934), in Lippman, *Interpretations: 1933–35* (New York: Macmillan, 1936), 253–55.
34. Roosevelt, *Public Papers and Addresses: 1928–32:* 751–54.
35. Ibid., 745.
36. Ibid., 746. The description and arrangement of FDR's predecessors received the most extensive revision by FDR through Berle's drafts. See "Individualism: Romantic and Realistic," in Adoplh Berle Papers, FDR Library, Hyde Park, N.Y.
37. Roosevelt, *Public Papers and Addresses: 1933:* 518.
38. Ibid., 342.
39. Ibid., 418.
40. Ibid., 380.
41. Ibid., 342.
42. Hannah Arendt, *On Revolution* (New York: Viking, 1965), 238. For a stronger interpretation of Jefferson's commitment to public happiness, see Gary Wills, *Inventing America* (Garden City, N.Y.: Doubleday, 1978), 248–55, and for a weaker one, see John Diggins, *The Lost Soul of American Politics* (Chicago: Univ. of Chicago Press, 1984), 39–47.
43. Arendt, *On Revolution,* 238.

44. Ibid., 258–59.
45. See, for example, William Appleman Williams, *The Contours of American History* (Chicago: Quadrangle, 1966), 4, 5.
46. Robert Sherwood, *Roosevelt and Hopkins* (New York: Harpers, 1948), 57.
47. See William Leuchtenburg's review of the public works programs in his "The Achievement of the New Deal," in *Fifty Years Later: The New Deal Evaluated*, ed. Harvard Sitkoff (Philadelphia: Temple Univ. Press, 1985), 165ff.
48. Sherwood, *Roosevelt and Hopkins*, 60.
49. Studs Terkel, *Hard Times* (New York: Bantam, 1970), 435, 450–51. It is useful to compare these accounts with the general passivity of the unemployed as revealed in depression studies cross-nationally. For example, see Paul Lazarfeld et al., who described depression Marienthal as "die mude Gemeinschaft" (the weary community) *Marienthal: The Sociology of an Unemployed Community* (Chicago: Univ. of Chicago Press, 1971).
50. Sherwood, *Roosevelt and Hopkins*, 57. Hopkins could, however, be more expansive in other contexts. See Jan De Hart Matthews, "Arts and the People: The New Deal Quest for Cultural Democracy," *Journal of American History* 62 (Sept. 1975): 324.
51. Matthews, "Arts and the People," 322; Hallie Flanagan, "Testimony before HUAC," in *Thirty Years of Treason*, ed. Eric Bentley (New York: Viking, 1971), 3–47; Holger Cahill, "American Resources in the Arts," in *Art for the Millions*, ed. Francis O'Connor (Greenwich, Conn.: New York Graphic Society, 1973), 43–44; Francis O'Connor, ed., *The New Deal Art Projects: An Anthology of Memoirs* (Washington, D.C.: Smithsonian Institution Press, 1972). The prints were destroyed or auctioned off to private investors in 1941.
52. Lincoln Rothchild, "The Index of American Design of the WPA/FAP," in O'Connor, *The New Deal Art Projects*; Nancy E. Allen, *The Index of American Design* (Washington, D.C.: National Gallery of Art, 1984).
53. Walter Quirt, "On Mural Painting," in O'Connor, *Art for the Millions*, 79.
54. I rely here upon the reproductions of murals in Marlene Park and Gerald E. Markowitz, eds., *Democratic Vistas: Post Offices and Public Art in the New Deal* (Philadelphia: Temple Univ. Press, 1984).
55. For analysis of competing visions of the TVA, see Philip Abbott, *The Exemplary Presidency: FDR and the American Political Tradition* (Amherst: Univ. of Massachusetts Press, 1990), 91–100.
56. Francis Perkins, *The Roosevelt I Knew* (New York: Viking, 1946), 213.
57. Roosevelt, *Public Papers and Addresses: 1936*: 16, 17.
58. Arthur Schlesinger Jr., *The Politics of Upheaval*, 291; Moley, *After Seven Years*, 332ff.
59. Roosevelt, *Public Papers and Addresses: 1936*: 566.
60. Ibid., 39, 40.
61. Ibid., 197.
62. Merill D. Peterson, *The Jeffersonian Image in the American Mind* (New York: Oxford Univ. Press, 1960).
63. Donald R. McCoy, *Landon of Kansas* (Lincoln: Univ. of Nebraska Press, 1966), 330.
64. FDR to John N. Gardner, Nov. 20, 1934, in Roosevelt, ed., *FDR: His Personal Letters* 1:433.
65. Schlesinger, *Politics of Upheaval*, pt. 1 vividly describes the "rise of the dema-

gogues." Also see, William E. Leuchtenburg, *Franklin D. Roosevelt and the New Deal* (New York: Harper and Row, 1963), chap. 5.

66. See Edward Pessen, *Jacksonian America* (Homewood, Ill.: Dorsey, 1969), 384–93 for a review of the findings of the "entrepreneurial" school, which emphasizes its economic policies. FDR's (mis)reading of Jackson was so successful, however, that many scholars came to see the Jacksonian movement as a precursor to the New Deal. See Arthur Schlesinger Jr., *The Age of Jackson* (Boston: Little, Brown, 1945) for the first formulation. Recently Robert V. Remini has repeated this viewpoint. In *The Legacy of Andrew Jackson* (Baton Rouge: Louisiana State Univ. Press, 1988) he concludes that the "specific proposals of the Jacksonian program," such as opposition to internal improvements, have "long since passed into history" and what remains is a "stirring and elegant defense of popular government and the means by which it could be realized" (43).

67. Alexis de Tocqueville, *Democracy in America*, ed. J. P. Mayer (Garden City, N.Y.: Doubleday, 1969), 531–32.

68. Roosevelt, *Public Papers and Addresses: 1936: 574.*

69. Roosevelt, *Public Papers and Addresses: 1935: 237.*

70. Leuchtenburg, *Franklin D. Roosevelt and the New Deal*, 132.

71. Roosevelt, *Public Papers and Addresses: 1937: 1–2.*

72. On the battle over the court reorganization plan, see William E. Leuchtenburg, "Franklin D. Roosevelt's Supreme Court 'Packing' Plan," in *Essays on the New Deal*, ed. Harold Hollingsworth (Austin: Univ. of Texas Press, 1969); Philip Abbott, *Exemplary Presidency*, chap. 7; Joseph Alsop and Turner Catledge, *The 168 Days* (Garden City, N.Y.: Doubleday, 1938) is still a valuable narrative.

73. *New York Times*, Aug. 22, 23, 1938. See Roosevelt, *Public Papers and Addresses: 1938: 435* for his remarks on southern feudalism.

74. William Starr Meyers, ed., *The State Papers and Other Public Writings of Herbert Hoover* (Garden City, N.Y.: Doubleday, 1934), 1:500, 504.

75. Charles A. Beard and Mary R. Beard, *The Rise of American Civilization* (New York: Macmillan, 1927), 2:51, 53.

76. Louis Hacker, "Revolutionary America," *Harper's Magazine*, Mar. 1935, 444; V. F. Calverton, "The American Revolutionary Tradition," *Scribner's Magazine*, May 1934, 354.

77. Frank L. Owsley, "The Irrepressible Conflict," in *I'll Take My Stand*, by Frank L. Owsley (New York: Harper and Brothers, 1930), 68.

78. Albert J. Beveridge, *Abraham Lincoln, 1809–1858* (New York: Victor Gollancz, 1928); Emanuel Hertz, *Abraham Lincoln: A New Portrait* (New York: Horace Liveright, 1931), 409 (Hertz used a quote by Lincoln against the Mexican War to support his assertion); Gilbert Hobbs Barnes, *The Antislavery Impulse, 1830–1844* (New York: Harcourt, Brace and World, 1933); Avery Craven, *The Repressible Conflict* (Baton Rogue: Louisiana State Univ. Press, 1939); James G. Randall, "The Blundering Generation," *Mississippi Valley Historical Review* 27 (June 1940): 27; George Fort Milton, *The Eve of Conflict* (1934) (New York: Octogon, 1963).

79. Archibald MacLeish, "The Irresponsibles," *Nation*, May 18, 1940, 619–23. Also see Lewis Mumford's *Faith for Living* (New York, 1940). Both Macleish and Mumford had expressed militant antiwar positions a few years earlier. "When America Goes to War: A Symposium," *Modern Monthly* (June–July 1935). See Philip Abbott, *"Leftward Ho!"*: *V. F. Calverton and American Radicalism* (Westport: Greenwood Press, 1993) for an account of the rapid switch on the part of the American intelligentsia on the war question.

80. Carl Sandburg, *Abraham Lincoln: The War Years* (New York: Harcourt, Brace, 1939), 2:333.
81. Burns, *Roosevelt: The Lion and the Fox*, 422–23.
82. Sandburg's speech is reprinted in his *Home Front Memo* (New York: Harcourt, Brace, 1943), 29–30. For FDR's relationships with Sherwood and Sandburg, see Alfred Haworth Jones, *Roosevelt's Image Makers* (Port Washington, N.Y.: Kennikat, 1974).
83. Jones, *Roosevelt's Image Makers*, 328–29. The *New York Times* headline the following day read: "President Bids Nation Awake to Peril / Roosevelt is Grim / Quotes Lincoln to Show a Parallel."
84. CW 2:268.
85. CW 2:461.
86. Roosevelt, *Public Papers and Addresses: 1940*: 298–300.
87. Ibid., 301–2.
88. Ibid., 302.
89. Ibid., 408.
90. Ibid., 408, 432–33, 436, 439, 472.
91. Ibid.
92. *New York Times*, Nov. 1, 1940, 18.
93. Samuel I. Rosenman, *Working with Roosevelt* (New York: Harper, 1952), 236, 245.
94. Roosevelt, *Public Papers and Addresses: 1940*: 531, 532, 544.
95. Ibid., 640.
96. Ibid., 634–36.
97. Ibid., 665, 666.
98. Ibid., 672.
99. James MacGregor Burns, *Roosevelt: Soldier of Freedom* (New York: Harcourt, Brace, Jovanovich, 1970) viii.
100. Roosevelt, *Public Papers and Addresses: 1940*: 281. In this earlier formulation at a press conference, the president paired the various freedoms against the philosophy of the "corporate state."
101. Roosevelt, *Public Papers and Addresses: 1941*: 3.
102. Basler, ed., *Collected Works* 1:115.
103. Roosevelt, *Public Papers and Addresses: 1941*: 3.
104. Ibid., 4–6.

PART II. SPIRITED PRESIDENTS

1. For a discussion of thymos and spiritedness in general, see Catherine H. Zuckert, "On the Role of Spiritedness and Politics," in *Understanding the Political Spirit: Philosophical Investigations from Socrates to Nietzsche*, ed. Catherine Zuckert (New Haven, Conn.: Yale Univ. Press, 1988), 1–29.
2. Plutarch, *The Age of Alexander* (Baltimore: Penguin, 1973), 256.
3. Allan Bloom, *The Republic of Plato* (New York: Basic Books, 1968), 440c–d.
4. Homer, *The Iliad*, trans. Marton Hammond (Baltimore: Penguin, 1987), 9:318–20, 173.
5. Ibid., 24:40–45, 394.
6. Machiavelli, *Discourses*, trans. Leslie J. Walker (Baltimore: Penguin, 1970), bk. 2, pt. 2, pp. 274–75.

7. James Parton, *The Life of Andrew Jackson*, 3 vols. (New York: Mason, 1860), 1:267–306.

8. Stefan Lorant, *The Life and Times of Theodore Roosevelt* (New York, 1959).

9. William Henry Harbaugh, *The Life and Times of Theodore Roosevelt* (New York: Collier, 1961), 107.

10. Louis Hartz, *The Liberal Tradition in America* (Harcourt, Brace and World, 1955), 230; Norman Mailer, *The Presidential Papers of Norman Mailer* (New York: Bantam, 1964), 46–47.

Chapter 4. Andrew Jackson: Will

1. Edward Everett, *Orations and Speeches*, 4 vols. (Boston: Little, Brown, 1878–79), 2:55; Douglas T. Miller, "Everything's Changed," in *The Nature of Jacksonian America*, ed. Douglas T. Miller (New York: Wiley and Sons, 1972), 7–8. Even Jackson was taken with the "experiment" at Lowell. Reviewing twenty-five hundred young women employees in parade from a hotel balcony, he exclaimed, "Very pretty women, by the Eternal" and left the town with "a more positive attitude toward manufacturing." Burke Davis, *Old Hickory: A Life of Andrew Jackson* (New York: Dial Press, 1977), 330–31.

2. Harbaugh, *Life and Times of Theodore Roosevelt*, 94–95.

3. John Spencer Bassett, ed., *Correspondence of Andrew Jackson*, 7 vols. (Washington, D.C.: Carnegie Institution of Washington), 1:153.

4. Ibid., 1:175.

5. Ibid., 1:255.

6. Augustine Buell, *History of Andrew Jackson*, 2 vols. (New York, Charles Scribner's Sons, 1904), 2:410; S. Putnam Waldo, *Memoirs of Andrew Jackson* (Hartford, Conn., 1820), 35. John William Ward examines Jackson's orphanage in terms of his self-made-man persona in his *Andrew Jackson: Symbol for an Age* (New York: Oxford, 1962), 166–80, and Michael Paul Rogin explores its psychological foundations: *Fathers and Sons: Andrew Jackson and the Subjugation of the American Indian* (New York: Vintage, 1975), chap. 2.

7. Rogin, *Fathers and Sons*, 41.

8. Alexander Walker, *Jackson and New Orleans* (New York, 1856), 13.

9. Ward, *Andrew Jackson*, 160.

10. Bassett, ed., *Correspondence of Andrew Jackson* 3:118–19.

11. Rogin, *Fathers and Sons*, 193–205; Ward, *Andrew Jackson*, 57–63. See Bassett, ed., *Correspondence of Andrew Jackson* 2:324–51 for Jackson's barely controlled disdain for the caution of Monroe, Calhoun, and Scott.

12. Schlesinger, *Age of Jackson*, 37.

13. U.S. Congress, *Annals of Congress*, 15th Cong., 2d sess., 1:653.

14. Davis, *Old Hickory*, 170–71; Bassett, ed., *Correspondence of Andrew Jackson* 2:443.

15. Ward, *Andrew Jackson*, 263; Bassett, ed., *Correspondence of Andrew Jackson* 3:199; Davis, *Old Hickory*, 191.

16. Bassett, ed., *Correspondence of Andrew Jackson* 3:278, 280.

17. Remini, *Legacy of Andrew Jackson*, 19–20.

18. Bassett, ed., *Correspondence of Andrew Jackson* 3:276.

19. Peterson, *Jeffersonian Image in the American Mind*, 69.

20. Bassett, ed., *Correspondence of Andrew Jackson* 3:280–81.

21. Adrienne Koch and William Peden, eds., *The Life and Selected Writings of Thomas Jefferson* (New York: Modern Library, 1944), 608–9; Parton, *Life of Andrew Jackson* 1:219.

22. Richard B. Lattner, *The Presidency of Andrew Jackson: White House Politics, 1829–1837* (Athens: Univ. of Georgia Press, 1979), 105, 86.

23. See Robert V. Remini, *Andrew Jackson and the Bank War* (New York: W. W. Norton, 1967) for a detailed account of the war generally sympathetic to Jackson.

24. Ibid., 81.

25. "Veto Message," in Richardson, ed., *Messages and Papers of the Presidents* 3:1144.

26. Ibid., 3:1153.

27. Ibid.

28. "Removal of Public Deposits," in Richardson, ed., *Messages and Papers of the Presidents* 3:1226.

29. Bassett, ed., *Correspondence of Andrew Jackson* 5:216.

30. Ibid., 5:217.

31. James C. Curtis, *Andrew Jackson and the Search for Vindication* (Boston: Little, Brown, 1976), 164; Davis, *Old Hickory*, 335.

32. Daniel Webster, *Speeches and Forensic Arguments* (Boston: Perkins, Marvin, 1835), 2:274.

33. "Protest," in Richardson, ed., *Messages and Papers of the Presidents* 3:1311.

34. Ibid., 3:1312.

Chapter 5. Theodore Roosevelt: Energy

1. Edmund Morris, *The Rise of Theodore Roosevelt* (New York: McCann and Geoghegan, 1979), 12, 13, 20, 21; Stephen Gwynn, ed., *The Letters and Friendships of Sir Cecil Spring-Rice* (Boston: Houghton Mifflin, 1929), 1:437; Bernard de Voto, ed., *Mark Twain in Eruption* (New York: Harpers, 1940), 8.

2. Theodore Roosevelt, "National Life and Character," in *American Ideals*, by Theodore Roosevelt (New York: Putnam's, 1897), 2:93.

3. Ibid., 2:123.

4. Elting E. Morison and John Blum, eds., *The Letters of Theodore Roosevelt* (Cambridge: Harvard Univ. Press, 1951–54), 1:136.

5. Governeur Morris, in Theodore Roosevelt, *The Works of Theodore Roosevelt: National Edition* (New York: Scribner's Sons, 1926), 7:469.

6. Morison and Blum, eds., *Letters of Theodore Roosevelt* 1:102; Morris, *Rise of Theodore Roosevelt*, 333.

7. Morris, *Rise of Theodore Roosevelt*, 374; Thomas Hart Benton, in Roosevelt, *Works* 7:5, 6, 232. Two years later in volume 1 of *The Winning of the West*, TR expanded his account of westward migration in terms of "race expansion." *The Winning of the West* (New York: Putnam's, 1889), 1:1–27.

8. Thomas Hart Benton, in Roosevelt, *Works* 7:233.

9. Ibid., 7:204.

10. Ibid., 7:75–76.

11. Ibid., 7:79, 92.

12. Morison and Blum, eds., *Letters of Theodore Roosevelt* 2:1047.

13. Governeur Morris, in Roosevelt, *Works* 7:458, 468.

14. Thomas Hart Benton, in Roosevelt, *Works* 7:79; 83; 156.
15. Theodore Roosevelt, "American Ideals," in Roosevelt, *American Ideals* 1:2.
16. Ibid., 1:4.
17. The Rough Riders, in Roosevelt, *Works* 11:80. Finley Peter Dunne's "Mr. Dooley" was one of the few Americans to see TR's act of self-promotion. Dooley claimed that the book was mistitled and suggested alternatives such as "th' Darin' Exploits iv a Brave Man be an Actual Eye Witness," "th' Account iv th' Destruction iv Spanish Power in th' Ant Hills." He settled upon "Alone in Cuba." *Mr. Dooley's Philosophy* (New York: R. H. Russell, 1900), 13–18. Roosevelt's account became more self-deprecating years later. See *Theodore Roosevelt: An Autobiography* (New York: Charles Scribner's Sons, 1929), 241–45.
18. Theodore Roosevelt, "First Annual Message," in Richardson, ed., *Messages and Papers of the Presidents* 14:6642–43.
19. Ibid., 14:6641, 6642, 6645.
20. At the close of his administration, TR compared America to the French Second Republic, with "Bryanites" and "Debsites" cast in the role of radicals who, given the opportunity, would act like their alleged French counterparts who "adopted every kind of impossible policy, including the famous national workshops for the unemployed." He cast himself as the heroic alternative to a Louis Napoleon, whose regime rested on "force, corruption, and repression." Morison and Blum, eds., *Letters of Theodore Roosevelt* 6:954.
21. "Fifth Annual Message," in Richardson, ed., *Messages and Papers of the Presidents* 14:6985–66.
22. Theodore Roosevelt, "Washington's Forgotten Maxim," in Roosevelt, *American Ideals* 2:66.
23. "Farewell Address," in Richardson, ed., *Messages and Papers of the Presidents* 1:215.
24. Roosevelt, "Washington's Forgotten Maxim," 89.
25. See Roosevelt's address to Spanish-American War veterans in which he described America as a "mighty young nation, still in the flush of its youth, and yet with the might of a giant." Richardson, *Messages and Public Papers of the Presidents* 14:6699.
26. "Speech at San Francisco," in *Presidential Addresses and State Papers of Theodore Roosevelt*, ed. Albert Shaw (New York: P. F. Collier & Son, 1910), 395–96.
27. Roosevelt, *An Autobiography*, 548.
28. Harbaugh, *Life and Times of Theodore Roosevelt*, 372, 373; John Morton Blum places major blame on Taft and his advisors for antagonizing this spirited man. *The Republican President* (Cambridge: Harvard Univ. Press, 1967), 145.
29. Morison and Blum, eds., *Letters of Theodore Roosevelt* 6:1087.
30. Ibid., 7:453.
31. Ibid., 6:1087.
32. "The Man with the Muck-Rake," in *Presidential Addresses* 5:712–24.
33. Elting E. Morison has thus concluded that TR's renunciation in 1908 was made in the context of a "flood tide of his personal and public powers" and Roosevelt came to regret the decision once out of power. In 1912 his "most natural urge" (a will to power) reemerged, and it was "frustrated, before it was satisfied, by the decision of 1908" and "forced itself forward to spend, in one of his favorite phrases, and be utterly spent." Morison speaks of the enormous act of will on Henry L. Stimson's part to resist participating in TR's "intense personal experience." *Turmoil and Tradition* (Boston: Houghton Mifflin, 1960), 188–89.
34. Harbaugh, *Life and Times of Theodore Roosevelt*, 396–97.

35. Roosevelt, *Works* 12: 19.
36. Roosevelt insisted that if Wilson acted courageously, he would support him "exactly as Thomas and Farragut had behaved in the days of the Civil War." Morison and Blum, eds., *Letters of Theodore Roosevelt* 8:1154. For Roosevelt's recurrence of belatedness and his application of Jefferson's as well as Buchanan's policies to Wilson's, see John Milton Cooper Jr., *The Warrior and the Priest* (Cambridge: Harvard Univ. Press, 1983), 303–11.
37. Edgar Lee Masters, "At Sagamore Hill," in *Starved Rock*, by Edgar Lee Masters (New York: Macmillan, 1919), 96–97.

Chapter 6. John F. Kennedy: Promise

1. "Introduction to President Truman," Jan. 9, 1956, John F. Kennedy Library, Boston (hereafter cited as JFKL).
2. Ronald Reagan, *Speaking My Mind: Selected Speeches* (New York: Simon and Schuster, 1989), 242.
3. William G. Carleton, "Kennedy in History: An Early Appraisal," *Antioch Review* 24 (Fall 1964); Henry Pachter, "JFK as an Equestrian Statue: On Myth and Myth Makers," *Salmagundi* 1 (1966); George Kateb, "Kennedy as Statesman," *Commentary*, June 1966; Gary Wills, *The Kennedy Imprisonment* (Boston: Little, Brown, 1981); Henry Fairlie, *The Kennedy Promise* (Garden City, N.Y.:Doubleday, 1973); Nancy Gager Clinch, *The Kennedy Neurosis* (New York: Grossett and Dunlap, 1973); Doris Kearns Goodwin, *The Fitzgeralds and the Kennedys* (New York: Simon & Schuster, 1987); Herbert S. Parmet, *Jack: The Struggles of John F. Kennedy* (New York: Dial, 1983) and *JFK* (New York: Dial, 1983); Harris Wofford, *Of Kennedys and Kings* (New York: Farrar, Straus, Giroux, 1980); Thomas C. Reeves, *A Question of Character* (New York: Free Press, 1991); Nigel Hamilton, *JFK: Reckless Youth* (New York: Random House, 1992). These are, of course, only representative. See Thomas Brown, *JFK: History of an Image* (Bloomington: Indiana Univ. Press, 1988) for a complete and insightful review.
4. The *New York Times* reported an approval rating of 58 percent at the end of Kennedy's term. In 1990, it stood at 84 percent, by far the highest of any twentieth-century president, including FDR. *New York Times*, Jan. 24, 1993.
5. Carleton, "Kennedy in History," 296.
6. Arthur Schlesinger Jr., *A Thousand Days* (Boston: Houghton Mifflin, 1965), 84.
7. Mailer, *Presidential Papers*, 46.
8. Ibid., 47.
9. McLuhan's remarks were made in an interview in the *Globe and Mail*. Philip Marchand, *Marshall McLuhan* (New York: Ticknor and Fields, 1989), 150. See also his analysis of the assassination, Kennedy, coolness, and television. "Murder by Television," *Canadian Forum* (Jan. 1964): 222–23.
10. John F. Kennedy, *The Burden and the Glory* (New York: Harper and Row, 1964), 195; Benjamin C. Bradlee, *Conversations with Kennedy* (New York: W. W. Norton, 1975). Kennedy immediately followed with an address that was so supportive of corporate capital that John Kenneth Galbraith concluded that it was the most "Republican speech since McKinley." No administration composed of rational men," said Kennedy, "can possibly feel it can survive without business." *Burden and the Glory*, 198; Reeves, *Question of Character*, 334.
11. Midge Decter, "Kennedyism," *Commentary*, Jan. 1970, 22; Mailer, *Presidential Papers*, 59.

12. "Radio Speech on Russia," JFKL.
13. Richard J. Whalen, *The Founding Father: The Story of Joseph P. Kennedy* (New York: New American Library, 1964) 402–3; Reeves, *Question of Character*, 150–52. Also see William E. Leuchtenburg, *In the Shadow of FDR* (Ithaca, N.Y.: Cornell Univ. Press, 1983), 63–120 for Kennedy's reluctant imitations of Roosevelt.
14. James MacGregor Burns, "John F. Kennedy, Candidate on the Eve: Liberalism without Tears," *New Republic*, Oct. 31, 1960, 14–16.
15. Parmet, *Jack*, 476.
16. Schlesinger, *Thousand Days*, 739–58.
17. Leuchtenburg, *In the Shadow of FDR*, 110.
18. In a flash of hostility, JFK once told Theodore White that TR's letters showed elements of good historical writing but his own histories were "low grade." *In Search of History* (New York: Warner, 1978), 469.
19. See Parmet, *Jack*, chap. 17 for the most thorough assessment. Also see Theodore Sorenson, *Kennedy* (New York: Harper and Row, 1965), 66–70.
20. John F. Kennedy, *Profiles in Courage* (New York: Harper and Brothers, 1955), 7–8, 18–19.
21. Ibid., 246.
22. Ibid., 237, 244, 246.
23. Ibid., 238–39.
24. Reeves, *Question of Character*, 128.
25. "Columbus Day Speech," 1949, JFKL. Kennedy returned to his Peter the Hermit reference thirteen years later when he complained to Ben Bradlee about the hostility of corporate capital. "There's no sense telling them I love them anymore. They don't believe it. Fuck 'em. It's like Peter the Hermit's day." *Conversations with Kennedy*, 101.
26. Sorenson, *Kennedy*, 14, 256. Kennedy employed the St. Crispian trope in his "Ich bin ein Berliner" speech. When the Cold War was over and Germany was united, "The people of West Berlin can take sober satisfaction in the fact that they were on the front lines for almost two decades." *Burden and the Glory*, 100. Michael Beschloss is so impressed with the address that he places it in poetic form for his analysis. *The Crisis Years: Kennedy and Khrushchev, 1960–1963* (New York: Burlingame Books, 1991), 605–8. Also see Will's comments on JFK's heroes. *Kennedy Imprisonment*, 72–83.
27. Kennedy, *Burden and the Glory*, 183; 109–10. JFK was fond, however, of citing Jefferson as the cosmopolitan young man of intellect. See, for example, his citation of a contemporary of Jefferson as "a gentleman of 32 who could calculate an eclipse, survey an estate, tie an artery, plan an edifice, try a cause, break a horse, dance the minuet, and play the violin" and his remark at a dinner honoring Nobel Prize winners that "this is the most extraordinary collection of talent . . . that has ever been gathered together in the White House—with the possible exception of when Thomas Jefferson dined alone." "Address at the University of North Carolina," Oct. 12, 1961, *Public Papers of the Presidents of the United States: John F. Kennedy*, 3 vols. (Washington, D.C.: Government Printing Office, 1962–64), 1:666; Sorenson, *Kennedy*, 384.
28. "The Vigor We Need," *Public Papers of the Presidents of the United States: John F. Kennedy* 1:558.

29. John F. Kennedy, *To Turn the Tide* (New York: Harper and Brothers, 1962), 4.
30. Sorenson, *Kennedy*, 157.
31. Reeves, *President Kennedy: Profile of Power*, 60.
32. Kennedy, *Burden and the Glory*, 181. Richard Reeves concludes that "for Kennedy, civil rights, were just politics, a volatile issue to be defused." *President Kennedy*, 62. For another view, however, see Carl M. Brauer, *John F. Kennedy and the Second Reconstruction* (New York: Columbia Univ. Press, 1977), who argues that if one were to draw up a ledger on these questions, Kennedy's achievements on the plus side are impressive (319–20).
33. Richard M. Nixon, *R.N.: The Memoirs of Richard Nixon* (New York: Grosset and Dunlop, 1978), 288.
34. "Speech before the Miami Junior Chamber of Commerce," Oct. 18, 1949, JFKL; "Polish American Congress Broadcast," June 16, 1947, JFKL; "The Foreign Policy of the United States," Oct. 21, 1946, JFKL; "Radio Speech on Russia," 1946, JFKL; "Speech before the Pennsylvania Young Democrats," July 16, 1949, JFKL; "China," *Congressional Record*, 81st Cong., 1st sess.
35. Sorenson describes the president as "depressed and lonely" and "angry and sick at heart" after the crisis. *Kennedy*, 308.
36. Ibid., 294.
37. Schlesinger, *Thousand Days*, 841.
38. Wills, *Kennedy Imprisonment*, 254. Also see Clinch, who argues that JFK brought the nation "perilously close to nuclear holocaust without rational need." *Kennedy Neurosis*, 198.
39. Wills, *Kennedy Imprisonment*, 269.
40. Robert Thompson Smith, *The Missiles of October* (New York: Simon and Schuster, 1992), 356.
41. For reexamination of these questions by some of the participants, see James G. Blight and David A. Welch, eds. *On the Brink: Americans and Soviets Re-examine the Cuban Missile Crisis* (New York: Hill and Wang, 1989) and *Back to the Brink: Proceedings of the Moscow Conference on the Cuban Missile Crisis* (Lanham, Md.: Univ. Press of America, 1992).
42. Bradlee, *Conversations with Kennedy*, 133.
43. Malcolm E. Smith, *John F. Kennedy's 13 Great Mistakes in the White House* (Smithtown, N.Y.: Suffolk House, 1980), 192–93. The comment about "high school thought" is Acheson's. Characterizations of the level of decision making among particular members of ExComm is, of course, tied to the nature of the narrative. See Larry Powers's complaint about "the inability of some to make thoughtful judgment and stick to it, without changing their minds impulsively the next day" in contrast to the president's coolness. Powers, *"Johnny, We Hardly Knew Ye"* (Boston: Little, Brown, 1970), 312. Scholars attending the 1987 Hawk's Cay conference were surprised by the disorderliness and irrationality on the part of ExComm in general. Blight and Welch, eds., *On the Brink*, 123–31.
44. Sorenson, *Kennedy*, 724; *New Republic*, Dec. 1, 1962.
45. Kennedy, *Burden and the Glory*, 92.
46. Smith, *Missiles of October*, 356.
47. Paul B. Sheatsley and Jacob J. Feldman, "A National Survey on Public Reactions and Behavior," in *The Kennedy Assassination and the American Public*, ed. Bradley S. Greenberg and Edwin B. Parker (Stanford, Calif.: Stanford Univ. Press, 1965), 156, 158. Poll respondents listed the death of a "strong young man" sec-

ond behind expressions of sympathy for the Kennedy family as their immediate reaction from a list of seventeen.

48. David Bellin is the most aggressive defender of the lone assassin theory. See his *Final Disclosure* (New York: Scribner's, 1988). Also see Jean Davison, *Oswald's Game* (New York: W. W. Norton, 1983). Henry Hurt's *Reasonable Doubt* (New York: Holt, Rinehart and Winston, 1985) is a powerfully argued theory of Cuban involvement. See also Anthony Sommer's *Conspiracy* (New York: Paragon, 1989) for a case for Oswald's deep involvement in the American intelligence apparat and Jim Marris, *Crossfire* (New York: Carroll and Graf, 1989), who extends the conspiracy to include other forces. G. Robert Blakey (chief counsel for the House Select Committee on Assassinations) and Richard N. Billings argue the case for organized crime figures as the assassins in *The Plot to Kill the President* (New York: Times Books, 1981). The exemplary statement of the relationship between the assassination and The Promise is Oliver Stone's *JFK*. His *JFK: The Documented Screenplay* (New York: Applause Books, 1992) includes much critical reaction on this point. See especially the essays by Alexander Cockburn, Arthur Schlesinger Jr., William Manchester, and Norman Mailer.

PART III. MINOR AND FAILED PRESIDENTS

1. For a review and standardization of numerous presidential "historical greatness" ratings, see Dean Keith Simonton, *Why Presidents Succeed* (New Haven, Conn.: Yale Univ. Press, 1987), 166–228.

Chapter 7. Thomas Jefferson: The Doubling Effect

1. Peterson, *Jeffersonian Image in the American Mind*, 444. Also see James MacGregor Burns, *The Deadlock of Democracy* (Englewood Cliff, N.J.: Prentice-Hall, 1963), 24–25.
2. Schwartz, *George Washington*, 5.
3. H. A. Washington, ed., *The Writings of Thomas Jefferson* (New York: Derby and Jackson, 1859), 6:286 (hereafter cited as *WTJ*).
4. Tom Wicker, *The Anas* in *Jefferson: Public and Private Papers* (New York: Vintage Books, 1990), 348, 352 (hereafter cited as *Jefferson*).
5. Jefferson's actual critique had been somewhat more narrow than the translation which reached America suggested. The letter, thrice translated, had read the "form" of the British government, while the original spoke of "forms" (parades, parties, etc.). The republican objections to the creation of a Washingtonian "court" were already widespread. *WTJ* 4:139–40. Jefferson offered an elaborate explanation of the letter to Van Buren in 1824, almost thirty years later. *WTJ* 7:365–72.
6. *WTJ* 4:139.
7. See, for example, Forrest MacDonald, *The Presidency of Thomas Jefferson* (Lawrence: Univ. of Kansas Press, 1976), 32.
8. *WTJ* 6:288–89.
9. Dumas Malone, *Jefferson and the Ordeal of Liberty* (Boston: Little, Brown, 1962), 271.
10. Henry Lee, *Observations on the Writings of Thomas Jefferson* (New York: C. de Behr, 1832), 89, 100, 106.

11. Henry Adams, *History of the United States of America* (New York: Scribner's Sons, 1890), 2:272, 289.
12. See Peterson, *Jeffersonian Image in the American Mind*, 112–61 for nineteenth-century antebellum evaluations of Jefferson.
13. *WTJ* 4:354. Dumas Malone, *Jefferson the President, First Term* (Boston: Little, Brown, 1970), 5–16 is one of the few historians to take threats such as this with any seriousness.
14. Malone, *Jefferson the President, First Term*, 274.
15. *Jefferson*, 167.
16. Malone, *Jefferson the President, First Term*, 22.
17. *Jefferson*, 167.
18. Garret Ward Sheldon, *The Political Philosophy of Thomas Jefferson* (Baltimore: Johns Hopkins Univ. Press, 1990), 86.
19. *WTJ* 4:386, 406.
20. *WTJ* 7:133.
21. *WTJ* 4:365–66.
22. *WTJ* 4:392–93.
23. *WTJ* 4:430.
24. Peterson, *Jeffersonian Image in the American Mind*, 136.
25. Robert M. Johnstone, *Jefferson and the Presidency: Leadership in the Young Republic* (Ithaca, N.Y.: Cornell Univ. Press, 1978), 67.
26. *WTJ* 4:432, 434.
27. Malone, *Jefferson the President, First Term*, 338.
28. Drew R. McCoy, *The Elusive Republic* (Chapel Hill: Univ. of North Carolina, 1980), 202.
29. Ibid., 203.
30. Merrill D. Peterson, *Thomas Jefferson and the New Nation* (New York: Oxford Univ. Press, 1970), 770.
31. *WTJ* 4:500–501.
32. *WTJ* 4:500.
33. Merrill D. Peterson ends his assessment by forgiving Jefferson. He asserts that his "dominant purpose remained what it had always been." *Thomas Jefferson and the New Nation*, 775–76. Alexander DeConde's *This Affair of Louisiana* (New York: Charles Scribner's, 1976) is less acquitting.
34. Peterson, *Jeffersonian Image in the American Mind*, 445.
35. Peterson, *Thomas Jefferson and the New Nation*, 777–89.
36. Peterson, *Thomas Jefferson and the New Nation*, 773, 745; *WTJ* 4:420–21.
37. *Jefferson*, 166.
38. *WTJ* 5:62.
39. Julian Boyd, "Thomas Jefferson's 'Empire of Liberty,'" *Virginia Quarterly Review* 24 (1948): 159.
40. MacDonald, *Presidency of Thomas Jefferson*, 73.
41. Adams, *History of the United States* 4:463, 289.
42. Albert Jay Nock, *Jefferson* (New York: Hill and Wang, 1926), 161.
43. *WTJ* 5:297.
44. *WTJ* 5:379.
45. Leonard D. White, *The Jeffersonians* (New York: Free Press, 1951), 433.
46. Dumas Malone, *Jefferson the President, Second Term* (Boston, Little, Brown, 1974), 591.

47. McCoy, *Elusive Republic,* 219–20.
48. *WTJ* 7:425.
49. *WTJ* 4:268, 6:606.
50. *WTJ* 7:356–57.

Chapter 8. Ronald Reagan: New Deal Shards

1. Felix Frankfurter Oral History, JFKL.
2. Dwight D. Eisenhower, *Waging Peace* (Garden City, N.Y.: Doubleday, 1965), 654. On the record of hostile accommodation of Republican presidents, see Leuchtenburg, *In the Shadow of FDR;* Alonzo Hamby, *Liberalism and Its Challengers* (New York: Oxford Univ. Press, 1985); Abbott, *Exemplary Presidency.*
3. *New York Times,* Aug. 17, 1980. Reagan here defended comments he made in 1976.
4. See Ronald Reagan and Richard G. Hubler, *Where's the Rest of Me?* (New York: Dutton, 1965) and Ronald Reagan, *An American Life* (New York: Simon and Schuster, 1990). Gary Wills uses the term "memory clusters" in his *Reagan's America* (Baltimore: Penguin, 1988), chap. 6.
5. Reagan, *American Life,* 54, 66.
6. Ibid., 69; Also see Reagan and Hubler, *Where's the Rest of Me?* 53–54 for a similar assessment.
7. Reagan, *American Life,* 105; Reagan and Hubler, *Where's the Rest of Me?* 139, 141.
8. Interview with Walter Cronkite, CBS, Mar. 3, 1981. Reagan made similar comments to David Brinkley, ABC, Dec. 22, 1981. Francis Lowenheim reviews and critiques Reagan's memory of the 1937 speech in "Reaganscribing History," *New York Times,* Mar. 23, 1981.
9. Interview with David McCullough, Dec. 1, 1981, cited in Leuchtenburg, *In the Shadow of FDR,* 214.
10. Ibid., 241–15.
11. Reagan and Hubler, *Where's the Rest of Me?* 119.
12. Reagan, *Speaking My Mind,* 224–26.
13. Ibid., 23, 213; Reagan and Hubler, *Where's the Rest of Me?* 123; Reagan, *American Life,* 135, 115.
14. Reagan compared himself to Whittaker Chambers when he remembered the opposition to his GE speeches. Reagan and Hubler, *Where's the Rest of Me?* 268. Twice before the Conservative Political Action Conference Reagan placed Chambers at the center of his analysis. *Speaking My Mind,* 99, 180. See Paul D. Erickson, *Reagan Speaks* (New York: New York Univ. Press, 1985), 80–82 for an interpretation of Reagan's use of Chambers as part of a prophetic narrative of America.
15. Reagan, *American Life,* 67.
16. Peggy Noonan, *What I Saw at the Revolution* ((New York: Random House, 1990), 157.
17. *New York Times,* Jan. 29, 1982.
18. Roosevelt, *Public Papers and Addresses: 1936:* 16, 17, 44. For an analysis of the second term as a "Jacksonian turn," see Abbott, *Exemplary Presidency,* 110–31.
19. Arthur Schlesinger Jr. presented the Jacksonians as precursors of New Dealers in his *Age of Jackson.* Other analysts have emphasized the entrepreneurial features of Jacksonianism. See Bray Hammond, "Jackson, Biddle and the Bank of

the United States," *Journal of Economic History* 7 (May 1947) and Richard Hofstadter, *The American Political Tradition* (New York: Knopf, 1948), chap. 3. Marvin Meyers describes the Jacksonians as "venturesome conservatives" in his classic account, *The Jacksonian Persuasion* (Stanford, Calif.: Stanford Univ. Press, 1957).

20. Daniel Webster, "Speeches in the Senate of the United States on the Resolution of Mr. Foote," in *Speeches and Forensic Arguments*, ed. Daniel Webster (Boston: Perkins, Marvin, 1835), 1:366–67.
21. Tocqueville, *Democracy in America*, 531–32.
22. Roosevelt, *Public Papers and Addresses: 1936: 272.*
23. Ibid., 459.
24. Reagan, *Speaking My Mind*, 34, 63.
25. Ibid., 272.
26. *New York Times*, Aug. 15, 1980.
27. *National Review*, Sept. 4, 1981, 999.
28. *New York Times*, Jan. 29, 1982.

Chapter 9. *Wilson/Hoover/Nixon: The Great Fall*

1. James David Barber, *The Presidential Character*, 3d ed. (Englewood Cliffs, N.J.: Prentice-Hall, 1985), 82–83. In addition to Wilson/Hoover/Nixon, Barber includes LBJ. From a belated perspective, Johnson is removed from the list, since his monumental failure, the Vietnam War, is poetically a shared one with JFK (who frequently escapes via the route of The Promise) and Nixon. On LBJ and belatedness, also see chap. 10.
2. Garry Wills, *Nixon Agonistes* (New York: New American Library, 1970), 396.
3. Herbert Hoover, *The Ordeal of Woodrow Wilson* (Baltimore: Johns Hopkins Univ. Press, 1992), 10.
4. Wills, *Nixon Agonistes*, 30–31.
5. Richard M. Nixon, *Six Crises* (Garden City, N.Y.: Doubleday, 1962), xvi.
6. John M. Mulder, *Woodrow Wilson: The Years of Preparation* (Princeton, N.J.: Princeton Univ. Press, 1978), 95–96.
7. Woodrow Wilson, *Congressional Government*, 68.
8. On Wilson's public and reluctant use of Jefferson and his private and admiring attitude toward Hamilton, see Cooper, *Warrior and the Priest*, 184, 217, 394.
9. Woodrow Wilson, *The New Democracy* (New York: Harper and Brothers, 1926), 2:140–41.
10. Ibid., 2:361.
11. N. Gordon Levin Jr., *Woodrow Wilson and World Politics* (New York: Oxford Univ. Press, 1968), 5.
12. Barber, *Presidential Character*, 65; Rosen, *Hoover, Roosevelt, and the Brains Trust*, 40; Roosevelt, *Public Papers and Addresses: 1928–32: 672.*
13. For a discussion of the pre-Depression Hoover persona, see Kent Scofield, "The Public Image of Herbert Hoover in the 1928 Campaign," *Mid-America* 51 (Oct. 1969): 285.
14. Joan Hoff Wilson, *Herbert Hoover, Forgotten Progressive* (Boston: Little, Brown, 1975).
15. Martin L. Fausold, *The Presidency of Herbert Hoover* (Lawrence: Univ. Press of Kansas, 1985), 25.

16. Williams, *Contours of American History*, 426.
17. Ellis W. Hawley, "Herbert Hoover and American Corporativism, 1929–1933," in *The Hoover Presidency: A Reappraisal*, Martin L. Fausold and George T. Mazuzan, eds. (Albany: State Univ. of New York Press, 1974), 102.
18. Murray N. Rothbard, *America's Great Depression* (Los Angeles: Nash Publishers, 1972).
19. Herbert Hoover, *American Individualism* (Garden City, N.Y.: Doubleday, 1923), 1–2, 6–7, 12.
20. Ibid., 39–40.
21. Ibid., 53–54, 59–60.
22. Ibid., 24, 30.
23. Herbert Hoover, *The New Day: Campaign Speeches of Herbert Hoover* (Stanford, Calif.: Stanford Univ. Press, 1938), 59–60.
24. Herbert Hoover, *The State Papers and Others Writings of Herbert Hoover* (Garden City, N.Y.: Doubleday, 1934), 2:264, 250, 470.
25. Hoover, *Ordeal of Woodrow Wilson*, 74.
26. Ibid., 207.
27. David Abrahamsen, *Nixon vs. Nixon: An Emotional Tragedy* (New York: Farrar, Straus and Giroux, 1977); Fawn Brodie, *Richard Nixon: The Shaping of his Character* (New York: W. W. Norton, 1981); Eli Chesen, *President Nixon's Psychiatric Profile* (New York: Wyden, 1973).
28. Tom Wicker, *New York Times Magazine*, Jan. 19, 1969, 21.
29. Garry Wills, "Richard M. Nixon," in *The Oxford Companion to the Politics of the World* (New York: Oxford, 1993), 644.
30. Wills, *Nixon Agonistes*, 31. Nixon frequently repeated the secrecy critique in his post-presidency foreign policy reviews. See Richard M. Nixon's *The Real War* (New York: Warner Books, 1980), 253; *Seize the Moment* (New York: Simon and Schuster, 1992), 229; and *1999* (New York: Simon and Schuster, 1988), 175.
31. The term is Kissinger's description of Bismarck, and Bruce Mazlish applies it to Nixon in his *In Search of Nixon* (Baltimore: Penguin, 1972), xxii.
32. Richard M. Nixon, *Public Papers of the President* (Washington, D.C.: Government Printing Office, 1971), 188. Stephen E. Ambrose reviews the immediate political context of the address in *Nixon: The Triumph of a Politician, 1962–1972* (New York: Simon and Schuster, 1989), 436–38. Again, Nixon reviews Wilson's project in his post-presidential books. See Nixon's *Real War*, 15, 21, 312; *Seize the Moment*, 300, 304; and *1999*, 16, 28.
33. Michael A. Genovese, *The Nixon Presidency* (Westport, Conn.: Greenwood Press, 1990), 136.
34. Tas Szulc, *The Illusion of Peace* (New York: Viking, 1978), 7–8.
35. Genovese, *Nixon Presidency*, 110–11.
36. See Stephen Garret, "Nixonian Foreign Policy: A New Balance of Power—or a Revived Concert?" *Polity* (Spring 1976): 389–421; Stanley Hoffman, "Will the Balance Balance at Home?" *Foreign Affairs* (Summer 1972): 60–86; James Chace, "The Concert of Europe," *Foreign Affairs* (Oct. 1973): 96–108; M. J. Brenner, "The Problem of Innovation and the Nixon-Kissinger Foreign Policy," *International Studies Quarterly* (Sept. 1973): 255–94.
37. Garret, "Nixonian Foreign Policy," 409.
38. Nixon, *Seize the Moment*, 229, 305.

Conclusion

1. Schwartz, *George Washington*, 22, 80.
2. For a masterful critical account of Adams's reevaluation, see Gordon S. Wood, *The Creation of the American Republic 1776–1787* (New York: W. W. Norton, 1969), chap. 14.
3. Charles Francis Adams, ed., *The Works of John Adams* (Boston: Little, Brown, 1856), 10:115.
4. See, for example, Ralph Adams Brown on this point. *The Presidency of John Adams* (Lawrence: Univ. Press of Kansas, 1975), 112–13, 210–15.
5. Kohn, *Eagle and Sword*, 257.
6. The best case for Van Buren as player in the quest against belatedness can be found in J. David Greenstone, *The Lincoln Persuasion* (Princeton, N.J.: Princeton Univ. Press, 1993, chap. 7. Greenstone argues Van Buren engaged in monumental gamble that he could transform what had become a prisoner's dilemma game on the question of slavery and sectional loyalty into a "chicken game" which he would win.
7. Sellars, *James K. Polk*, 213.
8. Ibid., 484–87.
9. Paul H. Bergeron explains that Polk's achievements are underrated because he could not understand how "expansionism, a great unifying force for the nation, as he saw it, could tear it apart." *The Presidency of James K. Polk* (Lawrence: Univ. Press of Kansas, 1987), 260. Ellis and Wildavsky trace Polk's limitations to his obliviousness to warring factions in the Democratic party. *Dilemmas of Presidential Leadership*, 145–46. Sellars reminds readers that the sectional crisis Polk helped precipitate was "hard to discern behind the facade of national party loyalty that dominated the visible surface of political reality" in the 1840s. *James K. Polk*, 476.
10. Kenneth M. Stampp has called Johnson the "Last Jacksonian" and a self-defined upholder of the "left" wing of the Democratic Party. *The Era of Reconstruction, 1865–1877* (New York: Vintage, 1967), 55.
11. Ibid., 63.
12. See William F. McNeely, *Frederick Douglass* (New York: W. W. Norton, 1991), 247–48 for an account of this famous exchange.
13. Hans L. Trefousse, *Andrew Johnson: A Biography* (New York: W. W. Norton, 1989), 337. The remark is all the more poetically significant since Johnson expressed a lifelong identification with the republican persona of Cato.
14. Ibid., 236.
15. Vaughn Bornet, *The Presidency of Lyndon Johnson* (Lawrence: Univ. Press of Kansas, 1983), 9; also see Eric F. Goldman, *The Tragedy of Lyndon Johnson* (New York: Dell, 1974), 301; Leuchtenburg, *In the Shadow of FDR*, 147–49. Leuchtenburg, in particular, emphasizes the obsessive patricidal relationship of LBJ in regard to FDR.
16. On this point, it is interesting that Stephen Skowronek compares LBJ to both Monroe *and* Polk. *The Politics Presidents Make* (Cambridge: Harvard Univ. Press, 1993), 330.
17. Joseph Califano Jr., *The Triumph and Tragedy of Lyndon Johnson* (New York: Simon and Schuster, 1991), 75.
18. Reeves, *President Kennedy: Profile of Power*, 504–5.
19. For Johnson's wartime shift, see Robert Dallek, *Lone Star Rising: Lyndon Johnson*

and His Times 1908–1960 (New York: Oxford Univ. Press, 1991), 253–54; for his fear of being charged with betraying Kennedy's anticommunism, see Doris Kearns Goodwin, *Lyndon Johnson and the American Dream* (New York: St. Martin's Press, 1976), 253.

20. *Public Papers of the Presidents of the United States: Lyndon Baines Johnson* (Washington, D.C.: Government Printing Office, 1965), 394–99.

21. Goodwin, *Lyndon Johnson and the American Dream*, 343.

22. *New York Times*, June 30, 1990. On the eve of American bombing of Iraq, Bush had briefly took on the Lincoln persona.

23. *New York Times*, Mar. 29, 1989. The *Times* reporter was skeptical of Bush's assertion that he was an "Oyster Bay kind of guy."

24. *New York Times*, Aug. 15, 1990, Oct. 24, 1990. Bob Woodward, *The Commanders* (New York: Simon and Schuster, 1991), 343. The White House announcement of the beginning of the war copied Eisenhower's D-day radio address: "The liberation of Kuwait has begun."

25. Stephen Skowronek examines "political time" as one of three major constraints upon presidential leadership. "Presidential Leadership in Political Time," in *The Presidency and the Political System*, ed. Michael Nelson (Washington, D.C.: Congressional Quarterly Press, 1984), 87–132. Six of our eleven strong presidents correspond to Skowronek's "firsts" in political time as "regime builders." Also see his *Politics Presidents Make*, which, except for its decided emphasis on the constraints imposed by political time, is required reading for belated presidents.

26. Rossiter, *American Presidency*, 108; Erwin C. Hargrove, *The Power of the Modern Presidency* (New York: Knopf, 1974); Michael Nelson, "Evaluating the Presidency" in Nelson, ed., *The Presidency and the Political System*, 8.

27. Bruce Buchanan, *The Citizen's Presidency* (Washington, D.C.: Congressional Quarterly Press, 1987), 31.

28. Edward Corwin, *President: Office and Powers* (New York: New York Univ. Press, 1957), 310.

29. Rossiter, ed., *Federalist Papers*, 437–38.

30. See Clinton Rossiter, *Constitutional Dictatorship* (Princeton, N.J.: Princeton Univ. Press, 1948); Carl J. Friedrich, *Constitutional Government and Politics* (New York: Harper and Brothers, 1937), 215–19; Arthur M. Schlesinger Jr., *The Imperial Presidency* (Boston: Houghton Mifflin, 1973).

31. Thomas E. Cronin, *The State of the Presidency*, 2d ed. (Boston: Little, Brown, 1975), 25–49; Also see Bruce Buchanan's discussion of the cultural expectations of "presidential greatness" and his recommendations for a "competent" presidency (*Citizen's Presidency*, 27–32, 101–34) as well as Jeffrey Tulis's attempt to constrict modern presidential rhetorical practice (*Rhetorical Presidency*.)

32. Jack Valenti, *A Very Human President* (New York: W. W. Norton, 1975), 45.

33. Bate, *Burden of the Past*, 133–34.

BIBLIOGRAPHY

* *

Abbott, Philip. "Do Presidents Talk Too Much?" *Presidential Studies Quarterly* 18 (Spring 1988):347–62.
———. *The Exemplary Presidency*. Amherst: Univ. of Massachusetts Press, 1990.
———. *Leftward Ho!: V. F. Calverton and American Radicalism*. Westport, Conn.: Greenwood Press, 1993.
———. *Political Thought in America: Conversations and Debates*. Itasca, Ill.: F. E. Peacock, 1991.
Abbott, W. W., et al., eds. *The Papers of George Washington*, vol. 1. Charlottesville: Univ. Press of Virginia, 1983.
Abrahamsen, David. *Nixon vs. Nixon: An Emotional Tragedy*. New York: Farrar, Strauss and Giroux, 1977.
Adams, Charles Francis, ed. *The Works of John Adams*. Boston: Little, Brown, 1856.
Adams, Henry. *History of the United States of America*. 2 vols. New York: Scribner's Sons, 1890.
Albanese, Catherine L. *Sons of the Fathers: The Civil Religion of the American Revolution*. Philadelphia: Temple Univ. Press, 1976.
Allen, Nancy. *The Index of American Design*. Washington, D.C.: National Gallery of Art, 1984.
Allen, W. B., ed. *George Washington: A Collection*. Indianapolis: Liberty Classics, 1988.
Alsop, Joseph, and Turner Catledge. *The 168 Days*. Garden City, N.Y.: Doubleday, 1938.
Ambrose, Stephen. *Nixon: The Triumph of a Politician, 1962–72*. New York: Simon and Schuster, 1989.
Anderson, Dwight. *Abraham Lincoln: The Quest for Immortality*. New York: Knopf, 1982.
Arendt, Hannah. *On Revolution*. New York: Viking, 1965.
Barber, James David. *The Presidential Character*. Englewood Cliffs, N.J.: Prentice-Hall, 1985.
Barnes, Gilbert Hobbs. *The Anti-Slavery Impulse, 1830–1844*. New York: Harcourt, Brace, World, 1933.
Basler, Roy P., ed. *The Collected Works of Abraham Lincoln*. New Brunswick, N.J.: Rutgers Univ. Press, 1953.

Bassett, John Spencer, ed. *Correspondence of Andrew Jackson*. Washington, D.C.: Carnegie Institution of America.

Bate, W. Jackson. *The Burden of the Past and the English Poet*. Cambridge: Harvard Univ. Press, 1970.

Beard, Charles A., and Mary R. Beard. *The Rise of American Civilization*. New York: Macmillan, 1927.

Bellin, David. *Final Disclosure*. New York: Scribner's, 1988.

Bergeron, Paul H. *The Presidency of James K. Polk*. Lawrence: Univ. Press of Kansas, 1987.

Berle, Adolph. "The Social Economic of the New Deal." *New York Times Magazine*, Oct. 29, 1933.

Berle, Beatrice Bishop, and Travis Beal Jacobs, eds. *Navigating the Rapids, 1918–1971: From the Papers of Adolph A. Berle* New York: Harcourt, Brace, Jovanovich, 1973.

Beschloss, Michael. *The Crisis Years: Kennedy and Khrushchev, 1960–63*. New York: Burlingame Books, 1991.

Beveridge, Albert J. *Abraham Lincoln, 1809–1858*. New York: Victor Gollancz, 1928.

Blakey, G. Robert, and Richard N. Billings. *The Plot to Kill the President*. New York: Times Books, 1981.

Blight, James G., and David A. Welch, eds. *Back to the Brink: Proceedings of the Moscow Conference on the Cuban Missile Crisis*. Lanham, Md.: Univ. Press of America, 1992.

———. *On the Brink: Americans and Soviets Re-examine the Cuban Missile Crisis*. New York: Hill and Wang, 1989.

Bloom, Harold. *Agon: Towards a Theory of Revisionism*. New York: Oxford Univ. Press, 1982.

———. *The Anxiety of Influence: A Theory of Poetry*. New York: Oxford Univ. Press, 1973.

———. *The Breaking of the Vessels*. Chicago: Univ. of Chicago Press, 1982.

———. *A Map of Misreading*. New York: Oxford Univ. Press, 1975.

Blum, John Morton. *The Republican President*. Cambridge: Harvard Univ. Press, 1967.

Borit, Gabor S., and Norman O. Forness, eds. *The Historian's Lincoln*. Urbana: Univ. of Illinois Press, 1988.

Bornet, Vaughn. *The Presidency of Lyndon Johnson*. Lawrence: Univ. Press of Kansas, 1983.

Boyd, Julian. "Thomas Jefferson's 'Empire of Liberty.'" *Virginia Quarterly Review* 24 (1948):538–54.

Bradford, M. E. *Remembering Who We Are. Athens*. Athens: Univ. of Georgia Press, 1985.

Bradlee, Benjamin C. *Conversations with Kennedy*. New York: W. W. Norton, 1975.

Brauer, Carl M. *John F. Kennedy and the Second Reconstruction*. New York: Columbia Univ. Press, 1977.

Brenner, M. J. "The Problems of Innovation and the Nixon-Kissinger Foreign Policy." *International Studies Quarterly* (Sept. 1973): 255–94.

Brodie, Fawn. *Richard Nixon: The Shaping of his Character*. New York: W. W. Norton, 1981.

Brown, Ralph Adams. *The Presidency of John Adams*. Lawrence: Univ. of Kansas Press, 1975.

Brown, Thomas. *JFK: History of an Image*. Bloomington: Indiana Univ. Press, 1988.

Buchanan, Bruce. *The Citizen's Presidency*. Washington, D.C: Congressional Quarterly Press, 1987.

Buell, Augustine. *History of Andrew Jackson*. New York: Charles Scribner's Sons, 1904.

Burns, James MacGregor. *The Deadlock of Democracy*. Englewood Cliffs, N.J.: Prentice-Hall, 1963.

———. "John F. Kennedy, Candidate on the Eve: Liberalism Without Tears." *New Republic*, Oct. 31, 1960, 14–16.

———. *Roosevelt: The Lion and the Fox*. New York: Harcourt, Brace and World, 1956.

———. *Roosevelt: Soldier of Freedom* New York: Harcourt, Brace, Jovanovich, 1970.

Cahill, Holger. "American Resources in the Arts." In *Art for the Millions*, ed. Francis O'Connor. Greenwood, Conn.: New York Graphic Society, 1973.

Califano, Joseph, Jr. *The Triumph and Tragedy of Lyndon Johnson*. New York: Simon and Schuster, 1991.

Calverton, V. F. "The American Revolutionary Tradition." *Scribner's Magazine*, May 1934, 352–58.

Campbell, Karlyn Kohrs, and Kathleen Hall Jamieson. *Deeds Done in Words: Presidential Rhetoric and the Genres of Governance*. Chicago: Univ. of Chicago Press, 1990.

Carleton, William G. "Kennedy in History: An Early Appraisal." *Antioch Review* 24 (Fall 1964):277–99.

Chace, James. "The Concert of Europe." *Foreign Affairs* (Oct. 1973): 96–108.

Chesen, Eli. *President Nixon's Psychiatric Profile*. New York: Wyden, 1973.

Childs, Marquis. "They Hate Roosevelt." *Harpers*, May 1936, 634–42.

Clinch, Nancy Gager. *The Kennedy Neurosis*. New York: Grossett and Dunlap, 1973.

Commins, Saxe, ed. *Basic Writings of George Washington*. New York: Random House, 1948.

Cooper, John Milton, Jr. *The Warrior and the Priest*. Cambridge: Harvard Univ. Press, 1983.

Corwin, Edward. *President: Office and Powers*. New York: New York Univ. Press, 1957.

Craven, Avery. *The Repressible Conflict*. Baton Rouge: Louisiana State Univ. Press, 1939.

Creel, George. *Rebel at Large*. New York: Putnam, 1947.

Croly, Herbert. "The Great Jefferson Joke." *New Republic*, June 9, 1926.

Cronin, Thomas E. *The State of the Presidency*. 2d ed. Boston: Little, Brown, 1975.

Cunliffe, Marcus. *George Washington: Man and Monument*. Boston: Little, Brown, 1958.

———. *In Search of America: Transatlantic Essays, 1951–1990*. Westport, Conn.: Greenwood Press, 1991.

Cunningham, Noble E., Jr. *Popular Images of the Presidency*. Columbia: Univ. of Missouri Press, 1991.

Curtis, James C. *Andrew Jackson and the Search for Vindication*. Boston: Little, Brown, 1976.

Dallek, Robert. *Lone Star Rising: Lyndon Johnson and His Times 1908–1960*. New York: Oxford Univ. Press, 1991.

Davis, Burke. *Old Hickory: A Life of Andrew Jackson*. New York: Dial Press, 1977.

Davis, Michael. *The Image of Lincoln in the South*. Knoxville: Univ. of Tennessee Press, 1971.

Decter, Midge. "Kennedyism." *Commentary*, Jan. 1970, 19–27.

DeConde, Alexander. *This Affair of Louisiana*. New York: Charles Scribner's, 1976.

Diggins, John. *The Lost Soul of American Politics*. Chicago: Univ. of Chicago Press, 1984.

Dunne, Finley Peter. *Mr. Dooley's Philosophy*. New York: R. H. Russell, 1900.

Eisenhower, Dwight David. *Waging Peace*. Garden City, N.Y.: Doubleday, 1965.

Ekrich, Arthur. *Ideologies and Utopias: The Impact of the New Deal on American Thought*. Chicago: Univ. of Chicago Press, 1969.

Ellis, Richard, and Aaron Wildavsky. *Dilemmas of Presidential Leadership*. New Brunswick, N.J.: Transaction Books, 1989.

Erikson, Paul. *Reagan Speaks*. New York: New York Univ. Press, 1985.

Everett, Edward. *Orations and Speeches*. 4 vols. Boston: Little, Brown, 1878–79.

Fairlie, Henry. *The Kennedy Promise*. Garden City, N.Y: Doubleday, 1973.

Fausold, Martin L. *The Presidency of Herbert Hoover*. Lawrence: Univ. Press of Kansas, 1985.

Ferling, John E. *The First of Men: A Life of George Washington*. Knoxville: Univ. of Tennessee Press, 1988.

Fehrenbacher, Don E. *Lincoln in Text and Context*. Stanford, Calif.: Stanford Univ. Press, 1987.

———. *Prelude to Greatness: Lincoln in the 1850s*. New York: McGraw-Hill, 1964.

Flanagan, Hallie. "Testimony Before HUAC." In *Thirty Years of Treason*, ed. Eric Bentley. New York: Viking Press, 1971.

Flynn, John T. *The Roosevelt Myth*. New York: Devin-Adair, 1948.

Forgie, George B. *Patricide in the House Divided*. New York: W. W. Norton, 1979.

Freeman, Douglas Southall. *George Washington*, vol. 5. Boston: Scribner's, 1948–57.

Freud, Sigmund. *Group Psychology and the Analysis of the Ego*. New York: Liveright, 1949.

———. *Moses and Monotheism*. New York: Knopf, 1947.

———. *Totem and Taboo*. New York: Random House, 1918.

Friedrich, Carl J. *Constitutional Government and Politics*. New York: Harper and Brothers, 1937.

Garret, Stephen. "Nixonian Foreign Policy: A New Balance of Power—or a Revised Concert?" *Polity* (Spring 1976): 389–421.

Genovese, Michael A. *The Nixon Presidency*. Westport, Conn.: Greenwood Press, 1990.

Goldman, Eric F. *The Tragedy of Lyndon Johnson*. New York: Dell, 1974.

Goodwin, Doris Kearns. *The Fitzgeralds and the Kennedys*. New York: Simon & Schuster, 1987.

———. *Lyndon Johnson and the American Dream*. New York: St. Martin's Press, 1976.

Greenberg, Bradley S., and Edwin B. Parker, eds. *The Kennedy Assassination and the American Public*. Stanford, Calif.: Stanford Univ. Press, 1965.

Greenstein, Fred I. "In Search of the Modern Presidency." In *Leadership in the Modern Presidency*, ed. Fred Greenstein. Cambridge: Harvard Univ. Press, 1988.

Greenstone, J. David. *The Lincoln Persuasion*. Princeton, N.J.: Princeton Univ. Press, 1993.

Gwynn, Stephen, ed. *The Letters and Friendship of Sir Cecil Spring Rice*. Boston: Houghton Mifflin, 1929.

Hacker, Louis. "Revolutionary America." *Harper's Magazine*, Mar. 1935, 444–46.

Hamby, Alonzo. *Liberalism and Its Challengers*. New York: Oxford Univ. Press, 1985.

Hamilton, Nigel. *J. F. K.: Reckless Youth*. New York: Random House, 1992.

Hammond, Bray. "Jackson, Biddle and the Bank of the United States." *Journal of Economic History* 7 (May 1947):1–23.

Harbaugh, William Henry. *The Life and Times of Theodore Roosevelt*. New York: Collier, 1961.

Hargrove, Erwin. *The Power of the Modern Presidency*. New York: Knopf, 1974.

Hart, Roderick P. *The Sound of Leadership*. Chicago: Univ. of Chicago Press, 1987.

Hawley, Ellis W. "Herbert Hoover and American Corporativism, 1929–1933." In *The Hoover Presidency: A Reappraisal*, ed. Martin L. Fausold and George T. Mazuzan. Albany: State Univ. of New York Press, 1974.

Hay, Robert P. "George Washington: American Moses." *American Quarterly 21* (1969): 780–91.

Hertz, Emanuel. *Abraham Lincoln, A New Portrait*. New York: Horace Liveright, 1931.

Higginbotham, Don. *George Washington and the American Military Tradition*. Athens: Univ. of Georgia Press, 1985.

Hoffman, Stanley. "Will the Balance Balance at Home?" *Foreign Affairs* (Summer 1972): 60–86.

Hofstadter, Richard. *The American Political Tradition*. New York: Knopf, 1948.

Hoover, Herbert. *American Individualism*. Garden City, N.Y.: Doubleday, 1923.

———. *The New Day: Campaign Speeches of Herbert Hoover*. Stanford, Calif.: Stanford Univ. Press, 1938.

———. *The State Papers and Other Writings of Herbert Hoover*. Garden City: N.Y.: Doubleday, 1934.

———. *The Ordeal of Woodrow Wilson*. Baltimore: Johns Hopkins Univ. Press, 1992.

Howe, Daniel Walker. *The Political Culture of the American Whigs*. Chicago: Univ. of Chicago Press, 1979.

Hurt, Henry. *Reasonable Doubt*. New York: Holt, Rinehart and Winston, 1985.

Jaffa, Harry. *The Crisis of the House Divided*. New York: Doubleday, 1959.

Johannsen, Robert W. *Stephen A. Douglas*. New York: Oxford Univ. Press, 1973.

Johnstone, Robert M. *Jefferson and the Presidency: Leadership in the Young Republic*. Ithaca, N.Y.: Cornell Univ. Press, 1978.

Jones, Alfred Haworth. *Roosevelt's Image Makers*. Port Washington, N.Y.: Kennikat, 1974.

Jones, Robert F. *George Washington*. New York: Fordham Univ. Press, 1986.

Kateb, George. "Kennedy as Statesman." *Commentary*, June 1966, 54–60.

Kendall, Willmoore, and George W. Carey. *The Basic Symbols of the American Political Tradition*. Baton Rouge: Louisiana State Univ. Press, 1970.

Kennedy, John F. *Profiles in Courage*. New York: Harper and Brothers, 1955.

Kernan, Alvin B. "'The Henriad': Shakespeare's Major History Plays." In *William Shakespeare: Histories and Poems*, ed. Harold Bloom. New York: Chelsea House, 1986.

Ketcham, Ralph. *Presidents Above Party: The First American Presidency, 1789–1829*. Chapel Hill: Univ. of North Carolina Press, 1984.

Koch, Adrienne, and William Peden, eds. *The Life and Selected Writings of Thomas Jefferson*. New York: Modern Library, 1944.

Kohn, Richard H. *Eagle and Sword: The Beginning of the Military Establishment in America*. New York: Free Press, 1975.

———. "The Inside History of the Newburgh Conspiracy: America and the Coup D'état." *William and Mary Quarterly*, 3d ser., 27 (1970):187–220.

Lash, Joseph P. *Dealers and Dreamers: A New Look at the New Deal*. New York: Doubleday, 1988.

Lattner, Richard B. *The Presidency of Andrew Jackson: White House Politics, 1829–1837*. Athens: Univ. of Georgia Press, 1979.

Lazarfeld, Paul, Marie Jahoda, and Hans Zeisel. *Marienthal: The Sociology of an Unemployed Community*. Chicago: Univ. of Chicago Press, 1971.

Lee, Henry. *Observations on the Writings of Thomas Jefferson*. New York: C. de Behr, 1832.

Leuchtenburg, William E. "The Achievement of the New Deal." In *Fifty Years Later: The New Deal Evaluated*, ed. Harvard Sitkoff. Philadelphia: Temple Univ. Press, 1985.

———. "Franklin D. Roosevelt's Supreme Court 'Packing' Plan." In *Essays on the New Deal*, ed. Harold Hollingsworth. Austin: Univ. of Texas Press, 1969.

———. *In the Shadow of FDR*. Ithaca, N.Y.: Cornell Univ. Press, 1983.

Levin, N. Gordon, Jr. *Woodrow Wilson and World Politics*. New York: Oxford Univ. Press, 1968.

Lewis, Lloyd. *Myths After Lincoln*. New York: Readers Club, 1941.

Lippman, Walter. "On Planned Planning." In *Interpretations: 1933–35*, by Walter Lippman. New York: Macmillan, 1973.

Locke, John. *Of Civil Government: Second Treatise*. Chicago: Regnery, 1971.

McCoy, Donald R. *Landon of Kansas*. Lincoln: Univ. of Nebraska Press, 1966.

McCoy, Drew. *The Elusive Republic*. Chapel Hill: Univ. of North Carolina, 1980.

MacDonald, Forrest. *The Presidency of George Washington*. Lawrence: Univ. Press of Kansas, 1974.

———. *The Presidency of Thomas Jefferson*. Lawrence: Univ. of Kansas Press, 1976.

Machiavelli, Niccolo. *The Prince and Discourses*. New York: Modern Library, 1940.

MacLeish, Archibald. "The Irresponsibles." *Nation*, May 18, 1940, 619–23.

McLuhan, Marshall. "Murder by Television." *Canadian Forum* (Jan. 1964):222–23.

McNeely, William F. *Frederick Douglass*. New York: W. W. Norton, 1991.

Macpherson, James M. "Abraham Lincoln and the Second American Revolution." In *Abraham Lincoln and the American Political Tradition*, ed. John L. Thomas. Amherst: Univ. of Massachusetts Press, 1986.

Mailer, Norman. *The Presidential Papers of Norman Mailer*. New York: Bantam, 1964.

Malone, Dumas. *Jefferson and the Ordeal of Liberty*. Boston: Little, Brown, 1962.

———. *Jefferson the President, First Term*. Boston: Little, Brown, 1970.

Mansfield, Harvey, Jr. *Taming the Prince: The Ambivalence of Executive Power*. New York: Free Press, 1989.

Marchand, Philip. *Marshall McLuhan*. New York: Ticknor and Fields, 1989.

Marris, Jim. *Crossfire*. New York: Carroll and Graf, 1989.

Marsh, Ebenezer. *An Oration Delivered at Wetherfield on the Death of General George Washington*. Hartford, Conn.: Hudson and Goodwin, 1800.

Masters, Edgar Lee. *Lincoln, The Man*. New York: Dodd, Mead, 1931.

———. "At Sagamore Hill." In *Starved Rock*, by Edgar Lee Masters. New York: Macmillan, 1919.

Matthews, Jan De Hart. "Arts and the People: The New Deal Quest for Cultural Democracy." *Journal of American History* 62 (Sept. 1975):316–39.

Mazlish, Bruce. *In Search of Nixon*. Baltimore: Penquin, 1972.

Meyers, Marvin. *The Jacksonian Persuasion*. Stanford, Calif.: Stanford Univ. Press, 1957.

Milton, George Fort. *The Eve of Conflict*. New York: Octagon Press, 1963.

Moley, Raymond. *After Seven Years*. New York: Harper, 1939.

Morison, Elting E. *Turmoil and Tradition*. Boston: Houghton Mifflin, 1960.

Morison, Elting E., with John Blum, eds. *The Letters of Theodore Roosevelt*. Cambridge: Harvard Univ. Press, 1951–54.

Morris, Edmund. *The Rise of Theodore Roosevelt*. New York: McCann and Geoghegan, 1979.

Mulder, John M. *Woodrow Wilson: The Years of Preparation*. Princeton, N.J.: Princeton Univ. Press, 1978.

Mumford, Lewis. "When America Goes to War." *Modern Monthly* (June–July 1935):198–99.

Nelson, Michael. "Evaluating the Presidency." In *The Presidency and the Political System*, ed. Michael Nelson. Washington, D.C: Congressional Quarterly Press, 1983.

Nelson, Paul David. "Horatio Gates at Newburgh." *William and Mary Quarterly*, 3d ser., 29 (1972):143–58.

Nicholay, John, and John Hay. *Abraham Lincoln: A History*. 10 vols. New York: Century, 1917.

Nixon, Richard M. *1999*. New York: Simon and Schuster, 1988.

———. *The Real War*. New York: Warner Books, 1980.

———. *R.N.: The Memoirs of Richard Nixon*. New York: Grosset and Dunlop, 1978.

———. *Seize the Moment*. New York: Simon and Schuster, 1992.

———. *Six Crises*. Garden City, N.Y.: Doubleday, 1962.

Nock, Albert Jay. *Jefferson*. New York: Hill and Wang, 1926.

Noonan, Peggy. *What I Saw at the Revolution*. New York: Random House, 1990.

Owsley, Frank L. "The Irrepressible Conflict." In *I'll Take My Stand*, by Frank L. Owsley. New York: Harper and Brothers, 1930.

Pachter, Henry. "JFK as an Equestrian Statue: On Myth and Myth Makers." *Salmagundi* 1 (1966):5–25.

Park, Marlene, and Gerald E. Markowitz, eds. *Democratic Vistas: Post Offices and Public Art in the New Deal*. Philadelphia: Temple Univ. Press, 1984.

Parmet, Herbert S. *J.F.K.* New York: Dial, 1983.

———. *Jack: The Struggles of John F. Kennedy*. New York: Dial, 1983.

Parton, James. *The Life of Andrew Jackson*. 3 vols. New York: Mason Brothers, 1860.

Perkins, Francis. *The Roosevelt I Knew*. New York: Viking, 1946.

Pessen, Edward. *Jacksonian America*: Homewood, Ill.: Dorsey, 1969.

Peterson, Merill D. *The Jeffersonian Image in the American Mind*. New York: Oxford Univ. Press, 1960.

———. *Thomas Jefferson and the New Nation*. New York: Oxford Univ. Press, 1970.

Pious, Richard. *The American Presidency*. New York: Basic Books, 1979.

Phelps, Glenn A. *George Washington and American Constitutionalism*. Lawrence: Univ. Press of Kansas, 1933.

Powers, Larry. *"Johnny, We Hardly Knew Ye."* Boston: Little, Brown, 1970.

Quirt, Walter. "On Mural Painting." In *The New Deal Art Projects: An Anthology of Memoirs*, ed. Francis O'Connor. Washington, D.C.: Smithsonian Institution Press, 1972.

Randall, James G. "The Blundering Generation." *Mississippi Valley Historical Review* 27 (June 1940):3–28.

Randall, J. G. *Lincoln the President*, vol. 1. New York: Dodd, Mead, 1956.

Reagan, Ronald. *An American Life*. New York: Simon and Schuster, 1990.

———. *Speaking My Mind: Selected Speeches*. New York: Simon and Schuster, 1989.

Reagan, Ronald, and Richard G. Hubler. *Where's the Rest of Me?* New York: Dutton, 1965.

Reeves, Richard. *President Kennedy: Profile of Power*. New York: Simon and Schuster, 1993.

Reeves, Thomas C. *A Question of Character*. New York: Free Press, 1991.

Reid, John Philip. *In Defiance of the Law: The Standing Army Controversy, the Two Constitutions, and the Coming of the American Revolution*. Chapel Hill: Univ. of North Carolina Press, 1981.

Remini, Robert V. *Andrew Jackson and the Bank War*. New York: W. W. Norton, 1967.

———. *The Legacy of Andrew Jackson*. Baton Rouge: Louisiana State Univ. Press, 1988.

Riccards, Michael. *The Ferocious Engine of Democracy: A History of the American Presidency*. Lanham, Md.: Rowman and Littlefield, 1994.

———. *A Republic If You Can Keep It: The Foundation of the American Presidency, 1700–1800*. Westport, Conn.: Greenwood Press, 1987.

Richardson, James D., ed. *Messages and Papers of the Presidents*. 20 vols. New York: Bureau of National Literature, 1897.

Rockman, Bert. *The Leadership Question*. New York: Praeger, 1984.

Rogin, Michael Paul. *Fathers and Sons: Andrew Jackson and the Subjugation of the American Indian*. New York: Vintage, 1975.

Roosevelt, Theodore. *American Ideals*. 2 vols. New York: Putnam's, 1897.

———. *Theodore Roosevelt: An Autobiography*. New York: Charles Scribner's Sons, 1929.

———. *The Winning of the West*. New York: Putnam's, 1889.

———. *The Works of Theodore Roosevelt*. 20 vols. National edition. New York: Scribner's Sons, 1926.

Rosen, Elliot A. *Hoover, Roosevelt, and the Brain Trust*. New York: Columbia, 1977.

Rosenman, Samuel I. *Working with Roosevelt*. New York: Harper, 1952.

Rosenman, Samuel I., ed. *The Public Papers and Addresses of Franklin D. Roosevelt*. 13 vols. New York: Harper and Row, 1938–50.

Rossiter, Clinton. *The American Presidency*. New York: Harcourt, Brace and World, 1960.

———. *Constitutional Dictatorship*. Princeton, N.J.: Princeton Univ. Press, 1948.

Rossiter, Clinton, ed. *The Federalist Papers*. New York: New American Library, 1961.

Rothbard, Murray N. *America's Great Depression*. Los Angeles: Nash Publishers, 1972.

Rothchild, Lincoln. "The Index of American Design of the WPA/FAP." In *The New Deal Art Projects: An Anthology of Memoirs*, ed. Francis O'Connor. Washington, D.C.: Smithsonian Institution Press, 1972.

Royster, Charles. *A Revolutionary People at War: The Continental Army and American Character, 1775–1783*. Chapel Hill: Univ. of North Carolina Press, 1979.

Sandburg, Carl. *Abraham Lincoln: The War Years*. New York: Harcourt, Brace, 1939.

Schlesinger, Arthur, Jr. *The Age of Jackson*. Boston: Little Brown, 1945.

———. *The Age of Roosevelt: The Politics of Upheaval*. Boston: Houghton Mifflin, 1960.

———. *The Crisis of the Old Order*. Boston: Houghton Mifflin, 1957.

———. *The Imperial Presidency*. Boston: Houghton Mifflin, 1973.

———. *A Thousand Days*. Boston: Houghton Mifflin, 1965.

Scofield, Kent. "The Public Image of Herbert Hoover in the 1928 Campaign." *Mid-America* 51 (Oct. 1969):278–93.

Schroeder, John H. *Mr. Polk's War: American Opposition and Dissent, 1846–1848*. Madison: Univ. of Wisconsin Press, 1973.

Schwartz, Barry. *George Washington: The Making of an American Symbol*. Ithaca, N.Y.: Cornell Univ. Press, 1987.

Schwarz, Jordan A. *Liberal: Adolph A. Berle and the Vision of an American Era*. New York: Free Press, 1987.

Sellars, Charles. *James K. Polk: Continentalist 1843–1846.* Princeton, N.J.: Princeton Univ. Press, 1966.

Shaw, Albert, ed. *Presidential Addresses and State Papers of Theodore Roosevelt.* New York: P. F. Collier & Son, 1910.

Sheatsley, Paul B., and Jacob J. Feldman. "A National Survey on Public Reactions and Behavior." In *The Kennedy Assassination and the American Public,* ed. Bradley S. Greenberg and Edwin B. Parker. Stanford, Calif.: Stanford Univ. Press, 1965.

Sheldon, Garret Ward. *The Political Philosophy of Thomas Jefferson.* Baltimore: Johns Hopkins Univ. Press, 1990.

Sherwood, Robert. *Roosevelt and Hopkins.* New York: Harpers, 1948.

Simon, Paul. *Lincoln's Preparation for Greatness: The Illinois Legislative Years.* Norman: Univ. of Oklahoma Press, 1965.

Skeen, C. Edward. "The Newburgh Conspiracy Reconsidered." *William and Mary Quarterly,* 3d ser., 31 (1974):272–98.

Skowronek, Stephen. *The Politics Presidents Make.* Cambridge: Harvard Univ. Press, 1993.

———. "Presidential Leadership in Political Time." In *The Presidency and the Political System,* ed. Michael Nelson. Washington, D.C: Congressional Quarterly Press, 1984.

Smith, Malcolm E. *John F. Kennedy's 13 Great Mistakes in the White House.* Smithtown, N.Y: Suffolk House, 1980.

Smith, Robert Thompson. *The Missiles of October.* New York: Simon and Schuster, 1992.

Sommers, Anthony. *Conspiracy.* New York: Paragon, 1989.

Sorenson, Theodore. *Kennedy.* New York: Harper and Row, 1965.

Stampp, Kenneth M. *The Era of Reconstruction, 1867–1877.* New York: Vintage, 1967.

Stoll, E. E. "Shakespeare's Presentation of a Contemporary Hero." In *Shakespeare: Henry V,* ed. Michael Quinn. London: Macmillan, 1969.

Stone, Oliver. *JFK: The Documented Screenplay.* New York: Applause Books, 1992.

Strauss, Leo. *Persecution and the Art of Writing.* Glencoe, Ill.: Free Press, 1952.

Strozier, Charles B. *Lincoln's Quest for Union.* New York: Basic Books, 1982.

Szulc, Tad. *The Illusion of Peace.* New York: Viking, 1978.

Taylor, Gary, ed. *Henry V.* Oxford : Oxford Univ. Press, 1982.

Terkel, Studs. *Hard Times.* New York: Bantam Books, 1970.

Tocqueville, Alexis de. *Democracy in America.* Ed. J. P. Mayer. Garden City, N.Y.: Doubleday, 1969.

Trefousse, Hans I. *Andrew Johnson: A Biography.* New York: W. W. Norton, 1989.

Tugwell, Rexford G. *The Democratic Roosevelt.* Baltimore: Penguin Books, 1969.

Tulis, Jeffrey. *The Rhetorical Presidency.* Princeton, N.J.: Princeton Univ. Press, 1987.

Valenti, Jack. *A Very Human President.* New York: W. W. Norton, 1975.

Van Doren, Mark. *Shakespeare.* New York: Holt, Rinehart and Winston, 1967.

deVoto, Bernard, ed. *Mark Twain in Eruption.* New York: Harpers, 1940.

Waldo, S. Putnam. *Memoirs of Andrew Jackson.* Hartford, Conn., 1820.

Walker, Alexander. *Jackson and New Orleans.* New York: 1856.

Ward, John William. *Andrew Jackson: Symbol for an Age.* New York: Oxford Univ. Press, 1962.

Washington, H. A., ed. *The Writings of Thomas Jefferson.* New York: Derby and Jackson, 1859.

Webster, Daniel. *Speeches and Forensic Arguments*. Boston: Perkins, Marvin, 1835.

Weisbuch, Robert. *Atlantic Double-Cross: American and British Literature in the Age of Emerson*. Chicago: Univ. of Chicago Press, 1986.

Whalen, Richard J. *The Founding Father: The Story of Joseph P. Kennedy*. New York: New American Library, 1964.

White, John Todd. "Standing Armies in Time of War: Republican Theory and Military Practices during the American Revolution." Ph.d diss., George Washington Univ., 1978.

White, Leonard D. *The Jeffersonians*. New York: Free Press, 1951.

White, Theodore. *In Search of History*. New York: Warner, 1978.

Will, George. *Cincinnatus: George Washington and the Enlightenment*. Garden City: Doubleday, 1984.

Williams, William Appleman. *The Contours of American History*. Chicago: Quadrangle, 1966.

Wills, Gary. *Inventing America*. Garden City, N.Y.: Doubleday, 1978.

———. *The Kennedy Imprisonment*. Boston: Little, Brown, 1981.

———. *Lincoln at Gettysburg*. New York: Simon and Schuster, 1992.

———. *Nixon Agonistes*. New York: New American Library, 1970.

———. *Reagan's America*. Baltimore: Penguin, 1988.

———. "Richard M. Nixon." In *The Oxford Companion to the Politics of the World*. New York: Oxford Univ. Press, 1993.

Wilson, Edmund. *Patriotic Gore*. New York: Oxford Univ. Press, 1962.

Wilson, Joan Hoff. *Herbert Hoover, Forgotten Progressive*. Boston: Little, Brown, 1975.

Wilson, Woodrow. *The New Democracy*. New York: Harper and Brothers, 1926.

Wofford, Harris. *Of Kennedys and Kings*. New York: Farrar, Straus, Giroux, 1980.

Wood, Gordon S. *The Creation of the American Republic 1776–1787*. New York: W. W. Norton, 1969.

Woodward, Bob. *The Commanders*. New York: Simon and Schuster, 1991.

Yeats, W. B. *Essays and Introductions*. London: Macmillan, 1961.

Zinn, Howard. "The New Left Views the New Deal." In *The New Deal: Analysis and Interpretation*. Ed. Alonzo L. Hamby. New York: Weybright and Talley, 1969.

Zuckert, Catherine H. "On the Role of Spiritedness and Politics." In *Understanding the Political Spirit: Philosophical Investigations from Socrates to Nietzsche*. Ed. Catherine H. Zuckert. New Haven, Conn.: Yale Univ. Press, 1988.

INDEX

* *

ADW0263

Emerson College Library